AN ATLAS OF JUVENILE MMPI PROFILES

AN ATLAS OF
Juvenile MMPI Profiles

BY

Starke R. Hathaway

AND

Elio D. Monachesi

THE UNIVERSITY OF MINNESOTA PRESS, MINNEAPOLIS

PRINTED IN THE UNITED STATES OF AMERICA AT THE
LUND PRESS, MINNEAPOLIS

Library of Congress Catalog Card Number: 61-8795

ISBN: 0-8166-0232-8

Second printing 1971

PUBLISHED IN GREAT BRITAIN, INDIA, AND PAKISTAN BY THE OXFORD UNIVERSITY PRESS,
LONDON, BOMBAY, AND KARACHI, AND IN CANADA BY THOMAS ALLEN, LTD., TORONTO

Acknowledgments

The research on which the data in this *Atlas* are based has been supported from two main sources. We have received liberal grants from graduate school research funds of the University of Minnesota, and a greater portion of the support has been granted by the National Institute of Mental Health. For these grants we should like to express our appreciation here.

It is obvious that the authors cannot properly accept full credit for the great amount of work in the completion of so extensive a task. Our first measure of appreciation is to the school personnel, police officials, judges, ministers, and others who have so much trusted us and believed in the significance of the project that they have given facilities, time, and confidential information. It is our greatest wish that the findings we can make available to aid in understanding the problems related to delinquency and mental health that confront these contributors may meet their expectations.

We also owe a debt to the ninth-grade students who were the subjects and who continue to provide data on their lives toward a mutually desired better, more healthy society. We are cognizant of the freedom we have had to administer a personality test that touches upon matters private to students and their families. We have soberly accepted the responsibility this entails and we believe that the data provided will adequately repay our subjects for their trust in us through the possible broadening of our understanding of the unhappy events that affect many families and persons.

The important inclusion of college MMPI's and many aptitude and SVIB records in the *Atlas* histories depended upon the invaluable and unlimited cooperation of the University of Minnesota Student Counseling bureaus in Minneapolis and Duluth. Several individuals from these staffs will need only to glance through this book to understand how much of the value of the work is due to their efforts.

To no small degree we owe much to the persons who have worked on the project both in Minneapolis and around the state. They are too numerous to be mentioned by name, but we would like to express special thanks to Alta Nupson and Sherman Iverson who each represent others in this region who helped us extensively and whom we do not forget. Directing the staff, and vitally interested in the work, was Lawrence A. Young. His knowledge of the field problems and

ACKNOWLEDGMENTS

his unrelenting pressure for accumulation of data are represented on every page. Among others who have contributed to management and planning of the project are Leona Erickson Dahlstrom, Lee Erickson Broehm, Larry Katz, and Mary Lyon Sutton.

Finally, in organizing and editing the *Atlas,* Phyllis Reynolds of our staff and Jeanne Sinnen of the University Press were exceedingly important to us.

STARKE R. HATHAWAY
ELIO D. MONACHESI

Minneapolis
December, 1960

Table of Contents

GUIDE TO THIS *ATLAS*

Guide to This *Atlas*

The *Atlas of Juvenile MMPI Profiles* is a collection of over a thousand short case histories selected and organized according to salient features of MMPI profiles represented by codes. The profiles are from inventories taken by ninth-grade juveniles.

In the decade since publication of *An Atlas for the Clinical Use of the MMPI* (8) the usefulness of the atlas method of presenting data for the interpretation of a personality test has become increasingly better recognized. Duker (4) has provided direct objective evidence for the clinical validity of atlas information, and Meehl (14) (15), Drake and Oetting (3), and others have made methodological contributions toward greater objectivity in the interpretation of personality test profiles.

All modern objective personality tests have several scales or measurement categories; a subject's score on each scale is expressed in terms of normative standard or percentile scores. The pattern (profile) of these several scores is expected to suggest to the test user significant information or a personality description about his subject. Each scale in the profile has been separately derived with a diagnostic or descriptive meaning, and profile interpretation may be done by attributing to the subject the diagnoses or descriptions that go with the separate scales. Many of those who work with personality theory have faith in the existence of separate scales or factors that can be combined additively to form an individual's personal description. Each scale would be added into the description in the degree of its profile score and the known correlates of the most deviant score would be the most significant items used to describe the subject. With MMPI scales, this would suggest that if one had a group of patients with diagnosed schizophrenia, ideally they all should have scale 8 (related to schizophrenia) as the largest score in their profiles.

Attempts to apply this approach to profile interpretation have been so unrewarding even with tests derived by factor analytic methodology that many psychologists have come to believe that no worthwhile validity has been developed for objective personality tests. But possibly it is the basic hypothesis that individual personalities can be synthesized from pure scales that is false; alternatively, scale interaction may be the basic rule for the synthesis of individual personalities. This interaction hypothesis in simple form would assert that although there are key variables (scales), such variables cannot be purified because they include an element of continuous generality (true factor meaning) and in addition they include an element of almost discontinuous meanings. These meanings appear only as constructs derived from sometimes one, sometimes another combination of several variables among those in the profile. Furthermore, the combinations divide into permutations of relative score (code orders) that also identify different constructs. With such a hypothesis, scale interaction could be so complex (although still orderly) that the interpretative contributions of single scales to a profile would approach being individual to each profile. The meaning of a score on one scale in a profile would depend on the scores obtained on other scales in the given profile. The generality of higher or lower scores on the scales would be very weak. Lykken has suggested some consequences of approaching this problem by partitioning the multidimensional test space into cells whose predictive meaning is determined by the accumulated observation about those persons whose profiles locate them in the several cells (13).

As a matter of fact, in practice, piecemeal description of the subject from individual scales is usually modified by the test user's experience with the test to allow to some extent for the blending of separate scale meanings. Descriptive terms appropriate to deviation on one scale interact with the descriptive terms for other scales to modify what would be said about deviations on the separate scales. But for most test users clinical experience with subjects having closely similar profiles of scores cannot be large because close similarities between the profiles of subjects are exceedingly rare as more than four or five scales are used. This assures that one can have at most only limited experience with closely similar profiles. Even if the scales have considerable covariance it becomes improbable that any one subject's sequence of values (his profile) will be found on another subject. Also it is difficult to categorize and remember the individual observations or facts associated with each of a large diversity of profiles.

An atlas is one way of bypassing all the above problems in personality test profile interpretation. It presents some significant personal data about a fairly large number of individuals who are classified by arbitrary similarities among the test profiles (an approximation of the Lykken cells) and the method, though cumbersome, is independent of test theory. It is a new approach to expressing the meaning and usefulness of personality tests and it provides a practical working stratagem. An atlas is a compendium of experience with a test: it presents the user with information about subjects who have previously obtained test profiles like the one he wishes to interpret. But what is new in the atlas method of interpretation is that the reported data have not been molded to the test. In a properly constructed atlas, the case history information about the persons with various test profiles are gathered and compiled without "contamination" from the test data on them — the test scores are not known to those collecting data or to those putting the data into history form. For the test user the interpretative sequence follows this pattern: S to be understood → test profile from S → atlas profiles like that of S → information generalized about persons who had these similar profiles → generalizations applied to S. The link between S and the generalizations does not include anyone's statements about what the test measures. In this sequence the test is an inarticulate link valid in merely establishing a degree of similarity between S and the other persons. Its usefulness for understanding S depends obviously upon the degree to which the test method of picking some similar persons to use in interpretation is valid for the desired interpretation. It seems inescapable that increasing the number of similarities in the test area between an S and the comparison group of persons used as a source of inferences about him will increase the probability that the inferences will be correct. At the same time it must be stated emphatically that the *Atlas* groups identified with every pattern of code similarity may not necessarily suggest helpful interpretations. It is not reasonable to expect that the validity of the test variables will extend to the point of assuring pertinent validity for every code class that can be identified.

The atlas method assumes the user of a personality test is able to abstract and apply the information from the case material in the histories. The user will read the accumulated cases having profiles similar to that of his subject. His statement about the subject will be based upon his immediate experience and he might say, "Some common elements that I see among these cases are . . . We will consider it more than randomly probable that S will show these elements."

Except for some technical jargon, useful information about a child with a given MMPI code can be gleaned from this *Atlas* by an untrained person; or, at least for preliminary interpretation, the atlas method lessens the training required of the user. This statement may startle those who would emphasize training as a requisite for even simplest uses of a test. In effect we are saying that if a counselor is competent to collect and interpret his clinical experience, he is probably competent to read and apply these case histories; thus he will be using the MMPI. This can be done even if the user never learns what the individual scales of the MMPI are said to measure. Assuming that the profile to be interpreted is valid, then both the correct and the erroneous inferences of the counselor in interpreting from code histories in the *Atlas* would be of the same sort that would characterize his other counseling work where he applies generalities of his experience toward understanding or controlling individual behavior. Of course, the more training a counselor has in the use of the MMPI, the better he will be able to interpret and apply MMPI data. In referring to the simpler levels of MMPI use, we are not at all advising less emphasis upon training; on the contrary, there is a rich and meaningful increase of value from the MMPI and other such tests that comes with experience and training.

The Cases

All the cases in this *Atlas* were drawn from the second phase of the Hathaway-Monachesi studies of ninth-grade Minnesota public school pupils and their later careers (9) (10) (11) (12). These studies, supported by grants from the National Institute of Mental Health, the University of Minnesota Graduate School research funds, and other sources, began in 1947 with a Minneapolis sample of about 4,000 boys and girls and were expanded in 1954 by a statewide sample of about 11,000 boys and girls. Data for the case histories of the *Atlas* were collected beginning about three years after the 1954 testing when these pupils were in the twelfth grade. Trained field workers interviewed teachers, ministers, parents, and others. Also there was a search of public records. For many children, the MMPI was repeated in the twelfth grade, and a later search of university and college admission records provided additional MMPI records for some. Data from a statewide high school testing program for high school seniors, carried out by the University of Minnesota Student Counseling Bureau, were also available. (Appendix Table 1, following the Case Histories section of this volume, provides general normative data on the MMPI profiles for the statewide sample.)

Every effort was made to gain good cooperation in data collection. Trained persons with high integrity were employed in the testing and the follow-ups. This tended to reassure everyone that information would not be carelessly handled and confidences would not be betrayed. Early coding of names and reduction of data to punched cards further protected individuals. The fact that no "incidents" or significant blocks occurred in the testing or follow-up programs indicates that there was understanding and cooperation on the part of the many contributing persons and agencies.

Finally, we have tried to assure anonymity in the case histories, and we are certain that no child can be identified, except perhaps for one or two notorious cases where news services destroyed all privacy. The subjects are mostly average boys and girls, normal or near it, and they and the events that are reported often sound similar to other persons and events. In the histories, identifying items were changed or distorted to destroy the personal identification but were kept similar enough to provide the reader with equivalent data. Death of a parent, for example, was often placed a year before or after the actual time; special offenses were changed in nature or at least displaced in time. This process occasionally so mixes events that a child or family might find common (but fictitious) elements between their own and another history.

We hope that no reader will find more than what we intended: a balanced depiction of mostly ordinary good boys, girls, and families, characterized without malice by those who knew them and presented in case histories to better equip the user of the *Atlas* to do his job. We could hardly expect to understand the individual problem case if we could not study and understand the majority who do not need special help. We hope and expect that this *Atlas* will far more often help to show the strengths of youth than to emphasize the weaknesses.

Selection of Cases

The *Atlas of Juvenile MMPI Profiles* differs from the first *Atlas* in the method by which the case histories were selected. We have tried to provide several representatives of every code type that can be encountered. Consequently, case selection started with the codes themselves. From the master list of about 11,000 boys and girls on whom we had enough descriptive data, a few boy and girl representatives were selected for each two-point code * type that occurred. Where possible, the selected codes were primed (highest T score greater than 70). In no instances were ninth-grade codes selected in which the two highest scales were tied or within one point of each other in score; only a few are included in which the second and third highest were tied. Some low-point codes and some invalid profiles were also chosen. Except for the special examples included to show the personality patterns associated with a question about the profile validity, the cases selected had L scores under 10 and F scores under 16.

After the preliminary selection, the information items from the follow-up notes were copied verbatim onto a single page. This fact sheet was labeled with the subject's file number and a gross indication of intelligence and the high school

---

* "Two-point code" refers to the two most deviant high-scale scores of a profile.

achievement rank when these measures were available. The fact sheet carried no indication of MMPI code or scores. First drafts of the case histories were dictated from these sheets, which had been shuffled into random order. Since the original field collection of facts was also done independently of MMPI scoring, there was no way in which the case history could be contaminated with MMPI data. As stated earlier, this freedom from contamination is necessary to proper development of any atlas of test profiles. It assures that only random or valid consistency can appear among the case histories of a certain code type.

After the preliminary dictation, the cases were individually checked against the history notes to assure factual accuracy. The MMPI codes and other information were then added and the cases were complete except for final editing. If the subject was a twin, the MMPI code(s) for the other member of the pair were added in brackets in the case history whenever they were available.

When a user can see common and distinctive elements among the exemplary histories for a code type, then it is likely that these elements are validly related to the code type. Sometimes the *Atlas* user will not discover any common elements among the histories given for a code class. Such diversity can easily happen from the random omission of cases that would have been more typical and it will often happen because the code really does not identify persons similar in the areas of record.

In using the case histories the reader should keep in mind that they are based upon the comments of informants. Most often the descriptive data came from teachers, counselors, ministers, and law officers, with parents, friends, physicians, business people, and social workers also contributing. It is exceedingly important, especially for counselors, to remember that the *Atlas* case histories were deliberately composed with little attention even to the intelligence of the child or his school record. For example, the follow-up reports may describe a pupil as an over-achiever or as not bright although these judgments are not supported by the test scores and high school rank. The counselor should note the occurrence of such discrepancies between observers and test data as a part of his evaluation of the whole case. The personalities and behavior of the children cannot be directly known. The descriptions tell how the juveniles appeared and were evaluated by the observers. This fact is an asset in application of the *Atlas*, since most users will have a greater need for evaluation of the children as those around them saw them than for evaluation of some hidden personality that was not interpersonally apparent. Because this descriptive view should be preserved and because the user must himself decide what some of the follow-up statements meant in the minds of the teachers and others who made them, direct quotations have been used liberally. They have been used especially when the original field note seemed obscure or unclear. If any informant likened a boy to "Jack Armstrong," we have passed on the statement. Including it may not be informing for some readers at all, but omitting it might impoverish the picture for others. Even when quotation marks are not used, the case histories are always close to the field notes, and the field workers tried to write down exactly what was said.

Many of the cases are very short. We tried to use only those cases where there was assurance that the field work was adequate, but to fill out categories, it was necessary to include some where no one said much. In the majority of the cases with short descriptions, the field worker could not get anything more because the boy or girl was not conspicuous. A troublemaker or an unusually nice and cooperative child was often described with detail; a boy or girl who neither made trouble nor contributed much to school or church or community left informants with little to say. To a degree, therefore, the brevity of a case history means that the child was inconspicuous, which is itself a helpful item for interpretation.

Descriptions apply mainly to behavior during the ninth, tenth, and eleventh grades. Our evidence abundantly supports the statement commonly made that this is a time often marked by rapid shifts in personality. These years cover a period when boys and girls are moving quickly from childhood toward adulthood, freeing themselves of home and other dependencies; and in these days of youthful marriage, the high school student often completes the transition to having a family of his own. Similarly, society changes its demands and expectations. Words in the histories that relate to maturity, to rebelliousness, and to sexual behavior, for example, betray the changing attitudes of teachers and others. The changes in cultural role that are reflected in the cases of this *Atlas* also appear in the MMPI codes (where more than one was available) which vary with the child's changes. We were only occasionally told that change was observable to the informants — teachers expect it and do not find it remarkable. Also, marked personality changes sometimes occurred just after testing and a year or two before the follow-up. Such factors tend to decrease the apparent validity of the test patterns. The long-term validity of any test or other assessment when applied to juveniles seems inevitably limited by these changes in the individuals and their society.

Fortunately, most personality change during these years is toward better adjustment. It has often been pointed out that if older men caused as much trouble as do fifteen- and sixteen-year-old boys, our police forces could not cope with the problem. Wirt and Briggs (16) have demonstrated the rapid decrease in incidence of law breaking as the boys of our Minneapolis sample aged from fifteen to twenty-two years. Some boys do, however, become temporarily worse in adjustment and behavior as they go on from the ninth grade. It is especially important for counselors to predict the direction and nature of changes. Retest MMPI's will occasionally help in this prediction, and counselors should recognize the value of obtaining frequent retests of their problem cases.

We want to emphasize that personality does change and part of the variability of MMPI codes expresses the differences. Appendix Tables 2 and 3 give some data about the more and less stable patterns. If counselors are disturbed to find so much change in MMPI codes between two testings, they should consider that a test showing only the stable elements in personality would be useless for most remedial or diagnostic guidance. We need to be aware of those important transitory phases that are such significant factors during the teens.

Coding

Although it is assumed that the user of this *Atlas* will have a general familiarity with the MMPI, the following is a brief review of the coding system adopted, that of Hathaway (7).

Coding begins with substitution of digit number symbols for the ten clinical scales usually scored (see the list below). These numbers are then used exclusively for designating the scales. In this volume the scales are in the customary order with the Si scale (code number 0) following 9.

1 = Hs (+ .5 K)	6 = Pa
2 = D	7 = Pt (+ 1 K)
3 = Hy	8 = Sc (+ 1 K)
4 = Pd (+ .4 K)	9 = Ma (+ .2 K)
5 = Mf	0 = Si

With the number symbols of the scales in mind, the code is prepared from the individual's profile (or a list of his T scores). First, all clinical scales within the T-score range 46 to 54, inclusive, are crossed off. The numbers of the scales that score in this middle range are not shown in the codes. Next, the high-point code is written. This begins with the number symbol of the scale with the largest T score and continues with the other number symbols of scales of progressively lower T score down to the limit, 55. A line is drawn beneath all adjacent scale numbers that are equal or that differ by only one point. A break in the underscoring, e.g., 12 738'46 ..., indicates that there is more than one point difference between the two numbers where the break appears. Finally, a prime is placed to indicate where the profile crosses T = 70, two primes where it crosses 80, three at 90, and so on. This placing of the primes leaves the numbers for all scales with a T score greater than 69 to the left of at least one prime mark. With insertion of the primes, the high-point code is completed. A dash always follows the high-point code unless only part of a code is given, in which case the partial code is followed by three dots to indicate that it is incomplete.

The low-point code follows the dash. This begins with the number of the scale with the smallest T score and continues upward until a T score of 45 is reached. Underlining is done as with high-point codes. A prime is placed to show where the profile crosses the T = 40 line.

A profile with no codable low points will end with a dash and, similarly, a profile that commences with a dash indicates that no T score exceeds 54.

A code is completed with the addition of the raw scores of the three validity scales, L, F, and K, in this order, and separated from the low-point code by a space or two. These scales are given in raw score form because the distributions of L and F are so greatly skewed. K is included for consistency, although this score is not usually used in defining a valid profile.

The limits for profile validity are shown below. Invalidity from unanswered items is not considered here because at the time of testing every effort was made to avoid more than fifty omitted items.

L Score		*F Score*	
Valid	0–9	Valid	0–15
Invalid (high L)	10–16	Invalid	
		High F	16–21
		Ultra high F (UHF)..	22 or greater

If both the L and F scores are within the valid limits, the profile is referred to as a valid one. If L or F is high, the three scores are followed by an X in the code to draw attention to the invalidity. Appendix Table 4 gives the observed rates of the degrees and forms of validity.

For illustration and some practice with codes, the reader may wish to study the following examples.

A code written 4′89–′5 3:6:20 gives this information: The highest point of this profile is on scale 4, and in MMPI jargon it is a "primed" code, which simply means that at least one scale exceeds a T score of 69. Scales 8 and 9 are here coded next. Since they are placed to the right of the prime, the T scores must be between 70 and 54. The scale 8 score is larger than the 9 score by at least two points (no under-scoring). Other scales of the profile, except scale 5, must be in the average range 46 to 54. Scale 5 is coded low, and the placement of the prime in the low-point code shows that this score lies between 39 and 46. Finally, the raw score on L is 3, the score on F is 6, and the K score is 20.

Another example is 5′968–3′12 3:10:7. From this code it can be deduced that the T score of scale 5 is above 69, the score on scale 9 is less than 70 but more than one point larger than the following score, the scores on scales 6 and 8 fall below that of scale 9 and are equal or within one point in value as shown by the under-scoring. The low-point code shows that scale 3 has a T value less than 40 (the 3 is at the left of the prime). Two scores, those of 1 and 2, are, in order, between the values 39 and 46. The three validity scores L, F, and K have the indicated raw scores. Both this and the code above are from valid profiles.

Additional data on the Hathaway coding system and on the more complete Welsh system are given in Dahlstrom and Welsh (1).

Key to the History Headings

The histories in this *Atlas* are arranged in numerical order according to the codes of the ninth-grade MMPI profiles, beginning with profiles that have no cod-able high points, followed by profiles that have 1 as the highest point, and ending with profiles that have 0 as the highest point.

A summary of data precedes each history. The discussion of the following example will serve to make clear the abbreviations used.

SAMPLE HEADING

a_1 a_2 a_3	b_1	c_1
M:14:2	ACE IX, 50; XI, 50	′98467– 2:1:13
a_4 a_5 a_6	b_2	c_2
N:III:4	ENG IX, 50; XI, 50	′4987–′0 1:2:12
	b_3	c_3
	HSR 50	′489–′50 2:1:12
	b_4	
	SVIB 4′58–10	

a. Personal Data. The subject was male, 14 years old, with two siblings. He lived with his parents, whose socioeconomic status was rated at the clerical, skilled, and retail business level, and he attended school in a community with a population of 2,500 to 5,000. Thus:

$a_1 =$ sex, either M or F.

$a_2 =$ age in years at the time of the ninth-grade testing.

$a_3 =$ number of siblings at the time of the ninth-grade testing.

a_4 = family status: N = not a broken home; B = broken home. A broken home means the parents were divorced or separated; one or both parents were dead; the child was in a foster home; the child was living with relatives or other persons; the child was adopted; etc. The use of N or B was determined at the time of the ninth-grade testing; subsequent divorce, death, or separation is noted in the history, not the heading.

a_5 = socioeconomic status. A modification of the Minnesota Scale for Parental Occupation (Institute of Child Welfare, University of Minnesota) was used, by which Roman numerals I through VII signify the following:

I = professional
II = semiprofessional
III = clerical, skilled, and retail business
IV = farmer (IVA = large, commercial farm, e.g., dairy, truck;
    IVB = average, substantial farm; IVC = small farm)
V = semiskilled, clerks, and minor business positions
VI = slightly skilled
VII = day laborer

When the letter N appears in this space, it indicates that the socioeconomic status could not be determined. This sometimes happened if the child's school record was incomplete or if death or separation of a parent had altered the socioeconomic status beyond adequate determination.

a_6 = community size. Arbitrary classification of communities into seven population categories was made:

1 = greater than 100,000
    and suburbs
2 = 10,000–100,000
3 = 5,000–10,000
4 = 2,500–5,000
5 = 1,000–2,500
6 = 500–1,000
7 = less than 500

The location of the child's school determined the community listed for him. Thus it is possible for a child whose home is on a farm, for instance, to appear, according to the a_6 entry, to be living in a community of some size. One should refer to the a_5 entry to find which children live on farms.

b. *Scholastic and Interest Ratings.* The subject's ranks on four measures are given.

b_1 = percentile ranks for the ninth (IX) and eleventh (XI) grade ACE Psychological Examination based on ninth- and eleventh-grade norms, respectively. The ranks were obtained from the Student Counseling Bureau of the University of Minnesota, which administers this examination. When all ACE (and ENG) scores are missing, an IQ percentile rank will often appear in their place. A percentile rank was used (identified as "IQ centile" in the case heading) to make the data comparable to the ACE ranks. The IQ rank was usually from a group test obtained at or before the ninth-grade level. When the word "none" is given it means that the child did not take the ACE even though it was offered, that the test was not given in his school, or that the child had dropped out or transferred before the time of the test.

b_2 = percentile ranks for the ninth (IX) and eleventh (XI) grade Cooperative English Test based on ninth- and eleventh-grade norms, respectively. The ranks were obtained from the Student Counseling Bureau of the University of Minnesota, which administers this examination also. "None" here signifies the same as "none" for the ACE score.

b_3 = high school percentile rank as determined in the eleventh or twelfth grade. DO = dropout, followed by time of dropout. Both a high school rank and dropout indication may appear if the child dropped out near the time of graduation. trans. = transfer to another school, followed by time of transfer. If a high school rank was obtained from the school of transfer, the rank appears and notation of the transfer is found only in the text. "None" sometimes appears in this space when a high school rank was not supplied even though obviously the child graduated. "None" may also mean that the child remained in school after being dropped back a year because of failure.

b_4 = Strong Vocational Interest Blank scores. These were made available by the Student Counseling Bureau of the University of Minnesota. The tests were given, generally during the eleventh grade, in approximately 50 per cent of the schools where our ninth-grade MMPI testing was done. However, not all the students in these schools elected to take the SVIB, and, in a few instances, almost no girls in a class took the test.

For the boys we have used the SVIB coding system of Hagenah and Clark (6), which is not unlike the MMPI coding system used in the *Atlas*. Darley and Hagenah's (2) occupation groups and primary, secondary, and reject patterns for males were adopted, with these modifications: production manager was included with occupation group 4, president of manufacturing concern with group 9, and C.P.A. with group 0 * (5). The scoring method may be described briefly as follows.

The profile code is formed by listing first all primary patterns (patterns for which there is a preponderance — plurality or majority — of A and/or B+ scores) and setting these to the left of a prime ('), followed by all secondary patterns (those with a preponderance of A, B+, and B scores). A dash ends the primary and secondary patterns. Reject patterns (those representing a preponderance of scores in any one occupation group that fall to the left of the "chance" or shaded area on a profile) are listed to the right of the dash. When no primary, secondary, or reject patterns are codable the symbol '– is used. The nonoccupation scales, i.e., interest maturity, occupation level, and masculinity-femininity, are not included in this coding system. A boy with an SVIB profile of 4′58–10 is thus shown to have a preponderance of A and/or B+ scores in occupation group 4. In both the occupation groups 5 and 8 he has a preponderance of A, B+, and B scores. His reject scores are in occupation groups 1 and 0.

Because there has been less research on the women's SVIB the problems of interpretation for the girls of our study were difficult. We chose to code the female blank as follows: We selected five interest categories — housewife, elementary teacher, office worker, steno-secretary, and nurse — and assigned them the letters "WR," which stands for Woman's Role. If a majority of a girl's scores fell in A

---

* The numeral 0 replaced 10 (X) as used by Darley and Hagenah to avoid confusion in code interpretation.

and/or B+ (office worker was counted only if in A since the "chance" area includes B+), the code was designated WR′, the letters going to the left of the prime. If a majority of the scores fell in A, B+, and B (steno-secretary was counted only if in B+ since the "chance" area includes B), the code was designated ′WR, the letters going to the right of the prime. A code ′– indicates that a majority of scores fell outside A, B+, and B. There was no instance of a reject pattern in the 217 female SVIB's coded for the *Atlas*.

Appendix Table 9 shows code frequencies for the boys and girls whose histories appear in the *Atlas*. "None" following SVIB signifies that the test was not taken.

c. *MMPI Profile(s)*. For this subject two MMPI profiles in addition to the one obtained in the ninth grade are available. The codes are listed in the following order:

c_1 = ninth-grade profile
c_2 = twelfth-grade profile
c_3 = a college (generally entering freshman) profile

If ninth-grade and college profiles are available, but none from the twelfth grade, dashes appear at c_2. The first profile is *always* from the ninth-grade testing.

How to Use the Atlas

Use of this *Atlas* begins with the MMPI code or codes to be interpreted. The user should turn to the *Atlas* and read the case histories that have codes most similar to the one that is under consideration. If underscoring occurs on the first two, or more, code numbers of the user's code, then these should be looked up in all permutations. For example, ′49 . . . should be considered also as ′94 . . . . As a further example, a code like 132′ . . . has six equally good possibilities, namely 123′ . . ., 132′ . . ., 213′ . . ., 231′ . . ., 312′ . . ., 321′ . . . . If the *Atlas* does not provide closely matching examples, the primes are necessarily disregarded in finding cases with similar codes.

The *Atlas* may be entered directly with a reference code by looking for closely matching ninth-grade codes in the body of the book where ninth-grade codes determine the sequence of the histories. In practice this arrangement is an index of ninth-grade codes. Three other indexes are provided at the end of the volume. The first of these shows the codes of the MMPI's taken in the twelfth grade and in college, mainly during the freshman year. This index permits one to find the histories of children with a given code at an older age. This process is retrospective, for, in contrast to the ninth-grade code, these codes came after most of the events recorded in the history. The ninth-grade code leads one toward what the child will be or do, the later codes suggest what the child has been or done. A second index shows the low points so that one may also locate histories corresponding with these. A final index shows the cases with high L and high F. One may find here some indication of the characteristic codes for these validity indicators.

For information on the relative frequencies of a given code, Appendix Tables 5 and 6 should be consulted. For example, the ′94 code is rather common and has a high-point frequency of twenty-one per thousand among male profiles. If the code is 9′4 . . . or higher, the frequency goes up to thirty per thousand, and the total incidence of 94 codes is fifty-one per thousand among those that are valid. It is interesting in this example that the more deviant code is commoner than is the one with lower scores. The low point of the profile can similarly be evaluated for frequency. The 94 code is infrequently a low code, with a rate of only two per thousand. For a whole code of 9'46–'2 0:10:15, the appendix table indicates the low point, scale 2, has a frequency of thirty-seven per thousand boys.

An important consideration should be noted in regard to the L and F scores. If these are in the valid ranges, the subject has cooperated and understood the task well enough. But if, for example, the L score is invalid, the procedure should be modified. High L profiles occur with a frequency of 2.4 per cent (Appendix Table 4). Invalid profiles should be checked by reading both the *Atlas* case histories of similar invalid codes and also those among valid codes.

For the example code cited just above, the *Atlas* includes one very close fit: 9'46–'2 2:4:15 F, Case Number 878. Unfortunately this is a girl and the example is from a boy. Possibly the sex difference is so determining on personality that one would not refer to a girl's history in interpreting a boy's code even with such close similarity of tests. (In one respect the similarity is not so close because if the girl's raw score on scale 5 were read on the male norms, the T score would be near 80 and the code would approach 5"9'46–'2, which suggests that sex could greatly affect the interpretation.) Turning to the codes of boys, one can find thirty-eight with 9' . . . . Of these boys, nineteen also have a low 2 as an additional similarity to the example code. If one wishes to check the indications of these two main similarities (9' high and 2 low), reading these nineteen cases should serve. Another possibly important category would be the cases of 94 . . . , considering only the combination of these two high points without the primes or low points. There are eighteen of these boys, and one of the profiles is invalid. Still another category could be 946 . . . –2, which includes three high points and one low point of commonality. The additional points of code similarity cut the number of cases to two boys. The L score in the example is a little higher, but otherwise these two *Atlas* codes have very close similarity to the example.

We do not yet have the evidence to say which categories of similarity are best for selecting informative case histories. The *Atlas* demonstrates the complexity of interpretation of the MMPI by the great variety of codes it lists. Probably if we had data on the problem, certain scales should be more heavily weighted for the purpose of selecting comparison case histories when a certain kind of information is desired; very likely the best categories of similarity should change for the different sorts of information. Predicting delinquency, for example, perhaps will depend on a different system for matching codes than that used for predicting mental illness. For the present, the user of the *Atlas* will usually need to depend upon arbitrary decisions.

In making notes about the cases to be used for interpretation, one should not fail to examine the additional information in the case heading material. Siblings, home structure, and the other data can be significant cues. Similarly, the test data on ability and interests and the high school rank can contribute to the summary.

Appendix Tables 5 and 6 provide two important additional rates that may be consulted in interpreting cases — rates for delinquency and for school dropout. Both of these rates are based on the frequencies of delinquency and school dropout in the statewide sample of our study. For high code 49, a delinquency rate of 54 per cent and a school dropout rate of 25 per cent are given. Since the general rates for the whole sample, as listed at the end of the table, are 34 per cent delinquency and

15 per cent dropout, one can say that, among boys with the 49 high-point code, the delinquency rate is 54/34 times the general rate and the school dropout rate is 25/15 times the general school dropout rate. Compare these data on the 49 boys with similar figures on the 05 boys: the latter have a delinquency rate of only 11 per cent and school dropout is only 5 per cent. These rates are 11/34 and 5/15, both low.

Other frequency data can be found in Appendix Tables 2 and 3, showing the stability of the ten profile high points. Here, for example, in Appendix Table 2, it may be seen that high 4 occurs in 18.2 per cent of the profiles of boys in our sample; 7.7 per cent of all the boys had primed codes with the high point 4 as high as 70 T score. On retest in the twelfth grade, 60 per cent of these 4 codes persist — 75 per cent among those that are primed. Finally, it is probably significant that none of the boys with high 4 changes so far as to have a low 4.

The appendix tables permit one other kind of comparison. Without reference to code, we checked every case history for the occurrence of any of the following descriptive terms:

erratic-unhappy	stubborn-hostile
lazy-undependable	truant
unlikable	follower-indifferent
introvert-quiet	mature
cooperative-conscientious	pleasing-well mannered
leader-very popular	peppy-scatterbrained (girls only)

This list gives one or two of the adjectives characteristically used to describe subjects in each of the single-high-point code classes. Originally a frequency tabulation was made for every adjective commonly used in the follow-up information. The resulting list of nearly one hundred adjectives had to be reduced in order to establish "families" of adjectives used frequently enough to permit statistical checks, although this meant some loss in precision of descriptiveness. Some adjectives had to be abandoned because they could not be fitted into any larger class. Where the groups of adjectives seemed to be fairly homogeneous, the reduction was accomplished arbitrarily, on face value. The class called cooperative-conscientious, for example, was a condensation from among such adjectives as dependable, hard working, and responsible. We used cooperative-conscientious as a rubric to which a case was assigned whenever any one of the adjectives of the family was actually used or, sometimes, when the sense of the case clearly supported assignment to the class.

Every case was read in random order (without knowledge of the child's MMPI scores) and tallied into the indicated class or classes. Of course, some of the cases were not tallied into any class, others were tallied into four or five. If contrasting descriptions by informants suggested it, a case was tallied into contradictory classes. For example, a boy could be called conscientious by one teacher and unreliable by another. Naturally such contrasts were rare, but we adhered to the system and included all descriptions without discrimination. Tables 1 and 2 show the number of cases put in each class under this system.

After these distributions were completed, we computed percentages to indicate the relative use of each description for each code group; that is, if there were forty boys in a code group, say high 2, and ten instances of introverted-quiet were noted in the case histories, it may be said that the frequency of use of this descriptive

Table 1. Number of Boys in Each Code Class That Fell in Each Descriptive Class

| Description | High Code | | | | | | | | | | High L | High F | Total in Each Descriptive Class |
	1	2	3	4	5	6	7	8	9	0			
Erratic-unhappy ...	3	5	4	3	1	3	6	9	11	0	7	5	57
Stubborn-hostile ...	9	5	3	18	6	5	3	14	16	4	4	16	103
Lazy-undependable	4	7	5	10	3	9	7	14	9	11	8	10	97
Truant	1	2	2	6	2	2	1	2	5	4	3	7	37
Unlikable	3	3	4	6	10	3	6	12	9	12	11	3	82
Follower-indifferent	3	7	1	13	7	8	9	12	7	9	10	15	101
Introvert-quiet	10	10	11	10	9	10	11	17	21	17	9	6	141
Mature	1	2	2	2	5	3	3	1	2	5	2	1	29
Cooperative-conscientious	8	11	13	11	12	9	12	18	11	14	11	5	135
Pleasing-well mannered ..	7	9	10	6	8	9	13	11	11	5	11	6	106
Leader-very popular	6	5	5	9	8	9	6	8	9	6	4	0	75
Total in each code class	29	40	30	58	38	41	45	75	63	42	27	30	518

Table 2. Number of Girls in Each Code Class That Fell in Each Descriptive Class

| Description | High Code [a] | | | | | | | | | High L | High F | Total in Each Descriptive Class |
	2	3	4	5	6	7	8	9	0			
Erratic-unhappy	2	3	4	5	1	2	8	6	8	5	9	53
Stubborn-hostile	0	2	12	3	5	3	7	10	1	2	7	52
Lazy-undependable	1	1	6	2	2	2	6	5	5	1	8	39
Truant	1	0	5	1	1	2	3	4	3	0	2	22
Unlikable	3	2	4	6	2	0	9	4	6	5	11	52
Follower-indifferent	1	2	3	6	3	3	4	1	5	6	8	42
Introvert-quiet	11	10	17	17	12	7	16	5	28	13	9	145
Mature	1	7	9	3	4	6	5	8	5	3	2	53
Cooperative-conscientious.	12	15	17	16	16	19	14	19	18	9	10	165
Pleasing-well mannered .	9	23	18	20	21	14	10	27	20	13	7	182
Leader-very popular	1	8	7	11	4	9	1	10	2	2	2	57
Peppy-scatterbrained ...	2	6	7	10	3	5	8	18	3	1	4	67
Total in each code class..	26	43	55	47	41	38	42	53	53	24	30	452

[a] There were not enough 1 . . . cases among the girls to be significant.

Table 3. Frequency and Percentage of Use of One Descriptive Class (Pleasing-Well Mannered) for Each Code Class of Boys and the Rank of Percentages

| Item | High Code | | | | | | | | | | High L | High F |
	1	2	3	4	5	6	7	8	9	0		
Frequency ..	7	9	10	6	8	9	13	11	11	5	11	6
Percentage ..	24	23	33	10	21	22	29	15	17	12	41	20
Rank	4	5	2	12	7	6	3	10	9	11	1	8

xvi

class for this code class is 25 per cent. We next ranked these percentages, giving rank 1 to the code group to which a given descriptive term was applied most frequently (in proportion to the size of the code group) and rank 11 (for girls — there were not enough 1 . . . cases among them to be significant) and 12 (boys) to the code group with the lowest frequency. As one example, Table 3 shows all the data for boys tallied in the pleasing-well mannered group. In this class, high L cases easily had rank 1, with scale 3 next. At the other extreme, cases with codes showing high scales 4 and 0 are rarely called pleasant.

Appendix Tables 7 and 8 list the descriptive terms under each code class in order of rank as thus calculated from highest (most frequently used description) down to lowest.

In interpretation, one may get a preliminary idea about a code class by noting from Appendix Table 7 or 8 the one or two most frequently used words as well as those infrequently used. Of course, judgment is involved here as in all other interpretative use of this *Atlas*. Although the adjectival usages are probably valid trends, not all cases in a code class were described by even the most frequently used adjective. Also, the adjectives for a given group appear at times contradictory. For example, in Appendix Table 7 the high L cases are equally described as pleasing and as unlikable. Possibly even the same boy was described by two informants with these contrasting words. It is more likely that the high L boys are really not homogeneous but divide into two types, separable in part by the way the high L trait is perceived in them by others. In view of such variation, interpretation of a high L case should be cautious. Finally, adjectives rarely used about a code group are not necessarily helpful in interpretation. High 6 cases are least often called unlikable among the possible classes of boys; this does not signify that a boy with a high 6 profile may not be unlikable, for some high 6 cases were so classed.

The *Atlas* user must integrate the information in his notes on its cases with the actual data on his case to be interpreted. Often it is best to have additional interviews with the subject or informants to inquire about points that are suggested by the *Atlas* cases but on which information is lacking or has been deliberately distorted or withheld. If suggestions from the *Atlas* fall in line with what is known of the case, this increases confidence in the user's summary built up from the *Atlas* information. Some items from the *Atlas* will not seem to apply, and certain of these may need as much explication as those that do apply. Sometimes it is important to know why a child does not exhibit a feature common among the *Atlas* cases with similar codes. If, for instance, for a given code class, the boys of the *Atlas* appear to be socially well liked and a boy being studied is not well liked, the counselor should attempt to understand why his subject is exceptional.

Drill in *Atlas* use is important. In practicing, it is helpful for several persons to work up an *Atlas* summary starting from some reference code and compare notes on the abstracted information. We are confident that there is a special skill involved in the task of abstracting information. This skill is probably similar to the clinical skill that aids in all professional evaluation of personality.

Liberal consultation of *An MMPI Codebook for Counselors* (3) and *An Atlas for the Clinical Use of the MMPI* (8) will also be of great aid to the counselor. *An MMPI Handbook* (1) should be available as well, and the work of Wirt and Briggs (16) is another useful source.

REFERENCES

1. Dahlstrom, W. G., and G. S. Welsh. *An MMPI handbook: A guide to use in clinical practice and research.* Minneapolis: University of Minnesota Press, 1960.
2. Darley, J. G., and T. Hagenah. *Vocational interest measurement: Theory and practice.* Minneapolis: University of Minnesota Press, 1956.
3. Drake, L. E., and E. R. Oetting. *An MMPI codebook for counselors.* Minneapolis: University of Minnesota Press, 1959.
4. Duker, J. The utility of the MMPI Atlas in the derivation of personality descriptions. Unpublished Ph.D. thesis, University of Minnesota, 1958.
5. Hagenah, T. A normative study of the Revised Strong Vocational Interest Blank for Men. Unpublished Ph.D. thesis, University of Minnesota, 1953.
6. Hagenah, T., and K. E. Clark. "A coding system for the Strong Vocational Interest Blank" (in press).
7. Hathaway, S. R. "A coding system for MMPI profile classification," *J. consult. Psychol.,* 11:334–337 (1947).
8. Hathaway, S. R., and P. E. Meehl. *An atlas for the clinical use of the MMPI.* Minneapolis: University of Minnesota Press, 1951.
9. Hathaway, S. R., and E. D. Monachesi. *Analyzing and predicting juvenile delinquency with the MMPI.* Minneapolis: University of Minnesota Press, 1953.
10. Hathaway, S. R., and E. D. Monachesi. "The personalities of predelinquent boys," *J. Crim. Law, Criminol. and Pol. Sci.,* 48:149–163 (1957).
11. Hathaway, S. R., E. D. Monachesi, and L. A. Young. "Rural-urban adolescent personality," *Rural Sociology,* 24:331–346 (1959).
12. Hathaway, S. R., E. D. Monachesi, and L. A. Young. "Delinquency rates and personality," *J. Crim. Law, Criminol. and Pol. Sci.,* 50:433–440 (1960).
13. Lykken, D. T. "A method of actuarial pattern analysis," *Psychol. Bull.,* 53:102–107 (1956).
14. Meehl, P. E. *Clinical versus statistical prediction: A theoretical analysis and a review of the evidence.* Minneapolis: University of Minnesota Press, 1954.
15. Meehl, P. E. "Wanted — a good cookbook," *Amer. Psychologist,* 11:263–272 (1956).
16. Wirt, R. D., and P. F. Briggs, "Personality and environmental factors in the development of delinquency," *Psychol. Monogr.,* 1959, No. 485.

CASE HISTORIES

1. F:14:5	ACE IX, 42; XI, 53	–<u>13</u>′	1:6:8
N:III:2	ENG IX, 75; XI, 85	′93<u>45</u>–2′	1:2:14
	HSR 86		
	SVIB ′WR		

This was a "chubby, sweet girl." She was reliable, cooperative, and active in sports, but she was not a leader. Occasionally she would flare up in anger, but her display of temper would quickly end with a laugh. She did not follow in the pattern of her family, who were "fanatically religious." After graduation she went to a junior college.

One of her brothers was considered one of the worst behavior problems the school had ever had; he was said to be like his father. The father sided with his son against authorities and was a problem to the police, who had the responsibility of controlling the boy. The parents were financially in good circumstances and paid the expenses incurred by the misbehavior of their children. Possibly the boy was favored over his sister.

2. M:15:1	ACE IX, 88; XI, 49	–1′<u>3429</u>	2:2:13
N:III:2	ENG IX, 80; XI, 81	′46–7′	3:2:19
	HSR 62		
	SVIB 4′28–		

This boy was "impersonal, imperturbable, and self-confident." He was indifferent and unmotivated in his schoolwork, in which he barely got by. He was courteous and neatly dressed. Outside of school he was a good worker; he played in a jazz band and worked as a mechanic. It is possible that he had little vitality left for school. He had a police record for stealing and traffic offenses. After graduation he went to college.

The father, a businessman, frequently helped school authorities with projects. The mother was "an outstanding person, very active in community affairs."

3. F:14:1	ACE IX, 21; XI, 26	–<u>136</u>′8	3:4:8
N:V:1	ENG IX, none; XI, 67	′<u>92</u>–<u>61</u>′	8:2:15
	HSR 39		
	SVIB none		

This girl was pretty, courteous, neat, friendly, pleasant, and well mannered. She was shy and timid until she reached the upper grades, when she appeared to outgrow these traits. Her teachers thought of her as an average student throughout high school. She was often tardy but did not present any real behavior problems. In her senior year she was married and had a child, but returned to school to graduate.

4. M:15:2	ACE IX, 77; XI, 89	–1'3689	5:2:15
N:III:5	ENG IX, 76; XI, 54	'94638–0'5	3:3:20
	HSR 42		
	SVIB none		

His teachers had talked to this boy many times in their efforts to understand him, but he remained an enigma to them. His performance was erratic in almost everything he tried to do whether scholastic or extracurricular. He would be good for two weeks and then he would slump. It was difficult to keep him working. He had no plans for the future. The prediction of delinquent behavior made by one ninth-grade teacher was not confirmed in the later check of police records.

5. F:14:2	ACE IX, 59; XI, 47	–1'385	2:0:14
N:I:4	ENG IX, 74; XI, 64	–9'4650	0:0:16
	HSR 70	–'460	2:1:14
	SVIB none		

This girl was a fiery redhead who always got her own way from her parents and others. She liked her freedom and she liked activity, but she was no discipline problem. Her behavior seemed to be well channeled and she had a small group of good friends. She continued on to university study.

6. F:16:5	ACE IX, 40; XI, 33	–1'387	1:3:14
B:VI:1	ENG IX, none; XI, 46		
	HSR 25; DO 12th gr.		
	SVIB none		

This girl was "sulky and unkempt." She "had a mustache problem." Her associates were "a motorcycle crowd." In her schoolwork she was indifferent and negative. Before her senior year she quit school to be married — "which was probably of necessity." One teacher predicted she would have legal difficulties.

   Her parents had been divorced before she entered high school.

7. M:14:2	ACE IX, 59; XI, 33	–14'7063	4:2:12
N:IVB:5	ENG IX, 33; XI, 34		
	HSR 49		
	SVIB 4'8–5		

In junior high school this boy was frequently sent to the principal's office for causing minor disturbances. By the time he entered senior high school, however, he was thought of as a good boy and was well liked, although he was not a leader. When one first met him he seemed more reserved than was actually the case. He was on the football team.

8. M:15:1   ACE IX, 93; XI, 88   –1'6<u>70</u>   1:5:16
    N:III:3   ENG IX, 38; XI, 76
                       HSR 41
                       SVIB none

Generally this boy was seen as making a good adjustment. He had a fine personality
and seemed socially at ease. Although sometimes noisy and not always dependable
in his schoolwork, he could be counted on to be cooperative and to display good
common sense. He was inclined to become overly familiar with his teachers.

    The father, a hard-working mechanic, was quiet and inarticulate although "a
fine person." The mother was very nervous and had hysterical outbursts. She took
an active part in community affairs and was well accepted within her circle of
friends.

9. F:14:1   ACE IX, none; XI, 97   –1<u>68</u>'<u>37</u> <u>042</u>   1:1:11
    N:III:2   ENG IX, none; XI, 100
                       HSR 100
                       SVIB '–

There were contrasts in the descriptions of this girl. To some she was talented,
mature, likable, outgoing and pleasant in manner, displaying remarkable integrity
and poise. She was a good student, a capable cook and seamstress. Others, while
agreeing with much of this description, emphasized her aggressiveness and stated
that she was opinionated and often rude, and that she had a streak of stubbornness.
Some teachers complained that while her scholastic achievement was high, she
did not make full use of or always properly channel her abilities. She liked to do
things her own way; she did not hesitate to correct others — even adults — although she did not take correction well herself. She became bored with routine and
was impatient with slow thinkers. In her senior year she declined membership in a
scholastic honor society because she did not agree with some of its policies. After
completing high school she married "an amiable but mediocre man."

    The father was a small businessman. The girl shared many things with him; she
claimed, however, that he was jealous of her boy friends.

10. F:14:2   ACE IX, 61; XI, 74   –1'9   4:2:18
    N:V:1   ENG IX, none; XI, 64
                       HSR 32
                       SVIB none

This girl was "wholesome and healthy looking." She had a nice personality and she
was extremely friendly and outgoing. Her main extracurricular interest was in
dramatics.

11. M:15:4   ACE IX, 94; XI, 99   –2′   3:1:15
    N:II:1   ENG IX, none; XI, 72
                    HSR 81
                    SVIB 8′–

Described as "the Jack Armstrong type," this boy was popular, outgoing, and talkative. He was a leader in many school activities, "a good school citizen."

12. F:14:4   ACE IX, 82; XI, 61   –21′509   4:2:15
    N:VI:4   ENG IX, none; XI, 98   ′34 89 67–5′2   4:1:21
                    HSR 78
                    SVIB ′WR

This girl was quiet, reserved, and not a leader. Most characteristically, she seemed to be trying to do a good job; she was always willing and eager to please. She had an average number of friends but was in few activities. She worked part time as a secretary and planned on a similar full-time position after graduation.

13. F:15:7   ACE IX, 84; XI, 87   –24′359   4:5:18
    B:VII:4   ENG IX, 91; XI, 93   ′67–5′24   6:2:18
                    HSR 100
                    SVIB WR′

This girl had few friends and no boy friends; she was "very reserved and very alone." She "went to school to study" and she became class valedictorian. She also worked after school hours. In her family she was distinguished as the only one who had achieved in any outstanding way.

Possibly because of the size of the family, the girl lived with her grandmother. The father was commonly unemployed. He was dull but nice and friendly — "too little pay and too many kids" was one comment on his situation. The mother, who was often ill, was hospitable and friendly, although she lacked social skills. She was interested in the children and she also worked outside the home when she could. All the other children seemed "faithful and likable but poor scholars." The family had "an old-fashioned sense of values."

14. M:14:2   ACE IX, none; XI, 82   –2614′35   2:1:14
    N:V:1   ENG IX, none; XI, 79
                    HSR 43
                    SVIB none

This boy was very interested in and good at athletics. He was bright and well liked by fellow students, although he was also said to be overbearing and outspoken. He was always attempting to monopolize situations with excessive talk. These characteristics led him to be a troublemaker in the classroom, where he was "always chattering and creating disturbances."

15. F:14:1	ACE IX, 78; XI, 41	–2'<u>65</u>	3:1:14
N:V:1	ENG IX, none; XI, 92	'0978–	3:4:9
	HSR 69		
	SVIB none		

This girl had a tendency to be overweight and only erratically tried to diet; however, her appearance was neat. She was well liked and a leader in many activities. In fact, she took on more than she could handle. Her scholastic work was not outstanding, but she had good ability in music and art. Her hobbies were sports and roller skating. One teacher saw her as a rather unstable and unpredictable but likable girl with a good sense of humor. She went with a group of girls whose main interest was boys, and it was said that she had "emotional problems concerning boys." There were episodes when she burst into tears, but she would quickly recover and seem happy. In her senior year she became pregnant but managed to finish school, after which she was married. The marriage was not a very happy one, and it was said that she contemplated divorce. One ninth-grade teacher had predicted that the girl would have legal problems.

16. F:15:0	ACE IX, 74; XI, 79	–2'8	5:1:18
N:III:1	ENG IX, 66; XI, 80		
	HSR 77		
	SVIB none		

This girl was well liked by fellow students and teachers. She was considered to be a nice girl although somewhat nervous. She was no particular problem in school and apparently wanted to do well, but she was not a very serious person. On one occasion she was caught cheating and she showed a feeling of guilt about this. Her teachers also thought she got more help from her mother than was appropriate for her development. She did not show much interest in boys during high school. She played in the school band, and after school hours she worked in a clerical position, in which she did very well.

17. F:15:1	ACE IX, 50; XI, 38	–3'<u>12769</u>	7:4:11
N:VI:2	ENG IX, none; XI, 51		
	HSR 80		
	SVIB none		

This girl was pleasant and friendly but very quiet. The most characteristic thing about her was that when a test was announced she got sick and missed school. When she made the test up she usually did well, but if she was forced to take it at the regular time, she did poorly. Other students teased her about "morning sickness." By her senior year her attendance record was better and she had matured somewhat.

18. M:15:3   ACE IX, 44; XI, 59   –3′<u>29</u>   2:6:15
    N:VI:3   ENG IX, 53; XI, 27   ′6–81′<u>79</u>   1:2:10
                  HSR 33
                  SVIB ′4–

A farm boy, this youth was described as friendly, respectful, and quiet. He did not participate in school activities and eventually became uncooperative and obviously uninterested in school.

The father was "flippant and unsettled," changing jobs quite often. The mother was a fairly good person who attended church regularly and "practiced her Christianity."

19. M:14:5   ACE IX, 44; XI, 26   –34′19   3:4:9
    B:IVB:5   ENG IX, 32; XI, 31
                  HSR 18
                  SVIB none

This boy began accumulating an extensive police record during the summer following the ninth grade. His offenses included breaking and entering, shoplifting, and traffic violations. He was committed to a correctional school but he later returned to complete high school with his class. His conduct after his return was good and he was described by some as a "cooperative and willing student." Teachers tended to differ rather markedly in their descriptions of him. One described him as having "a lot of personality; a likable, friendly, and outgoing boy who was something of a show-off and did anything on a dare." Although admitting that he did not have much "moral fiber," teachers with this point of view believed his difficulties resulted from a broken home and too lenient foster parents. Others characterized him as "very mouthy," antagonistic, uneasy, having a chip on his shoulder. They saw him as undependable, sneaky, and always ready with excuses. After completing high school he married and began training for a semiprofessional career.

The boy grew up in the home of relatives after the death of his mother. His foster father was described as sociable and easygoing but a drinker who chased around with other women when he had enough money. He was also criticized by some for his business practices. The foster mother was "very strict, matronly, average in dress but not too neat." Her own children were said to be well behaved and well looked after.

20. F:14:2   ACE IX, none; XI, 52   –3′<u>9461</u>   3:2:10
    N:III:2   ENG IX, none; XI, 81   ′2<u>06</u> <u>47</u>–95′   2:3:13
                  HSR 68
                  SVIB none

Although this girl had good motivation, she was quiet and retiring, and had "a nondescript personality." She worked hard and was a good student but did not take part in any activities.

21. M:14:1	ACE IX, none; XI, 84	−4′	2:4:12
N:VI:3	ENG IX, none; XI, 80	−′2178	2:2:14
	HSR 81		
	SVIB none		

This boy was active in school affairs. He was particularly interested in singing. His best academic subjects were mathematics and science, and he was interested in becoming an engineer. Friendly and courteous, he was generally well liked. "He was grateful for small favors."

22. M:15:1	ACE IX, 82; XI, 87	−41′25 67	8:2:15
N:III:3	ENG IX, 73; XI, 77		
	HSR 85		
	SVIB 4′2–90		

President of his class, this boy took part in many activities. He was always pleasant, polite, and courteous. "They do not come any better."

23. M:15:2	ACE IX, none; XI, 52	−4′1856730	3:0:14
N:V:1	ENG IX, none; XI, 39		
	HSR 05		
	SVIB 4′−		

Minor disciplinary infractions were noted for this boy: sometimes he talked too much, he ran around a lot, and he "had a few sex problems." At times he could be surly. Sometimes he was impetuous and he had a tendency to give up easily. In contrast to the poor work in his studies, he was an outstanding athlete. One could describe him as a friendly person who spent too much time daydreaming.

24. F:14:0	ACE IX, 94; XI, 94	−429′57	4:1:16
N:IVB:7	ENG IX, 98; XI, 94		
	HSR 100		
	SVIB ′WR		

This girl excelled in scholarship but she was relatively inactive socially. She never was a conduct problem and she seemed to be completely stable. Her school activities were curtailed in part because she had responsibilities at home where she cared for her sick mother. Her parents gave her little liberty and she was often called for after games or other events. She wanted to be a teacher.

Before the girl entered high school the father had been a heavy drinker and had trouble keeping a job. He then had a period of illness and shortly after this inherited considerable money and property. From this time on he became a good parent and an acceptable citizen.

25. F:15:1   ACE IX, none; XI, 98   –4'31528   5:0:14
    N:V:3   ENG IX, none; XI, 100
               HSR 97
               SVIB none

This girl was emotionally stable and a good student, "very dependable and fine." She was active in school affairs and was particularly interested in music.

26. F:14:4   ACE IX, none; XI, 76   –5'1   4:4:12
    N:VII:4   ENG IX, none; XI, 84   '8937–'5   4:6:16
               HSR 87
               SVIB none

This girl was bright and she worked up to her ability, but she was not a leader. She was well dressed and was popular in her group. Very religious, she refused to wear makeup and she had no dates with boys.
    The mother was said to be very emotional. There was "good home supervision."

27. F:14:1   ACE IX, none; XI, 90   –51'429   7:5:16
    N:IVB:3   ENG IX, none; XI, 95   '08–259'14 4:1:17
               HSR 90
               SVIB none

This girl was quiet and shy, and so inconspicuous in school that the teachers considered her not very bright. She was very small in stature; this may have troubled her some and made her more retiring. She was not a conduct problem, and she did what she was expected to do. The students neither welcomed nor rejected her from their groups. She took part in few school activities.

28. M:14:3   IQ (centile) 33   –51'768902 8:2:14
    N:III:2   HSR DO 11th gr.
               SVIB none

This boy was guilty of many relatively minor offenses such as disorderly conduct, various traffic violations, and driving his father's car without permission. In school he was obscene in language, belligerent toward other students, insubordinate, and frequently truant. He was "unable or unwilling to succeed." Both emotional maladjustment and delinquency were predicted for this boy by his ninth-grade teachers. In the eleventh grade he quit school to join the Navy.

29. F:15:2   ACE IX, 11; XI, 41   –54′21   0:1:6
     N:VI:1   ENG IX, none; XI, 60
                  HSR 47
                  SVIB none

This girl was cooperative and reliable. She was considered an average student who worked almost up to her capacity. She was socially active and well liked. She hoped to go to college after her graduation.

30. M:15:3   ACE IX, 42; XI, 62   –5980′37   0:10:3
     N:VII:1   ENG IX, none; XI, 23
                  HSR DO 12th gr.
                  SVIB none

This boy "had common sense, but didn't like school." He had a nice personality most of the time, but would occasionally become sullen. He was completely indifferent and negative in school. "He tried to get by with a lot." His grades were poor and he finally dropped out in the beginning of his senior year. Two teachers predicted he would develop legal or emotional trouble. In his sophomore and junior years he was guilty of a number of traffic offenses.

31. M:14:9   ACE IX, 74; XI, 82   –6′23   0:1:17
     N:V:7   ENG IX, 68; XI, 78
                  HSR 74
                  SVIB 4′–90

One teacher saw this boy as "probably better mannered than any young man known." Another said of him, "You name it and he has it." The faculty "dreaded having him graduate because he was so fine and honorable." He placed team and school before his own desires. He was a talented person whose observations were keen; he was original and courageous. His excellent contributions to the school included activities in music, drama, and athletics. After graduation he went on to a small college.

32. F:14:2   ACE IX, 85; XI, 72   –62′7   7:4:16
     N:IVA:5   ENG IX, 69; XI, 90   ′46837–0′29   2:0:24
                  HSR 92
                  SVIB ′–

"She was an all-American girl, topnotch in every way," said one informant. Attractive, poised, and charming, this girl was dependable and faithful, excellent in school and church work. She had a warm, winning personality. Because of her beauty and exceptional qualities, some students, both boys and girls, resented her. The only shortcomings mentioned about her were that she seemed to lack leadership and possibly was not tactful with other students. She went to college after graduation and there was chosen homecoming queen.

The father, though "pompous and opinionated," was likable enough and a good businessman. The mother was tactlessly honest and critical of faculty members. She was very active in church and community. The home was considered a fine one and the parents were financially able to give their children many things. However, rules were laid down and enforced.

33. M:14:5	ACE IX, 88; XI, 82	–67'5<u>23</u> 4:4:15
N:IVB:2	ENG IX, none; XI, 64	
	HSR 70	
	SVIB 4'1–0	

Small in stature, this boy resented his size. Although he was not a conduct problem, he was "scrappy and took no guff." He was immature in manner. He was moderately popular and an above average student.

34. M:14:2	ACE IX, 74; XI, 86	–7'2<u>10</u> 2:0:14
N:V:2	ENG IX, 89; XI, 98	
	HSR 90	
	SVIB 90'–4	

This boy had nice manners and was socially poised, articulate, and generally friendly. He had high moral and scholastic standards. He was described as not particularly masculine but "never thought of as feminine." He was active in drama. Other students tended to seek him out, but he was not a strong leader.

35. M:14:7	ACE IX, 100; XI, 100	–7'3<u>0125</u> 1:5:12
B:VI:2	ENG IX, 100; XI, 99	
	HSR 36	
	SVIB none	

This boy seemed defensive about both his home and his abilities, although he tested very high in intelligence. He was an indifferent student. His school attendance was irregular and he needed to be constantly urged to do his schoolwork. "He was not belligerent, merely indifferent." He made little effort to be socially accepted, and he tended to associate with the "wrong crowd." He was weak and pale in appearance and a heavy smoker. In an earlier grade he had entered a house and stolen some money, but he gave no further known trouble of this kind. After completing high school he entered college.

The father had deserted the family. The mother had not only her own children to care for but those of a relative as well. The home situation was described as "confusing." The children were said to be bright and they worked to help support themselves.

36. F:16:2	ACE IX, 26; XI, 06	–76'93	4:7:8
N:VII:4	ENG IX, 15; XI, 26		
	HSR DO 11th gr.		
	SVIB none		

This girl was neat in appearance and sweet and friendly in manner. She had a number of good friends in her own small group. In her junior year she became pregnant and dropped out of school to be married. She had been very slow in her schoolwork, but she tried hard. Her marriage seemed to be a happy one.

The father was unimaginative, easygoing, and indulgent with the children. The mother was "just a child intellectually," a friendly, dull, harmless chatterer; however, she seemed to be the dominant member of the family. The parents were very devoted to their children and, within the very limited means of the family, the girl was overindulged. Both parents worked but their income was low and they were often unrealistic in their planning and handling of financial matters.

37. F:14:3	ACE IX, 44; XI, 79	–78'624 93	5:2:13
N:V:2	ENG IX, none; XI, 81		
	HSR 68		
	SVIB WR′		

This was a large, motherly girl, a "domestic type." She was shy and retiring and in no activities. She had a few friends, mostly farm girls.

38. M:15:2	IQ (centile) 92	–9'17	4:1:16
N:V:3	HSR 96		
	SVIB ′4–		

This boy was responsible, reliable, and mature. In his schoolwork he was a good student — hard working and helpful. He had a fine disposition. After completing his junior year he transferred to a school in another state.

39. F:14:1   ACE IX, none; XI, 71   −9′<u>41</u>   2:0:19
    B:IVB:6   ENG IX, none; XI, 53
                  HSR none
                  SVIB none

This was a commonplace, "comfortable type" of girl with better than average grades. She was well liked and rated high on all general personality traits except that of leadership.

40. F:14:2   ACE IX, none; XI, 25   −′96   6:3:21
    N:III:1   ENG IX, none; XI, 59   ′498<u>367</u>−′2 3:3:18
                  HSR 60   ′8475−   3:2:22
                  SVIB none

Because of her religious affiliation this girl did not mix well and her social life centered in her church associations. Her conduct and effort in school were satisfactory. Her strongest work was in orchestra; she was weakest in science. She enjoyed sewing and did well in it. For recreation she liked outdoor activities. While in school she had part-time jobs doing office work or selling. In appearance she was "not particularly attractive."

The mother was considered to be overly solicitous for her daughter, but it was said that the daughter was "okay in spite of her mother." The mother was a pleasant, outgoing woman. Another daughter was much more socially comfortable and active.

41. F:15:3   ACE IX, 52; XI, 77   −9′<u>713</u> 6:2:17
    N:IVB:4   ENG IX, 87; XI, 85   ′<u>64</u>−51′2 4:4:15
                  HSR 38
                  SVIB none

This girl had a "Bohemian attitude." She was independent and an individualist. Although she took some liberties in school, she was not a real conduct problem. She was lacking in tact and was thought of as "a little busybody."

42. M:15:4   ACE IX, 17; XI, none   ′1−<u>25</u>′6 4:3:15
    N:VII:1   ENG IX, none; XI, none
                  HSR DO 11th gr.
                  SVIB none

This boy was well liked "in his particular crowd" and his teachers described him as an "average and friendly kid." His ability in schoolwork was poor and, because of his poor marks and lack of interest, he dropped out in his junior year. While still in school he was charged with operating a motor vehicle without a driver's license.

43. M:14:5	IQ (centile) 58	′1–5′9	5:3:18
N:II:1	HSR none	′0<u>9873</u>–′12	3:10:6
	SVIB none		

"Fat and lazy in appearance," this youth was tired all the time and one teacher wondered if "something might be wrong with him." He did not try in class and was very poor in his schoolwork. Another teacher said that all the members of this family were "good as gold but dumb." In his senior year this boy got into some trouble because he was caught drinking beer.

44. F:16:3	IQ (centile) 21	123<u>40</u>′8769–5′	8:11:10
N:VI:1	HSR DO 11th gr.		
	SVIB none		

This girl was well mannered, neat, and friendly, and she tried hard in school. In spite of her effort, she was slow and lacking in self-assurance. She seemed to do best when she was praised, and she resented criticism.

45. F:14:3	ACE IX, none; XI, 11	123″7860′45–9′	6:10:11
N:VII:4	ENG IX, none; XI, 35	1<u>203</u>′784<u>65</u>–9′	9:5:15
	HSR 48		
	SVIB none		

Several teachers predicted that this "inactive, lethargic, and inert" girl would become emotionally maladjusted, and at the time of testing she was already judged to be so. She had ulcers, and it was believed that she was unhappy, probably about her home. She was regarded as needing help, as standing apart from the rest of the students, and as having few or no friends. One teacher felt that she was a typical case of someone who worshipped a teacher. She was not a conduct problem in school and she was a hard worker at her studies, possibly an overachiever for her ability.

1'28573496–

The family was considered a "bad one." The father was chronically ill and the mother was apparently inadequate. One of the brothers was in a considerable amount of trouble, and another "had gone berserk."

46. M:16:7	IQ (centile) 16	1'28573496–	9:3:24
N:IVC:5	HSR trans. 12th gr.		
	SVIB none		

This was a small and physically immature boy, described as "sneaky, shifty, and having a poor attitude." He appeared arrogant and "always had an answer." He once stole a bicycle and painted it so that it could not be recognized. It was said that he could not be convinced of his wrongdoing. He was lax in school attendance, and when present he was annoying because of inattentiveness which was upsetting to the entire class.

47. M:14:3	ACE IX, 99; XI, 100	'13–'5	6:3:17
N:VII:6	ENG IX, 97; XI, 90	——	——
	HSR 71	'43–'05	1:2:22
	SVIB 4'–		

Although he was likable most of the time and had many friends, this boy did not take an active part in school affairs. Sometimes he was an aggressive show-off and "tangled" with the school principal. His teachers described him as sarcastic, sharp-tongued, and outspoken, and yet they also characterized him as conscientious, as "responsible to a point," and as "honest and straightforward." He was moderately handicapped by poor eyesight. He continued on at a university in an engineering course.

48. M:15:4	ACE IX, 38; XI, 56	'1348–5'920	8:6:21
N:III:1	ENG IX, 38; XI, 34	'48–5'209	5:4:21
	HSR 59		
	SVIB 4'8–5		

His teachers found this boy cooperative, reliable, and conscientious; their descriptions included phrases ranging from "extremely quiet" to "rather quiet." Some teachers called him withdrawn and perhaps depressed. They could give no reason for the depression. Others called him likable, friendly, well balanced, pleasant, happy, well adjusted. "He did a job well but it was tough for him"; he was a conformist with "good self-discipline." A twin sister in the same class was described as a slightly more able student. [The MMPI codes for the twin were, ninth grade,

08″726′43–'9 3:11:4, and, twelfth grade, 8″7204′6913–'5 2:11:11.] While attending school he had a part-time job. After graduation he went to a small college.

The family was a "close-knit" one. Although one person described the whole family as shy and retiring, it was repeatedly emphasized that the home was a fine one — "outstanding for this day and age." The parents were very interested in the school activities of the children.

49. M:14:1	ACE IX, none; XI, 53	'135078962–	7:6:16
N:III:2	ENG IX, none; XI, 46	'8396–'05	1:4:18
	HSR 66		
	SVIB none		

About the only distinctive thing said of this boy was that he was very active in the Boy Scouts. He worked up to his capacity in school, was pleasant and well motivated. He got into no trouble but contributed nothing in particular. He "had his friends" among the students, and seemed to be generally well liked.

50. F:14:6	ACE IX, none; XI, 44	'13607284–'5	9:5:17
N:VI:2	ENG IX, none; XI, 42		
	HSR 47 DO 12th gr.		
	SVIB none		

In most instances, descriptions of this girl were mildly negative. She was "very quiet and just filled a seat in the classroom." She did not care about school and did very little work. She was unreliable and frequently absent from school, finally dropping out in the winter of the twelfth grade. Shortly after this she was married. Throughout her high school days she was regarded as a girl mainly interested in boys and marriage.

51. M:14:5	ACE IX, none; XI, 41	'137–2'56	2:4:15
N:IVC:3	ENG IX, 63; XI, 64	'834 671–0'592	1:2:24
	HSR 57		
	SVIB none		

This boy liked farming and was active in the 4-H Club; he was indifferent in school and did not work hard. In class he was unaggressive and "a talker although easily subdued." He was somewhat mischievous and occasionally "sassy." He "tested authority." He did not have many friends and was in very few school activities.

52. M:14:5   ACE IX, 28; XI, 50   13'7268590–'4   5:6:13
    N:VII:1   ENG IX, none; XI, 28
                HSR 04
                SVIB none

One teacher said of this boy: "He shows little ability and even less ambition." His teachers had to constantly prod him to do his work because of his slow, easygoing, and lazy attitudes. He was continually failing or on the verge of failing in school, but this seemed not to bother him — he would go to a movie during the afternoon rather than spend the time on his schoolwork. He did not graduate with his class but was later granted a diploma after doing additional work. When he did complete assignments, his work was neat, always in ink and written with an irregular hand. A nice-looking boy, he caused no trouble around school. He was described as shy, nonaggressive, and always very polite. He respected school authority and readily conformed to its rules and regulations. Noted for having a pleasant disposition, he appeared happy, cheerful, friendly, and ready with a smile. He went out for track, but dropped it after an injury. He was never a leader but did take part in some church youth activities. It was believed that he did not date.

During high school his expressed vocational goals became increasingly less ambitious. Throughout his youth he worked at odd jobs and reportedly turned the money over to his father to help with the family finances. After finally completing high school he entered the armed services. Several teachers expressed the view that the boy had a lot to overcome and that, everything considered, "he had done well in spite of his background."

When in the eighth grade, he and several other boys had entered and ransacked a cabin, for which he had been brought to juvenile court and placed on probation. He had himself earned the money to make restitution. Reports called him "a pretty good boy," except for this one offense.

The family had always received some kind of supplemental public assistance. The father was "irregular" and at times alcoholic. Because of his drinking he had only a series of odd jobs; however, the welfare agency felt that he "did all he could under the circumstances." The family had had some bad luck: the father was disabled for a year because of an industrial accident; the mother was ill with a chronic condition, although she sometimes worked outside the home at menial jobs. An older sister of the boy had been seriously delinquent; she was possibly a bad influence on the other children. The home was described as messy and dirty.

53. M:15:2   ACE IX, none; XI, 38   1'387249–'5   7:14:16
    N:VI:2   ENG IX, none; XI, 06   '6890–'2   3:8:12
                HSR 31
                SVIB none

Described as "an automobile bug," this boy was in a number of auto accidents during high school. He sometimes created a problem in class by his talking. Enthusiastic, always happy and smiling, he had many friends with him at all times. He would not work in class, and outside of class he went with a group of "leather-jacket boys" during his last years of high school.

54. F:14:2   IQ (centile) 88   '130724–95'   3:2:18
    N:IVB:3   HSR 35   –9'781   2:2:16
                    SVIB none

This farm girl was a "wholesome 4-H type, well adjusted in all ways, with some good friends." Her interests were domestic, and she was going steady with a nice boy.

55. F:15:1   ACE IX, 38; XI, none   '130867–9'4   4:3:17
    N:II:4   ENG IX, 50; XI, none
                    HSR trans. 11th gr.
                    SVIB none

A significant change occurred in this girl during her high school years. Originally shy, colorless, and "overshadowed by her older sister," she "blossomed into a charming, poised, and capable young woman" after the older sister graduated. Her quietness developed into dependability and self-assurance, and she made lasting, sincere friends. A teacher commented that "it was marvelous to watch her steady and sure development." The family moved when she was in the eleventh grade, and she graduated in another state.

The family presented a "fine social front," but there was inner tension and bad feeling between the mother and some of her in-laws, who lived nearby. The mother was crippled and used her illness to "enslave" the family. The older sister was said to have made life miserable for the entire family by taking advantage of the mother's illness. The father was a more stable person. He was a successful businessman and a good provider. It was "in order to ensure his family's happiness and his wife's health" that he sold his business and moved to another state.

56. M:14:1   IQ (centile) 93   1'4237 6890–'5   2:5:18
    N:III:1   HSR trans. 9th gr.
                    SVIB none

The special interests of this boy were sports and music. In his schoolwork he was a fair student, best in mathematics and art. He never caused any difficulty. He was always neat, polite, cooperative, and cheerful. He hoped to go to college after graduation.

57. M:14:5   ACE IX, none; XI, 22   1"432'7806–'5   2:8:19
    N:V:2   ENG IX, none; XI, 01
                    HSR 03
                    SVIB none

This boy associated with bad companions and was often absent from school. While in school he caused frequent disturbances — by putting gum in a girl's hair, using foul language in the hallway, kicking his locker. He drank and was considered untrustworthy and unreliable. His main extracurricular activity was wrestling. The boy was once caught shoplifting a valuable object. He was guilty of several traffic offenses and was caught by the police purchasing whisky. He had a record of vandalism, having broken a window with a snowball and having willfully destroyed school property.

58. M:14:2	ACE IX, 75; XI, 56	'1<u>43589</u>–'0	3:6:18
B:VI:5	ENG IX, 90; XI, 74	'2<u>7163458</u>–'0	2:5:15
	HSR 63		
	SVIB '589–		

Eighth-grade reports about this boy revealed he was "a conduct problem and a show-off; undependable and without pride in his work." In his early high school years he was often absent, possibly because of frequent illness. He "never talked over his problems with the counselor," and the minister reported that he "could not reach the boy, who had a hard shell of indifference." The boy was "never home and always aimlessly driving around." At the time these unfavorable impressions were formed he was going with "the wrong crowd." However, after "the principal talked with the boy, he changed, becoming pretty well adjusted." He subsequently began to work, becoming more steady and reliable. He appeared more outgoing and friendly, and he developed an interest in athletics. Apparently he became active enough so that other students accepted him, and at least one person called him "a normal, natural boy." He entered military service after high school.

Both the social status and the reputation of the family were poor. The parents were described as "tramps," and the father was an alcoholic. The mother's behavior was considered very irregular by local moral standards, and neither she nor the husband supervised the children, although it was mentioned that the mother babied the boy. The mother's health was not good; she was very obese and was always complaining. The parents had been divorced while the boy was in elementary school.

59. M:14:1	ACE IX, none; XI, 82	14'8<u>6357</u>–'90	6:14:16
N:VI:3	ENG IX, 73; XI, 73	4'536–2'0	5:3:19
	HSR 32		
	SVIB none		

This boy had two appearances: To the students he had qualities making for popularity and they elected him to high school offices. To the teachers he had an offensive personality; he was argumentative and a "wise guy"; he expected favors from them. He associated with "the hoodlum element," and he was described as a "sharp kid." He had a steady girl friend. He had a record of traffic violations, of possession of beer, and of possessing an uncased gun.

60. M:14:0	ACE IX, 77; XI, 97	1'637502–	7:5:17
N:I:4	ENG IX, 71; XI, 61	'135–'09	3:2:18
	HSR 80		
	SVIB none		

This was a very active boy; "in fact, it seemed that he had to be active." He gave the impression of being extroverted and aggressive; however, he was never belligerent. He characteristically spoke in a big loud voice that some persons described as "grating." During his early high school years he was considered "mouthy," but he had "tamed down" quite a bit by his senior year. He had many friends and displayed a great deal of initiative and ability to accept responsibility both in his schoolwork and in extracurricular activities. One person, observing him outside the school setting, said that he "liked to be alone and was a bookworm." A teacher had felt when he was in the ninth grade that he was likely to become emotionally maladjusted.

61. M:14:8	ACE IX, 03; XI, 04	'16390–2'75	4:8:14
N:IVC:5	ENG IX, 10; XI, 05	'3856742–	8:6:23
	HSR 35		
	SVIB 1'2–5		

The oldest child in a large family, this boy had the responsibility of running the family farm while his father worked in town. He was described as "a really fine boy," but quite reserved, unaggressive, shy, and a follower rather than a leader. In part these qualities were thought to be the result of a somewhat overpowering home situation. At school he was a hard worker and "a top student" in vocational shop courses.

The home situation was described as very poor. The father, a "hotheaded" man, had been jailed on several occasions for stealing. The boy's many positive characteristics were said to be in sharp contrast to those of the other members of his family.

62. M:14:9	IQ (centile) 23	168'4239–	7:7:15
N:VII:5	HSR none		
	SVIB none		

The "pool-hall type," this boy had little ambition and made no attempt to gain acceptance by others. He disliked school and was deliberately absent much of the time. When he was present, he was inconsiderate and inattentive. He threw things while the teacher's back was turned and he sat with his feet in the aisle so that others stumbled over them. He was described as "inadequate." Always in the "center of trouble," he was responsible for "the small irritations that are usual with this type of person." Five teachers expected that he would get into difficulty with the law, and two others expected that he would develop emotional problems. He did, in fact, get into legal trouble in his junior year and he was placed on probation for theft. In this offense he was an accomplice to a brother.

The family environment was "inadequate and unclean." The father was a heavy drinker and there was very little money for his family. The boy was not decently clothed. In addition to the brother who had been caught stealing, there was another brother who had had an "interesting emotional breakdown."

63. M:15:3	ACE IX, 87; XI, 78	1″7′435280–	0:4:16
N:VI:1	ENG IX, none; XI, 51	′74213–′6	1:1:19
	HSR 81		
	SVIB ′8–9		

Well balanced, well liked and accepted, this boy showed "outstanding" cooperation in his schoolwork, doing supplementary assignments and "arriving at good conclusions." One person, however, thought him to be a little on the effeminate side, lacking in drive, and somewhat lazy. He was active and talented in dramatics. In his freshman year he got in trouble when he was caught stealing. He continued his education at an out-of-state university.

The boy's father died while the boy was in high school. The father had had two years of college but, nevertheless, worked in a low-level occupation. The mother worked as a waitress. There was a younger brother who had been much closer to the father than had this boy.

64. M:16:3	ACE IX, none; XI, 50	1′74820–′6	1:7:18
B:VII:1	ENG IX, none; XI, 34		
	HSR 24		
	SVIB none		

Two of his ninth-grade teachers expected that this boy would get into legal difficulties. In school he made a very poor adjustment: he was truant and disrespectful, "a tough guy," belligerent, and antagonistic.

65. M:14:2	ACE IX, 85; XI, 87	′176835–2′9	0:6:14
N:VI:2	ENG IX, none; XI, 98		
	HSR 88		
	SVIB 8′4–		

This boy was quiet, conscientious, and a hard worker. A "sharp" student, he liked school and hoped to become an engineer. He did not take any part in activities and was known as a "bookworm." He had only a few good friends, all of whom were described in similar terms.

66. M:15:3	ACE IX, 08; XI, 06	1'768<u>093</u>–'4	8:9:17
N:III:4	ENG IX, none; XI, 04	'47<u>136</u>–'5	8:3:22
	HSR 15		
	SVIB '–		

While in junior high school this boy mentioned in an account of himself two difficulties: asthma and, in his own words, "I don't read good." The school counselor at that time described him as depressed and concerned about grades, slow in expressing ideas, introvertive, and in need of social development. His failure to pass mathematics was attributed, by his teacher, to "lack of application" and interest in "little boy activities." Despite these shortcomings he remained in school and was described in his senior year as "docile, nice in appearance, and pleasing in personality." He got along well with other students and was never a conduct problem. His poor scholastic achievement and reading deficiency persisted throughout his high school career.

67. M:14:8	ACE IX, none; XI, 25	18'''2''<u>367</u>'450–	7:15:23
B:III:3	ENG IX, none; XI, 05	8'46–'5	4:10:17
	HSR 20		
	SVIB '48–0		

This boy's home life was very deficient. He had been placed in a foster home when he was four years old because of parental neglect. In the ninth grade he was described as having "tremendous inferiority feelings resulting from his seriously disturbed life history." He had a minor physical handicap and suffered from severe acne. Very immature, "he acted like an eight-year-old," always associating with younger children. He was energetic, but he seemed to have no skills or other resources and he did not take an active part in school affairs. He was a "poor loser and not a gracious winner." He seemed to show little concern over the consequences of his actions. He stole things and, after admitting his guilt, would repeat the act. In addition to this misbehavior he was also accused of sexual molestation of a young girl.

The father, who had been convicted of several criminal offenses, was described as a "likable, disarming person." After a long illness, he died when the boy was in high school. The mother was alcoholic and inadequate.

68. M:14:1	ACE IX, none; XI, 19	18''723'<u>4906</u>–	5:15:16
N:VI:3	ENG IX, none; XI, 01		
	HSR 13		
	SVIB –5		

A surly, not too pleasant disposition was the personality feature most characteristic of this boy. He appeared outgoing, for he was never alone and he liked to talk. He tended to argue rather than accept authority. Academically he was poor, and his teachers believed that he got most of his work from other students. "He must be constantly watched." He was interested in sports and was a member of one of the school's athletic teams.

69. M:15:1   ACE IX, none; XI, 40   '18̲7̲4̲–5'2   5:5:15
    N:VI:1   ENG IX, none; XI, 21
                    HSR 20
                    SVIB none

"Well adjusted, an all-around boy," was the way this youth was described. He was cooperative and a hard worker both in school and outside. He impressed others as "a very neat and responsible individual." In spite of his good attitudes and hard work, his academic achievement was not good, and it was said that he "aspired to a higher level of work but lacked ability." In some contrast, he was also described as "easygoing."

70. M:15:7   ACE IX, 57; XI, 72   1'87̲5̲9̲ 2̲3̲ 64̲–   2:1:20
    N:IVB:5   ENG IX, 56; XI, 43
                    HSR 55
                    SVIB none

This boy "worked up to his capacity" and was active in school affairs, although he had religious principles that kept him from attending parties or dances (he hoped to enter the ministry). He was particularly interested in music and photography.

71. M:16:3   ACE IX, 08; XI, 02   18'0̲3̲ 27̲6̲4̲5̲–   5:9:15
    N:IVB:4   ENG IX, none; XI, 01   1"3487'26905–   9:7:27
                    HSR 12
                    SVIB '4–5

This boy was popular, had many friends, and appeared happy, although he was a poor student. He was successful in school athletics, but he did not study. He promised to get his assignments in, but just did not follow through despite the fact that he had the same opportunities to do the work as his more responsible classmates. It had been recommended that he take remedial reading. One teacher observed that he was average in most traits but that he never assumed a leader's role and somewhat lacked good judgment and common sense. The boy was older than his classmates and when he was in the ninth grade his teachers considered him a potential school dropout. He had been a victim of polio during early childhood. The school counselor noted that at one period during junior high school he had to miss classes because of an injury and that he had been depressed about this. He had attended school in two other states before entering this junior high school.

72. M:14:5	ACE IX, none; XI, 06	'1984236–	2:7:11
N:III:1	ENG IX, none; XI, 08		
	HSR 24		
	SVIB none		

This boy had "some sort of disease in the seventh grade, but he seemed to recover fully from this illness." His ability was low and he was a poor student, although he seemed to work up to his capacity in school. He was a little noisy, but fairly well liked. He played in the band.

73. M:15:1	IQ (centile) 24	1984'07326–'5	5:8:11
N:I:2	HSR 06		
	SVIB none		

In high school this boy appeared to be "extremely introverted." He had very few associates and was a daydreamer in class. "He attached no value to school" and stubbornly refused to do required schoolwork or to give oral reports. His scholastic achievement was so poor that his teachers requested he be separated from his class. School records indicated a deterioration over the years in both aptitude and achievement tests, as well as in his general school performance. At the time of the ninth-grade testing several teachers predicted the boy would become emotionally maladjusted. Numerous brushes with the police, which began when he was ten, continued throughout his high school years, their frequency increasing with his age. Offenses included petty thefts, traffic violations, disorderly conduct, and acts of vandalism committed without apparent reason.

The boy's father was a professional man and both parents were highly educated. An older sister was a very successful student. The father was described as being "very busy with community affairs." The parents were called in frequently by both school and juvenile authorities to discuss their son's behavior. The father took the position that the boy would outgrow his behavior problems.

74. M:14:3	ACE IX, none; XI, 26	1'037825–	1:7:6
N:VII:3	ENG IX, none; XI, 22	2'''1''07'38–'96	5:2:13
	HSR 20		
	SVIB –5		

"One of the better students in the low-ability group," this youth was dependable and responsible. He had always lived on a farm and wanted to continue farming after graduation. He was often absent from school, apparently to help at home, where his family depended heavily upon him. In school he was quiet, polite, and inconspicuous.

The family had never been in any difficulties and "kept to themselves pretty much." The father was a very hard working man; he maintained a small farm and worked as a laborer in town. The boy worked with his father both before and after graduation.

75. M:14:3   ACE IX, 28; XI, 07   '1056–   5:7:12
     N:III:3   ENG IX, 35; XI, 05   12'80374–'59   7:7:18
                   HSR 02
                   SVIB '1–5

This was a short, small-featured boy, who was extremely quiet, withdrawn, and easily depressed. His school behavior was described as indifferent, erratic, and negative. He was frequently absent from school. His teachers felt that he did not make full use of his limited ability and was in constant need of prodding. Some observers said he was lazy, uninterested, and had an "I-don't-care attitude." In class "he contributed nothing — he just sat." One teacher commented that the boy was unable to read or write and that since the sixth grade he had just been "passed along." The boy did not create disturbances in class and was never considered to be a discipline problem. He seldom spoke, but when he did, one teacher observed, there was a suggestion of a speech impediment. It was also noted that he never associated with any of his classmates.

The parents were considered to be somewhat like the boy, and the family was not respected too highly by the community. The parents let the children do as they pleased. At the same time the father was considered to be a hard worker and the mother to be pleasant, cheerful, and articulate. The three brothers were also very much like the boy: "introverted and unimaginative."

76. M:15:4   ACE IX, 06; XI, none   1'0873–'5   0:6:8
     N:V:2   ENG IX, none; XI, none
                   HSR DO 11th gr.
                   SVIB none

While he was in school, this boy was a borderline conduct problem although never a severe one. Though unexcitable, he had a "little chip on his shoulder" and "rough edges that might jab you now and then"; he made himself obnoxious by asking irritating questions. He was also likable and somewhat gregarious, and he had several close friends. In appearance he was tall and dark and had prominent teeth. He generally had a "big toothy grin." He got into mild trouble at one time by violating his driver's permit. He dropped out of school in the eleventh grade to join the service.

77. F:14:9	ACE IX, 44; XI, 41	'2–1'3	6:3:9
N:IVB:4	ENG IX, none; XI, 51	'9354–1'2	0:2:11
	HSR 73		
	SVIB none		

Almost all that was said about this girl was that she was a "wonderful girl with a fine personality." She was good looking and friendly. In her schoolwork she was described as industrious and dependable.

78. M:14:1	ACE IX, 32; XI, 62	'2–18'73	5:5:7
B:IVB:4	ENG IX, none; XI, 45		
	HSR 64		
	SVIB 4'–90		

This was "a good boy, active in athletics." He was never exceptionally good in sports but he tried hard and was dependable. Similarly, he worked hard at his studies and seemed conscientious and interested, although he never volunteered in class. One ninth-grade teacher expected that he would become emotionally maladjusted.

The father died when the boy was in the ninth grade. He had been a fine parent. The mother had been previously married to a man much older than herself — "a cold, disinterested person." She was fun-loving and gay, and the second marriage had produced a good home situation, in which the family had done things together. After the death of her second husband, the mother became serious and "thought her children most important."

79. M:15:1	ACE IX, none; XI, 41	'2–'19	3:2:13
N:VI:3	ENG IX, none; XI, 23		
	HSR 72		
	SVIB none		

This boy's scholarship and personality improved as he went through high school. He was "a fine-looking boy," very poised and trustworthy. He was active in athletics. A steady worker outside of school, he owned a car and showed maturity and adult judgment.

80. F:15:0	ACE IX, none; XI, 58	'2–'19	6:1:15
N:V:2	ENG IX, none; XI, 57		
	HSR 12		
	SVIB none		

Although nothing very bad was reported about her, the only good things that were said about this girl were that she was pleasant and neat. Her schoolwork seemed difficult for her, but her teachers thought that she worked up to her ability. Lacking in leadership qualities, she was withdrawn, seemed to lack confidence, and did not participate in school activities.

81. F:14:2	ACE IX, none; XI, 49	'2–19'35	3:2:8
N:V:1	ENG IX, none; XI, 38		
	HSR 30		
	SVIB none		

This girl was not a school problem. She was a shy person and exhibited no interest or pep.

82. M:15:6	ACE IX, none; XI, 49	'2–7'9016	8:8:13
B:III:1	ENG IX, none; XI, 44	'3495–0'	9:1:21
	HSR 33		
	SVIB none		

The only favorable thing said about this boy was that he had "a good mechanical mind"; otherwise he was described as causing disturbances, lazy, and extremely indifferent. He appeared languid and lacking in motivation. At one time he had a contest with another student to see who could accumulate the most absences.

83. M:15:2	ACE IX, none; XI, 52	'2–'8163	6:2:15
N:I:3	ENG IX, none; XI, 38		
	HSR 42		
	SVIB none		

This boy "could have been a fine leader with all his potentials." Although he was a good athlete, he did not obey training rules and was excluded from athletic participation during his junior year. In spite of the fact that he had previously earned a letter, he did not bother to go out for the team in his senior year. Lazy, he showed little initiative and "needed watching." He "got by," doing as little as possible.

He came from "a fine home" and had good parents. In fact, it was suspected that some of his difficulty may have been caused by the parents' indulging and pampering him.

84. M:15:3	ACE IX, 16; XI, none	'2–'971	9:5:17
N:IVB:2	ENG IX, none; XI, none		
	HSR DO 10th gr.		
	SVIB none		

This was a farm boy with outdoor interests and mechanical skills who did not like English, history, and other academic subjects. He quit school in order to work on the farm, but he took evening courses to continue his mechanical training after he had dropped regular schoolwork. He was serious-minded, hard working; he knew what he wanted and headed for it. He had friends among other farm boys and was well liked. After a while he enlisted in the armed services.

The farm home was a good one and well kept up, although the yard was littered and the buildings were old. The father was a hard worker (though considered only a fair farmer), talkative, and temperamental, "a little moody." He was not close to his children. The mother, outgoing and pleasant, was a peacemaker between the father and son.

85. M:14:1	ACE IX, 24; XI, 24	2″1′78043–	7:4:21
N:II:1	ENG IX, none; XI, 19		
	HSR 66		
	SVIB ′24–0		

This physically immature boy was tall, slender, even frail in appearance. His teachers used such terms as extremely quiet, retiring, withdrawn, and introverted to describe his general demeanor. He seemed especially shy and insecure in social situations, and when talking to teachers, he "fidgeted and bit his fingernails." Although this pattern of behavior was reported by both elementary and high school teachers, improvement was also noted, for he was said to have many friends and a steady girl by his senior high school year. Considered to be a responsible and conscientious student, he did his best work in mathematics and science. He worked hard at his studies but was severely handicapped in reading. He was reportedly under heavy pressure from home, especially from his mother, to achieve. At one time during his high school career his parents obtained special training in remedial reading for him. Athletics interested him and he participated in several sports. In these activities he was also a hard worker but too physically immature and unskilled ever to make a varsity squad.

The father, mild and soft-spoken, was said to be somewhat like the boy. The mother was "a tremendous pusher, the driving force behind the whole family." She dominated the home and was thought by some to neglect housekeeping in order to run the children's lives. Both parents were college graduates.

86. M:14:3	ACE IX, none; XI, 68	2″178′0634–′5	3:15:8
N:VI:2	ENG IX, none; XI, 83	′76034–	3:4:6
	HSR 42		
	SVIB none		

Although this boy was easy to talk to and well liked by his fellow students, he was not so successful in relationships with school and other authorities. Generally uncooperative and occasionally unreliable, he smoked, drank, and caused disturbances in class. He was caught breaking into a room at school and was warned by the police. In his senior year he was involved in more serious offenses of speeding, drunkenness, and grand larceny. He was active in school athletics and once became very bitter when expelled from the hockey team. In spite of all these difficulties one report said that he received discipline well and was not belligerent.

87. F:15:5   IQ (centile) 50   '23–'179   3:4:9
    N:III:2   HSR DO 10th gr.
                 SVIB none

Unaggressive and quiet, this girl rarely took the initiative. She was neatly dressed and made a nice appearance, but she had an unimpressive personality. Her friends were among the more undesirable students. She finally dropped out of school sometime during the tenth grade.

88. M:15:3   IQ (centile) 38   '23–'9   4:3:17
    B:VII:1   HSR DO 10th gr.
                 SVIB none

This little, red-haired, freckled boy did not do well as a student. He was not much better in shop courses than he was in other academic work. He was a "nice kid who was in no trouble — he just did nothing in school." He dropped out of school to go to work after finishing the ninth grade.

89. F:14:4   ACE IX, 34; XI, 20   2'317 60 548–'9   7:3:14
    B:IVC:2   ENG IX, 49; XI, 37
                 HSR 26
                 SVIB none

This "unimaginative and stolid girl" was very ordinary and had no high hopes for her future. She was described as a good worker, although she was not considered strong in her behavior traits. After the death of her father she had worked in order to continue in school.

During this girl's pre-adolescent years the father had committed suicide and, following a period of severe grief, the mother remarried. During this time the children had lived with a relative. One sibling had a congenital defect in development. The income of the family was low and the mother received public aid.

90. F:14:3	ACE IX, 48; XI, 58	'23517–	1:3:16
N:III:1	ENG IX, 73; XI, 64	'578–'6	2:1:21
	HSR 49		
	SVIB none		

This "dependable and reliable" girl was a "very nice follower." She was neat in appearance, somewhat adult for her age, and generally a very responsible person, although she lacked drive and was nonaggressive and inactive in school groups. Her friends, who were few in number, were superior to her in ability and oriented toward college and the achievement of a higher scholastic rank than this girl was able to attain. She eventually got a small scholarship to a college, which she went on to attend after graduation.

She came from what was described as "a nice family," active in school functions. However, the father was considered overly active and aggressive. One older brother got into some trouble and the father made ostentatious efforts to "fix things" with the police. The only comment relative to the mother was that she had a severe sensory impairment.

91. F:14:3	ACE IX, 81; XI, 85	236'07 14–59'	6:4:14
N:V:1	ENG IX, none; XI, 68		
	HSR 81		
	SVIB none		

Although it was said that this girl's "very presence helped the class" and she "contributed a lot to her class," she was also described as introverted. She had few friends and was withdrawn and unsure in manner. She expressed the wish that she had joined more school activities and that she had a boy friend. As she continued in school she became a little more active and, as a senior, she worked on the school paper. "She had definite creative ability but used it only as a hobby." After graduation she became a nurse.

An older sister had been very successful in school activities; she was beautiful and popular. The family's income was inadequate and they were burdened with sickness and relatives.

92. M:14:5	ACE IX, 89; XI, 86	'24–5'9	3:8:15
N:V:5	ENG IX, 57; XI, 42	'436–'05918	1:4:12
	HSR 75		
	SVIB none		

"He was one of the finest boys in the school and it hurt to lose him." This comment referred to the fact that this boy left the high school in his senior year to attend a preparatory school. He had a "scintillating personality and a fine sense of humor"; he was generous, articulate, and fair. Possessing much poise and social grace, he had been active in student organizations.

He did very well in the preparatory school and went on to attempt a higher level of training in order to make a career in the armed forces. However, at this higher level he failed. His failure was attributed to a minor physical illness and a lack of the necessary emotional stability to keep up the pace. Discouraged, he returned home. Summarizing the experience, one person said that he was "too immature and his parents had expected too much of him." After his return he went to work with his father and appeared to be gaining more maturity. It was said that he expected to return to school after a while.

The family situation seemed good. There was "sensible, fine control of the children" and the parents had a wholesome interest in them. The parents were compatible, and the whole family got along well together. The father was a small businessman who was outgoing and friendly, although he was also said to have a high opinion of himself and to be a bit domineering. The mother was called "fair and kind," and was more reserved than her husband.

93. M:14:5	ACE IX, none; XI, 33	24'1087 63–'5	3:12:14
N:VI:3	ENG IX, none; XI, 04		
	HSR 02 DO 12th gr.		
	SVIB none		

The teachers found this boy sullen and hard to handle. Apparently not much interested in school, he abandoned it in his senior year and joined the Navy. After a short term in the service, he returned to the community and went to work. His employer considered him an excellent worker. Before quitting school he had got into some trouble when he was caught stealing a part from a car.

The home situation was generally good. The father had died while the boy was in high school and the mother, who had taken over the management of the family, had apparently done a good job. "All members of the family pulled together."

94. M:14:9	ACE IX, 17; XI, none	'243–'50 67	5:2:18
N:IVC:3	ENG IX, 27; XI, none	'948–52'6	3:2:16
	HSR 24		
	SVIB '24–5		

A "lone wolf and definite introvert," this boy was very quiet, never volunteered, merely occupied a chair, and responded only when spoken to. Although indifferent to schoolwork, he had a "friendly and congenial personality, always carrying a smile." He was "kept out of school to help with farm work," but it was suspected that he "really ran wild at night." His work in junior high school was much better than his later work; he seemed to "slide backwards as he went on in school, becoming more lazy, unreliable, and uncooperative." He was considered a "great underachiever" who was capable of doing good work if he wanted to. His only interest was in the Future Farmers movement. He had a police record for driving an automobile without a license.

In spite of the fact that the family had a low economic status, they were quite active in the community and were hard working and well respected. All the members of the family had to "dig in and help."

95. F:14:4 ACE IX, 81; XI, 79 2430′86719–5′ 4:9:7
    B:VI:4 ENG IX, none; XI, 86 ′78964230–1′ 1:4:6
                  HSR 79
                  SVIB none

In the ninth grade, this girl seemed to live in a shell and a majority of her teachers expected her to develop emotional problems. She continued to be nervous and unhappy, and received professional help because of her poor mental health. She "needed self-confidence and recognition." By her senior year she had greatly improved and was extremely popular: "a real lady." There was, however, still an "undercurrent in her personality" and she was becoming a little "'big-headed."

The family situation had been bad. Before the parents separated, the father had left the home whenever he took a notion. At the end of her freshman year the girl moved "outside her family."

96. M:16:9 ACE IX, 10; XI, 23 24′70–9′ 5:9:17
    N:IVB:5 ENG IX, 12; XI, 14 854′3679–′0 7:9:17
                  HSR 17
                  SVIB ′49–

This was a slow, "average" student who was ambitious and wanted to go to college. He worked very hard and was thought of as a pleasant, mature, levelheaded boy who possessed a good sense of humor and presented no problems. He was active in class discussions and was liked by both faculty and students. Illness caused him to miss a large number of days in the eleventh grade. He had "a wide knowledge of agriculture." After graduation he went into the Marines.

Although the father was described as "a strong personality and easy to get along with," the family was not considered a particularly good one by the community. The parents "hung around beer parlors a bit" and the house "was filthy inside — messy, littered, and smelly." Apparently some of the difficulty was due to the mother, who was more likely to work in the fields than in the house. She was "very interested in her children being good, but would protect them even when they were wrong." The family did not push the children, being "just as glad if they stayed around home."

97. F:14:0   ACE IX, none; XI, 49   2‴48″3176′09–   3:15:13
    N:V:3   ENG IX, none; XI, 43
              HSR 14
              SVIB ′WR

This "cute" girl, "bouncy and full of pep," was too active in outside things to care about school. She was frequently truant and was finally expelled, in the twelfth grade. "Her night life interfered with getting to school in the morning." Other students didn't like her; they didn't approve of her standards. She was flighty and irresponsible and liked to dramatize herself. She was thought to be sexually promiscuous.

The father was hard working, talkative, and a heavy drinker. The mother was an attractive woman who frequented the local taverns, often in the company of other men; she was "peppy, wild." There was little parental supervision. Neither parent was willing to accept responsibility for the girl or the home.

98. F:14:0   ACE IX, 03; XI, 07   2′483506–′9   6:8:15
    N:IVC:3   ENG IX, 13; XI, 36   ′50–91′687   3:1:11
              HSR 76
              SVIB none

Reliable, pleasant, and very cooperative, this girl was good in "business courses." She was tall and angular but did not seem to feel inferior because of this. She had many friends among both students and teachers.

99. F:14:2   ACE IX, 99; XI, 100   2483′710–′5   4:5:21
    N:VI:3   ENG IX, 100; XI, 100
              HSR 91
              SVIB ′–

This was a "helpful, considerate, smart, reliable, and honest" girl. In manner she was retiring, but as she continued in high school, she "came out of it." She was interested in speech.

100. F:14:2   ACE IX, 16; XI, 43   2′408135697–   3:14:11
     N:III:1 ENG IX, 26; XI, 47   ′5089–′31   2:4:11
              HSR 20
              SVIB none

Although this girl was described as lovely, "a perfect lady, cooperative, attractive in personality, and loyal," she appeared to contribute little to the school situation "and just went her own way." In spite of the fact that she tried very hard in her schoolwork and did get her assignments done, her achievement remained poor. In particular, her work in English was "hopeless," and she was believed to lack the capacity for doing better. Her friends and activities seemed to be outside the school. After graduation she married.

101. M:15:7	ACE IX, none; XI, 17	'24089–5'6	3:7:12
N:VI:3	ENG IX, none; XI, 17	'47<u>53</u>–	2:5:16
	HSR 42		
	SVIB –5		

This boy was small and very quiet. Always trying hard to do what was expected of him, he was a "worker" but not an academically strong student. His teachers liked him because he was always smiling and respectful. When he finished school he hoped to become a mechanic. In his junior year he got into some trouble because of driving a car without a license. After graduation he went to work in a manufacturing plant.

The family had a good reputation in the community and both father and mother were good and steady people.

102. F:15:2	IQ (centile) 35	'25–'6	6:4:11
N:IVB:4	HSR 03		
	SVIB none		

This girl had a poor academic record. She was well liked and was active as a cheerleader. She was interested in "sports, good times, and the outdoors."

103. M:14:2	ACE IX, 44; XI, 61	'25–6'<u>341</u>	2:2:13
N:IVA:6	ENG IX, 39; XI, 37		
	HSR 58		
	SVIB '89–2		

This boy was very small, even "tiny" in stature. He had a pleasing personality and was not a conduct problem in school. A willing and good worker, he was only a fair student. He did not engage in any extracurricular activities, although he had some musical interests. One of his ninth-grade teachers rated him as likely to have emotional difficulties. He had several close friends, all of whom had good reputations.

104. M:15:1
    N:II:1

ACE IX, 85; XI, 79   2'5376–'90   5:3:18
ENG IX, none; XI, 61   ——   ——
HSR 97   '364–0'95   6:1:21
SVIB '8–

"One of the school's better boys," this youth was active on the student council and in dramatics and music. He had a nice personality and was liked by everyone. His teachers thought him dependable and a good worker without being "an apple polisher." He did very good schoolwork and was on the honor roll, but he cheated in one test in order to keep up his grades. It was said that he was pushed hard by his parents. After graduation he registered at a university, but there appeared to be doubt that he would succeed in keeping up with the requirements of the work.

The father was "a polished individual" who had been an athlete and was sorry his son was not one also. The father tended to be a heavy drinker. The parents were "hard to get to know except on the social side." In most ways, however, the home was considered to be a very good one.

105. M:14:3
    N:III:1

ACE IX, 84; XI, 71   254'731–   3:5:14
ENG IX, none; XI, 75   '598463–20'   5:10:16
HSR 59
SVIB 4'8–

Called a "lazy underachiever," this boy labored under the handicap of having a brilliant brother. He got along fairly well and had a steady girl friend. The only specific complaint about him was that he had been often tardy without an excuse.

106. M:14:2
    N:III:3

ACE IX, 99; XI, 99   '256378 40–'9   1:1:17
ENG IX, 93; XI, 98   '35467–   2:2:17
HSR 98   '736 2458–'0   1:1:15
SVIB none

Although serious, this boy was known for his dry sense of humor. He had a fine personality, was popular, and took part in a great many activities. He was a "top student," had an "inclination to do a great deal of deep thinking on many issues," and was outstanding in debate. After graduation he registered at a university to study engineering.

107. F:14:4
    N:V:2

ACE IX, 89; XI, none   '25679–'41   2:2:12
ENG IX, 81; XI, none
HSR DO 10th gr.
SVIB none

Of interest in this case is the fact that the girl eventually quit school in order to buy more clothes. This behavior was sanctioned by the girl's mother. The teachers felt that the girl had every promise of becoming a very successful high school graduate, and they rated her highly. In particular, she was described as outstanding in cooperation, emotional control, judgment, and reliability.

108. M:15:2   ACE IX, 94; XI, 90   '26–'47 93   2:0:13
     N:II:3   ENG IX, none; XI, 94
                  HSR 89
                  SVIB '–

The only criticism of this boy was that he acted "a little wise" once in a while. A good student and athlete, he made a satisfactory school adjustment. Outside of school he was in intermittent trouble: he was guilty of breach of the peace against a man's property, of molesting the man, and of stealing. As a result of these acts he was placed on probation for a year.

109. M:14:4   ACE IX, 42; XI, 59   '26–'5   4:1:15
     N:III:1   ENG IX, none; XI, 42   '132748–9'5   5:1:21
                  HSR 54   '1–9'75   6:3:17
                  SVIB none

This boy was "normal and average." His teachers regarded him as adaptable, retiring, cooperative, courteous, dependable, and industrious. It was stated that "he needed to be a little more aggressive and needed encouragement in his school-work." He did not participate in any school activities, but he worked as a gardener outside of school and liked to hunt and fish. He hoped to take training in engineering. After graduating he entered a university, where he was maintaining a C average.

110. M:15:2   ACE IX, 44; XI, 32   '2649–'51   1:4:13
     N:VI:4   ENG IX, none; XI, 15   '965–2'   3:2:18
                  HSR 20
                  SVIB '9–5

This boy "had to have attention — craved it, and wanted to be everyone's friend." He "tried to be a hero and badly needed approval." Unsure of himself, he was "a puppy dog who let others control him." In class he "jabbered all the time but was not malicious." Active in athletics, he was fairly well liked but neither admired nor respected by his fellow students. He got into trouble several times during his junior and senior years by committing traffic offenses; he was also caught at a beer party.

111. F:14:0   ACE IX, 07; XI, 03   '2650–'1̲3̲ 7:7:12
   N:III:1   ENG IX, none; XI, 05
         HSR 08
         SVIB none

"On the unattractive side," this girl was "a little mouse," quiet but usually smiling. She had a habit of chewing her fingernails. Although she was very conscientious and concerned about grades, she was a poor student and accomplished little, apparently unaware of the fact that she was not doing well in her academic work. About her only school activity was playing in the school band.

112. M:14:2   ACE IX, 42; XI, 17   2'684973– 9:2:21
   B:IVB:3   ENG IX, none; XI, 17
         HSR 12
         SVIB '890–5

"Sly and a time waster," this boy was indifferent and had a poor attitude toward school. He caused slight disturbances in the school halls and he ran with a "bad crowd." His interest was in sports and he was captain of an athletic team. His mother died when he began grade school and he never accepted his stepmother.

113. M:15:2   ACE IX, none; XI, 52   2'71409853̲– 1:5:9
   N:VI:1   ENG IX, none; XI, 17
         HSR 39 DO 12th gr.
         SVIB none

"Negative and antagonistic toward authority," this boy was cocky, indifferent, and had an I-don't-care attitude. He was truant from school and "would stretch and break the rules." In his senior year he dropped out of school to join the armed services. One ninth-grade teacher expected that he would become emotionally maladjusted, and another thought that he would have difficulties with the law.

114. M:14:3   ACE IX, 92; XI, 92   2'746318̲–'5 7:6:22
   N:II:2   ENG IX, none; XI, 74   '304725̲–'9 3:0:17
         HSR 55
         SVIB '4–

The over-all adjustment of this boy was reported to have improved through the years. Before the ninth grade he had been considered nervous; he had been prone to disturbing dreams and enuresis. It was said that he had been badly frightened and beaten by older boys during this period. At this time a minor offense — destruction of property — was noted in police records. One of his ninth-grade teachers expected him to become emotionally maladjusted. Later he was characterized with many good descriptive terms, although it was still said that he "tried to be brusque and tough, but was not." He did not take part in sports or extracurricular activities, but he cooperated well, "worked for good morale, and was social-problem-minded." In general, he was reliable, fairly dependable, and well liked without being either a leader or a follower. He was a sensible, responsible student who could be trusted, but "he never pushed himself too hard." He mixed well with both boys and girls and talked easily. The teachers considered him to be "definitely of college ability." He was above average in mathematical and scientific interests and ability and considered a career in either the Army or engineering. Follow-up information did not show evidence that he pursued these interests, and it seemed likely that he did not go on to further his education.

The family, although seemingly harassed by more than the normal amount of physical illness, was reasonably stable. The father was a hard worker and a personable, relaxed man.

115. M:14:1	ACE IX, 82; XI, 89	2'75683–9'	4:2:18
N:III:1	ENG IX, 89; XI, 72	'2678540–'9	0:1:17
	HSR 97	6'87 4105–'9	1:3:17
	SVIB 12'4–		

Many praiseworthy things were said about this boy. He was a good student and one of the leaders in his class. Physically large, he was active in athletics and was described as a likable, friendly, clean-cut boy who was well rounded and well adjusted. He was always polite, respectful, cooperative, and dependable. Very mature for his age, "he stuck to his business and did not waste time." In matters of judgment he displayed "a lot of good common sense." He was the president of one group and did a good job; "he always leads in the right way." He was concerned about many things and "quite engrossed in plans for the future." Despite his many fine qualities he was not too well known because he was quiet in manner and did not project himself; he was "always humble and unassuming." A hard-working boy, he found a job during his summer vacations. After graduation he registered at a university.

The boy was described as "just like his dad"; it was said that he had "wonderful parents."

116. F:15:5	ACE IX, none; XI, 21	2'76408–59'	6:7:17
N:IVB:2	ENG IX, none; XI, 66		
	HSR 69		
	SVIB none		

An average student who was very quiet and cooperative, this girl was "quite conscious of boys and vice versa." She belonged to a number of student organizations and hoped to become a nurse or secretary. She had a pleasing personality.

117. F:14:3   ACE IX, 63; XI, 52   '2780–'63   4:4:8
     N:II:1   ENG IX, 72; XI, 79
                     HSR 62
                     SVIB none

This popular girl was pleasant and nice. She was unusually reliable and cooperative, and she was active in numerous school group affairs. Always conscientious,
she was ambitious and volunteered quickly. Although she "did have her slumps,"
these did not last long. She wanted to become a private secretary after graduation.

The father was "very inventive, creative, and meticulous of details." The family
was hard working and conscientious and had a good reputation, although they
were not outgoing leaders in the community.

118. F:14:5   ACE IX, 36; XI, 18   278"031'469–5'   5:10:10
     N:IVA:4   ENG IX, none; XI, 43   '20 4678–5'9   3:2:18
                     HSR 33
                     SVIB WR'

Described as "buxom," nondescript, and not very neat, this girl was not a conduct
problem. She "filled a chair," did what she was told, listened fairly well, but engaged in no activities. She went with a "funny crowd" who were considered a
"bunch of wallflowers."

119. M:16:7   ACE IX, none; XI, 08   2'79–'1   6:2:15
     B:V:3   ENG IX, none; XI, 16
                     HSR 28
                     SVIB none

"Never frivolous, a boy who takes school and life seriously." Small and very thin,
he was quiet and retiring in his manner. He stuttered severely and, although his
speech showed gradual improvement during high school, he "blocked completely"
when in a group. One person observed that "he appeared so insecure," and another
called him "a boy with many problems." He generally associated with boys much
younger than himself. He had a hobby of working with motors. One teacher anticipated emotional problems for him. When he had to register for the draft, "he went
to pieces."

One of eight children, he had been removed from his parents' home to live with
relatives because of parental neglect. Both foster parents were said to be genuinely
interested in the boy; however, the foster father tended to be somewhat severe
and critical in dealing with him. His wife was considered to be more understanding.

120. M:15:2	ACE IX, 93; XI, 98	'2705 84–'9	7:0:21
N:III:1	ENG IX, 90; XI, 61	'8563–9'	4:1:22
	HSR 71		
	SVIB none		

"Just too quiet, he lived in his own little shell," was the way one teacher described this boy. He got top grades in those classes where no speaking or recitation was involved. Another teacher described him as "quiet, reserved, conscientious, and doing a good job; one of the best in the school and never in trouble." He actively participated in athletics and music while in high school. Small, but physically rugged in appearance, he was said to be accident prone. His teachers felt that he was the kind of boy who would make a good teacher and should go on to college. After graduation, however, he worked with his father in the small family business. Not long after graduation it was reported that he was suffering from an incurable disease that would probably soon be fatal. In the spring of his sophomore year he had been guilty of a moderately severe traffic offense.

The family was well regarded in the community. The father was described as a "sensitive man with high standards." He was very close to his sons, taking them with him on fishing and hunting trips. The mother was also said to be a responsible parent, but more of a "crisis type" than her husband. Neither of the two other children in the family was as capable a student as was this boy. The family had had a number of severe adjustments to make in recent years, and they also had a struggle to make ends meet financially.

121. F:15:12	IQ (centile) 43	2'83719–	7:7:11
N:VII:3	HSR DO 11th gr.		
	SVIB none		

During early high school years this very pretty girl was considered a "nice girl" — friendly and well liked. However, she was not a good student and had no interest in school. Although she had "academic possibilities," her school attendance was irregular, she became "boy crazy," and she left school in the eleventh grade to be married. After the marriage she continued to live in the community.

The family was large and none of the children finished high school. The parents were unusually old; they were apparently conscientious but not very intelligent. Although both parents worked, the family was poor.

122. F:15:2	IQ (centile) 31	28'4671 390–	6:15:15
B:III:1	HSR DO 10th gr.		
	SVIB none		

This girl was absent for three months of the ninth grade and eventually dropped out of school in the middle of the tenth grade. The reason for her absences was not given. It was stated that she had received private instruction at home during this period. In junior high school she was a D student, but her "school citizenship and industry were fair." Her favorite subject was mathematics, but she did not like English or home economics. Her outside activities included baby sitting and a knitting club. About a year after she dropped out of school she married; she was later divorced. A child had been born to her several months before her marriage. Following the divorce, she got what work she could, but found it difficult to obtain positions.

The mother was twice divorced, and at least one of her husbands was a "worthless drunk." The mother and the girl lived in one small room. One of the girl's half-sisters was also in a considerable amount of trouble, moving from one foster home to another.

123. M:15:5	ACE IX, 87; XI, 79	'28473–'95 8:1:24
N:V:2	ENG IX, 66; XI, 51	
	HSR 39	
	SVIB none	

Because of his happy nature and his "witty sayings," this boy had some friends and followers, but he was certainly not popular. He was not considered to be very dependable, trustworthy, or responsible, and in his schoolwork he was lazy and showed "weak character." His only school activity was wrestling, relative to which he said, "No coward can take beatings." He got into trouble because of an incident in which he committed some vandalism of a minor nature.

The father was a heavy drinker, but not to the extent that it interfered with his work. The mother was an unusual woman, hard working, never discouraged, always striving with great endurance and vitality. It was a happy-go-lucky family in a run-down home where there was never a worry and always genuine hospitality.

124. M:17:1	ACE IX, 05; XI, none	2'''84''731'06–'9 5:10:12
N:III:3	ENG IX, 07; XI, none	2''48'67013–5' 4:11:16
	HSR 02	
	SVIB '0–	

A large, good-natured boy with a fine disposition, this youth was also a good worker. His scholastic achievement was poor, however, and he was noted for sleeping in class. He "looked dull," and he had a moderate hearing loss. He was a football player.

The father was active in community clubs and liked to attract attention. The mother was also helpful in the community. The home was generally a good one for the boy. The parents realized some of his problems and attended conferences to discuss his handicaps.

125. M:14:3   ACE IX, 61; XI, 68   '285–6'91   4:7:15
    N:III:1   ENG IX, none; XI, 39
                 HSR 84
                 SVIB '48–

A dependable and consistent student, this boy was so quiet and noncommunicative that he had to be drawn out. He was cooperative, obedient, shy, and not very social. The teachers considered him the most intelligent member of his family. He worked part time while going to school.

126. F:14:3   ACE IX, 37; XI, none   28"739'40 165–   1:11:7
    N:VI:1   ENG IX, none; XI, none
                 HSR DO 11th gr.
                 SVIB none

Since the seventh grade this girl's school achievement had been poor and she was uninterested and uncooperative. She finally dropped out of school in her junior year. In class she appeared retiring and timid, and she was repeatedly tardy or absent. When she was at school she loitered in the halls. She had a negative attitude and seemed indifferent to what others thought. Although she was attractive, usually well dressed, and seemed to have a number of positive qualities, she did not apply herself and appeared unwilling to accept any kind of steady responsibility. Outside of school she associated with a wild group of boys and girls, gradually getting into more and more trouble because of her behavior with them. She would run away from home and stay out all night, and she was repeatedly in trouble because of drinking and sexual misbehavior. She did not see herself as having any faults and she blamed her parents for her behavior, saying that her mother was "old-fashioned and nagging." The girl was hostile and rude to everyone in authority. She became illegitimately pregnant and was sent to a correctional school.

The father was a poor provider and was often unemployed. He admitted that he had been unable to control his daughter. He seemed fond of the children and apparently made a real effort to work with them. The mother appeared to be a much less adequate person and was described as immature, frivolous, and highstrung. The father tended to blame much of the family trouble on the mother. The family was frequently on relief and was often guilty of buying things for which they could not pay. One other sibling had a record of theft and delinquency.

127. F:14:1   ACE IX, none; XI, 52   '287406–   5:4:8
    N:V:3   ENG IX, 65; XI, 54   '4798–'65   4:2:13
                 HSR 22
                 SVIB none

This girl was low in energy and very obese — "so heavy that she was sick." Although she was not a conduct problem, she was a poor student. She "worked hard but it didn't soak in" and she worried about her low marks. Apparently she was friendly enough with others, more so with teachers than with students. One teacher said that she was a "nice girl and nondescript." Another report claimed that she was "a little snooty." She had a steady boy friend.

128. F:14:3	ACE IX, 57; XI, 69	2′870315–′9	3:6:9
N:VI:3	ENG IX, 62; XI, 69		
	HSR 35		
	SVIB WR′		

This girl was called "pleasant, peppy, very neat, and dependable." She was also described as courteous and self-reliant.

129. M:14:9	ACE IX, 21; XI, 20	2′897406–	5:10:16
N:VI:3	ENG IX, 02; XI, 10	48″6′7923–′5	3:10:13
	HSR 36		
	SVIB none		

Most of the reports about this boy were adverse. He did not work up to his capacity; he was indifferent toward school, often being truant and frequently leaving the building without permission; he was discourteous and erratic in his dependability. He was called "crafty and cantankerous," and was suspected of being responsible for many "underhanded activities that occurred around the school." In his senior year he was arrested for illegal possession of intoxicating liquor. One of his ninth-grade teachers suggested that he might become emotionally maladjusted.

130. M:14:4	ACE IX, none; XI, 15	2′807194–′6	1:10:8
N:VII:3	ENG IX, none; XI, 17	2′4017 89–	1:3:8
	HSR 06		
	SVIB none		

This boy had a serious visual handicap, and it was felt that the fact that he was a very poor student and poor reader was related, in part, to this handicap. He was "nice and pleasant" and had a number of friends. Apparently he tried to cooperate in schoolwork but was in no extracurricular activities.

131. M:15:2	ACE IX, 26; XI, 33	′294678–	4:4:18
B:VI:1	ENG IX, 12; XI, 17		
	HSR 35		
	SVIB ′48–		

When under supervision this boy behaved fairly well, but when in the corridors or in an unsupervised room, he created a disturbance. He had a poor attitude in school and was somewhat sarcastic. Throughout his high school years he developed into more and more of a procrastinator and failed frequently to complete his assignments. As part of an English assignment in his senior year, he wrote a short account of a gasoline stealing expedition in which he and other boys had taken part. They "borrowed (to put it mildly) from persons who used regular gasoline because they preferred it. Therefore, he said, rich people who used ethyl did not have to worry." The account was full of very bad spelling and grammatical errors. It spoke of the stealing as "really fun." (Later he was convicted of stealing gas and, subsequently, of car theft.) After graduation he went to work as a day laborer.

The family was well known to welfare authorities. The home had no modern facilities. The father, who had legal custody of the children, taught them that society was against them. He was bitter because he felt he had not received compensation for an injury by which he was disabled. He was considered a pest at the school. The mother's reputation was no better. She "entertained other men." One of two brothers was also in trouble with the law, but the other brother had high ability and was apparently a very active and contributing student in the school.

132. M:14:1	ACE IX, 70; XI, 86	'29486 75–1'3 3:8:8
N:VI:3	ENG IX, 68; XI, 74	
	HSR 32	
	SVIB 4'–	

This boy was "fat and pudgy," but neat. Of a retiring nature, he minded his own business and made a good general adjustment in school. He preferred manual labor to schoolwork, however.

133. M:16:1	ACE IX, 46; XI, 13	'297–65'83 6:3:18
N:V:1	ENG IX, none; XI, 12	
	HSR 41	
	SVIB none	

This boy "had a good personality but did not know how to apply it." Babied by his family, he was somewhat of a whiner who always had excuses if things went wrong. Having grown up with the idea that his father would protect him, he was unable to accept responsibility. He was interested in athletics but did not achieve as well as he could have in this area. After graduation he registered at a technical school but soon dropped out to enter the service.

The father was a small businessman who was successful in his business and his family affairs. It was felt that the father pushed the son toward greater achievement. The mother was said to have a tendency toward alcoholism.

134. M:15:2	ACE IX, 91; XI, 79	29″7438′61–′0	3:11:10
N:II:1	ENG IX, 66; XI, 19	94″7328 51′6–	4:10:13
	HSR 28	495′372861–	2:8:11
	SVIB 5′0–2		

A great deal of variance occurred in the behavior of this boy between the ninth and twelfth grades. A small boy with very poor posture, he was described as "the class jester," a role that he fitted both in appearance and in behavior. "Where he was, trouble just happened." He was the kind that "spoke out of turn." He had obnoxious mannerisms and was one of a fringe group, from whom he seemed unable to break. He described himself as a follower who was pulled along by the group. He further stated that he wasn't happy with his friends, but that they were able to lead him astray. He got into trouble because of disturbing the peace and at one time he was found possessing a bottle of whisky. However, he never had any officially recorded contact with the authorities. He lacked self-confidence and was unable to work under any pressure at all. When his friends boasted of their sexual exploits, he complained that he lacked confidence with women.

In contrast, he was capable verbally and widely read. He attended lectures when he could, and seemed to find it important to make a good impression. He considered himself to have the ability to belong among intellectuals, and he wanted to spend time in an intellectual atmosphere. He could be friendly and witty. Both he and his family visited social workers to get help with his over-all adjustment. During his last two years of high school he got into no trouble, and he seemed to be well motivated, although he continued to do a good deal of daydreaming. After graduation he went to a university, hoping to become less attached to his home and looking forward confidently to his future.

His father, who was self-employed, was a hard worker and a good provider. The mother was a nervous person who had migraine headaches and "took tranquilizers." She had a part-time job outside the home even though it was not financially necessary. The parents were very concerned over the boy and his progress.

135. M:16:4	ACE IX, 14; XI, 09	′290–5′1	5:8:12
N:VI:3	ENG IX, 09; XI, 03		
	HSR 05		
	SVIB ′4–		

Several of his ninth-grade teachers predicted that this boy would become emotionally maladjusted. He was handicapped by an ill-fitting glass eye, and he "probably had an inferiority complex." In his desire to be accepted by the group and, apparently, to gain status, he associated with some rather undesirable companions who easily influenced him. A lazy boy who worked in spurts, he did not push himself. At least one person described him as sincere, however. His general schoolwork was poor, and he was particularly poor in reading. He got into repeated trouble because of careless driving and speeding, but the police said he was basically a good boy.

136.	M:15:4	ACE IX, none; XI, 15	2'904–'1	8:4:12
	B:V:3	ENG IX, none; XI, 09	'149–	7:1:16
		HSR 48		
		SVIB none		

An orphan, this boy lived with an uncle. He was well dressed and clean, and his hair was always well combed. He could be pleasing, but "he had no manners and was usually discourteous to young and old." Blustery and seeming to crave attention, he was not accepted by others. Scholastically he was a poor student. He was active in football. After graduation he went to work at a factory.

The uncle was described as a rough and ready, outspoken man who "had done a good job bringing up the boy."

137.	M:14:3	ACE IX, 84; XI, 16	'204–6'9	6:4:15
	N:III:1	ENG IX, none; XI, 22	48'725 30–'9	4:3:22
		HSR 34		
		SVIB none		

This boy apparently needed glasses when in grade school but did not get them until he was in high school. He was well liked, courteous, friendly, but more a follower than a leader. Although he was not a good student, he belonged to clubs and did well in such subjects as art and mechanical drawing. His general school adjustment seemed to deteriorate as he continued through high school. He was suspended for truancy at one point, and in the eleventh grade was said to lack friends. Outside of school he liked to fish and hunt. After graduation, he took a full-time job which required little skill.

138.	M:16:7	ACE IX, 13; XI, none	'20473–'9	3:11:15
	N:VII:1	ENG IX, none; XI, none		
		HSR DO 10th gr.		
		SVIB none		

In the elementary grades this boy had been shy and timid, but dependable and hard working. His ability for schoolwork was low and he lacked interest in academic pursuits. He dropped out of school in his sophomore year. He was well behaved, neat, and courteous. Although he liked art, music, mathematics, and English, he was not outstandingly successful in any of these subjects. He had failed the first grade and later he also failed a physical education course. He enlisted in the armed services and, after expiration of his first three-year period, he re-enlisted.

The family was often on relief because the father was irregularly employed, owing in part to his alcoholism. The father also deserted his family for short periods of time. The children were reported to be in need of clothing and medical care. The mother was stronger and contributed more to the family welfare. She worked efficiently, but at least one caseworker thought that she might be mentally dull.

139. F:14:1   ACE IX, none; XI, 93   2′0648–′19   5:0:15
     N:V:1   ENG IX, none; XI, 86
                HSR 70
                SVIB none

The only things said of this girl were that she was interested in music, was no problem in the school, and was "shy and wholesome."

140. F:14:6   ACE IX, none; XI, 40   20′67438–9′   6:5:16
     N:III:2   ENG IX, none; XI, 44   ′274 603–5′1   2:3:12
                HSR 76
                SVIB none

This girl was quiet, friendly, cooperative, and charming. She was thought to work up to her capacity and she was an altogether acceptable person.

141. F:14:2   ACE IX, 26; XI, 64   ′20678–9′   8:4:18
     N:II:1   ENG IX, 68; XI, 74   — —   — —
                HSR 45   ′43986–0′   5:1:25
                SVIB none

This was "a girl you think of as being well adjusted, no problems showing." She was attractive and worked part time as a model. She was interested in dramatics but never had any actual success in acting. In manner she seemed mature, quiet, and not boisterous.

142. M:14:3   ACE IX, 13; XI, none   2′07–′1549   5:7:6
     N:IVC:5   ENG IX, 13; XI, none
                HSR DO 11th gr.
                SVIB none

At least one of his ninth-grade teachers expected this boy to become emotionally maladjusted. He was headstrong, uncooperative, and felt imposed upon. He was known to drink when in the ninth and tenth grades, but after his parents showed some concern, this became less of a problem. His parents did not, however, care whether he went to school or not, and he quit after the tenth grade to go to work in a local factory.

The father, a farmer, was "a know-it-all but not well educated." He was not well regarded in the town and was "lax about everything except his farm and his home." He tended to let his wife and sons do the hard farm work as he "ruled the roost." The mother was nervous and complained about having to work too hard. The home was well kept both inside and out.

143. M:14:1	ACE IX, 69; XI, 61	'20738–'9	0:4:15
N:III:1	ENG IX, 70; XI, 56	'3–'0496	1:2:17
	HSR 67	'346897–0'	1:1:22
	SVIB 9'80–		

His teachers reported that this boy "had problems" in the eighth and ninth grades. He appeared worried, he was extremely sensitive, and he brooded. He was also overly conscientious and too concerned with little things. These tendencies gradually disappeared and he became much more mature and better adjusted. He was quiet and a little self-conscious and withdrawn, yet he usually seemed likable, pleasant, respectful, and cooperative. He made a good showing in school athletics. In his schoolwork he did quite well "for his ability," but needed to be prodded or he would do just what he had to do to get by and consequently contribute very little. His friends were mostly boys with higher academic ability than he. After graduation he continued his education in the field of engineering.

The father was "a big, robust, glad-handing sort of man." In general, the father and mother were considered to be very good parents and they had a nice home. The mother was concerned over the adjustment of the boy when he was in the eighth and ninth grades and went to the school for frequent conferences.

144. M:16:1	ACE IX, none; XI, 77	'2093–6'48	4:3:8
N:IVA:7	ENG IX, none; XI, 47		
	HSR 50		
	SVIB none		

In the tenth and eleventh grades this boy was "the wise-guy type." He was immature in class, making frequent wisecracks, and was generally "a snippy and saucy show-off." During the twelfth grade he greatly improved. Also at this time he became a class leader for the first time. This change was attributed to the fact that he had set himself a goal: he wanted to become a teacher. When in the ninth grade he was involved in an automobile accident, but he was not arrested. After graduation he registered in a university agricultural training program.

145. M:15:1	ACE IX, 61; XI, 66	'3–'20	2:0:17
N:III:1	ENG IX, 60; XI, 06	'9438–0'25	3:0:19
	HSR 02		
	SVIB none		

Almost nothing good was said of this boy. A constant source of trouble, he shuttled between several public and private high schools, usually failing his subjects. It took him five years to get through high school, but getting a diploma at all was considered "quite an accomplishment for him." "He acted the part of a big wheel"; his chief interests were fast cars and girls. Some informants said very harsh things of him: "a yellow coward," "a whiner," "a squealer," "the type who would cut your throat on Skid Row," "the rottenest egg in the whole school." Physically large, well built, and "in robust health," he showed some interest in athletics but was unwilling, in several attempts, to make the necessary sacrifices or to stick with it long enough to make a team. His associates were well known to the police and were often in trouble. He himself seemed "always able to smell trouble and keep just shy of getting caught." He was also very adept at talking his way out of difficulties and using his father's money and influence to get himself out of jams. Delinquencies he was reportedly involved in included drinking, molesting girls, forgery, and fighting with a switch-blade knife. The best thing said of him was that he was "a bewildered kid, low in reliability and initiative, spoiled by his father's protection."

During his last year of school some improvement was reported. He was quiet, seemed to make some effort, and, with tutoring, did just enough work to get by. After graduation, while he was attending a junior college, he was involved in a court proceeding where he was charged with carnal knowledge for fathering the child of a junior high school girl. One ninth-grade teacher had predicted subsequent delinquency for him.

The boy dominated the home. The father, a businessman, was protective toward his son. The mother was said to be more cooperative with school authorities. However, the family had a great deal of money and both parents were considered to be much more interested in social activities than in the children.

146. M:14:4	ACE IX, 59; XI, 74	'3–5'6	5:2:18
N:IVC:5	ENG IX, 53; XI, 60	'36–9'	5:3:18
	HSR 87		
	SVIB 4'8–90		

This boy was neat, pleasant, and well liked. He was described as mature and both personally and socially well adjusted. A good student, he worked hard in school as well as after school on his family's farm. He wore his hair long and dressed in leather jacket and boots, but he was "not a hood in school." He took part in some athletics. In his sophomore year he was accused of malicious destruction of property on Halloween. Although it seemed very likely that he was guilty, he was released for lack of proof. After graduation he took a job and it was believed that he subsequently joined the armed services. "He was interested in school and would have continued if he had been given the chance."

The family had a marginal income. The father was "talkative and happy-go-lucky."

147. F:14:1	ACE IX, 30; XI, 46	'3–5'62	2:2:15
N:II:1	ENG IX, 62; XI, 40	'934–'057	4:1:16
	HSR 61		
	SVIB none		

This girl was in many activities. She was described in glowing terms: "a wonderful girl, a leader, respected, well liked, gracious, popular, attractive, and always pleasant." Well groomed, much alive and outgoing, extremely cooperative, she appeared adult and mature. In many ways she was one of the top girls in the school. She had a "genuine interest in people and their problems and would never do or say anything to hurt anybody." One teacher remarked that she was "a little hyperactive and not always too dependable because of her many activities." Good in class discussions, recitations, and written reports, she often surprised her teachers by not doing well in tests of ability or academic achievement. Her closest friends were persons of high ability and "she seemed to compensate by participating in many activities." She began a home economics course at college after graduation.

Both parents took an active part in school affairs; the family was a "well-rounded group."

148. M:14:0	ACE IX, none; XI, 91	'3–'6<u>79</u>	6:2:18
N:III:3	ENG IX, none; XI, 93	'54–'61<u>780</u>	5:2:17
	HSR 94	'5–7<u>81</u>'	5:2:14
	SVIB '89–		

This boy took part in many activities. He was pleasant, cooperative, and not a conduct problem. "He tried very hard and was rewarded by success." After graduation he continued his education at a university.

149. F:14:1	ACE IX, 90; XI, 96	'3–'6<u>05</u>	7:1:18
N:III:1	ENG IX, 97; XI, 98		
	HSR 55		
	SVIB none		

More mature than the other girls in her class, this girl was an individualist in behavior and appearance. She was tall and very nice looking, but she dressed differently from the other girls. An "outsider" in the class, she seemed self-sufficient. Her grades varied from very good to low, her poorest work being in social science. According to her language teacher, "She never made mistakes — she was an amazing creature." Her family did not have much money and she had to work outside of school.

150. F:15:1	ACE IX, 75; XI, 68	'3–'798	5:3:16
N:II:1	ENG IX, none; XI, 93	'6–'9	2:1:18
	HSR 81	'4–'2<u>90</u>	4:1:22
	SVIB none		

This was an "all-around girl," a good worker and socially active in school. She was "very normal and nice" and her school record was excellent. She was further described as well mannered, serious, and willing. In many ways she was a leader. After graduation she began university work and hoped to become a school teacher.

The father was a college graduate and a teacher. The mother was very active, doing volunteer work in the community, but "her home always came first." The family was considered to be "as fine as they come" — the parents ideal and the homelife excellent.

151. F:14:2	ACE IX, none; XI, 36	'3–'871 69	7:2:11
N:IVC:3	ENG IX, 40; XI, 51	'7–'2	5:4:16
	HSR 52		
	SVIB none		

Although nondescript, this girl had many friends and was in an average number of activities. She was not a conduct problem but was said to be somewhat irresponsible and lazy.

152. M:15:3	ACE IX, 75; XI, 89	'3–'9	5:1:19
N:IVB:4	ENG IX, 97; XI, 94	'6435–'92	6:4:22
	HSR 88		
	SVIB none		

While attending high school, this boy did most of the work at home on a farm. At school he was somewhat reticent; however, he could speak well and there was a certain "air of authority about him." He was usually "very negative" in his approach, frequently saying, for example, "I don't suppose you would let me . . ." He appeared brusque and often stubborn. It was suggested that he was sensitive and that his behavior was "a cover for his sensitivity."

The father's reputation may have contributed to the boy's sensitivity. He was a "soapbox orator" who made himself conspicuous with his unorthodox views. Because of the father's continuous speech making and outside activities the boy had to do the work on the farm.

153. M:15:0	ACE IX, none; XI, 56	'3–9'24 580	7:1:18
N:V:1	ENG IX, none; XI, 66	——	——
	HSR 84	'3–1'045	2:4:14
	SVIB none		

This boy apparently gained in strength as he went through high school. During his freshman year he was an average student and did his best work in history. He failed in mathematics, although it was a favorite subject. He later transferred to another school and its principal described him as "outstanding in cooperation, unusually well balanced, sound in making decisions; absolutely reliable, doing extra work; a leader who was sought out by others." He was active in Scout work and went to camp in the summer. After graduation he continued on to a university, where he was a C student. He wanted to be a teacher.

154. F:14:2	ACE IX, 94; XI, 89	'3–'925	5:5:16
N:VI:4	ENG IX, none; XI, 77	'95–4'62	3:3:16
	HSR 82		
	SVIB '–		

Termed a "career girl," this youngster worked outside of school as a receptionist and did a good job. She was active, industrious, and responsible, and had many friends. She took part in numerous school activities. Her teachers described her as having a "nice personality and sunny disposition." She was once lectured by the police for participating in a rowdy beer party.

155. M:15:1	ACE IX, none; XI, 43	'3–'926	5:1:19
N:V:1	ENG IX, none; XI, 36	'4372–'60	3:1:19
	HSR 10		
	SVIB none		

This boy had seriously defective vision and this handicap undoubtedly contributed to his poor schoolwork. Descriptions of him were rather contradictory. Some described him as "useless," lazy, and a general nonparticipant. Very much withdrawn, he was a lone wolf. Others, however, saw him as trying hard to do good work in school and as a pleasant, nice boy. He was not a discipline problem. His teachers practically "lifted him through school" because of his efforts. Outside of school he was interested in science and outdoor activities.

156. F:15:2	ACE IX, none; XI, 94	'31247–9'	6:3:21
N:II:1	ENG IX, none; XI, 99		
	HSR 100		
	SVIB '–		

From being shy and bashful in the ninth grade, this girl developed in her own quiet way to win the respect and admiration of fellow students and adults. Early in her high school years she was unresponsive socially — a sober person, businesslike in manner. By the end of her senior year, however, she came to be recognized as hav-

'31<u>2</u>675849–

ing a great deal of potential, and she was voted one of the outstanding students. After graduation, she entered a university.

The parents were very much interested in the children and their education. The family all took an active part in church and community and they spent much of their leisure time together.

157. M:15:1 ACE IX, 85; XI, 89 '31<u>2</u>675849– 5:0:16
     N:III:1 ENG IX, none; XI, 69
              HSR 94
              SVIB '12–

This was a tall boy who had a "bad skin problem." He was dependable, cooperative, courteous, and had a pleasing personality. "He always did the right thing but only spoke when spoken to," and he was regarded as withdrawn and not at all active. Outside of school he worked for his father. After graduation he went to a small college.

The family was well accepted in the community and active in civic affairs. The father owned a small business and was described as overly aggressive, outspoken, and loud. A sister had a great deal of drive and was not well liked because of her outspokenness; she was a good student, but she alienated people.

158. M:14:2 ACE IX, none; XI, 41 '31<u>4</u>207–'5 7:7:15
     N:III:5 ENG IX, none; XI, none <u>72</u>'01<u>3</u>85–'9 5:8:15
              HSR 31
              SVIB none

"Carefree, happy-go-lucky," this youth paid little attention to the consequences of his behavior. Usually very gentlemanly, he was sometimes defiant but respected authority when it was displayed. His teachers found that he showed little initiative and needed prodding. He was an athlete but chose his friends from his church group rather than from the team. He also played in the band. He transferred to a school in a neighboring community for his senior year.

The home life was "very good." The parents, who were very religious, were cooperative with school authorities.

159. M:15:1 ACE IX, none; XI, 99 '31<u>4</u>59–'206 3:1:12
     N:I:1   ENG IX, none; XI, 82 9'3<u>64</u> <u>18</u> <u>75</u>–0'2 5:1:18
              HSR 69
              SVIB none

One teacher described this boy as a good, well-adjusted student who was quick-witted and witty, more lively than most, but not to the point of causing trouble.

Some other persons thought of him as insecure. His high school coach said that he needed and constantly sought encouragement and support to bolster his underlying inferiority feelings. He was also described as "a social climber." He was known to the police for several boyish peccadilloes. A juvenile officer described him as a good boy but one needing a "firm and steady hand to keep him on a straight path because he is easily led." It was easy to reason with him when he was in trouble, and he seemed appreciative of things that were done for or with him. His special interests were athletics, in which he excelled, and science. He expected to continue on to college for professional training. It was suggested that he might be "almost too high-strung to be a professional man."

The father and grandfather were both professionally trained. The father's work kept him out of the home a considerable amount of the time; however, the family was frequently observed together, and the parents seemed to be making a definite effort to keep the family closely knit despite the father's frequent absences from home. The mother had been hospitalized several times for alcoholism. She was high-strung and nervous.

160. M:15:2	ACE IX, 93; XI, 96	′314̲6̲–	2:1:20
N:V:1	ENG IX, none; XI, 93	′63̲9̲14̲8̲–0′	4:1:21
	HSR 73		
	SVIB 8′4–		

This boy was quiet, likable, and cooperative. He would "clown around in class but he was never malicious." In his junior year he got into trouble for the malicious destruction of property, but he made restitution. After graduation he went to a small college and in his second year there received a scholarship for partial financial support.

The family had a good reputation except for one older sister, who "turned into a tramp and became very promiscuous." The whole family worked hard and the parents were sociable and reliable.

161. F:15:10	ACE IX, none; XI, 24	3″1′4̲7̲8̲ 9̲6̲2̲–′0	3:6:14
N:V:1	ENG IX, none; XI, 22		
	HSR 53 DO 12th gr.		
	SVIB none		

Sweet and likable though sometimes temperamental, this girl dropped out ol school in her senior year to go to work. She married shortly thereafter. Full of fun and friendliness, she worked hard to compensate for what she seemed to lack in ability. In grade school, her reading ability had been so low that she had needed special tutoring. Although she was not a conduct problem, she was for a time involved with a boy who was considered "no good." She got into some trouble because she would borrow things and not return them. She had a twin sister who had somewhat higher academic ability; she also married young. [The MMPI codes for the twin were, ninth grade, 8149'62730–'5 3:5:16, and, twelfth grade, '968–'0 2:3:17.]

The father was known as somewhat of a fanatic about religion. The mother was more lenient. The family was at a low economic level, and since both parents worked outside the home, the children had to shift for themselves.

162. M:15:3	ACE IX, none; XI, 94	'3148567–'09	9:2:23
B:I:1	ENG IX, none; XI, 78		
	HSR 52		
	SVIB none		

This was a boy with many problems. He could be pleasant to talk to one minute but then become moody and dissatisfied. He was an underachiever, often skipping school and refusing to work when he was in school. This behavior eventually resulted in school suspension. He would often agree that he should straighten out but would not act upon his resolves. On first impression, he seemed a top personality, but this view was quickly modified on closer acquaintance. He was good looking and he was "greatly affected by girls; it seemed his ideal to have a girl for a companion." He had a girl friend who was said to have had a good influence on him. (She eventually became pregnant, and they married.) He liked to excel as an individual but could not participate as a member of a group. Other boys shied away from him. At home his stepfather gave him everything, but he was in frequent conflict with his mother. He was not a happy boy. He would go to his room, locking himself in and refusing to come out. He would later slip out and go for a long drive without a set purpose. At his worst he was very sullen and unable to talk to anyone in a civilized manner. He was in repeated difficulty with the law, at first because of traffic violations, but later because of theft and breaking and entering. He was also brought into court because of incorrigibility at home.

163. F:14:2	ACE IX, 30; XI, 29	31'74 28960–'5	9:5:21
N:V:1	ENG IX, none; XI, 45	'12348–'596	1:4:15
	HSR 55	'34 518–'90	4:2:23
	SVIB none		

Teachers generally described this girl as well adjusted, popular, pleasant, sparkling, poised, and conscientious. Never a disciplinary problem, she was open to suggestion and a leader in her own home room. She was active in musical affairs and never complained about the great amount of time spent in rehearsals. One or two teachers, however, described her as "lazy and somewhat nervous and high-strung."

They did not recognize her leadership and questioned the maturity of her judgment. After graduation, she began university work, in which she was reported to be doing well.

164. F:14:3	ACE IX, 15; XI, 26	3′178–′20	4:3:14
N:VII:1	ENG IX, none; XI, 45	7″21′43805–	2:5:18
	HSR 37	7′8290–′6	1:3:14
	SVIB none		

Although this girl was frequently absent from school, her absences seemed to be justified. The majority of the descriptive words applied to her were complimentary: friendly, diplomatic, conformist, industrious, obedient, and self-controlled. One teacher thought of her as "erratic, retiring, aloof, and timid." She appeared to lack self-confidence and was more a follower than a leader. One person felt that she needed to "become more active." She took some part in extracurricular activities, chiefly orchestra. Her main school interests were in sewing, dancing, and swimming. In most academic studies she received C's and D's. During her school years she had an outside job and also worked as a baby sitter. After graduation she registered at a university but later withdrew because of failing grades. Subsequent to this she took a regular job as a waitress but planned to go into subprofessional training.

165. F:15:3	ACE IX, 93; XI, 69	3′17954–′0	4:5:20
N:III:1	ENG IX, 89; XI, 85	43′19782–5′	2:5:21
	HSR 22		
	SVIB none		

While in the ninth and tenth grades, this girl had attitudes and friends that were "not the best." She seemed unhappy much of the time and was often absent from school. Although she apparently caused no great trouble, she did smoke and she restricted her social associations to a small group of friends. At one time a counselor secured part-time work for her, but she quit this job after two months. She improved somewhat during her later high school years and developed a degree of interest in training for a vocation. After high school graduation she began working for a large commercial concern in a clerical capacity.

166. F:14:1	ACE IX, 17; XI, 55	'32–'90	7:0:22
N:III:6	ENG IX, 34; XI, 59		
	HSR 42		
	SVIB none		

This girl had a special interest in clothes, and she wore her many clothes well. "She had a lot of poise." Quiet and unassuming, she did not put herself out to be friendly, but she was "receptive."

167. F:15:4   ACE IX, none; XI, 28   3'21–'09   7:4:18
     B:N:1   ENG IX, none; XI, 52
                     HSR 25
                     SVIB none

There was very little information about this girl. She had a "very sweet personality," but she was "scatterbrained." Her father was dead and because she was neglected by her mother she was placed in a foster home.

168. M:14:3   ACE IX, 99; XI, 91   '32416–'09   8:3:16
     N:I:5   ENG IX, 90; XI, 87   3'481679–'05 4:4:24
                     HSR 95
                     SVIB none

This was the most spirited boy in the class and a top student. A well-liked youth,
he was in many activities ranging from band and chorus to athletics. He did
everything well, had a good sense of humor, and was never mean or malicious.
He was described as "very alive" and as articulate.
     The parents were both college graduates, the father a professional man.

169. F:15:4   ACE IX, none; XI, 79   32'40 817–'5   7:7:6
     N:VI:3   ENG IX, none; XI, 93   3"21'0784–5'9 6:4:10
                     HSR 96
                     SVIB WR'

This girl was intelligent with "a head of her own," but she also "had a little chip on
her shoulder." She was a "live wire," had a strong character, and took part in many
activities. Although she would challenge teachers, her attitude in doing so was sincere. She was not a conduct problem, and she had a number of good friends.
     The father was described as "mean." Because the home was "poor," the girl
stayed with a relative most of the time.

170. F:14:1   ACE IX, 84; XI, 79   '32670–5'4   5:3:17
     N:III:1   ENG IX, 75; XI, 72   '3790–'5   3:3:15
                     HSR 80
                     SVIB none

Friendly, talkative, socially well adjusted, and "happy-go-lucky," this was a conscientious student who was considered a leader among the girls. A little unrealistic
and idealistic in her ideas, she would appear ashamed if she felt she had said
something foolish and the other students laughed at her. She was very active in
her church and maintained her interest in its youth groups. For a time she went

steady with a boy from her church, but later broke up with him. After graduating from high school she entered a subprofessional type of training.

The family was closely knit and of average middle-class socioeconomic level. Both parents were friendly and competent. The mother was said to be an outgoing person with a lot of "sparkle." It was mentioned that the father was sometimes "temperamental."

171. F:14:3	ACE IX, none; XI, 40	'32719–'6	9:4:16
B:V:3	ENG IX, none; XI, 33	341'782 506–	9:3:24
	HSR 42		
	SVIB WR'		

Shortly before the ninth-grade testing this girl was in an automobile accident in which her father was killed and she was severely injured. After the accident she became high-strung and her scholarship deteriorated. Disfigurement that resulted from the accident seemed to make her unduly self-conscious and she grew more unsure of herself in every way. However, even before the accident she had never asserted herself and had always asked permission before doing things. She had always been a serious girl who was not "distracted by foolishness." Neat and tidy in appearance, she was considered nice and respectable, and, although her school achievement was not good, she engaged in some school activities, primarily musical. After graduation she obtained a clerical position and was reported to be slow in her work. Shortly thereafter she was married.

There was not much information about the family as it was before the death of the father; the mother remarried and established a good home for the children.

172. M:14:2	ACE IX, none; XI, 07	32'814769–	9:6:22
N:IVA:5	ENG IX, none; XI, none		
	HSR 06		
	SVIB none		

This "mischievous" boy was easily led into foolish horseplay and he was often sent to the principal's office. His teachers described him as awkward, lazy, and dull. Reputed to be "a hard drinker," he was "very nervous" and "suffered from St. Vitus' Dance."

173. F:14:5	ACE IX, none; XI, 69	'34–'905	2:2:17
N:IVB:5	ENG IX, none; XI, 84		
	HSR 84		
	SVIB none		

The "principal's helper," this girl was dependable, accurate, and mature, with "much common sense." She met people and situations well and with poise.

174. M:15:3	ACE IX, none; XI, 100	341'8672–'09	6:3:26
N:III:3	ENG IX, none; XI, 87	'3416 57–	3:3:19
	HSR 99		
	SVIB none		

This handsome boy had few friends and took part in no school activities except a science club; he seemed not to need people and did not mix with his fellow students. He was an ardent reader, and his curiosity kept the teachers on their toes. He was "not smooth," but could get his point across. His scholarship placed him very high in the class, and after graduation it was expected that he would continue into engineering or scientific research.

175. F:15:4	ACE IX, 41; XI, 41	'34256–'09	7:1:21
N:II:1	ENG IX, none; XI, 62	'34618–'0	3:0:23
	HSR 29	'8946–0'2	3:4:23
	SVIB none		

In her freshman and sophomore years this girl was not very well behaved; she did things spontaneously, without thinking, and "talked out of turn." At the same time she needed to be pushed, and, although she was well liked, she was not a leader. As she continued in high school, her behavior improved, and she became very active, especially in art work. She "seemed to sense when a teacher could use good assistance and was right there to lend a hand." Calm and mature in behavior, she seemed more stable than most girls her age. She worked part time after school and was ambitious and friendly. After graduation she went to a university, where her grades were somewhat above average. One teacher predicted legal difficulties for her.

The father was described as calm and stable, but the mother seemed to be a "nervous type." She had "terrific determination," and when she worked at something, she neglected her family.

176. M:14:3	ACE IX, 82; XI, 95	'3426–	3:3:13
N:VI:1	ENG IX, none; XI, 84		
	HSR 95		
	SVIB 2'4–		

Two ninth-grade teachers predicted that this boy would become emotionally maladjusted. Although he was quiet and retiring to the point where it caused some concern to his counselor and teachers, he was described as a fine boy, mature and persistent in completing tasks. He was a good, cooperative, and considerate student. After graduation he attended a technical college.

177. M:14:1   ACE IX, 77; XI, 92   '34517-'9   4:3:17
N:I:1   ENG IX, 85; XI, 81   '9485-0'21   1:1:15
               HSR 98
               SVIB 4'15-90

One person said of this boy, "There are not enough good adjectives to describe him — he is one of the best." He was well groomed, poised, friendly, and well liked. Although he was somewhat shy and quiet, he was a fine leader and was president of his class. He worked hard and achieved very well. In activities he assumed responsibility and was "very, very conscientious." After graduation he attended a university.

The family's economic status was above average. Both parents were described as conscientious citizens of the community, participating in many activities but never becoming particularly prominent. The father gave the boy much companionship.

178. M:15:2   ACE IX, none; XI, 96   '3467-   8:2:22
N:N:1   ENG IX, none; XI, 55
               HSR 83
               SVIB none

This boy had a good sense of humor and was not a school problem. Although he was considered to be bright, he was erratic in work and moody in temperament.

179. M:14:1   ACE IX, none; XI, 82   '346719-0'   4:0:16
N:II:2   ENG IX, none; XI, 68   '9436-205'   5:4:19
               HSR 81
               SVIB none

The teachers thought of this boy as an underachiever and as one who lacked drive. He was, however, characterized by dependability and good judgment. Popular yet unobtrusive, he apparently made no outstanding impression on anyone.

180. F:15:2   ACE IX, 88; XI, 86   3'4678-5'0   3:7:13
N:V:1   ENG IX, 87; XI, 52   '479 683-'50 2:4:17
               HSR 61   4'367819-5'0 2:6:17
               SVIB none

This girl, it was said, "wore her hair too long, wore too much makeup, and was too stylish in dress." She gave an impression of snobbishness. Some people were of the opinion that she created this impression to cover a feeling of inferiority. In her dealings with people she "tried too hard." She expressed much concern about her social relationships with other students, feeling that she was more of a failure than she was in actual fact, since she appeared to be generally well liked. She was more interested in boys "than she should have been" and wanted to be in certain activities that would help her gain social recognition. She had many activities, both in church and in school, and her teachers said she was "a nice person to have around." A good student, she was very conscientious, although she appeared to have no strong direction in life. She attended college after graduating.

The parents had marital difficulties, chiefly because of the father's alcoholism. It appeared that the girl's seeming inferiority feelings may have been related to the general home situation. The mother was described as an emotional, nagging wife who had great difficulty in showing affection toward anyone. The girl once told her mother that she had sympathy for the father because the mother made him feel so inadequate. When the girl was a senior in high school, the father, under threat of separation from the mother, received outside help and reformed rather suddenly. At the same time the mother made a considerable effort to change. As a result the family was much more harmonious. The mother, however, suffered severely from guilt over her past behavior and required medical care.

181. F:14:2   ACE IX, 74; XI, 82   '347–'2   8:1:22
     B:V:2   ENG IX, 90; XI, 98   '368–2'50   11:2:24X
                 HSR 90
                 SVIB WR'

The most outstanding fact about this girl was that she was deeply religious and motivated to enter actively into a training program to do recruiting for the church. She affiliated with a fundamentalist Christian sect contrary to her mother's wishes. She was quiet, had a pleasant personality, and was well liked by the other girls in her class. In school she was not a leader, nor did she engage in many activities. She had musical talent. Her teachers considered her a perfectionist in everything. She had a slight congenital physical handicap.

The father was dead and the mother worked. The mother had a tendency toward alcoholism, and because of this, the girl often lived outside the home with an older sister.

182. F:14:3   ACE IX, none; XI, 98   '34867–5'20   4:3:26
     N:III:3   ENG IX, none; XI, 100
                 HSR 98
                 SVIB none

All statements about this girl were complimentary. She was talented, "completely reliable, and a very fine personality." She was an outstanding student, good in everything. She was salutatorian of her class. Her particular accomplishments were in music.

183. M:15:1   ACE IX, 77; XI, 90   3'486715–   5:5:25
    N:IVB:2   ENG IX, none; XI, 94
                     HSR 08
                     SVIB '89–2

"An accomplished liar," this boy was often truant from school. He seemed to prefer farming to going to school, and it was suspected that he feigned illness to justify
his truancy. Although he was lazy, he was not a conduct problem in the school. In
general, he went relatively unnoticed. He had few friends, but he did have some
dates.

184. F:15:0   ACE IX, none; XI, 44   '3489–'0   13:1:25X
    B:V:1   ENG IX, none; XI, 59   '38–'05   7:1:20
                     HSR 83
                     SVIB '–

This obese girl did average schoolwork, and she seemed willing to work, but she
never showed any leadership. Her teachers thought she might be a perfectionist.
She enjoyed writing poetry. She was quiet and her mood was variable, easily fluc-
tuating between depression and elation.

185. F:14:2   ACE IX, none; XI, 77   '35–'1   2:2:17
    B:N:1   ENG IX, none; XI, 85
                     HSR 93
                     SVIB none

One of the brighter students, this girl was well liked and she had a nice personality.
She also had a temper, however, and sometimes lost it, after which she always
apologized.

186. F:15:1   ACE IX, 95; XI, 95   '35–2'017   3:0:18
    N:II:1   ENG IX, none; XI, 96   '564–0'2   3:0:21
                     HSR 90
                     SVIB none

This big, tall girl was possibly sensitive about her size, though she was described
as "happy." There were "signs of emotional upset whenever she felt she had done
something less than perfect." She had a "terrific drive to be 100 per cent perfect."
Some pupils may not have liked her well because of her compulsiveness. Generally,
however, she was very active in school affairs. Frequently a leader, she could initi-

ate constructive ideas and was a good organizer. She was dependable and not a discipline problem. She was "an all-around fine girl," and "knew her p's and q's."

The father, a successful small businessman, encouraged his children to take advantage of available opportunities. The home life was closely knit.

187. M:15:0	ACE IX, 90; XI, 95	'35–8'1	6:1:14
B:VI:1	ENG IX, none; XI, 53	'956–'238	0:6:9
	HSR 22		
	SVIB none		

An underachiever, this boy had a few minor scrapes with teachers. For example, he once went hunting without permission from school or parents. In general, he was well adjusted, "except for the occasional need of prodding." At some time in his freshman year he apparently was involved in a burglary episode, although no details were available.

188. F:15:6	IQ (centile) 16	'3587–'1	2:5:11
B:VI:2	HSR DO 10th gr.		
	SVIB none		

"Heavy and big boned," this girl was friendly and well liked by her own group. She sometimes talked out of turn, although she was fairly well mannered. Uninterested in school, she dropped out to take a job and was married soon afterward.

The parents, who were separated, both worked at low-level jobs, and the family situation was described as "disorganized." A twin brother, who was characterized as frequently truant and insubordinate, especially to women teachers, also dropped out before completing high school. [The twin's ninth-grade MMPI code was 8'"64"9702– 0:29:9X.]

189. M:14:1	ACE IX, 36; XI, 18	'36–5'09	6:5:16
N:V:1	ENG IX, none; XI, 34		
	HSR 26		
	SVIB none		

This boy was congenitally lame and small in stature. Interested only in automobiles, he was lazy and inattentive toward schoolwork. He clashed with the teachers, used abusive language, and was generally disagreeable and negative.

190. F:15:3   ACE IX, 21; XI, 20   '36<u>14</u> <u>78</u>–'59   2:5:21
    N:V:2   ENG IX, none; XI, 45
                     HSR 21
                     SVIB none

Although she was not a conduct problem, this girl was withdrawn, shy, and bashful, and she made a poor social adjustment. She had difficulty in doing her schoolwork and engaged in no activities outside of class. Her only friends were a couple of farm girls. Shortly after her graduation from high school she married.

This girl's family was believed to be fairly typical. The mother occasionally worked outside the home, and with this help the family managed to maintain an income consistent with the community's average. The mother was said to be somewhat flighty and unreliable.

191. F:15:6   ACE IX, none; XI, 86   3'6<u>27</u><u>81</u>–5'   6:2:17
    B:V:1   ENG IX, none; XI, 95
                     HSR 83
                     SVIB 'WR

Dependable and mature, with good ability, this girl was pleasant and cooperative. She did not participate in many extracurricular activities, however, and was very quiet. Outside of school she worked every day. She was actively religious, although she found this to be unacceptable to her mother and stepfather, who "did not respect her views." In spite of these differences, she made a good adjustment and pursued her own interests. After graduation she went to a Bible school.

192. F:15:4   ACE IX, 87; XI, 72   '364–   3:8:12
    N:III:2   ENG IX, none; XI, 96
                     HSR 75 DO 12th gr.
                     SVIB none

Described as "very mature, a little fleshy and plump," and as "motherly, pleasant, and nice," this girl was not a conduct problem in school and was considered intelligent, cooperative, and a steady worker. During her last year of school she was forced to drop out in order to marry.

193. F:15:3   ACE IX, 88; XI, 84   '364–<u>29</u>'5   4:0:17
    N:I:1   ENG IX, none; XI, 95   — —   — —
                     HSR 86   '6–5'   4:2:14
                     SVIB none

Only good things were said about this girl. Popular with both boys and girls and respected by the teachers, she was a leader in school and church. A good musician, she took part in both school and community programs. Nice in appearance and mature in manner, she was a "solid citizen." She was a "wonderful help" to her mother with the younger siblings. A teacher said she "would like to have a building full of girls like this." Later at a university she made a B average in a home economics curriculum.

The father was a college graduate. Although he was a "little prim and shockable," he was, nevertheless, "very well meaning." The mother put her home first but was active outside of it in community affairs. There seemed to be every possible advantage given the children.

194. M:14:3	ACE IX, 50; XI, none	'36412 789–5'	6:9:16
N:V:1	ENG IX, 35; XI, none		
	HSR trans. 11th gr.		
	SVIB none		

A very quiet boy who was somewhat withdrawn, this youth had few friends and seemed to feel inferior to other boys. Schoolwork was difficult for him. He was unable to do better than average work and often did not reach even this standard. The family moved to another state and he completed his last two years of schooling there. Authorities from this school reported that "he seemed to be a well-adjusted boy." In his freshman year he had got into some trouble because of vandalism.

195. F:14:3	ACE IX, none; XI, 26	'36417280–9'5	5:2:24
N:VI:2	ENG IX, none; IX, 55	'64–5'	6:1:21
	HSR 82		
	SVIB none		

Responsible, reliable, and a leader, this girl was not a school problem. Her teachers said that she talked too much, however, and that she was domineering.

196. M:16:1	ACE IX, none; XI, 07	'369718–	6:6:14
N:VI:2	ENG IX, none; XI, 05	0'687239–'4	4:5:14
	HSR 27		
	SVIB none		

This boy had been very ill as a child and, as a result, was handicapped by a "heart condition." He had a pleasing personality, was neat and well liked by others. In school he was cooperative; he tried hard and was a responsive but very slow student.

197. F:14:1	ACE IX, 79; XI, 74	'37–'25	4:2:20
N:III:1	ENG IX, 90; XI, 87	'9–'45 10	3:4:19
	HSR 89	'49 83–'0	2:1:23
	SVIB none		

Although quiet, shy, and without a "flashing personality," this girl was described as having many good qualities. She was "sweet, lovely, a perfect lady, and tops in every way." She was extremely stable and a conscientious worker who "went out of her way to please." After high school graduation she went on to a university.

There is no information about the family beyond the fact that the father had a period of sickness when this girl was in the twelfth grade. The girl was said to have been clearly disturbed by her father's illness, but she did not break down to the point where her schoolwork deteriorated.

198. F:15:1	ACE IX, none; XI, 97	'37–2'0	4:0:19
B:III:2	ENG IX, none; XI, 93		
	HSR 94		
	SVIB '–		

Extremely popular and attractive, this girl was one about whom mostly good things were said. She was active in and out of school — a cheerleader and willing to carry responsibility in extracurricular activities. Sometimes she seemed "deadpan," and early in high school she had some minor trouble with one teacher.

199. F:15:2	ACE IX, 59; XI, 77	'37–'052	3:2:17
N:V:4	ENG IX, 77; XI, 73	3"918'647–'0	5:4:18
	HSR 87		
	SVIB 'WR		

This girl was peppy, vital, athletic, and characterized by so much poise that people overlooked her occasional misbehavior. For the most part she was described as very fine, with good abilities and a responsible and capable approach. She "sought for facts and wanted things right." By contrast, a few saw her as moody and outspoken, suffering from an inferiority complex. Even these persons recognized that the girl would quickly apologize and be sorry for her behavior. Her conduct outside of school was not beyond reproach and it was believed that she drank, smoked, and stayed out late. After graduation she went to a university.

The father was an outgoing, fine person. The mother also was considered a fine person, and, although she had a full-time job outside the home, she took time to be with the family whenever possible. If the girl was engaging in any bad behavior, it was believed that the parents were completely fooled by her because they were trusting and had high ideals.

200. F:14:1	ACE IX, none; XI, 92	3″71<u>8654</u>–	4:5:17
N:III:2	ENG IX, none; XI, 80	′78 <u>6032</u>–′9	1:5:18
	HSR 87		
	SVIB none		

The few notes about this girl say that she was a good student who was sensible and used good judgment. She mixed well with her classmates.

201. M:15:1	ACE IX, none; XI, 13	3″7<u>4189</u>–′06	5:4:19
N:IVB:3	ENG IX, none; XI, 12	′<u>34</u>–′05	3:3:19
	HSR 32		
	SVIB none		

Physical illness caused this boy to miss a year of school before the ninth grade. He was small in stature and did not look well. Although he was friendly and had a fair sense of humor, he was not interested in activities and did not take part in school affairs. After graduation he expected to become a farmer.

202. M:15:12	ACE IX, none; XI, 50	3″7<u>841</u>′26–′0	8:7:21
N:IVB:3	ENG IX, none; XI, 68		
	HSR 11		
	SVIB none		

"So normal that he went unnoticed," this boy was modest, quiet, dependable, reliable, well mannered, and fair. Never pushing himself and excelling in nothing, he was taken for granted. Although he appeared to apply himself, he was a comparatively poor student. After graduation he hoped to join the Army.

203. F:15:2	ACE IX, 74; XI, 78	′3<u>79</u> <u>2468</u>–	3:2:15
N:III:2	ENG IX, none; XI, 85	4″39′<u>85612</u>–	0:5:17
	HSR 93		
	SVIB ′–		

An attractive blonde, "pouty, spoiled, and saucy," this girl had to "get her sleep or she became crabby." Her personality was described as rather "neutral and colorless" and yet she was accepted by everyone. She seemed to have a considerable number of friends, and she took part in an average amount of extracurricular activity. Regarded as "boy crazy," she was always possessive of her current boy friend and several boys had trouble "shaking her." She was not a conduct problem and she seemed to work close to her capacity in school. She was allergic to many foods and frequently got sick, developing rashes and other symptoms which required clinical treatment. After graduation she continued training toward a semiprofessional job.

Perhaps to a fault, the children in this family were considered important. They were pampered and given everything, and the girl's boy friends were accepted into the home at once as though they were already members of the family. One of the sisters became illegitimately pregnant and was forced to quit school in order to marry. Otherwise all members of the family seemed to be well adjusted.

204. M:15:1	ACE IX, none; XI, 49	'37984–'05	7:4:19
N:III:3	ENG IX, none; XI, 43	'94–52'0	2:4:20
	HSR 40		
	SVIB 4'1–		

This quiet, unobtrusive boy was not a conduct problem and he minded his own affairs. In his schoolwork he was an average student but he did not engage in any extracurricular activities. He had "an average circle" of good friends.

205. F:14:3	ACE IX, 82; XI, 85	'38–'05	5:3:20
N:V:1	ENG IX, none; XI, 55		
	HSR 35		
	SVIB none		

Because she was "very fat" this girl went on a strict diet and became ill as a result. She was not very interested in school and was frequently absent. Not easy to get along with, she had few friends. Her short temper seemed to be a problem in her social relationships.

206. F:15:0	ACE IX, 65; XI, 58	'38–'05	7:3:22
N:III:1	ENG IX, none; XI, 95		
	HSR 81		
	SVIB none		

An honor student with a fine personality and a pleasing manner, this girl was termed "extremely sweet." She was a good musician and won a contest in musical performance. She was also described as serious and well behaved.

207. M:15:3	ACE IX, none; XI, 24	'381–0'2	1:3:19
N:III:1	ENG IX, none; XI, 29	'34–'079	6:1:19
	HSR 51		
	SVIB '8–		

This boy was generally well behaved, but he did cause some disturbances in the ninth and tenth grades. He had a good personality and was well liked by the other students. He was dependable. In class he never volunteered to recite. By his senior year his behavior had improved and he was no problem.

208. F:14:0   ACE IX, 52; XI, 59   '3856–'20   5:3:14
    N:VII:4   ENG IX, none; XI, 72   '438–   11:4:23X
                 HSR 90
                 SVIB WR'

Only good things were said about this girl. She was mature, well liked, and considered a "lady." "Smart and fine looking," she was moderately active in school affairs and had a select group of friends. She expected to go to a business college after she graduated from high school.

209. F:14:1   ACE IX, 42; XI, 55   '386–'7   4:9:11
    N:IVC:5   ENG IX, 55; XI, 68   '53–2'768   3:2:15
                 HSR 68
                 SVIB none

In her earlier high school years this girl had a bad reputation. She lied to school authorities and was guilty of peddling an obscene story that she had typed. It was in these early years that one teacher predicted that the girl would become emotionally maladjusted. Near her final year in high school she "realized her mistakes and began to try very hard to make up for them." This resulted in her being considered a fine student by the time she graduated.

210. M:15:1   ACE IX, none; XI, 93   '386–'0   13:2:22X
    N:V:2   ENG IX, none; XI, 84   — —   — —
                 HSR 88   '5–'72809   3:1:17
                 SVIB 4'–0

This was a polite, industrious boy. Pleasant, friendly, and well liked, he was "an average classroom citizen" and was considered completely honest and reliable. He was easy to talk with, courteous and amiable. He was not active in extracurricular affairs. After graduation he began the study of engineering at a university.

211. M:14:2   ACE IX, none; XI, 87   '387954–'02   5:4:16
    N:V:1   ENG IX, none; XI, 79   '1439–'076   8:3:18
                 HSR 77
                 SVIB 4'8–0

Described as outstanding in cooperation and motivation, this quiet boy had a pleasant personality and got along very well with his peers. He was a good student and would volunteer in class.

212. F:14:1   ACE IX, none; XI, 85   '38974–'20 3:1:17
  N:VI:2   ENG IX, none; XI, 63   '3–0'2   2:1:16
          HSR 87
          SVIB none

Called "always busy," this girl was dependable, polite, and responsible. She was "a very wholesome and nice girl, and she knew her place."

213. F:14:4   ACE IX, none; XI, 44   '39–'5   2:2:11
  N:V:2   ENG IX, none; XI, 96   '374812–5' 2:6:17
          HSR 66
          SVIB none

This girl was very popular, pleasant, and "well adjusted." She was a reliable, responsible, and good student. The only additional comment reported was that she was "attractive, shy, and quiet."

214. F:14:1   ACE IX, 70; XI, 73   '39–'528 3:3:18
  N:III:1   ENG IX, 79; XI, 81
          HSR 57
          SVIB none

This was a well-groomed, well-dressed girl who was relatively quiet. Although her teachers thought this quietness might give the impression of aloofness, they claimed she really "wasn't interested." Instead of having a large group of friends, she had one or two close friends. She seemed to be satisfied with these and with a boy friend. After graduation she went to a university.

215. F:15:3   ACE IX, 97; XI, 97   '395687–20' 3:0:21
  N:III:1   ENG IX, 89; XI, 92   — —   — —
          HSR 97   '3469–02' 6:0:22
          SVIB none

A "sort of bubbly type" who could "pull a person out of the dumps," this girl had a good deal of enthusiasm. She was intellectually curious, poised, and confident. She was "an ideal student to have, always appreciative and enthusiastic." Although one person said that there was possibly some social maladjustment, this was not readily apparent.

71

216. F:15:1   ACE IX, none; XI, 79   '3974–2'56   5:2:12
    N:VI:3   ENG IX, none; XI, 69   '70–8'9   3:1:12
               HSR 52
               SVIB none

This girl considered marriage more important than school. She had a tendency to "chase around" and was involved with a group that had interests like her own; this did not, however, interfere with her schoolwork. Although she was described as articulate and realistic, several teachers predicted that she would have some emotional disturbance. Before graduation she became engaged to a responsible and stable boy and expected to marry him after graduation.

The only reference made to the family concerned the father. He had requested the police to escort the girl home sometime during her tenth-grade year.

217. F:15:3   ACE IX, 57; XI, 52   39'748261–'0   5:3:15
    N:V:1   ENG IX, none; XI, 23
               HSR 22 DO 12th gr.
               SVIB none

Described as "very domestic," this girl had been engaged for one and a half years when she quit school in the spring of her final year. In the school setting she appeared quiet and withdrawn. She had a high character and morals and displayed considerable indignation over what she considered to be the immoral behavior of others. It was mentioned that she had had "much domestic training" at home. An underachiever in school, she apparently quit in order to be married.

218. M:14:1   ACE IX, 98; XI, 100   '3976458–0'2   6:2:23
    N:II:2   ENG IX, 96; XI, 98
               HSR 94
               SVIB 90'–12

This boy was a "wholesome, apt student who did wonderful work." Usually pleasant, friendly, and dependable, he was also quiet and did not often volunteer in class. He worked in cycles and his attitude toward school vacillated between good and poor, his disposition between sulky and happy. He "kidded and teased even the teachers in a quiet, fun sort of way." This kidding gave him the reputation of having a sharp tongue; "he would try to be clever but it would backfire."

219. F:14:0   ACE IX, none; XI, 44   '30–95'81   3:4:7
    N:VI:2   ENG IX, none; XI, 76
               HSR 82
               SVIB none

Although it was said that this girl was quiet and seemed in general to make a good adjustment, all other information was to the contrary. She did not take part in school activities, and there were instances in which she skipped classes. She kept company with a "tough girl," and had to be warned about "tight clothes."

220. F:14:0 B:N:5	ACE IX, none; XI, 99 ENG IX, none; XI, 99 HSR 92 SVIB none	3'0<u>168</u>–'<u>49</u>	1:3:11

This girl was "always dependable." She caused no problems but also entered into no school activities. She worked part time at a school job.

221. M:15:1 N:III:3	ACE IX, 95; XI, 99 ENG IX, 96; XI, 84 HSR 89 SVIB 48'–	'305–9'	7:5:18

Purposeful, quiet, hard working, cheerful, and pleasant, this boy was interested in radio and mechanics. He was also described as well balanced and conscientious.

222. F:15:0 B:V:1	ACE IX, 74; XI, 62 ENG IX, none; XI, 73 HSR 87 SVIB none	'4–'1 4"9'67–52'01 '4–<u>17</u> 80'5	7:1:15 5:2:15 3:2:7

Elected queen of an event in her senior year, this girl was always popular, helpful, eager, and pleasant. She was very conscientious about her studies and worked hard at them. Her manner was modest and happy. She worked after school hours and she wanted to be a librarian, although she sometimes seemed too gay and exuberant for such a quiet job. After graduation she went to a university, where she was reported to be doing well.

Her father had died just before she entered the ninth grade. The mother had to work. She seemed somewhat unstable, with more interest in her own good time than in her daughter's welfare. The mother later remarried and her husband considered his stepdaughter to be an expensive liability.

223. F:15:1 N:V:1	ACE IX, 93; XI, 68 ENG IX, none; XI, 99 HSR 98 SVIB none	'4–'15 4'36–'50<u>29</u> '48–<u>50</u>'<u>29</u>	8:4:17 7:1:24 8:0:26

This "large, chunky girl" was more interested in good grades than in friends. She achieved high scholastic honors apparently because of her seriousness, good judgment, hard work, and persistence. She was neat and nice in appearance but was very reserved and timid, even to the point of appearing to be stubborn. An episode was reported in which she had engaged in some vandalism involving the destruction of school property. She had good ability in music and could have had a career in that field if she had so wished. One person spoke of her as having something of suspicion in her attitude and as not being willing to trust people readily. After graduation she continued on to a university, where she made good grades. She was interested in teaching.

Both parents were excessively reserved and unobtrusive in all ways. Attempts to draw them into community activities did not succeed in overcoming their tendency to isolation. Within the family there was a high degree of closeness. Her brother was even more timid than the girl. In summary, the family were "good people but not very friendly."

224. F:14:2	ACE IX, 55; XI, 41	'4–1'79	8:2:16
N:I:1	ENG IX, none; XI, 52	— —	— —
	HSR 45	'5–2'	5:2:20
	SVIB none		

Descriptions of this girl were somewhat contradictory. She was characterized as "a very nice girl, an average student, pretty and pleasant." She was also described as "not very bright" and as "using her cuteness to pass academically." All agreed that she was not a leader and was somewhat erratic, but she was well enough liked and active in the school. She was a conformist, unusually willing and with fair judgment, but sometimes she "needed prodding." She had a very deep emotional attachment to a boy who readily returned her affection. They continued this close association into college, where she was said to have developed physical symptoms as a result of the intensity of the relationship. These physical complaints led to her parents' transferring her to another university, where her grades were reported to be C's.

The parents were college graduates and active in community affairs. They had a nice home and were interested in the welfare of their children. There was a good family atmosphere. One older sister had been a behavior problem in high school, but after going away to college she had seemed to outgrow the bad behavior.

225. F:15:1	ACE IX, 92; XI, 87	'4–'2	1:4:16
N:V:1	ENG IX, 93; XI, 89	9'–0'2̲6̲1̲	1:2:15
	HSR 52		
	SVIB none		

This tall, large, and somewhat heavy girl was bothered by her appearance but did not compensate by dressing appropriately. Instead she wore loud colors and unsuitable styles. She liked to be the center of attraction. Active within her own group, she was not, however, a leader. "Her mind seemed to be elsewhere." She would appear to be listening, even enthusiastic, then would suddenly lose interest. She found it hard to concentrate in class or in any other steady activity. She did not put her good intellectual ability to use and she never showed any interest in college. She appeared to be mature but caused trouble in a minor degree, rejecting assignments expected of her by teachers. Her chief associates, girls not in the school, went with older boys. There was one occasion when she may have been involved in a drinking episode. After completing high school she did office work.

226. F:14:2	ACE IX, 74; XI, 52	'4–2'507	3:2:20
N:III:4	ENG IX, 70; XI, 85	'438–0'	1:4:19
	HSR 76		
	SVIB '–		

Described as "a very fine girl," this student dressed attractively and was poised and courteous. She was "loved by everyone in school." She talked well and was able to share her happinesses and troubles with others.

The father was characterized as pleasant and energetic, perhaps too interested in his business. He was also described as domineering in the family, stern, strict, and without respect for his wife. He was a heavy drinker. The mother was an alcoholic who had made many efforts to overcome the habit. Apparently her alcoholism was tied, in some degree, to her husband's behavior. The girl had great faith and pride in her mother's attempt to cure herself. In general the children seemed relatively unaffected by the alcohol problem in the family.

227. M:14:18	ACE IX, 52; XI, 46	'4–5'36	8:3:12
B:IVC:5	ENG IX, 18; XI, 17	'27084–'3	6:6:12
	HSR 19		
	SVIB –5		

This boy "seemed to want to be accepted as a deviate." He was "bizarre" and neurotic, and he had difficulty with his speech when he was nervous. He fought with a brother, injuring him so severely that he was sent to the hospital, yet he was afraid of hurting himself when he worked with machines. On one occasion he sat on the floor and cried uncontrollably when he couldn't have his way at school. The teachers thought he was mentally ill and he was referred to a mental health clinic for study. He continued in school, however. He was found guilty of having liquor in his possession and of operating an automobile recklessly.

The father, a farmer, felt he had no control over the boy. The mother was dead. It was a large family.

228. M:14:0   ACE IX, 44; XI, 68   '4–'59   3:6:21
      N:VII:3   ENG IX, 57; XI, 42   '634–5'0   6:3:21
                       HSR 27
                       SVIB '24–5

This boy "kicked other students and created disturbances with his big, heavy boots." He wore a leather jacket and walked with a swagger. Although he was a lone wolf around school, he went with a rough crowd of boys. He refused to take direction, was easily offended, antagonistic, and contemptuous, always rebelling against authority. In schoolwork he was lazy and lacked motivation. One teacher said that he was "a headache in school, he should join the Army." In his senior year he went with and finally married a girl who was on probation and was considered to have a poor reputation. The marriage was against the wishes of his overprotective mother. The father was more understanding of his son than was the mother. After the marriage the mother would have nothing to do with the couple but the father gave them some help. The mother was described as "neurotic as can be," and it was thought the marriage might work out if she did not interfere.

229. M:15:9   ACE IX, 36; XI, 30   '4–6'8   4:2:14
      N:IVC:5   ENG IX, 33; XI, 17   '43–'6   4:2:17
                       HSR 17
                       SVIB –5

This boy was peppy and enthusiastic about everything except schoolwork. Friendly and a lively conversationalist, he got along well with others, but he often gave trouble in class, where he was "a kind of a pest." He was always in mischief of a playful sort — a "smart aleck who thinks he knows more than he does but who is not disliked for this trait." He simply did not apply himself in school and fooled around most of the time; but he was not a malicious troublemaker or sneaky.

The father was described as shiftless, slovenly, unclean, unshaven, and a weak personality. The mother was also called slovenly, although she was somewhat stronger than her husband. The home was run-down, badly in need of repair, and the yard was a junk heap. The family, however, was a close one. The mother, "warm and devoted," apparently held the children together.

230. M:15:6   ACE IX, 88; XI, 61   '4–819'73   1:3:8
      B:VI:3   ENG IX, 71; XI, 80   –05'6   2:2:18
                       HSR 46
                       SVIB 4'5–

"An asset to any community," this student was the most active boy in his class. A fine leader, he organized activities well and had the respect of fellow students and teachers. He took an active part in athletics, being captain of one of the varsity teams, and he was president of the student body. In schoolwork he was an underachiever during his first two years of high school. However, he showed steady improvement through the twelfth grade. He received an athletic scholarship and went to college.

The family situation was poor. The father had deserted when the children were young and the mother received public assistance for herself and her children. "A fine woman," she did a good job with great difficulty.

231. M:14:3	ACE IX, 59; XI, 77	'4–9'	6:5:19
N:IVC:3	ENG IX, 41; XI, 21	'3–'<u>56</u>	5:1:18
	HSR 65		
	SVIB –5		

Descriptions of this boy varied from "a terrific personality with average ability" to "a very shy country kid, not dependable in school." As seen by the teachers, he was lazy and irregular in his enthusiasm. He was considered to be working below his capacity. Although he lacked industry and was called just "average" by some, he was well liked. He wanted very much to farm after his graduation.

The father was a farmer and a skilled workman. He never took much interest in farming. The mother was greatly handicapped by deafness. She was a faithful person, very serious and hard working.

232. M:15:2	ACE IX, 10; XI, none	'4–9'6	9:1:17
N:III:1	ENG IX, none; XI, none	'79–	5:1:19
	HSR none		
	SVIB none		

One of apparently identical twins, this boy worked hard and was pleasant and well mannered. [His twin's ninth-grade MMPI code was '4<u>708</u>–'6 3:6:10.] He was quiet — almost withdrawn in manner — and not a very competent student. He worked outside of school. Both he and his brother were on active duty with the Army for a short time and then returned to school. He enjoyed his Army experience and later re-enlisted. The twins did not "hang" together either in or out of school.

The father was a skilled tradesman who had a good income. He had a good relationship with his boys.

233. F:14:6	ACE IX, 54; XI, 72	'4–'9<u>63</u>	3:6:15
N:IVC:5	ENG IX, 87; XI, 70	4'35<u>78</u>–	4:2:22
	HSR 73		
	SVIB none		

This girl had been "kind of a problem but straightened out." The nature of the problem was not indicated beyond a statement that she "sometimes goofed off when given a task to do." It appeared, however, that she was usually reliable and conscientious. Her teachers found her mature, popular, careful, and well liked. In appearance she was neat and well dressed. She was active in many school affairs and she worked in the school office, where she was considered efficient and able to go ahead on her own initiative. After graduation she took a secretarial job.

The father was considered somewhat dull but a good worker. "His wife plans and manages, and he works." He was a withdrawn but devoted parent. The mother was aggressive and the chief in the home. She was hard working and ambitious for her family; as a mother she was warm and attentive.

234. F:14:2	ACE IX, 75; XI, 91	'4–'0<u>27</u>	4:2:22
N:V:1	ENG IX, none; XI, 98	'9<u>348</u>–'<u>20</u>	5:0:24
	HSR 95		
	SVIB none		

This "tall, angular girl" was of average attractiveness. She dressed well, was liked by boys and girls, and seemed "perfectly normal in every way." By nature she was cheerful and outgoing and she had a good sense of humor. Interested in sports, reading, and music, she had some difficulty developing good study habits and for a while "felt sorry for herself and thought she was overworked." After a period of adjustment, the situation cleared up. The girl hoped to become a teacher. She went on to college, where she was reported to be doing well.

The parents were "easy to meet, sociable people." The home life seemed good and the economic level was above average.

235. F:15:1	ACE IX, none; XI, 79	'41–'<u>50</u>	5:2:20
N:V:1	ENG IX, none; XI, 49	43'96<u>187</u>–5'0	4:1:13
	HSR 96		
	SVIB none		

Although always well dressed and a good student, this girl had a bad habit of insulting the teachers. She was "snippy and a pusher" and she never finished anything. She was expelled from student activities because she was always absent from meetings and the like. She wanted to be active and a leader, but "this behavior frustrated her." One person described her as "a nervous wreck."

236. M:15:5	ACE IX, 88; XI, 82	4'12<u>8376</u>–'0	5:5:23
N:III:1	ENG IX, none; XI, 68		
	HSR 59		
	SVIB none		

The descriptions of this boy varied. He was elected to high class offices and was very popular, getting along well with all the other students, although he was not specifically a leader. He was considered to have "a lot of guts to stand out and up to teachers." The teachers described him as showing indirect resistance and having a poor attitude. They thought him to be too much of an individualist and to be headstrong and arrogant. He caused numerous disturbances and was guilty of several minor infractions both in and out of school.

237. M:14:8   ACE IX, none; XI, 16   '41298–'6 5:8:14
  B:VII:4   ENG IX, none; XI, none
       HSR trans. 11th gr.
       SVIB none

This boy simply did not like school. He had a negative attitude — he was "anti-everything." Belligerent, headstrong, and often truant, he associated with a "rough crowd." He never applied himself.

238. M:16:6   IQ (centile) 23   4'1328067–'9 7:6:22
  N:VII:3   HSR DO 10th gr.
       SVIB none

The mother of this boy died in his sophomore year. An aunt moved into the home to take care of the children and later became their stepmother. The boy was carefree and irresponsible, a poor student who dropped out of school shortly after his father's remarriage. He had been permitted a great deal of liberty. After leaving school he joined the Navy.

 The father was considered congenial and likable but unable to understand his children. He was generally ineffective. The four boys of the family tended to follow a pattern on the edge of delinquency, all being wild and irresponsible. The home was meager in furnishings and had few homelike comforts. The family was not well regarded in the community.

239. F:14:6   ACE IX, none; XI, 36   '4135–'0 4:3:22
  N:VI:2   ENG IX, none; XI, 47
       HSR DO 11th gr.
       SVIB none

Lazy, "slovenly, sloppy, and with no pride," this girl dropped out of school in the spring of her junior year after many absences. It was said of her that "she had good intentions but the results were poor," and her schoolwork was marked by many failures. She often went to the counselor for help and seemed to expect him

to do her work. She said that she wanted to earn enough money to finance training for a job, but the counselor doubted the sincerity of this goal. He also doubted
the girl's "high morals."

240. F:15:0   IQ (centile) 38   '4136957–0'   6:0:18
      N:V:2   HSR DO 10th gr.
                     SVIB none

This girl was a poor student who was described as unreliable and irresponsible.
She was "sort of scatterbrained." In class she was guilty of at least slight disturbances, and in one case she was with a group that broke a store window.

241. F:14:1   ACE IX, 77; XI, 77   '41389–'02   4:1:22
      N:III:1   ENG IX, none; XI, 64
                  HSR 67
                  SVIB 'WR

The few notes about this girl emphasized that she was well liked and a leader.
She took part in many activities, accepting responsibility and being very helpful.

242. M:16:8   ACE IX, none; XI, none   4'1620 83–5'   9:3:19
      N:VII:3   ENG IX, none; XI, none
                  HSR 17 DO 10th gr.
                  SVIB none

This was a boy with a nasty disposition and temper. He was sullen, seeming to
have a chip on his shoulder much of the time. He did not like school and the
teachers considered him a very poor student with poor ability. In appearance he
was stocky and dark. He left school while in the tenth grade and went into the Navy.
Before entering the service, however, he got into trouble and was charged with
assault and battery. After his return from the service, he began to work in the community and was married. One ninth-grade teacher had predicted he would have
legal problems.
     The father and mother were also both described as sullen and ill-tempered.
The family was "looked down upon" by the community and was often on relief.
None of the children graduated from high school.

243. F:16:6   IQ (centile) 19   41'783059–   7:11:14
      B:VII:4   HSR DO 9th gr.
                  SVIB none

Her teachers described this American Indian girl as "languid, lazy, sullen, uninterested, and constantly truant. She just wanted to live like an Indian." No one knew

her well. The only available intelligence test showed her to have an IQ of 39. This test apparently seriously underestimated her ability, for school records contained papers written by her that showed a fairly adequate command of the English language. Shortly after the ninth-grade testing, she was expelled from school and was later committed to a correctional institution because of truancy and incorrigibility. At the correctional school she made a rather good adjustment and got along well, particularly with other Indian girls. When she was with this group she appeared "happy and playful, tending to become loud and boisterous at times." While at the school she complained frequently of headaches and other minor ills; medical examination, however, revealed no physical bases for these complaints. She felt that her commitment was unjustified and, although she cooperated with the requirements of the school, she never participated in larger group activities. A new intelligence test at this time confirmed the earlier impression of her capability, for she achieved an IQ of 86. After a year the girl was put on parole and later she asked permission to marry. Following an interview with the girl and her prospective husband, the authorities granted permission. The latest information indicated that the couple were making a satisfactory adjustment.

The family was described as "wild." Both the girl and others in her family were known to the judge and sheriff and were described as guilty of misbehavior and of drunkenness. The home living conditions were inadequate and primitive.

244. M:14:3	ACE IX, 95; XI, 94	41′93 86–	6:12:11
N:II:5	ENG IX, 70; XI, 77	′317–′5	6:0:20
	HSR 83		
	SVIB 4′–90		

There were inconsistencies in the account of this boy. He was described, on the one hand, as well adjusted, quiet, and studious, and he was successful in some school activities that made him appear rather popular. By contrast, he was also described as "conceited, cocksure, a show-off, and stubborn." He had a tendency to argue and talk back even with the teachers. Sometimes he could be a mixture of silly and very outspoken. Apparently the more unacceptable behavior was most marked in his early high school years. He frequently fainted throughout his four years of high school. The cause of this fainting was not clear, but at least one counselor felt that it was a way of escape from problems. After graduation the boy went on to a small college where he was said to be well adjusted and studious.

The father was active in business and community and was thought to be more preoccupied with such interests than with his children. "He thought himself the most important man in town and lived beyond his means." He expected a good deal from his children and put pressure on them to produce. The mother was very socially conscious and expected to be treated by the community according to her husband's station. A brother was described in the same terms applied to the boy.

245. F:14:1   ACE IX, 20; XI, 24   423'167805–   13:10:24X
      N:III:1   ENG IX, none; XI, 19   '648–90'7   4:7:17
                      HSR 45
                      SVIB none

When she was in the seventh grade this girl suffered a head injury with a loss of memory for a few hours. In the ninth grade she was obese, quiet, and shy. As she continued in school she changed considerably and her quietness was supplanted by "giggling, flighty, boy-crazy behavior." In this role she was an even worse student than formerly, and she seemed to have no power of concentration. She was fairly popular with other girls because of this somewhat entertaining flightiness. Her moods were constantly changing and she was easily discouraged, seemingly needing encouragement and craving attention.

246. F:15:0   ACE IX, 38; XI, 21   '4235–'6   5:1:19
      N:V:3   ENG IX, 70; XI, 65   '534–'029   6:0:22
                      HSR 60
                      SVIB none

A runner-up in a local beauty contest, this girl had much charm and a fine personality. She was very active in school affairs and was a cheerleader. She worked outside of school and earned the reputation of being an excellent sales clerk.

247. F:14:2   ACE IX, none; XI, 78   4239'768–'5   3:3:15
      N:VI:3   ENG IX, none; XI, 80
                      HSR 63
                      SVIB none

This was an attractive and physically mature girl. In school she was stable and dependable, although she did flush when reciting and was considered shy. She was not a leader and did not volunteer, but she did well enough when she was asked. She had a tendency to "overdress." Her "attitude" sometimes evoked resentment from other girls.

248. M:14:0   ACE IX, 57; XI, 76   '42531–9'   3:2:22
      N:II:1   ENG IX, 70; XI, 66   '84536–2'0   3:4:21
                      HSR 78
                      SVIB 4'8–0

"One of the most popular boys, he had everything." This was a "clean-cut" youth, always well groomed and in good spirits. Very tall, he was an outstanding basketball player and his main interest was athletics. He was dependable and well liked by his fellow students, among whom he was a leader, although never an officious one. During his high school years he gained a number of scholastic and athletic honors. He went steady with a girl who was a couple of years older than he. Although he was "car crazy" and was active in hot-rod clubs, he was not a traffic offender and had no difficulty with the police. He bought his own car and worked on it himself. After graduation he took an engineering course in a university.

Both parents were college graduates and were considered to have made a "wonderful home" for the boy.

249. F:14:1	ACE IX, 44; XI, 76	4'2583 0617–'9	9:5:23
N:IVA:4	ENG IX, none; XI, 50	'532–'90	9:4:20
	HSR 88		
	SVIB WR'		

This girl was a "very ladylike, mature person." She had many friends, was well adjusted, and created no problems in school. She entered into a few activities, and it was said that she was "very steady and drove herself hard." Other descriptive words used about her were "intelligent, dependable, and responsible."

250. M:14:6	ACE IX, 81; XI, 81	4"26'5791 830–	1:5:13
N:VII:1	ENG IX, none; XI, 85	'26–'930	2:2:16
	HSR 83		
	SVIB none		

Generally friendly and well mannered, this boy was well liked by fellow pupils and teachers. His chief interests were in art and music; he was "not the athletic type." Most of his extracurricular activities were concerned with music, and outside of school he worked part time. Although unaggressive, he was a leader. He did get into some minor difficulties in his sophomore year: on one occasion he was caught cheating, and on another occasion he was found guilty of petty larceny outside the school. For the most part, he was a good, average, normal boy. After graduation he started university work with the hope of becoming an illustrator.

251. M:15:1	ACE IX, 57; XI, none	426'7 983–'5	3:7:15
N:VI:2	ENG IX, 71; XI, none		
	HSR none		
	SVIB none		

"His athletic ability covered this boy's whole family with glory" was one comment about this youth. The boy seemed to have little academic ability, however. He was self-conscious about this lack and tended to be withdrawn. Because of his failures in several subjects, he was unable to graduate with his regular class. He had a pleasant enough personality and was accepted by his classmates.

The father was very interested in the athletic achievements of his son and was himself an active spectator at athletic contests. He was considered a devoted father. The mother was quiet and talked rarely except when it was necessary to defend her son. At one time she had a conference with the school authorities when the boy was failing in several subjects and she was said to have accused the teachers of expecting too much of him.

252. M:16:6   ACE IX, none; XI, 34   '42693–'0   10:2:18X
     N:III:3   ENG IX, none; XI, 28   '4317982–'05   9:0:24
                  HSR 63
                  SVIB '4–5

This boy "attended school but was never part of it." He was well liked but not sought out nor was he a leader. One description said that "he was the type of boy who would be a good, substantial citizen and community member." His personality was charming, and when, after graduation, he got a full-time job in a supermarket as a clerk, the customers liked him to help them.

The father was a skilled workman who had made his way up to better jobs. The mother was social and jovial in manner. It was a substantial and good family, in which the parents and children enjoyed each other's companionship.

253. M:14:2   ACE IX, 48; XI, 25   42'7130 96–   7:11:12
     N:VII:2   ENG IX, 55; XI, 35   '8261349–'5   4:9:8
                  HSR 61
                  SVIB '4–5

In the ninth grade this boy was quiet and "a lone wolf." He had "terrific motivation" and tried very hard. He felt sensitive because he could not express himself well and he was not very well liked by other students, especially boys of his own age. He tended to associate with younger children. He got into trouble for possessing obscene pictures and later for shoplifting. In the shoplifting spree he was apprehended while returning some of the merchandise to the store. He was active in his Sunday school and was always considered to be courteous. After graduation he went to a junior college where his hard work and persistence led to a place on the honor roll.

The father was a factory worker, quick-tempered and an excessive drinker. He was very strict with the family and "considered stealing next to murder." The mother was "mousy and shy." One sister was described as "eccentric and high-strung."

254. M:15:2   ACE IX, 42; XI, none   '42783–5'9   4:3:21
     B:V:5   ENG IX, 39; XI, none   74"8'2963–'1   1:11:11
                  HSR DO 12th gr.
                  SVIB '90–5

This boy went to school until the twelfth grade because his mother wanted him to, but he did not like school and engaged in "passive rebellion." He was not, however, a school conduct problem. In town he was observed drinking, but he managed to stay clear of the authorities. Outside of school he seemed more friendly, and he did become somewhat more likable as he continued in school; one of the teachers who worked with him said that there had been some improvement. When he received a certificate instead of a graduation diploma, he was not troubled over the fact. He did good work on a job he took after quitting school.

The boy's father was killed before the time of testing and his mother remarried. The stepfather was resentful of the boy and his brother and was disliked by them. Considered "short-tempered and puny," he was physically ill and unable to work full time. The mother was a "very wonderful person who bore up under all pressures with a level head." She ran the home and the family business and accepted many responsibilities.

255. M:16:2	ACE IX, none; XI, 14	42″879′6351–	6:18:10X
N:V:1	ENG IX, none; XI, 04	<u>87‴431</u> 62′9–	3:11:19
	HSR 08		
	SVIB none		

This boy was cooperative and his conduct was fairly acceptable, although he was not, in general, a good school citizen. He did not associate much with other students. He was absent a number of times and he caused a few minor disturbances. His academic motivation was poor, his work habits were careless, and he seemed to be especially handicapped in arithmetic.

256. F:14:1	ACE IX, 46; XI, 49	4′207<u>8</u>63–	6:6:20
N:V:1	ENG IX, none; XI, 42		
	HSR 64		
	SVIB none		

"A very fine person and a fine school citizen," this girl was pleasing, open, and frank in manner. She had "a delightful smile and was sweet." Very friendly and cooperative, she was willing to be helpful on service projects. She was also described as "a very determined girl."

257. F:14:1	ACE IX, none; XI, 21	'42<u>09</u>–'3	4:9:15
B:III:1	ENG IX, none; XI, 43		
	HSR 37		
	SVIB none		

Teachers resented the fact that this girl got by with things. She was often absent from school and did not apply herself. Although she was friendly, she was also a "lone wolf," a more mature girl than the others in the class. Her standards were not too high. During her high school years she had a part-time job in a café.

258. M:14:4   ACE IX, 44; XI, 47   '43–'1   3:7:13
     B:III:1   ENG IX, none; XI, none
                     HSR 18
                     SVIB none

This boy was physically small for his age. He seemed to put in a great deal of effort when he did anything, and he limited the number of his activities. Quiet, likable, and well adjusted, he was usually not noticed because he was so unobtrusive.

His parents were separated or divorced.

259. M:15:4   ACE IX, 57; XI, none   '43–'9   6:2:21
     N:VII:1   ENG IX, 71; XI, none
                     HSR DO 11th gr.
                     SVIB none

After transferring from one school to another, this boy finally dropped out altogether when he was in the eleventh grade. He had the ability to do good work but accomplished little. He was sensitive and became upset when he made mistakes, but he seemed to gain more poise as he went through school. His attendance record in high school was poor. He received no encouragement from home and lacked personal drive. He was always untidy in school, never clean or satisfactorily dressed. He never got into great difficulty in or out of school, however, and he was always a friendly boy with a good disposition. One teacher predicted he would have emotional problems.

The father was a laborer, often unemployed, who "would call the police to discipline his daughters." The mother was a more steady person and worked to support the family. The older sisters were described as "dumb" and their behavior was not very acceptable. The home was described as a "pigpen."

260. M:14:2   ACE IX, 67; XI, 47   '43159–6'0   3:3:18
     N:V:1   ENG IX, 49; XI, 36
                     HSR 04 DO 12th gr.
                     SVIB 589'0–12

This boy was repeatedly described as having abilities that he didn't use. "He had a lot to give but gave nothing." He could be pleasant and friendly, but he seldom was. His school behavior was very unacceptable: he had a tendency to be disrespectful, he was repeatedly truant, he wanted special attention and when he couldn't get it he rebelled. He was caught cheating, and, though he denied it at first, he later confessed. "He dyed his hair"; he was immature and "had a filthy mind." By his senior year he was getting failing grades and had been suspended several times. Finally he was dropped from school. His expulsion was due in part to his frequent truancy in going to see a girl in a nearby community. He entered the armed services but had spoken of ultimately taking a course in engineering. One teacher predicted future emotional maladjustment.

The father was irregular as a worker, although he provided fairly well for the family needs. He seemed unconcerned that his family was "going downhill." The mother was a complainer. She was concerned about the boy's behavior but was unable to offer any specific suggestions to remedy the situation.

261. M:16:1	ACE IX, 05; XI, 14	4'3186027–	6:13:13
N:IVC:5	ENG IX, 01; XI, 01	84'159036–	6:11:20
	HSR 02		
	SVIB 4'–90		

This boy was dull and unable to achieve very much — "just plodded along." His grades were "gifts" and he received a certificate rather than a diploma. Honest, well meaning, and somewhat drab, he did his best, however.

The father, a farmer, was much like the boy. The mother was quiet and simple, and her housekeeping standards were low. The whole family seemed to be mentally dull, but they seemed to have done as well as could be expected with their potentialities. The reputation of the family was good.

262. M:14:2	ACE IX, 96; XI, 85	4'32165–'09	6:0:22
N:II:1	ENG IX, none; XI, 96	'543269–0'	1:1:17
	HSR 75	'469823–0'	4:0:23
	SVIB none		

There was general agreement that this boy was easily led and ran with the wrong companions. A member of a "car club," he was obsessed with his automobile. One person described him as "a drinker and a party boy." "He felt it necessary to be ornery to be well liked." Balancing these opinions was the agreement that he showed promise and would probably be a worthwhile person when he matured. He never got into much trouble and usually responded to firmness. He seemed eager to learn and he actively engaged in some of the school's activities. He worked outside of school, saving his money to buy a car and to go to college. After graduation he went to a university.

The father was considered compulsive and a "griper." He tried to be a good father and was unhappy about the boy's buying a car, but apparently he did not find it possible to be firm with the boy. The mother, the weaker of the parents, was considered to be eccentric. The parents showed a tendency to blame the school for some of the boy's difficulties.

263. F:15:5   ACE IX, none; XI, 30   4"3<u>21</u> 789–'65   8:1:25
     B:VII:3   ENG IX, none; XI, 53   '374<u>85</u>–'9   5:4:19
               HSR 61
               SVIB WR'

This girl was short and heavy. She had few clothes but she tried to be attractive with what she had. Although quiet and unaggressive, she could stand up for herself when necessary. She was a hard worker and generally a "good girl." She reacted very strongly against her poor home situation and, finally, in her senior year she went to live with relatives, where she was satisfied. She wanted to be a nurse, and her teachers thought that she should go to college. After graduation she began a nurses' training course.

The father had abused his wife and children and had deserted his family when the girl was eight. The mother also neglected the children and eventually a guardian had to be appointed. This guardian, worse than the parents, finally had to be replaced and it was at this time that the girl went to live with relatives.

264. F:15:3   ACE IX, 10; XI, 20   '4320–   6:7:15
     B:III:3   ENG IX, 15; XI, 26   '<u>374</u>–'65   7:4:19
               HSR 30
               SVIB WR'

Described as "a fine girl and a very normal youngster," this student was accepted and considered ambitious, reliable, and working up to her capacity. However, she was not a leader and engaged in no activities. She was said to have been illegitimate, but the putative parents had married, only to be divorced when the girl was about eleven years old. She then went to live with her grandparents, who apparently provided a good home and were solid, responsible people. After high school graduation she began to work as a technical aid.

265. F:14:1   ACE IX, 95; XI, 92   '436–'509   5:1:20
     N:III:5   ENG IX, 93; XI, 93
               HSR 91
               SVIB '–

Although this girl was a fine student — one of the best in her class — and had "all the social graces," she was "a little too bossy and inquisitive." "She liked to lord it over other students" and she was once caught eavesdropping. Although she was accepted by her own group, she was not popular with the entire student body. Very active and talented, she seemed to excel in anything she attempted. Similar remarks were made about her achievement and leadership in church activities. After graduation she enrolled in a small college and "wrote the first perfect English paper ever written in that school."

The family lived in a large and attractive house. At home the parents appeared poised and self-assured. Although very different in their personality characteristics, they gave the impression of compatibility. Both parents were thought of as exceedingly talkative, and if they had a fault, it was that they were self-satisfied, critical, and opinionated. A younger brother was described as obnoxious and a problem in school.

266. M:15:2	ACE IX, 71; XI, 69	'436817–'0	3:3:23
N:III:1	ENG IX, none; XI, 55	'346–2'9	4:2:21
	HSR 54		
	SVIB none		

This clean-cut, nice-appearing boy had a fine personality. An outstanding athlete, a good leader, and mature for his age, he was popular at school and president of his class. Described as courageous and dependable, he was a good student, not because things came easily for him but because he worked hard. His grades, however, were not outstanding because his many activities took too much of his time. He had an especially good relationship with his father. After graduation he continued his studies with the expectation of entering a military school.

The father was a very fine man, always cooperative and helpful with school projects. The mother was considered to be pleasant and sociable.

267. F:14:4	ACE IX, 94; XI, 94	'437–0'2	3:1:19
N:V:2	ENG IX, 95; XI, 80	'437896–0'5	2:3:21
	HSR 51		
	SVIB 'WR		

"Interesting looking and lots of fun," this girl was socially minded to a fault and was particularly anxious to please her teachers. She managed to attract a lot of attention. She seemed childish and flighty at times and "had a temper but was not volatile." The other girls liked her, although her steady boy friend was most important to her. After graduation she went to work.

The father, although a pleasing person, had been involved in some minor difficulties with the law. In spite of these problems he was a moderately good provider. The girl was given everything that she wanted, and the home discipline was considered lax.

268. M:15:4	ACE IX, 36; XI, 17	'4378152–	5:2:18
N:IVA:5	ENG IX, 04; XI, 14	'38–'6	7:2:17
	HSR 28		
	SVIB 4'–0		

In junior high school this boy caused mild disturbances by jostling pupils and other such behavior. He had a speech defect that resulted in his sounding babyish. Actually the baby of his family, he was very attached to his mother. As he continued in school his behavior improved and he became relatively popular, responsible, and active in school affairs. He had a great and mature interest in farming and was particularly active in farm organizations. After graduation he hoped to go to an agricultural school.

The father was self-assured and respected. He was domineering at times and it was thought this trait had an adverse influence on the boy. The mother, although friendly and a good housekeeper, lacked warmth and was not very well accepted in the community. An older brother of the boy had been a very definite school problem and was thought to have influenced the subject during his early high school period.

269. F:15:5	ACE IX, 61; XI, 58	'43869-'05 5:1:21
N:V:3	ENG IX, 66; XI, 69	
	HSR 44 DO 12th gr.	
	SVIB none	

This attractive girl was described as active, very steady, and levelheaded, but quiet. She was in a good many activities and had a number of different interests. In her senior year she dropped out of school to be married. Although this was a forced marriage, reports indicated that it worked out well.

The father was described in primarily good terms, but the mother was considered "aggressive and domineering." She appeared to push the father very hard and wished to live beyond his income level. Although attractive and charming in her many social contacts, she was apparently trying to "keep up with the Joneses." She became chronically ill during her daughter's later years in school. Several of the younger children had been in trouble because of petty thievery and other minor misbehavior.

270. F:16:2	ACE IX, none; XI, none	'439-6'0 9:1:18
N:V:3	ENG IX, none; XI, none	
	HSR DO 9th gr.	
	SVIB none	

Several ninth-grade teachers predicted that this attractive girl would become emotionally maladjusted. She was wild, undisciplined, and a poor student. At the end of the ninth grade she left to attend a vocational school. When she was nineteen she had an illegitimate child and abandoned it with a welfare association, which subsequently brought charges of nonsupport and abandonment against her. Before entering the ninth grade she had been arrested for petty larceny. The latest information about her was that she had married a college graduate.

The father was a steady, hard-working man who took little interest in his children. He was, however, much concerned when a son was expelled from grade school. The mother came from a "nervous and unstable" background. She had been "wild and flighty" in her youth, but became more quiet and respectable after her marriage. The home situation was said to be very lax. In addition to the brother who was expelled, an older sister died in a situation which "could have been an accident or suicide."

271. M:14:1	ACE IX, none; XI, 50	'45167–'2	0:3:14
N:I:1	ENG IX, none; XI, 57	'4579–'6	2:2:17
	HSR 04		
	SVIB none		

This was a tall, gangling boy who appeared ill at ease and was moody and unstable in temperament. In school he had a poor academic record; he was absent a great deal and was a discipline problem. He seemed unable to follow through in things and showed a complete disregard for school regulations. He was a liar. A friend in the class seemed to be influencing him in an undesirable direction. It was suggested that this friend was attracted to him because of the higher status of his family. During his sophomore year he broke with a girl friend and, taking the family automobile, ran away to the West Coast. He returned in a short time on his own and was repentant. In succeeding years he was repeatedly in trouble because of traffic offenses. One teacher predicted legal difficulties for him.

The father was said to "go along for the ride" in critical situations. The mother was the dominant person and she wanted her son to go into the armed services, but she also expected him to continue in school, despite his poor school record.

272. F:15:1	ACE IX, none; XI, 71	'453–'09	5:0:21
N:V:3	ENG IX, none; XI, 74		
	HSR 87		
	SVIB none		

Neatly dressed and well mannered, this girl was fairly popular. Only occasionally a leader, she was more often a follower. Her outstanding characteristic was a need to do things precisely. She disliked making errors and became upset when she did make them. Sometimes she was haughty and other times she was apologetic.

273. M:14:6	ACE IX, none; XI, 67	4'53167289–0'	6:6:21
N:I:1	ENG IX, none; XI, 77	'98 53–0'	5:5:19
	HSR 67		
	SVIB none		

This plump, rather short boy slouched when he walked and was somewhat clumsy. He felt there was a desirable group to which he did not belong, although this was denied by his teacher, who commented that he was well liked. He was pleasant, friendly, well mannered, and "a reflection of his good family background." He was never a school behavior problem, although on one occasion he appeared inappropriately dressed in shorts. He carried a great deal of responsibility in his home, and he was hard working and serious both in school and outside. A little timid, he was always ready to be helpful; "he was democratic, not a snob." After graduation he went to a university.

The father was away from the home a great deal because of his business. He had been an alcoholic, although he later managed to control this problem. The mother was calm and unhurried, pleasant, but not particularly attractive in appearance.

274. M:15:1	ACE IX, 84; XI, none	4'5<u>387</u>–'6	5:4:21
B:I:1	ENG IX, none; XI, none		
	HSR trans. 10th gr.		
	SVIB none		

This boy had a difficult time adjusting to his father's death, which had occurred shortly before the boy entered the ninth grade. As a result he was seen a number of times in a mental hygiene clinic. Even earlier than this he had seemed not to be at ease in making friends within his own age group and showed a preference to be with adults. His school record was satisfactory, in fact well above average. There was said to be competition between him and his twin sister. [The twin's ninth-grade MMPI code was 4'<u>37682</u>–'5 4:3:26.]

The father had been a professional man. The family moved from the community after the boy completed the ninth grade.

275. F:15:3	ACE IX, 30; XI, 17	'457–'2	3:3:20
N:V:2	ENG IX, none; XI, 20	'6–'92<u>10</u>	3:0:16
	HSR 29		
	SVIB 'WR		

Seen as vivacious by some, this attractive girl was also courteous and mature. It was particularly mentioned that she had high moral standards and that she made a very fine adjustment. Others saw her as not outgoing in social relationships and said that she gained popularity by being quiet and steady. Although her mother had encouraged her to get some sort of professional training, she was not capable in schoolwork and after graduation she took a job.

A good worker and an adequate person, the father was retiring but could be drawn out. Of the two, the mother was more outspoken and aggressive. She was considered to be a good mother and housekeeper. The family members kept to themselves, limiting social affairs to family gatherings.

276. F:14:0	ACE IX, none; XI, 99	'4572038–'91	6:3:19
B:III:2	ENG IX, none; XI, 98	— —	— —
	HSR 82	–21'75	3:0:16
	SVIB '–		

This girl's background was somewhat unusual. Her father had been killed during political strife in Europe and she and her mother had emigrated to America. The mother, who had professional training, was considered a responsible person. The girl was neat in appearance, well balanced, and a trustworthy person who was realistic in her outlook and had a good sense of humor. A good worker, she was willing to take responsibility and was well thought of in all ways. After graduation she went on to attend a university.

277. F:16:8	ACE IX, 06; XI, none	4'57819–6'3	6:5:22
N:III:5	ENG IX, 15; XI, none		
	HSR DO 10th gr.		
	SVIB none		

This girl was nice looking, but she wore too much makeup and was loud and giggly. Her teachers called her impenetrable: they couldn't talk to her and she "shrugged off counsel." She seemed to lack confidence and was often erratic and depressed. She couldn't conform to the requirements of the school and dropped out after the ninth grade. She was "boy crazy" and forward with boys. Although she was not known as a delinquent, her marriage was a forced one. Her husband had a very poor reputation in the community. Several of her ninth-grade teachers had predicted emotional and legal problems for her.

Her father, an unstable man, drifted from job to job. He indulged the children and did not control them closely.

278. M:14:3	ACE IX, 48; XI, 37	4'5867931–'2	11:6:21X
N:VI:5	ENG IX, 23; XI, 19	'678–'09	7:1:21
	HSR 34		
	SVIB 89'4–0		

In his freshman year this boy was shy and ill at ease until he got to know people. He was never forceful and did not add much to class discussions, although he was no problem. "He had a somewhat shifty look." He was, in general, hard working and conscientious; as he continued in school, he became more outgoing. His activities were limited by the fact that he worked very hard at home. He did play basketball, and he was a good competitor in that sport. After graduation he became a farmer.

The father, like the son, was uneasy in conversation, said little, and had a "shifty look." However, people who had dealings with him knew him as an honest person. He had an unskilled job and also farmed. The mother was friendly, talkative, and at ease. The house was disorderly and unclean, and the farm was not well kept up.

279. M:15:1	ACE IX, 55; XI, 52	'4580–1'793	3:5:12
N:VI:1	ENG IX, none; XI, 42	'4365–2'	2:4:17
	HSR 45	'349 56–20'7	2:2:18
	SVIB none		

This boy had moderate scarring from a facial repair done when he was a baby, but he did not seem conscious of it. He was well liked, reasonably industrious, and interested in outdoor activities such as Scouting and forestry. In school, though he showed no particular leadership, he was not a discipline problem, and he was a fairly good student. He was active in athletics and band. In his senior year one teacher said that he had become so independent that it was difficult at times to restrain him; he was loud and talkative. After graduation he went on to a university with plans to become a forester. He was reported to be making a B average.

The boy had a good family. The parents were interested in the children and the family was active together in many things.

280. M:14:5	ACE IX, 89; XI, 91	'459–6'20	1:1:14
N:V:2	ENG IX, none; XI, 77	4'''968753–'0	1:5:18
	HSR 67		
	SVIB 8'9–12		

This boy did not cause much trouble until the ninth or tenth grade, when he became a severe behavior problem. He developed "a persecution complex and felt like everyone was gunning for him." He did anything for attention and he always wanted to argue. He was a leader in gang fights and had no respect for law and order. He was cocky, defiant, and smarty. Most of his escapades were outside the school, but he also caused trouble in school and he was often truant. "He was anti-everything." He had a "terrific temper," to the point where he became destructive, malicious, and vicious. In the school he did get letters for sports and he was occasionally a class officer. His teachers said that "he could be very likable and personable if he didn't feel compelled to be so." In his senior year he was several times picked up by the police for creating public disturbances, but, in spite of repeated warnings, he continued to engage in fights and destructive activities. He wanted to go into the Army and later attend college and become a salesman.

The father, a temperamental man, disciplined the children erratically, sometimes harshly and sometimes not at all. He also was hotheaded and frequently in fights. Like the boy, he could be loud and blustering, and he had a "persecution complex." The mother was "more levelheaded" and cooperative, but she would side with her sons when they got into trouble, feeling that they were being picked on. An older brother was "just as ornery" as the boy.

281. F:14:8	ACE IX, 50; XI, 83	'46–'29	3:2:18
N:IVC:3	ENG IX, 71; XI, 95	'3–9'45	3:3:21
	HSR 81		
	SVIB WR'		

Characterized as having very good morals and a high character, this girl could readily adapt herself to almost any situation. She was conscientious, efficient, and dependable. Socially she was rather quiet and retiring, but she had a good many friends. The students liked and respected her, often turning to her for help. As a freshman she had some flippant tendencies, but she improved in this respect in her later school years. She worked hard in school and excelled in one or two subjects. She did any task well. She worked part time while going to school and made a very good impression on her employers.

The family was foreign in origin. They were hard working but their income was low because of much "hard luck." It was a good family, steady, solid, civic-minded, and well liked in the community.

282. M:14:2	ACE IX, 46; XI, none	4'61378 59–	4:1:22
N:I:1	ENG IX, none; XI, none	4'38567 29–0'	1:4:15
	HSR none		
	SVIB none		

Throughout his earlier years up to the junior high school level this boy's conduct and personality were very good and he was well liked. He then began to change, however, and to become an increasing problem to both school and community. He left the public high school to attend a military academy but was so homesick that he was unable to adjust in this new setting and he came home often. He was also guilty of misbehavior. When he was not permitted to continue in the academy, he returned to his original school, where he was popular with a group of "party boys who did a lot of drinking and carousing." A liar and in constant trouble, he was generally considered to be "a rotten, shifty character." He had few dates, drank heavily, and was in trouble with the police on one or two occasions. It was believed that he was putting up a front and that much of his behavior was a reaction against his parents. He was not well liked, and gave the appearance of currying favor with his crowd of boys. Another possible factor in his behavior was his feeling of inferiority to an older brother, who was socially and academically outstanding. One teacher who knew him well felt that in time the boy would turn out all right. After graduation he went on to study at a university.

The father, a leading professional man in the community, blamed the school for his son's problems and was very abusive toward the principal and teachers. The mother was a fine person. Both parents were thought to "mean well," and the two brothers were very well behaved and successful. It was a nice home and the parents were well thought of in the community.

283. M:15:7	ACE IX, 30; XI, 11	46'183725–	8:18:15X
B:IVB:4	ENG IX, 04; XI, 10	'6–5'7	6:5:12
	HSR 33		
	SVIB –5		

In class this boy's behavior was completely uninhibited and unpredictable. He was never tense. He would "mug," wiggle his ears, stamp his feet, and make loud remarks — often in bad taste — "whenever and about whatever he wished." He thought of himself as a clown and "would do anything to provoke a laugh." He was afflicted with nystagmus. "Not too bright," he was a poor reader and a poor student, and yet "he sometimes showed brilliant insight." He was stubborn. Reportedly some of his actions were guided by religious convictions at variance with those predominating in the community, but he was not known to have discussed religious matters at school. Although he was annoying, he was liked by everyone. The teachers' stratagems did not eliminate his disturbing behavior, but he could be dealt with quite easily. He responded to praise but not to scolding, and when he caused a disturbance, his teachers could divert him by requesting assistance with a small task. He showed improvement as he continued through school. By his senior year he demonstrated leadership qualities, was quite responsible, and "though he continued to be a wit, he lost some of his juvenile antics."

The home, everyone agreed, was a good one. The father had died when the boy was a child. The mother and children had done a good job of running the farm and keeping the family together. The father had been at one time a heavy drinker, but he had been a hard-working man with a zest for life and a "wonderful sense of humor." He had been a leader in his church. The family maintained their close church ties after his death. The mother, aggressive, pleasant, and friendly, dominated her household. The children were all said to be "a little irresponsible but witty and fun-loving kids." The family "kidded each other from morning to night."

284. F:15:1	ACE IX, none; XI, 71	'463–95'02	1:21:3X
N:II:2	ENG IX, none; XI, 85		
	HSR 57		
	SVIB none		

This large girl was very cooperative and reliable. She was well liked although her activities were limited. Her general adjustment was considered to be good. Sometimes she seemed aloof, particularly toward certain teachers. She wanted to be an elementary school teacher. On several occasions she was identified as one of a group caught drinking beer.

285. M:14:1	ACE IX, none; XI, 61	'46381–'5	2:5:18
N:VII:1	ENG IX, none; XI, 37	4'786 913–'20	1:1:24
	HSR 49		
	SVIB none		

This boy was extremely careless and "sacrificed accuracy for speed." His teachers considered his schoolwork to be below average. He did not like to take directions and never did more schoolwork than was necessary. He "tended to follow the gang." Likable and pleasant, however, he did not create any discipline problem.

286. M:14:0   ACE IX, none; XI, 97   4'6398–'0   3:2:18
     N:VI:2   ENG IX, none; XI, 58   '496–750'812   2:5:13
              HSR 57
              SVIB none

This boy was very quiet and in no school activities. He was indifferent and "only filled a seat." He was late in making up his school assignments. One of his ninth-grade teachers expected that he would develop emotional maladjustment. He was guilty of a careless driving offense.

287. M:15:2   ACE IX, 07; XI, 03   4'67–'95   6:4:15
     N:III:2   ENG IX, none; XI, 14   '42807–'53   8:5:16
              HSR 15
              SVIB '8–5

This boy was the "show-off type," meticulous in dress, outgoing, and active, but a follower who was frequently in trouble. Friendly and likable, he had a nice smile. He was a poor student — noisy, inattentive, immature, and always doing something wrong. He got satisfaction out of breaking small rules and regulations but he was never a major discipline problem or malicious. He was able to do well in a job he liked. He was popular with his classmates and was elected to a class office. When he was in the seventh grade he got into some trouble for vandalism; in his sophomore year he and some other boys were involved in misconduct with a girl. He also got into repeated trouble because of traffic offenses, with his license finally being restricted. After graduation he joined the armed services, where he made a good adjustment.

The father exercised little control over the boy and seemed relatively unconcerned. A younger boy in the family seemed likely to present the same general pattern of behavior as his brother.

288. F:16:5   IQ (centile) 38   4"678320–   3:8:14
     N:VII:2   HSR DO 10th gr.
              SVIB none

This girl was a poor student and a continuous truant — "really absent." She engaged in no school activities and had only a few friends. Finally, in her sophomore year, she quit school to get married. This was "a matter of necessity." One teacher expected that the girl would develop emotional maladjustment.

289. F:15:1   ACE IX, none; XI, 84   4'6798–5'2   3:5:15
     N:III:3   ENG IX, none; XI, 73   '3416–'09   4:1:21
              HSR 59
              SVIB 'WR

Voted the most talkative in her class, this girl was noisy and gossipy but very agreeable. She would flit from one group to another, gathering and dispersing bits of news. She was somewhat erratic in behavior and "her intentions were often better than her fulfillments." She was not, however, a problem in the school and she was a hard worker and in a number of activities. After graduation she entered teachers' training.

The father, a skilled workman, was well liked and a "nice fellow." The mother, like the girl, was loud, talkative, and outspoken. She tended to "put on airs," but she had a good sense of humor.

290. F:15:3	ACE IX, 84; XI, 58	46'70823–'5	9:4:14
N:III:2	ENG IX, none; XI, 91		
	HSR 90 DO 12th gr.		
	SVIB none		

This girl was "plain." She had good ability and she achieved well in school, but she was occasionally truant. One description called her a "hard leader." Her most active work was in the Future Homemakers of America, in which organization she was a state officer. Late in high school she "fell in love and lost her perspective." The boy was "a wonderful guy"; she dropped out of school in her senior year in order to marry him.

291. F:14:2	ACE IX, 36; XI, 59	'468–2'0	2:2:17
B:V:4	ENG IX, 58; XI, 75	4'87936–'50	0:2:19
	HSR 68		
	SVIB '–		

This mature and pleasant girl had a fine personality. She was the type of person teachers have faith in. She was known as an excellent baby sitter, and, although not a leader, she contributed well in school and she was always reliable and courteous. She was particularly gifted in art. After graduation she continued on to a teachers' college.

The community considered the father and mother to be morally lax. There was much turbulence at home and the girl was considered to have made a fine adjustment in spite of very bad home circumstances. This girl and another had been adopted; the other girl caused considerable trouble and was finally put out of the home when she became illegitimately pregnant.

292. F:15:1	ACE IX, 88; XI, 93	'468375–0'	6:3:24
N:III:1	ENG IX, 84; XI, 85	'9–0'25	1:2:20
	HSR 84		
	SVIB none		

This was a tall, somewhat reserved girl who was likable but not a leader. She was intelligent and cooperative, and she always did extra work. She was somewhat mature for her age and was the "kind of girl you would expect to marry well." A competent musician, she earned a good income professionally while still a student. This work kept her relatively busy and she was not a part of active school groups. After graduation she continued on to university study.

293. F:14:3   ACE IX, 40; XI, 15   46'871209–   5:6:11
    N:III:4   ENG IX, none; XI, 14
    HSR 52 DO 12th gr.
    SVIB none

This girl was bored and passive in her schoolwork and she did not take part in school activities, but she was not a conduct problem. She had some friends, although she was not socially active. In her senior year she quit school to get married. She had been very interested in marriage throughout her later school years. Although there wasn't any official record on her behavior, both the police and the sheriff commented that she was "wild, boy crazy, and possibly sexually indiscreet."

294. M:14:3   ACE IX, 96; XI, 99   4"6'8793215–   3:7:21
    N:V:1   ENG IX, 94; XI, 93   87'45263019–   2:6:20
    HSR 90
    SVIB '2–5

This boy was so quiet and reserved that one could not get to know him well. He was "a deep thinker," and a better than average student who "would try not to displease." He had nice manners and came from a fine home. He was well liked by his classmates who got to know him. He was not a leader; in fact, he was guilty of petty thievery and of curfew violation because he followed others. In his later high school years he became more socially comfortable and aggressive. After graduation he went to a sectarian university.

295. F:14:5   IQ (centile) 33   46'8790 52–   5:12:9
    N:V:2   HSR none
    SVIB none

The school career of this girl was highly irregular. On several occasions she was expelled for truancy, and at other times she quit for short periods on her own volition. Not attractive in appearance but fairly well dressed, she was quiet in school and seemed sober, rarely smiling. Outside of school her reputation was very bad. She drank and went about with an undesirable group. The police questioned her about the possession of strong beer, and she was known to lead "a fast life." There was some suggestion that she was becoming better behaved in her senior year. A majority of her ninth-grade teachers predicted that she would develop emotional problems and become delinquent.

296. F:15:1	ACE IX, 72; XI, 94	46'8702–'1 1:9:8
B:V:6	ENG IX, 84; XI, 75	
	HSR 82	
	SVIB none	

The chief thing emphasized about this girl was that she was conceited and held herself aloof. She liked to do things without consulting others. She considered herself above others — for example, she felt that it was all right for her to be tardy to class. She tended to attach herself to the "big wheels" and to play up to important people. She never seemed to put herself out to help anyone and she liked to have things entirely her own way. This behavior was reportedly characteristic of her actions at home too. Some persons questioned her moral standards. The other students did not accept her very well although she did have a small group of friends. An attractive girl, she was a school cheerleader.

The father died when she was young and for some time she lived with the mother and grandmother. Her mother's remarriage was a shock and the subsequent arrival of a child was reportedly at first especially resented by her.

297. F:14:4	ACE IX, 32; XI, 77	'46897–'213 2:5:17
N:VII:6	ENG IX, 63; XI, 77	
	HSR 74	
	SVIB WR'	

This girl's behavior was better in the ninth grade than it was later in high school. She was "very big with a bovine appearance." A giggly gum chewer, she was immature and loud and a little obnoxious. She was outspoken and gossipy. Possibly she was malicious in this gossip. She was also described as stubborn. It was chiefly her constant talking that made her a problem in the classrooms. She once reported to the police that she had been assaulted, but no action was taken by the authorities because her claim was questionable.

298. F:15:3	ACE IX, none; XI, 69	46'89057–'1 2:15:11
N:VI:3	ENG IX, none; XI, 51	
	HSR 55 DO 12th gr.	
	SVIB none	

This girl was very emotional; she had been observed "screaming and crying on the street." She was quite unattractive and was teased a great deal by other students. There were many instances when she was "in trouble or troubled." The family pattern was one of instability. After completing her junior year she dropped out of school and was married.

299. M:15:4   ACE IX, 81; XI, 93   '4680–2'135   2:2:13
    N:III:3   ENG IX, 73; XI, 73   9'463–02'5   3:4:20
                     HSR 52
                     SVIB none

This boy was a "wise guy," a "needler," a show-off. Obstructive and belligerent, he had a "terrific temper" when he was reprimanded. In all ways he was rather dissipated: he smoked, drank, ran around, and used profane language. He only satisfied his own whims and fancies. Although he liked sports, he would never work hard enough to make more than a minimum contribution to a team. Considered to have tremendous mental ability, he was hostile to teachers and subject matter. The majority of the time he caused disturbances in class. Once in a while he would seem to make an attempt to do better, and in these periods he could be friendly and more likable. In his senior year he got into trouble as one of a gang that broke into a building.

The father was described as erratic. He had "given up" on the boy, who certainly did not get along with him. Two other children were outstanding students, and the boy seemed to have reacted to this.

300. M:15:1   ACE IX, 63; XI, 59   '4697–5'1   1:2:13
    N:III:2   ENG IX, none; XI, 51
                     HSR 33
                     SVIB '8–

This neat, clean-cut boy made a fine impression and was easygoing and friendly. He showed some ambition and considerable drive to succeed. He caused no trouble in school, but before entering junior high he had been guilty of destruction of property, and in his sophomore year he was again in some minor trouble.

The father was somewhat arrogant and demanding of his own way. The mother was pleasant and easygoing. There was a good relationship among the members of the family and they maintained a nice middle-class home.

301. F:15:2   ACE IX, 76; XI, none   '47–'95   5:1:17
    N:VI:3   ENG IX, 71; XI, none
                     HSR DO 11th gr.
                     SVIB none

Uninterested in school and irregular in attendance, this girl finally dropped out in the eleventh grade. She was married shortly thereafter. While a student she associated with a minority group that got into some trouble with the authorities. Because of this behavior she had been put on probation for six months.

302. M:14:5   ACE IX, 54; XI, 67   4'7189 63–   4:5:24
    N:IVB:4   ENG IX, 62; XI, 65   4'87963–'0   1:2:22
                HSR 52
                SVIB '89–2

Small in stature, but good looking, well dressed, well mannered, and immaculate, this boy was "a lot sharper looking than most students." He was a bit sly and untrustworthy. Although he did not actually cause much of a problem in classes, he sometimes created disturbances; he was smart enough to get out in time, however, and was more a nuisance than anything else. He seemed to respect authority and to need control. As he went on in school, he became more likable and mature, and his personality generally improved.

The father, a farmer, was dominant and wary. He could be pleasant but in a brusque way. The mother was pleasant, hospitable, and a good manager. She was dominated by the father. The home was considered a good one, and the community reputation of the family was good.

303. M:15:3   ACE IX, 55; XI, 47   47'28 361–   2:4:19
    N:II:1   ENG IX, none; XI, 64
                HSR 18 DO 12th gr.
                SVIB none

This boy never liked school and he finally left it to enter the service during his senior year. He had been lazy in most of his schoolwork and was unresponsive to the teachers' attempts to make him see the need of applying himself. He was so lazy in fact that he was not respected by the other pupils and was not popular. He was a disturbance in the classroom; when scolded, he did not show resentment but went his indifferent way. He did not show any leadership and was undependable, unreliable, and untrustworthy. He played a musical instrument well, and this was his chief interest. He had a very close relationship with the orchestra teacher and at one time showed considerable emotion because he thought he had got the teacher into trouble. This incident was considered quite unusual for him, since he did not ordinarily let anything bother him. He was said not to be a bad boy but was easily led. He had got into minor trouble when he was younger over malicious damage to public property. After a warning no further action was taken.

The parents were not known to be bad, but they were relatively inactive in community affairs. The family lived in a large, old house with an unkempt yard and a "generally messy appearance." An older brother of the boy was very similar to him; he had married but was soon divorced.

304. F:16:3   ACE IX, none; XI, none   '47398–'5   9:1:20
    N:V:3   ENG IX, none; XI, none
                HSR DO 10th gr.
                SVIB none

A "flighty, giddy girl, her only aim was to leave school and her family and get married." She did quit school in the tenth grade and got married shortly thereafter. The father did not approve of the marriage and went to school authorities for help, but a social worker found the girl "set in her ways" and there was nothing that could be done. The girl and her husband lived on a farm and were considered to be unstable and immature. One ninth-grade teacher thought the girl would have later emotional maladjustment.

The father was an honest and earnest man who was concerned about the welfare of his children. He was particularly upset over this daughter's behavior. He was well thought of in the community and took an active part in numerous affairs. The mother, although an acceptable person, was lazy in disciplining her children.

305. F:14:7	ACE IX, 44; XI, 55	'475–'9	4:1:21
N:VI:3	ENG IX, 53; XI, 52	'79845–	3:2:16
	HSR 46		
	SVIB 'WR		

This girl, quiet in voice and colorless in personality, was said to be handicapped by poor economic conditions in her home. She was willing and dependable and showed some initiative. Her schoolwork was satisfactory.

The family as a whole was also colorless and soft-spoken. They were all hard workers and there was a strong loyalty among the family members. It was said that they were all of low intelligence. The mother sometimes took menial jobs outside the home to supplement the family income.

306. F:14:3	ACE IX, 88; XI, 74	'476–'902	5:2:22
N:VII:3	ENG IX, 92; XI, 94	4'17832–'9	2:1:27
	HSR 96	'481736–'9	1:1:26
	SVIB '–		

Small in stature and "very cute," this girl had a pleasant personality, a high character, and good potentiality for achievement. She was, however, also described as moody and easily bored, a person who frequently exhibited a "holier than thou attitude." She seemed a little spoiled and impulsive. Erratic in her work, she would speak out on the spur of the moment. She was a follower rather than a leader. When she did not want to do a thing, she would give some feeble and indirect excuse rather than an open and direct refusal. After graduation she began to attend a university.

The family was considered "high type" and a good one, interested in the children. The mother particularly tried to do a great deal for this daughter.

307. M:14:1   ACE IX, none; XI, 96   '4763–'509   6:2:22
    N:IVB:3   ENG IX, none; XI, 93
                HSR 96
                SVIB none

Badly disabled by an illness that left him bedridden during most of his sophomore year, this boy was nevertheless happy, well adjusted, and popular. He was an A student and "a delight to teach." In spite of his physical difficulties he was active in the school and he had a girl friend. Attractive, nicely dressed, and well mannered, he wished to become a physicist.

308. M:14:4   ACE IX, 42; XI, 58   4'7813–'56   7:2:25
    B:IVB:3   ENG IX, 35; XI, 15
                HSR 23
                SVIB 48'–5

An orphan since infancy, this boy lived with a foster family. Although he could be a good student, he did no more than was necessary and he cheated to get by. He was shy, mild mannered, and a little flighty. He always looked tired. His teachers found it hard to reach him.

309. F:14:2   ACE IX, 85; XI, 77   '4785–'01   2:2:22
    N:III:1   ENG IX, 91; XI, 66   '68–1'0   3:2:16
                HSR 69
                SVIB none

This was a tall, attractive girl with "a little girl manner of speaking that did not suit her stature." She had a slight speech defect. She was in the "upper social set," but was not snobbish and was a more thoughtful person than were others in her group. She had much vitality and plenty of energy to work in school activities. Eager to know, she had a tendency to question things, but if she found she was wrong, she gave in gracefully. In general, she worked well with others and was exceptionally cooperative and reliable. She was a little excitable, talked fast, and seemed at times to be in a big rush. At some moments she was a bit domineering, but this seemed to be a result of her wish to do things herself instead of getting others to help. "She grew on you and was extremely interesting." She won a small scholarship to a college and went to that school.

310. M:15:1   ACE IX, 59; XI, 37   47'98625–   3:8:11
    N:V:1   ENG IX, 48; XI, 22   6'''4"28'39705– 6:22:9X
                HSR 10
                SVIB none

Throughout high school this student was in a considerable amount of trouble. He drank and liked to have other people know about it; he was disrespectful and untrustworthy, sullen and defensive. He "always looked at a person as if he were laughing at them." He was reprimanded for many misdemeanors and was involved with a gang that destroyed property at the principal's home. He was also in repeated trouble because of careless driving. Despite his mischievous behavior, the other students liked and accepted him fairly well. After graduation he registered at a junior college and on several occasions returned to consult with his high school counselor.

311. M:15:3	ACE IX, 61; XI, 79	4'81357–'60	1:1:20
N:V:1	ENG IX, 69; XI, 46	'459 63–0'	1:3:19
	HSR 22		
	SVIB 8'4–		

"A football player and all boy" and "he could be a perfect gentleman" were two of the statements made about this boy. He was well liked, a natural leader, although "occasionally he led in the wrong direction." Early in his high school years he was loud in class and rather lazy. He was never in severe trouble nor was he malicious, but he was always on the edge of mischief. Teachers differed in their estimates of him, but most seemed to agree that he did not make the best use of his abilities. On one occasion he was involved, with three other boys, in an episode that included drinking and disturbing the peace. He was also fined for speeding. He was interested in commercial courses and hoped to go into business after serving in the Marines.

The mother was very strict with her children, but she did not know how to handle them and commonly asked for help from the school. An older brother had a record of minor delinquency similar to this boy's.

312. M:14:2	ACE IX, none; XI, 37	4'819–5'0	2:7:15
N:V:3	ENG IX, none; XI, 41	'482 37–5'60	4:6:22
	HSR 14		
	SVIB 4'8–0		

This boy and his brother, an identical twin, were given a great deal of attention in school because of their physical attractiveness. [The twin's MMPI codes were, ninth grade, '943–'5062 3:3:16, and, twelfth grade, 49'1378–'02 2:5:19.] Both were "full of the devil, as was their father when a boy," and they constantly fought with each other, even in church. This boy was said to be more mature than his twin. He had once been convicted of speeding. After graduation he was known to be staying at home and not working.

The parents were of south European origin and they had strong family ties. The family was considered to be a very desirable one at the lower middle-class level.

313. F:16:2
N:V:3

ACE IX, none; XI, 33
ENG IX, none; XI, 31
HSR 38 DO 12th gr.
SVIB none

4'8235–   3:4:15

A large brunette with an unhealthy complexion, this girl partly compensated for the defects in her appearance by always dressing well and neatly. She was a poor student and frequently skipped school. On several occasions she brought forged excuses. In her senior year she finally left school because of illness. She had wanted to study piano and spoke vaguely of a career in music. After quitting school she worked as a waitress.

The father was a steady worker described as "thrifty but not very bright." The mother became seriously ill when the girl was in her junior year. Since the mother was bedridden for a long time the girl had to shoulder much of the burden of housekeeping.

314. F:14:3
N:VI:2

ACE IX, 36; XI, 56
ENG IX, none; XI, 68
HSR 83
SVIB WR'

'4835–'0   3:3:21
'10 236478– 5:4:12

This farm girl was shy and inconspicuous to the point of being called timid. Nevertheless, the other students liked her and she was considered to be making a very fine adjustment. She was small and always very neatly dressed.

The family lived on a small farm but the father was primarily occupied as a construction worker. There were many chores for the girl to do at home.

315. F:14:0
N:I:1

ACE IX, 03; XI, 14
ENG IX, none; XI, 67
HSR 14
SVIB none

'485693–'1   4:7:13
'476–1'5   2:3:13

This girl was described as "rural" and the "domestic type." She was unattractive, overweight, and socially introverted. She would have liked to be more popular, but she did not know how to achieve popularity. She had a pleasant personality but was not a "good mixer." One of her teachers said that she was "the type of girl who seemed to yearn for affection and who would probably jump at any chance of marriage with any sympathetic man." A low-ability student, she had to work hard to achieve minimum grades. Scholastic success, however, seemed to be secondary in her interests. After graduation she married.

316. M:14:4   ACE IX, none; XI, 43   '486–5'20   4:3:20
    B:III:1   ENG IX, none; XI, 17
                     HSR 80
                     SVIB none

"A real eight-ball" and "just plain nuts," this boy was belligerent and not well liked
He was often sent to the principal. Careless and easily led, he could do good work
but was undependable. Even before the eighth grade he had a police record for
breaking and entering. Later he was involved in a gang fight.

The father had died and the boy lived with a stepfather; the two did not get
along well. It was "a bad home situation."

317. F:14:3   ACE IX, none; XI, 03   48'671–'295   0:8:23
    N:IVB:3   ENG IX, none; XI, 04
                     HSR 02
                     SVIB none

In the ninth grade this girl was obese and untidy, but in her later high school years
she improved in appearance. The home environment was apparently a slovenly
one and the girl learned cleanliness and social graces as she went to school. She had
considerable initiative, and she was friendly and pleasant. She was also described
as envious and not entirely trustworthy. One person said she could not carry on
an intelligent conversation and several teachers expected that she might develop
emotional or legal difficulties.

318. M:16:4   ACE IX, 17; XI, 06   486'72015–   2:9:22
    N:VI:2   ENG IX, none; XI, 03
                     HSR DO 11th gr.
                     SVIB none

This was a tall, mature-looking boy who was interested in hunting, fishing, and
sports. His scholastic record was poor. He was not an active troublemaker, but he
was uninterested in schoolwork and had no friends. Outside of school he was described as "a lone wolf — very quiet, an unsavory character." At his best he was
a cooperative boy who tried to be careful but who was slow in thinking and possessed no compensatory assets. He had a long delinquency record, beginning before the ninth grade and including repeated theft, drinking, and traffic infractions.
When he drank he became violent and malicious. He was married under the pressure of an illegitimate pregnancy and was almost immediately put in jail because
of theft.

The father was "weak and characterless and mentally dull." He could hold
only poor jobs. He was not positive or firm with the children and gave them a great
deal of freedom. The mother was a poor housekeeper and slovenly in appearance.
The house and family were generally subnormal.

319. M:14:5   ACE IX, 87; XI, 88   4'867935–'02   4:5:22
     B:I:1   ENG IX, none; XI, 81   '439 587–0'   6:4:24
                   HSR 54   '49538–0'2   5:4:23
                   SVIB none

This boy was adopted. He was quiet and he seldom smiled. "Most children would have cracked under the home pressure to achieve put on this boy." He was well liked, willing, and dependable beyond the ordinary. His ability in music was expressed in good performance, both with the orchestra and as a soloist. When his adoptive father died, he seemed to mature rather suddenly and take a great deal of responsibility in the home. Some of his ninth-grade teachers expected he might later have emotional problems.

The adoptive father, a professional man, had been a perfectionist; he expected his children to be perfect as well. The mother had technical training also, but she considered her children first, encouraging them in all worthwhile activities. The home was well organized, almost to the point of regimentation.

320. M:15:7   IQ (centile) 92   4'869731–'5   3:6:22
     N:N:2   HSR DO 11th gr.
                   SVIB none

This boy was "likable and alive," but his school attendance was poor and he felt that he was being held back — "life was not moving fast enough for him." He was erratic and had many "ups and downs." He appeared to be dissatisfied with life, but he did not seem to be angry about his lot. He finally quit school in the middle of his junior year. The home situation was said to be poor.

321. M:15:1   ACE IX, 28; XI, 58   '48602–   4:1:16
     N:IVC:4   ENG IX, 10; XI, 36   0'56–913'   2:3:7
                   HSR 26
                   SVIB 2'1–5

This boy "could have been at the top of his class if he had developed his talents." He was a fine musician but never performed, a good football player but never played, a good artist but never did anything artistic. He was very quiet and reserved; one could not get close to him. There seemed to be a shell about him and he betrayed no evidence of his feelings. In appearance he was big, tough, and good looking. He seemed to be an introvert who felt the world was against him; he never smiled or showed any evidence of pleasure. He was a member of a "gang." In his senior year he developed an interest in girls that tended to make him more sociable. After an altercation with an athletic coach who criticized him, he "let everyone down by quitting the team." He was guilty of careless driving on one occasion.

The father was a "happy-go-lucky farmer" who liked to hunt, loved to play cards, and was never serious. The mother, more intelligent and better able to lead, was an active and dominant person. She accepted the father's weaknesses.

322. F:14:1	ACE IX, none; XI, 64	'487–	2:1:21
N:III:1	ENG IX, none; XI, 38	'54–0'2	3:1:20
	HSR 77	'9–02'	3:1:23
	SVIB none		

This girl had a record of absences from school. She was concerned about her health and seemed nervous and highly emotional. Often she looked depressed. In her senior year she "fell in love and went for a loop."

323. M:15:4	ACE IX, 24; XI, 47	4'87123–'0	6:1:24
N:V:3	ENG IX, 49; XI, 51	'42–	5:2:17
	HSR 25		
	SVIB 4'–		

This boy exhibited little leadership ability and was quiet and reserved. He took part in some school activities and he seemed to be congenial, mature, and easy in manner. At times, he was somewhat moody, however, and he clashed in personality with at least one of the teachers. His stronger abilities were in manual arts.

The father was hard working and conscientious but often unemployed because of the seasonal nature of his work. The mother, also hard working, was mainly interested in her family. She was a capable civic leader and active in many community projects. It was a good, average home situation where the children were well behaved.

324. F:15:5	IQ (centile) 31	4'87316–	6:5:27
B:VII:3	HSR DO 11th gr.		
	SVIB none		

Described as "stubborn and bullheaded," this girl "ran wild when she was in school." She liked to read "love story and true confession" magazines. Before quitting school in the eleventh grade she went to the counselor to say she wanted to leave home. Further investigation revealed that she was trying to escape an incestuous relationship with her father. The mother was dead. After dropping out of school the girl married; two years later she was still considered "immature."

The father was a poor provider and the family lived in a run-down farmhouse.

325. M:14:2	ACE IX, 98; XI, 93	4"8739–'5	3:3:20
N:V:2	ENG IX, none; XI, 88	'94–'250	2:1:17
	HSR 94		
	SVIB '48–		

Very popular with students and teachers, this boy was outstanding in every way. He came from a good family and he had a close relationship with his parents. Not only was his school achievement high, he was an outstanding athlete and a leader in extracurricular activities both in and out of school. With all these qualities, he was also described as quiet, hard working, and confident. He was guilty of a traffic offense in his senior year. After graduation he went to a small sectarian university.

The father held two jobs. He was "a solid citizen, a good and likable mixer." He was interested in his son and he went to all events in which the boy participated. The mother was friendly, outgoing, and intelligent; she was likewise close to the children. She was the dominant person in the home.

326. F:14:3	ACE IX, 88; XI, 88	'4876–'5	3:3:20
N:III:1	ENG IX, 92; XI, 80	— —	— —
	HSR 35	'3861–25'0	2:2:21
	SVIB none		

This girl was popular, friendly, and "a nice person to have in class." She was, however, a "chatterer" and the other students did not have respect for her because they thought she was out for what she could get. She had "plenty of confidence but not much reason for it." She failed some courses but this did not bother her. She liked boys. After graduation she went to a university.

327. F:15:7	ACE IX, 48; XI, 81	4'879–	3:6:18
B:V:1	ENG IX, 72; XI, 62	— —	— —
	HSR 58	'849–5'23	3:1:20
	SVIB none		

This girl "went through inner contortions when she had to recite." She was "conscientious but very shy." She was not rejected by others but she did not really fit in. Never a problem in class, she was friendly, direct, polite, and gracious, always doing the work expected of her. After graduation she went to a university. Her father had died shortly before she entered the ninth grade.

328. M:15:3	ACE IX, 65; XI, 78	48'792–'6	6:3:19
N:VI:2	ENG IX, none; XI, 43		
	HSR 43		
	SVIB none		

Even in his senior year, it was said of this boy that he had "not grown up yet." His behavior was marred by tardiness and he had to be watched because he engaged in "horseplay." He was, however, likable and pleasant, and he was a fair student. One of the teachers expected that he would later develop emotional maladjustment.

329. M:14:0   ACE IX, 70; XI, 84   487'93 15–'0   1:7:15
     N:III:1   ENG IX, none; XI, 95
               HSR 49
               SVIB none

In the early years of high school this boy was belligerent, antagonistic, and arrogant. He had few friends and he engaged in no school activities. His behavior improved as he continued in high school. His teachers said he had "great leadership potential if he would use it." He came from a good family.

330. F:14:5   ACE IX, none; XI, 92   48'706 329–'5   1:9:10
     N:V:1   ENG IX, none; XI, 69   '94–'5   3:7:7
               HSR 71
               SVIB none

This girl was likable and pleasant. She "wrote beautifully," but she was frequently absent from school and seemed to lack ambition. Though definitely not a leader, she was a member of a clique in school. She got into trouble when she was caught with beer in her possession.

331. M:14:1   ACE IX, 82; XI, none   4'89–'5   3:6:20
     N:IVC:4   ENG IX, none; XI, none
               HSR DO 11th gr.
               SVIB none

This boy "had a certain friendliness about him," but he was untrustworthy, sly, and sneaky. He broke school rules, fought with other boys, and was lazy and unmotivated. After being repeatedly truant, he dropped out of school to join the armed services. Both delinquent behavior and emotional problems were predicted for him by ninth-grade teachers. He had a record of repeated delinquent offenses during his high school years: he was guilty of breaking windows, breaking and entering, and slugging the proprietor of a store during an attempted theft.

332. M:14:6   IQ (centile) 67   4"8956 17–0'2   7:7:22
     N:VI:1   HSR trans. 11th gr.
               SVIB none

This boy "liked swimming and boxing" and had "some talent" in these interests. Generally he was described as inadequate, sneaky, dishonest, aggressive, and lacking in self-control. He was a constant truancy problem in school. There were a number of items in his police record: he had been guilty of larceny, drinking, curfew violation, and other similar offenses.

111

333. M:15:2   ACE IX, 32; XI, none   48'96 5073–   1:3:13
    N:VI:2   ENG IX, 31; XI, none
           HSR DO 10th gr.
           SVIB none

This boy's parents tried to get him to stay in school, but he was uninterested and hence a poor student, and he dropped out at the end of his freshman year. He was not mean or malicious, but he was said to be "just too fast for his parents." He was in repeated trouble because of traffic and other minor infractions of the law. After quitting school he got a full-time job and worked until he went into the armed services.

The father was hard working and a good provider. Both parents were congenial persons of average financial means. They were cooperative with the school in attempting to persuade the boy to continue his studies.

334. F:14:2   ACE IX, 52; XI, 58   4'8967–'10   0:7:11
    N:V:1   ENG IX, 88; XI, 92   3784'261–'5   7:10:16
           HSR 34
           SVIB none

This girl was described as having good points and bad points. She was neat in appearance and was "very sweet, ladylike, and quiet." She wrote well, was sensitive and appreciative of literature. She was considered to be trying hard in her schoolwork, but she lacked confidence, often giving up and not preparing her work properly. Another description said she was "quiet, shy, and very artistic." As a freshman she was a conduct problem at times and was characterized as being bossy and having a bad temper. It seemed clear that in her early high school years she was "a spoiled child and immature." Frequent absences from school were sometimes attributed to ill health, but she was more often suspected of "skipping." As she continued through school, she improved in her achievement and cooperation. One ninth-grade teacher foresaw emotional maladjustment for her.

A younger sister was opposite in many ways, being vivacious, active, and a leader, but like her sister in that she was irresponsible in her schoolwork and attendance. The family was "middle class" and placed a high value on money. They were "striving upward."

335. F:15:5   ACE IX, 13; XI, 12   4"896'703–   3:7:16
    N:V:1   ENG IX, none; XI, 34   8"469'075–1'23   3:12:3
           HSR 10
           SVIB none

Ninth-grade teachers described this girl as quiet, apparently happy, and relatively cooperative. Scholastically she worked up to her ability, which was not high. One teacher commented she had so little money that she could not engage in some of the school activities. This statement about her was modified by another teacher who said that she did have money but that she had no sense of value in its use. Although she could be pleasing, her personality was generally not attractive, her manner was swaggering and arrogant, and she "never looked neat." As she continued in school, she became more tidy and made a better appearance but her behavior was less acceptable. She was ultimately suspended from school for a time for truancy; she shoplifted and generally deteriorated in her social contacts. The misbehavior appeared as "sort of an explosion." She had one very close friend, who had similar traits, and the two were always together, whispering to each other in a secretive fashion. Her only special interest was in music. After graduation she went to business college and finally took a job as a secretary.

It was a large, happy family, with the children generally reflecting a nice home atmosphere. The family worked hard but did not have much money, partly because of an illness of the father.

336. M:14:3	ACE IX, 57; XI, 65	'489713–	3:3:18
N:III:2	ENG IX, none; XI, 48	489'63–0'	1:2:15
	HSR 43		
	SVIB 9'8–		

This boy's school behavior was not very bad, but he got into a great deal of trouble outside of school. In school he was friendly and fairly cooperative. His grades varied from the best to the poorest. He was active in music and interested in sports, although his achievement was not outstanding. Outside the school he was a member of a gang and was immature and unstable. People thought of him as sullen, belligerent, and somewhat obnoxious. He had no respect for authority and took advantage of the fact that his father was on the school board. He got into repeated trouble. Among his offenses were damage of property, traffic violations, disorderly conduct, and drinking. After graduation he went to a university, where he attempted to begin professional training. He was not admitted to this program and it seemed likely that he was better suited to a business or sales career.

The father, a prosperous businessman, was good-natured. He felt that he had been overindulgent with his boys. Although he regretted this, he was unable to be severe with them. The mother also admitted that she had no control over her children. The parents were socially outgoing and community leaders. An older brother had also been involved with the police; a sister was reportedly making a good adjustment.

337. M:15:2	ACE IX, 57; XI, 18	4'8976–	4:5:19
N:V:1	ENG IX, none; XI, 18		
	HSR 51		
	SVIB '4–		

This boy would get out of line occasionally, but he could be straightened out with a few words. He was "a little strong-willed" but never obnoxious. He had a good character and was well liked. One teacher said, however, that he was "on the shady side and not to be trusted." Occasionally he put forth some effort to get help. He was active in all athletics. One of his teachers expected that he might develop emotional maladjustment.

The parents on occasion visited the school and were "fine and interested." The boy spoke well of his parents.

338. F:14:0   ACE IX, 70; XI, none   48′9<u>76</u>230–′5   2:9:11
     N:II:1   ENG IX, 74; XI, none
                HSR trans 10th gr.
                SVIB none

In the ninth grade, or a little before, this girl was a troublemaker and, in particular, was defiant at home. She was in general conflict with her parents. She was socially and physically well developed and her boy friends were older. "She had a lot of boy trouble." In her sophomore year she became a nicer girl and more willing to conform; she also got along better at home.

339. M:14:2   ACE IX, 63; XI, 58   4′<u>89763</u>–′0   5:2:25
     N:VI:2   ENG IX, 47; XI, 65
                HSR 52
                SVIB none

A "typical hot-rodder," this boy was immature, lazy, and a follower. He cooperated no more than was absolutely necessary in schoolwork. He would not take responsibility and would "brush aside any obligations." One junior high school teacher expected him to have emotional problems. Ultimately he was badly hurt in a motorcycle accident.

340. F:14:3   ACE IX, 11; XI, 03   489′<u>76025</u>–   3:3:17
     N:V:1   ENG IX, none; XI, 04
                HSR DO 12th gr.
                SVIB none

A teacher described this girl as having "peculiar mannerisms; she was restless, overactive, and dreamy; she felt inferior, and was a nonconformist with an over-developed social urge." She "needed firm management" and was very "boy crazy." She was lazy, and her social interests interfered with her school achievement, which was poor. In her sophomore year she and her family moved to another community. By the time she entered the twelfth grade she had attended three schools, and her record of achievement was the same in each one. She dropped out of school one month before graduation to be married.

There was considerable irregularity in the home background. The father had not been steadily employed. He drank excessively and accumulated many debts. The mother was apparently a better person, but she lacked balanced judgment. The relationship between the parents was not a solid one.

341. M:14:2	IQ (centile) 60	4'89076–'1	2:10:8
B:II:2	HSR DO 10th gr.		
	SVIB none		

An adopted child, this boy was a real problem to his adoptive parents. He "hated every moment of school" and had the ability to "get under the teacher's skin." He did not participate in any school activities. In the tenth grade, after failing, he dropped out of school and ran away from home. He was guilty of several minor destructive acts, careless driving, and racing cars. Ninth-grade teachers anticipated both delinquent behavior and emotional problems for him during his later career.

342. F:15:4	ACE IX, 36; XI, 16	4'806793–'2	5:7:12
N:VI:1	ENG IX, none; XI, 15	'46953–	2:4:8
	HSR 31		
	SVIB none		

Relatively uninterested in school, this girl was absent frequently without satisfactory reason. She was "snippy" at times, especially when corrected, and she was stubborn, wore a sullen expression, and did only as much work as was absolutely necessary. "She was not a leader and was a time waster." Sometimes she seemed to feel that she was dealt with unjustly. It was suspected that she was "wayward" with boys. Her appearance was described as average and she was usually neatly dressed. "Her one good feature was her loyalty to her church choir." Apparently her adjustment improved somewhat during her school years, although she never developed an interest in school and continued her truancy. After graduation she worked as a clerk.

343. F:14:1	ACE IX, 88; XI, 84	'49–'32	1:2:15
N:IVB:4	ENG IX, 99; XI, 98	'3–'025	6:3:20
	HSR 100		
	SVIB 'WR		

Valedictorian of her class, this girl "deserved the honor in every way." She was most attractive and was several times selected as a queen or as a winner in beauty contests. In spite of these many honors she was humble and characterized by poise, charm, and social grace. She was never silly or giddy but always mature and endearing in her comportment. In summary, she was "absolutely a fine, outstanding girl — the type everyone would like for a daughter." After graduation she continued her education at a small college.

The father was a farmer with limited ambition, a very hard worker but not progressive. The mother, pleasant and attractive, seemed more capable than the father. She had self-confidence and poise and met people well. A younger brother also seemed to have many good qualities, and, in general, the home situation was stable and good.

344. M:15:1	ACE IX, 89; XI, none	4'9260–	1:6:4
N:V:2	ENG IX, 79; XI, none		
	HSR DO 11th gr.		
	SVIB none		

"Black jacket, boots, hot-rod, and girls" constituted the main interests of this boy. A defiant person, he disliked anyone who expressed an opinion that differed from his own. He would argue with anyone, student or adult. In school he was resentful and could not take directions. In general, his teachers spoke of his volatile temper and nonconforming attitude. He felt several of the teachers picked on him. He did not like school and finally dropped out. Some of his difficulty was attributed to the fact that he was very ill during preschool years and had been spoiled as a result of the attention he got. He was in repeated difficulty, mostly through traffic infractions, which varied from minor ones to accidents of such severity that his license was suspended. He wanted to be a printer, and hunting and fishing were his hobbies. After leaving school he went to work in a shop where he seemed to mature and became a responsible worker.

The father and mother both worked in a small business, and they were described as good community members. The family was well respected.

345. M:15:5	ACE IX, 20; XI, 55	'493–05'	11:4:21X
N:VI:3	ENG IX 47; XI, 51		
	HSR 12 DO 12th gr.		
	SVIB none		

This boy was "physically and mentally lazy" and thoroughly undependable. "A lone wolf" who seemed to suffer from inferiority feelings, he was not a part of any social group but ran around uncontrollably and was interested only in hunting and fishing. He was temperamental; he "blew up" and quit when faced with even minor difficulties. He was disrespectful to some teachers and occasionally he pulled pranks. He finally quit school in his senior year. In spite of this behavior his minister felt "there was good stuff in him." After leaving school he joined the armed services.

The father was "sickly and lazy." Nevertheless, he was not too sick to hunt and fish. The mother, who took most of the family responsibility, was aggressive and dominant but generally pleasant and agreeable in community contacts.

346. M:14:3 ACE IX, 28; XI, 37 4'93876–0'25 4:7:18
   N:III:1 ENG IX, none; XI, 29
      HSR 05
      SVIB '48–

This student was neat, likable, and, in general, well behaved, although he could be impertinent and often he seemed "self-important." On several occasions he was caught smoking and skipping school and at times he belligerently questioned rules. He seemed to be serious-minded. Easily discouraged when he tried to achieve scholastically, he puzzled over why he did not do better. His vocational aims were out of line with his abilities. He was involved in an episode of vandalism at the school and several of his ninth-grade teachers predicted that he would become delinquent.

347. F:14:6 ACE IX, 67; XI, 90 '495–'21 5:4:13
   N:VI:2 ENG IX, 85; XI, 97 '45 73 869– 4:2:18
      HSR 51
      SVIB WR'

Dependable, reliable, and quiet, this girl was "a fine school citizen" who got along well with her classmates. In spite of this her grade achievement was far below her ability. When she was a junior there was an incident in which she was guilty of "swearing in class." Because of a poor home situation, she moved out in her senior year and lived in an apartment with another girl. After graduation she went to work and was said to be considering marriage.

The father was a problem drinker who had a good job but spent most of his money on drink. He was several times brought into court because of creating a disturbance in the family. The mother finally commenced divorce proceedings. The home was crowded but neat and clean.

348. F:14:3 ACE IX, 94; XI, 93 '496–1'53 5:3:16
   N:III:1 ENG IX, none; XI, 94 9'4768–1' 0:3:13
      HSR 96 9'4687–30'2 1:0:21
      SVIB none

Very well dressed and smart looking, this girl was popular and well liked. "She had everything" and was not a conduct problem. A younger sister had a "mental

117

breakdown," but this girl took the problem in a mature and understanding way. In her senior year there was a period in which she was tearful and her grades went down. She blamed this upon business difficulties that her father was having, but when she was transferred out of a science course, she changed and her grades went back up. She referred to the episode as having a "mental block." After graduation she attended a university and hoped to go into teachers' training.

349. M:14:8	ACE IX, 88; XI, none	4′96–1′0	3:3:11
N:V:2	ENG IX, 82; XI, none		
	HSR DO 10th gr.		
	SVIB none		

This boy had a physical irregularity that resulted in a speech defect and a cosmetic problem. He was subject to violent temper tantrums that sometimes became uncontrollable; he used obscene language, destroyed things, and sometimes even "passed out." After such episodes he was repentant. His behavior was so bad that he was considered to be in need of psychiatric help. His school attendance was irregular, and he was finally expelled from school in his sophomore year. Although he brought his schoolwork up to date and tried to re-enter at a later time, at the last minute he "chose to go hunting instead." His only friends were much younger than he, and one teacher said that his only real friends were his dog and his gun.

The father, a college graduate, was a skilled workman. The mother, like the boy, had a severe speech defect. The parents were very uncooperative with the school and community regarding the problems caused by the boy. There was some indication of resentment between the boy and his mother.

350. M:14:1	ACE IX, 70; XI, 77	′496–2′15	4:2:15
N:III:4	ENG IX, 58; XI, 56	′6498–′0	2:2:14
	HSR 33		
	SVIB –5		

This boy was well mannered, courteous, and fairly well liked. He was a follower, not a leader, and seemed to have little motivation toward his schoolwork or any extracurricular activity. His greatest interest was his car. It was thought that he was spoiled by his mother, and at one point he had charged a large amount of merchandise for his car to his mother's account. When he was finally forced to work this out he did a good job. In summary, he did not seem to be so much a bad boy as an immature one who would probably do all right later, although it was said that his schoolwork was better in his early high school years. He was guilty of minor traffic offenses. After graduation he went into the armed services.

The father was stern in manner but was likable and jovial in practice. The mother was considered to be too easy on the children. Although it was not financially necessary, she worked outside the home. She did not, however, neglect her housekeeping.

351. F:16:2   ACE IX, 11; XI, 06   4'96<u>325</u>–   3:2:14
     N:V:1   ENG IX, 31; XI, 23
                  HSR 25
                  SVIB none

This girl realized she did not have much ability and felt inferior because of it. She was courteous, friendly, and well poised. If she disliked a thing, she would keep it to herself; she was not one to "blurt out her feelings." One teacher expected that she might get into trouble with law. She hoped to go to business school after her graduation.

352. F:14:2   ACE IX, 88; XI, 84   49'6378–'5   4:7:12
     N:IVA:4   ENG IX, 79; XI, 79   68"<u>473</u>'9<u>02</u>–'5   2:11:10
                  HSR 82
                  SVIB 'WR

This petite and vivacious girl was resented by some of the other students because she was "an apple polisher with charm." She was unusually gracious, poised, and mature, and she did many things well. She had, according to another informant, "a very sweet quality that endeared her to students and teachers." Early in high school she had aspirations to be a social worker or a teacher, and after graduation she attended a small college where she probably did take teachers' training.

The family was a good one, proud, alert to new methods, and interested in making progress with a good farm. The children were all well mannered and well behaved.

353. M:14:1   ACE IX, 98; XI, 84   4'9<u>638</u>–02'   3:1:18
     N:I:1   ENG IX, none; XI, 78
                  HSR 59
                  SVIB '9–

This boy was described as "narcissistic" and impressed with his own appearance. He was popular with fellow students and was active in chorus. In contrast to his popularity among students, the faculty found him not very cooperative, definitely "talky," too self-conscious, confident, and very childish. When he was dismissed on one occasion from a group activity, he "pouted" and bragged that the teacher would ask him back. This did not happen and he eventually returned to the activity on his own initiative. "He was quick to accept honor but not the responsibility that went with it." He got into some difficulty because of traffic offenses, and two of his teachers expected that he might develop emotional maladjustment.

354. M:15:3	ACE IX, none; XI, 52	4″9′67283–′15	4:12:10
N:III:3	ENG IX, none; XI, 17	′02–5′13	5:5:12
	HSR 54		
	SVIB 4′8–0		

This small, stocky boy was an ambitious youngster and "a regular hustler." He worked part time while going to school and full time in the summers. His actions were mature and his achievement was better than the average. Many people considered him to have "a lot of common sense." Several ninth-grade teachers, however, expected that he would have emotional or legal problems. After graduation he married a classmate and went into the armed services. The couple was considered very congenial.

355. F:14:3	ACE IX, 59; XI, 64	4′9678–′1	1:5:11
B:III:1	ENG IX, 83; XI, 72	4″9′67832–5′0	0:1:20
	HSR 57	4′63–′5170	1:1:15
	SVIB none		

The most important factor in this girl's adjustment was her reaction to the bad home situation. Her parents had separated sometime before she entered the ninth grade. Her allegiance was to her father and there was some evidence that her mother abused her. She was just an average student, but she was neat in appearance, friendly, and respectful most of the time. She had "a lot of strength" and was relatively popular. She was, however, "basically an unhappy child" and there were many times when she appeared depressed. Her home problems caused her to miss school frequently. She took considerable responsibility as the oldest child in caring for a younger sister. The disputes of the parents that led to a divorce when the girl was a junior appeared to make her feel guilty. After graduation she went to a university.

The father was successful in a competitive business. He felt that the mother was unstable and should not have custody of the children after the divorce. He appeared to have warm feelings for his children. Apparently he had tried hard to hold the family together. The mother was emotional and domineering. She was a problem to the police because she called them frequently to make a suicide threat or for some other reason. All the children appeared to react unfavorably to the situation.

356. M:14:1	IQ (centile) 26	4″96′8 270–′1	3:12:10
N:V:2	HSR DO 11th gr.		
	SVIB none		

Interest in "hot-rods" and racing far exceeded this boy's interest in school. Besides general indifference and low motivation, he was characterized by apparently poor ability. He was guilty of excessive talking and other disturbances in class. After dropping out of school he enrolled in a vocational course and then joined the Navy. One teacher predicted that he would get into trouble with the law.

357. F:15:4 ACE IX, 08; XI, none 4'96857–'2   5:2:9
    B:VII:2 ENG IX, none; XI, none
             HSR DO 10th gr.
             SVIB none

This girl was popular, attractive, and never a conduct problem. She did need "prodding" to get her schoolwork done and she was sensitive when criticized. At times she could be "a bit pouty." She dropped out of school in her sophomore year. Two of her ninth-grade teachers expected that she would have emotional or legal problems later.

358. M:14:7 ACE IX, 05; XI, 20   '49728–'3   8:6:15
    N:IVC:2 ENG IX, none; XI, 02 '43906–   7:5:15
             HSR 11
             SVIB 4'–

With little aggressiveness or initiative, this boy "did not have enough ambition to get into trouble." He was "a nonentity who would not respond to anything." He did not mix well with the other students, although he was easygoing and had a fairly good attitude. In his quiet way he was polite, neat, cooperative, and reliable. He was very anxious to join the armed services and did so immediately after graduation.

359. F:15:2 ACE IX, 42; XI, 32   '4978–'0   1:2:21
    N:IVC:5 ENG IX, 79; XI, 61   4'9875–'0   3:4:23
             HSR 59
             SVIB none

"The girl of 1,000 excuses" was the expression used by teachers to characterize this student. Large and quite obese, she tended to shy away from group activities. She had an answer for everything and could always give many reasons for not participating in school activities. She did well in her schoolwork. In her senior year she seemed more confident, poised, and sure of herself. She "hung around with a tough group at times." After finishing high school she took a job in a factory.

The father was considered opinionated and hard to get along with, but he was relatively successful and active in community affairs. The mother was less well known. She did not have much control over the children. The parents often kept the children away from school to do chores.

360. M:15:6 ACE IX, none; XI, 96   4'9785 63–'20   2:6:10
    N:VI:3   ENG IX, none; XI, 80   84'753 69–'02   2:2:12
             HSR 69
             SVIB 4'1–

Although bright, this boy was never a good student. He often created disturbances by being noisy in the halls, and the teachers considered him undependable. Artistic and original, he made no attempt to develop these qualities. He was fairly popular with his own group, which tended to be a little wild. He took a moderately active part in school affairs.

The father was a likable man, slow but dependable and respected. The mother was energetic and quick. The other children were bright and did well in school. All the children worked part time while attending school, and the entire family was described as "nice and hard working."

361. F:14:4	ACE IX, 88; XI, 93	'498–'5	8:4:22
N:IVA:4	ENG IX, 79; XI, 89	'6–'9	5:2:20
	HSR 97		
	SVIB WR'		

This girl had a fine personality; she was dependable and worthwhile in every way. She was in many activities, both in the school and in her church. After graduation she seemed to have difficulty starting out on her own. She delayed college to work for a while and then began to study to be a practical nurse, although her capabilities far exceeded the requirements of this training.

The father was a "genuine and wholesome person," and the mother, too, was described as a fine person. They were both painfully shy. It was a stable home; the family, although somewhat reticent, aloof, and "different," was well enough accepted in the community.

362. M:14:0	ACE IX, 48; XI, 14	'498–'623	4:6:16
N:V:5	ENG IX, 12; XI, 05		
	HSR 01		
	SVIB none		

In his early high school years this boy was a severe problem. He defied and despised authority. He occasionally drank to excess and he could not, or would not, study. He accumulated a record of traffic offenses. This generally unacceptable behavior ended rather abruptly when he had a severe automobile accident. Following this accident he became more reserved and seemed to develop social poise. He "changed from a problem to an angel." He took an interest in sports and was particularly good in mechanical work. After graduation he worked as a mechanic and hoped to go to a technical school.

The father was a heavy drinker, but drunk or sober he always seemed pleasant in his manner. The mother appeared emotionally unstable, dull, and uninteresting. She seemed to have "a persecution complex." The boy was thought to be resentful of his father's alcoholism, and he had no apparent love for either parent.

363. M:15:1   ACE IX, 34; XI, 15   '49813–5'02 6:2:25
  N:III:3   ENG IX, 31; XI, 20   '423–9'6 8:2:22
         HSR 21
         SVIB 4'–0

In the ninth grade this boy presented an adjustment problem. He was big, blustery, noisy, and suffering from an inferiority complex. He went with a tough bunch of boys and he had an antagonistic attitude. As he continued in school he remained relatively uninterested and was "very lazy." He became, however, more dependable and cooperative so that some persons described him as having a nice personality. Outside of school he was a fairly good and hard worker. There was a record of a traffic offense; otherwise he did not get into any great trouble. He drank some.

  The father was an older version of the boy. The mother was a strong person who controlled the children and the father.

364. M:14:0   ACE IX, 79; XI, 62   4"98172635– 4:5:19
  N:I:5   ENG IX, 78; XI, 71   94'8327– 2:5:14
         HSR 80
         SVIB '4–

The evaluation of this boy seemed to change somewhat from class to class. He was a good student who "at times did above average work." He was described by some as very mature and as "a wholesome, all-American boy." Some teachers thought of him as cooperative, but others disagreed and characterized him as "not very dependable." He also was said to lack "staying power." He was independent, and although he could be "good when he wanted to be," he could not be pushed once he had made up his mind. His school attendance was good and he was not a discipline problem. His most successful activities were in athletics, where he was on the football team. Some persons said that even in this area he "had a tendency to take the easy way out." He was popular but not a leader. He did not begin to date girls until shortly before his graduation. During his high school years he worked part time with his father. After graduation he went into the armed services and began to study electronics.

  The father was generous with his son, but strict in regulating his deportment and insisting on his conformity to religious principles. The father was "always on the go and did everything at a run." He stuck close to his home and his job and did not mix with others. The mother had a very strong personality and "ran the show in the family."

365. F:15:3   ACE IX, 88; XI, none   49'835167– 4:5:21
  N:V:2   ENG IX, 98; XI, none
         HSR trans. 10th gr.
         SVIB none

The most recurrent items about this girl related to animosity toward her parents and her rebellion against them, which spread, in part, to the school setting. Both she and her sisters were characterized by this rebellion. The girl went around with an older married man and kept late hours, apparently just to make the parents angry. She was popular with boys but had no close girl friends. A hard girl to talk to, she paid no attention to anyone. In the presence of teachers she was quiet and withdrawn. Uninterested in school, she was not in any activities and her scholastic achievement was far below her capabilities. According to her own statement, she would rather be popular with fellow students than work for grades. She was intelligent and a very good musician; she hoped to be a music teacher. Although she never got into any severe difficulties, authorities considered sending her to a correctional institution, but they felt that she would not benefit by this. The parents finally transferred her to a more strict parochial school, where she was reported to be making a good adjustment.

The father was considered to be dictatorial and the cause of rebellion in the daughters. He checked up on them constantly, and every time they went out he required that they report back to him. The mother always agreed with the father and took his side in the discipline of the children. Both parents seemed very determined; they had set ideas about discipline and high goals for their children. It was generally felt that the difficulty with the children was attributable to the parents.

366. M:14:2	ACE IX, 59; XI, 53	'4985<u>137</u>–'6	3:4:14
B:VII:3	ENG IX, 63; XI, 59	'80<u>2934</u>–'5	1:3:11
	HSR 41		
	SVIB none		

This boy had rheumatic fever when he was a child. Before he entered the ninth grade, his parents were divorced. He accepted his stepfather fairly well. In school he was very reticent, never saying much, but he was well liked and reliable. The minister described him as "one of the finest boys — he did fine work with boys." He apparently had no interest in girls. He got into a little trouble, which was not specified.

The father was an "oddity." He was frequently in jail for one or another reason. The father blamed the mother for all his troubles. Although there were conflicting opinions, the majority of informants felt that the mother was a dependable and conscientious person.

367. M:15:1	ACE IX, 98; XI, 99	49'8523–'1	5:3:13
N:II:1	ENG IX, 97; XI, 85	49"5876–'1	5:6:13
	HSR 38	5'94–'02	5:5:19
	SVIB 0'15–		

A great deal of ability coupled with poor motivation characterized this student. Any showing of interest or enthusiasm came in flashes. He was a healthy, well-groomed boy with much poise, and he was popular with his classmates. He took an active part in athletics, public speaking, and dramatics but neglected his studies. As he continued in school he became more conscientious and started to grow up, his grades going from low to very satisfactory in some subjects. After graduation he enrolled at a university. As a college freshman he took part in athletics for a while but then dropped this activity.

The parents did not seem to demand much of their children. The family was a closely knit group and there was a very close relationship between father and son. Although financially it was not necessary, the mother worked outside the home.

368. F:15:2	ACE IX, 17; XI, none	4‴9″8′576–	6:9:20
N:III:1	ENG IX, 30; XI, none		
	HSR DO 11th gr.		
	SVIB none		

In grade school this girl was accused of stealing, cheating, and blaming others when she was caught. She was a very poor student. She worried her parents and others because she spent so much time "chasing boys," with whom she stayed out all night. The parents were concerned about her behavior and they asked the police to investigate when they could not discipline her.

369. M:15:6	IQ (centile) 08	4′986–2′05	3:11:16
N:VII:2	HSR DO 10th gr.		
	SVIB none		

Guilty of a long line of minor offenses and some more severe ones, this boy had a record that began early of larceny, traffic violations, assault, intoxication, and other items. He had no interest in his studies or respect for authority and he was frequently absent from school. He was a disturbance in classes and in the halls, starting fights with other boys. He dropped out of school at the beginning of the tenth grade. A majority of his teachers thought that he would have future legal and emotional problems.

370. F:15:7	IQ (centile) 69	4‴98″6′507231–	3:26:8X
N:VI:3	HSR DO 10th gr.		
	SVIB none		

By the ninth grade this girl had a bad reputation. She kept bad company, was out every night, and was guilty of repeated offenses which included drinking and shoplifting. She seldom attended school and finally dropped out during the tenth grade. Soon after this she was placed on probation by the juvenile court. Her probation supervisor said that she distrusted adults and was slow to respond to offers of help.

It took her six months to express any feelings about herself or her future. "She smoldered and then wanted to strike out and break the rules." She had, however, shown some responsibility and ability to plan on a job she held during this period. Emotional difficulties had been predicted for this girl by one of her ninth-grade teachers.

The home was a poor one with uninterested but nagging parents. According to some reports, the girl had few opportunities for normal development.

371. F:14:3	ACE IX, none; XI, 14	'49860–1'27	0:9:10
N:III:1	ENG IX, none; XI, 74	9'54–21'0	2:6:9
	HSR 46		
	SVIB '–		

This was a popular, nice girl who took part in some activities and, among other things, tried out for cheerleading. She was only an average worker, and in certain school relationships she was rude and arrogant. There were some eccentric traits in her school behavior. Police said that she "ran with the wrong company and was out all night, but she was a nice girl."

372. M:16:3	ACE IX, none; XI, 79	4'987–'25	4:6:14
N:V:1	ENG IX, none; XI, 74		
	HSR 80		
	SVIB none		

This boy was described as mature, conscientious, industrious, and well mannered. He was quiet and unobtrusive in the school. During his sophomore year he was caught and charged with larceny but was released after a warning.

373. F:15:5	ACE IX, none; XI, 13	4'987621–	4:5:18
N:IVB:3	ENG IX, none; XI, 02		
	HSR 06		
	SVIB none		

This girl got married while she was in school and apparently wanted to quit, but her husband insisted that she continue. Although she tried hard, she was very slow and a poor achiever. In manner she was quiet, and she had a "negative personality." She was not well liked, but this did not bother her after her marriage. Two of her ninth-grade teachers expected that she would develop emotional maladjustment later.

374. M:14:8   IQ (centile) 78   4′987623–5′01   2:7:15
    N:VI:1   HSR DO 11th gr.
                  SVIB none

This boy traveled with a tough group. He was belligerent and defiant of authority in and out of school — a real conduct problem. In the middle of his junior year he dropped out of school to join the Navy. By that time he had accumulated a record of traffic violations and had been involved in one episode of pilfering.

375. M:16:2   IQ (centile) 60   4″9′8706–   1:11:6
    B:III:1   HSR DO 11th gr.
                  SVIB none

A little lazy and uninterested in school, this boy quit after his sophomore year. When in school, he was "saucy and snappy." This behavior got him into occasional trouble with the teachers. Several teachers expected that he would later develop emotional or legal difficulty.

376. F:15:5   ACE IX, none; XI, 52   49′87065–13′2   0:12:3
    N:VII:3   ENG IX, none; XI, 80
                  HSR 54 DO 12th gr.
                  SVIB none

A very attractive, tall brunette of Indian descent, this girl seemed to have possibilities as a student, but her interests were only in marriage. She was described as "a fine girl" but she started "chasing around" when she was a junior, and she left school to be married when a senior. Several teachers had predicted that she would be in legal or emotional difficulties.

The father was a laborer who was neither very dependable nor a good provider. The mother had to hold a job; she worked nights and consequently could not supervise the girl, even though she was interested in her children. All the children were above average students.

377. M:14:4   ACE IX, 27; XI, 33   ′490–6′5   8:6:16
    N:III:1   ENG IX, none; XI, 65   ′94–615′208   5:4:14
                  HSR 26
                  SVIB none

This student was happy and relatively pleasant, getting along well if no work was involved. His teachers characterized him as independent, at times belligerent; they thought he had the attitude that the world owed him a living. He did not recognize authority and always strove to establish himself as an equal. He had a

127

kind of negative attitude, lacking initiative to go ahead on his own, even in extra-curricular activities. He occasionally smoked and violated other school regulations. He was often absent from school. Outside of school he was interested in sports and automobiles. He went into the Marines after graduation.

The parents seemed to show little concern about their children's schooling.

378. F:14:7	ACE IX, 24; XI, 07	'49<u>087</u>–	3:3:14
N:VI:4	ENG IX, 23; XI, 36	'95–'<u>17</u>	5:2:15
	HSR 50		
	SVIB WR'		

One of twins, this girl was more attractive, outgoing, and intelligent than her twin sister. [The twin's MMPI codes were, ninth grade, '<u>40</u> <u>58</u>–1'<u>236</u> 3:5:10, and, twelfth grade, '<u>389</u>–'10 3:1:16.] They were apparently compatible, but they had no close relationship. At school this girl demonstrated a good deal of initiative and determination in all her activities; consequently she had a record of achievement that was higher than her abilities. She was particularly interested in physical education. After completing high school she took further training at a trade school.

The home was described as cluttered and lacking in modern conveniences. The father, thought to be not very bright, was a meek-appearing but hard-working man who yielded the family leadership to his wife. The mother was an easygoing, talkative person with considerable religious zeal. Though bright enough, she apparently was not a very good manager. Both parents were very interested in their children's welfare. There was a disabled child in the home who was well accepted by all members of the family. An older brother of the twins, although not a gifted student, had achieved well in college. In summary, it may be said that while the home suffered from poverty and disorder in material ways, the family had a good reputation and the parents had an acceptable relationship with the children.

379. M:15:1	ACE IX, 85; XI, 65	'401–'8	4:5:11
N:VI:1	ENG IX, none; XI, 77	20'<u>785</u>–	2:4:7
	HSR 70	'07<u>468</u>–'9	2:4:10
	SVIB none		

Appearing more physically mature than the average, this boy was quiet and rather introverted. Generally he was well liked; he had a nice personality, although he could be sullen at times. He was not a leader. In summers he worked at a resort, where he was described as willing, well balanced, and capable of doing his own work. In school he was no problem; he was a good student and worked hard to maintain high grades. He liked sports and was moderately active in them. After graduation he majored in engineering at a university. His first-quarter grades were only average.

380. M:15:1   IQ (centile) 48   '402–56'9   6:3:19
     B:III:1   HSR trans. 10th gr.
                   SVIB none

A "complete nonconformist" who had traveled widely with his parents, this boy transferred to another school at the end of his freshman year. His work in school had been unsatisfactory in nearly every respect. His behavior was equally unsatisfactory and he was called incorrigible and a habitual truant. He also ran away and was in trouble with the law a number of times. On one occasion he was charged with "malicious mischief involving girls." He was in jail for a short time because of violation of probation. He worked outside of school at odd jobs. A psychiatrist to whom he was taken during the worst of his school behavior attributed much of his trouble to the twenty-six times that the mother had moved, taking him with her. A majority of his teachers predicted both legal and emotional maladjustment.

The mother had divorced the father when the boy was ten years old. Another marriage lasted for a short period, and she remarried for a third time. The mother was very nervous; but she appeared to have matured considerably after the second divorce.

381. F:14:1   ACE IX, 22; XI, 72   4″02'678–'15   5:8:10
     N:V:1   ENG IX, none; XI, 50   '406879–   2:5:12
                   HSR 57
                   SVIB none

From the ninth grade on this girl wanted to be a policewoman. She was a neat, somewhat timid girl who was never a disciplinary problem; she was a follower. For the most part, she was well adjusted, cooperative, well mannered, and friendly. Poor in her academic work, she did well in sports, music, and dancing. When her best friend quit school to get married, she also wanted to quit and had to be persuaded to return after several weeks of absence. After graduation she took a job for a short time and then made application to the armed services.

382. F:14:4   ACE IX, 99; XI, 98   '406–'5   3:2:21
     N:IVB:4   ENG IX, 100; XI, 88   '0–9'2   3:3:19
                   HSR 85
                   SVIB WR'

This girl was described as large and quite pretty, although not attractive. Her teachers wondered if she might be bothered by her size. She did not dress as well as some of the other students and one teacher felt that her attire may have made her self-conscious. Although studious and sincere, she was so shy and reserved that it was difficult for her to recite. Her teachers found her difficult to know or describe because of her reserve and inarticulateness. It was believed that her shyness may have begun with a childhood disease. Some saw this shyness as curtness, to the point of unfriendliness. There was conflicting evidence about her mood. She

129

was said to show anger easily but was also described as calm and quiet. She did work up to her capacity in the school setting and never asked for help. She was deeply religious and expected to go into church work after her graduation. She carried out this ambition by going to a religious school, and it was reported that she was growing less shy as she began to find herself.

The reputation of the family was very good, and the parents were considered to be unusually fine people who were very active in their church. The father came from a family in which there was a considerable history of mental illness, but he himself was dependable and a good worker, with both mechanical and musical talents. The mother, who limited her social activities to her church, was friendly, hard working, and generally a competent person.

383. M:15:3	ACE IX, none; XI, 32	'4062378–'9	4:3:17
N:V:3	ENG IX, none; XI, 19	'24–'5	3:3:15
	HSR 25		
	SVIB none		

A very poor student, this boy did not like school and his relationships in the school were very poor. He cheated, and if caught, he would beg for mercy and promise never to do it again, but he was repeatedly caught. In his first three years of high school he was frequently tardy or truant. He "always had something to say and was always interrupting with irrelevant questions." Most adults did not like him. He was mainly interested in cars and spent most of his time with them. After graduation he continued to work around automobiles, showing little interest in further education.

The father, a small businessman, was high-strung and jittery. He had spent at least one short period in a mental institution. The mother was also said to have had a nervous breakdown, but she was never hospitalized. Two brothers were reckless drivers. All the boys were described as "dark, dashing, and good looking." The family income was above average so that the children had many things of a material nature but received little love or supervision from the parents.

384. M:15:1	ACE IX, 82; XI, 72	'4068–'31	1:9:10
N:VI:5	ENG IX, 75; XI, 62	'6954–173'	2:9:5
	HSR 41		
	SVIB 4'1–		

This boy was a "bad actor." Exceedingly sensitive, he could not take criticism. He was sneaky and had temper outbursts that were vicious and irrational. At one time he wrecked his car because it would not start. He seemed to try to be more mature than he was in fact; when people tried to help him, he behaved as though he was being persecuted, blaming his difficulties on his teachers and family. He was "a thorough hell raiser." A few teachers were able to get along with him, and a sympathetic person could sometimes talk with him and get him to cooperate. He did better in social studies and art than in other subjects. There were repeated offenses on his record, including wrecking of cars and various thefts. He wanted to join the Navy, and it was thought that this experience might have a maturing influence upon him.

The father was alcoholic, shifty, shy, and a lone wolf. He was very ugly and violent when he was drunk and treated the boy badly. He was a capable worker but frequently lost jobs because of his drinking. The mother was a good person but was mild and ineffectual. A younger brother, also in high school, seemed well adjusted.

385. F:14:3   ACE IX, 57; XI, 44   '407–39'81   6:2:15
    N:IVB:2   ENG IX, none; XI, 78   7'2068 43–'59   7:0:15
             HSR 80
             SVIB WR'

Quiet, unaggressive, and not a leader, this student had many friends and was well liked by the teachers. She was well dressed and neat. In her schoolwork she was judged to have average ability and to be working at her proper level. She was "an efficient, good, steady girl" who worked willingly and who was cooperative and mature. She was also well balanced and pleasant and expected to become an office worker after she graduated. One year after graduation she was married.

The family situation was satisfactory. The house was well kept. Although she was a little "uppish," the mother was pleasant and relaxed, and she "kept a close eye on the children." The father was described in similar but somewhat more positive terms.

386. M:15:5   ACE IX, 98; XI, 99   4'072658 31–'9   3:6:10
    N:V:1   ENG IX, 91; XI, 94   '4568 2790–   1:5:18
           HSR 55
           SVIB 124'–

This boy had good ability, but he did not work up to it and was considered lazy. He was repeatedly described as shy and self-conscious. He recognized this shyness and tried to overcome it, and was said by some to be self-confident and occasionally stubborn. Other students had to urge him to get him to participate in activities. Shortly after his graduation he was involved in a serious automobile accident, to which his own careless driving may have contributed. He started college but soon dropped out to attend a trade school.

The father was ill at ease in social situations, apparently somewhat like the boy. The mother was easy socially and seemed to be interested in the children, but she was "tired and frustrated." She could not get involved in community activities because of the father's resistance to any kind of social relationships. The other children in the family seemed intelligent and were not behavior problems.

387. F:14:2   ACE IX, none; XI, 52   4'076–   4:4:16
     N:VII:3   ENG IX, none; XI, 84   '4391 78–   3:1:20
                 HSR 84
                 SVIB WR'

This "chubby" girl liked to talk and was always enthusiastic about any activity in which she was engaged; she was described as jolly, with a "bouncing personality." Within the school her activities were numerous, and both teachers and peers enjoyed her and found her "fun to be with." The teachers particularly described her as hard working, a good student, and a very acceptable girl. Her outstanding social traits may have contributed to her school achievement so that it appeared better than would have been predicted from her measured intelligence. Upon graduation she attended a small teachers' college. Although her family could afford to support her in college, the girl had to work in order to pay her expenses.

The family was well respected and hard working. Her father had a chronic illness but managed to continue daily labor. The mother ran a small business partnership with another woman. The parents did not push the children very hard and were indifferent about whether they went to college or not, evoking a statement which claimed the children were "self-made."

388. F:14:1   ACE IX, 28; XI, 44   '40875–'6   3:4:13
     N:IVB:2   ENG IX, none; XI, 43
                 HSR 33
                 SVIB none

This obese girl was conscientious and she tried very hard in school but was a low achiever. Withdrawn and quiet, she had few friends and was never a conduct problem. It was said that she was pushed by a domineering mother.

389. M:15:2   ACE IX, 84; XI, 87   '5–   7:2:18
     N:V:1   ENG IX, 81; XI, 64   '2453–'6   5:7:19
                 HSR 82   '238–'4   9:3:21
                 SVIB 0'1–

During his first two years of high school, this boy was shy and withdrawn. He caused no trouble, but he didn't offer anything. He found mathematics to be very difficult, although he was good in physics. His junior and senior years were a period during which he "really blossomed out to realize his own abilities." He was described as a good thinker, a boy with a "deep mind." He enrolled in a university after graduation.

The father, an extroverted person, was "very antagonizing." The family had a religious background. The parents encouraged their children.

390. M:14:3	ACE IX, 98; XI, 96	'5–<u>12</u>'43 <u>90</u>	2:1:11
N:III:2	ENG IX, none; XI, 93	'<u>354</u> <u>69</u>–'<u>270</u>	5:0:16
	HSR 84		
	SVIB 8'59–2		

A "mature, popular, very polished, gentlemanly, and sophisticated" student, this boy was active and successful in many school activities. His participation in these activities was enthusiastic, and he exhibited "nervous energy" to the point that he sometimes appeared "a little brash." Although a leader, he never quite achieved the highest positions of leadership among his peers because of a reserve "just on the edge of stuffiness." He accepted responsibility well and was a willing and fairly hard worker, although sometimes he started things that he did not finish. During his high school career he won scholarships and other awards; he earned a letter in football; and he held a part-time job. He dated but did not have a steady girl friend. He was once reprimanded by the police for racing another car — "the kind of thing you would not expect of this boy." He entered college to study for a professional career.

The family was one of close relationships and worked as a unit. The father was said to be solid, moderately gregarious, and personable. He participated in community affairs, as did his wife, who was "sweet, quiet, friendly, and somewhat more aggressive than her husband. She never seemed tense or nervous and handled the children very well."

391. M:15:0	ACE IX, 70; XI, 40	'5–<u>18</u> 69'72	2:4:6
N:VI:3	ENG IX, 65; XI, 72		
	HSR 48		
	SVIB none		

Reports about this boy were somewhat conflicting. He was described as "big, ornery, and needing handling with kid gloves" by one person while another saw him as a good leader who was well liked. He could be "bold and saucy," but again appeared as "always a gentleman" and a "great kid." He expressed his intention to continue into college after high school graduation.

The father was an invalid with an incurable and progressive illness. The mother had to work, and she cared for her husband and the boy in her spare time.

392. F:15:3   ACE IX, 61; XI, 59   5"–2'37 19   6:3:13
     N:V:4   ENG IX, 33; XI, 36   59'8–'1   6:4:18
                     HSR 36
                     SVIB '–

The girl was "wholesome, sincere, attractive, and modest." She stayed in the background but was interested and active. Her main skills were in physical education and group recreational work. After graduation she went to a commercial college.

The father was a competent skilled workman with a pleasant disposition. The mother, also pleasant and acceptable, took no leadership in her home or in the community. The home was a good one in spite of the mother's lack of initiative and a low income.

393. F:14:2   ACE IX, 90; XI, 79   '5–24'13768   4:1:16
     N:IVB:5   ENG IX, 82; XI, 75   '57–1'32   1:1:16
                     HSR 21
                     SVIB WR'

In the ninth grade this girl was heavy and unattractive. Her personality was unpleasant; she was not well accepted socially and she was giggly. Boys seemed more important to her than school and she started to hang around town with a poor crowd. By the twelfth grade a number of changes had taken place. She had established relationships with a better group of students, had lost weight, and had improved her appearance. Throughout high school, however, she never worked up to her capacity. After graduation she began nurses' training.

The mother was quiet and retiring. She had several relatives who were mentally retarded. In the case of the mother, however, it was lack of personality rather than mental dullness which more adequately described her. The father was quiet, responsible, and respected in the community. One of the girl's brothers was considered to be dull, immature, and friendless.

394. F:15:1   ACE IX, 24; XI, 11   '5–246'1   4:1:9
     N:III:4   ENG IX, 29; XI, 46   9"08367–24'   4:1:13
                     HSR 24
                     SVIB '–

This girl was thought to be "achieving far beyond her ability." Although she was attractive and charming, she was so unobtrusive that people were not much aware of her. She had a fine sense of humor and of values. Her friends were few but loyal and acceptable. She was helpful at home unless it kept her away from her boy friend. She was a good seamstress and cook and was considered to have fine potential as a homemaker. She attended a business college but withdrew when she was married.

The father was a businessman, quiet and reserved but likable. The mother, although physically not very attractive, had a "wonderful personality" — she "bubbled over." She was deeply appreciative of what was done for her family. The family presented a united front, always together and always happy.

395. F:14:1	ACE IX, 74; XI, 82	5'–273 10'468	0:1:14
N:III:3	ENG IX, 78; XI, 85	9"874–6'20	3:1:11
	HSR 79		
	SVIB WR'		

This girl, who was in many extracurricular activities, was an "aggressive-leader sort" of person. She was gracious and reliable. Ordinarily she had a nice personality, but she was somewhat erratic. A bit egotistical, she governed her actions apparently according to what she thought of each particular teacher. Very careful of her companions, "she was never seen hanging around town in any unsavory place."

The home was a fine one. The family did many things together and they were close-knit.

396. F:14:2	ACE IX, 54; XI, 64	'5–'39	3:1:13
N:V:2	ENG IX, none; XI, 61	'3–'20	7:4:20
	HSR 90		
	SVIB WR'		

This girl, who had high moral standards, was active in her church and serious about wanting to become a missionary. Well liked, she was "a very fine girl in too many activities." As indicated by these descriptive statements, she was vivacious and peppy and belonged to numerous clubs, although she was considered a follower. Her manner was gentle and she was "sweet-natured." In schoolwork she was very good; her grades were high despite her numerous activities. In her later school years she began to date steadily a boy from a good family who was a little older than she. He was not well liked. He was considered "smart-alecky and amorous," resentful of authority; he "had a chip on his shoulder." In her senior year this association resulted in a pregnancy and the couple were married. Later reports indicated that they were reasonably well matched, although there were some difficulties.

The father, a small businessman, was aggressive, personable, and a smooth talker; he drank more than he should. He was often away from the home. When he was home the parents frequently quarreled. The mother was gregarious, likable, and attractive. She effectively disciplined the children in the absence of the father. The daughter was particularly close to her mother and it was a blow to her mother when the pregnancy occurred.

397. M:14:4   ACE IX, none; XI, 96   '5–'6   9:3:19
     N:III:3   ENG IX, none; XI, 83   '843127–'9   11:5:24X
                     HSR 73
                     SVIB none

This "mousy" boy wore thick glasses and "talked out of the corner of his mouth in a confidential manner." He was tolerated by the other students but he was not well liked. He was not athletic and had a "touch of femininity." He took responsibility well. His expressed goal was to become a music teacher. Outside of school he helped in his father's business and seemed to be a good boy. In the latter part of his senior year in high school he appeared in juvenile court because of careless driving; the case was dismissed.

398. F:15:2   ACE IX, none; XI, 25   '5–613'942   3:3:10
     N:V:2   ENG IX, none; XI, 78   '831645–'9   6:7:22
                     HSR 24
                     SVIB WR'

When compared with her classmates, this girl seemed to be quite mature. She was always neat and well groomed, but, although pleasant and sociable, she was "in a class by herself" and was never quite one of the school group. Apparently her isolation came in part from the fact that she spent most of her time either with a boy to whom she was engaged or in a job that she held after school hours. Her marriage was put off until the couple were of legal age. The boy was described as "a fine fellow." The girl continued to work after her marriage. During high school she was excused from athletics because of rheumatic pains.

The father owned a small business; both he and his wife were active in the operation of this enterprise. Their income was average and neither parent was very active in community affairs.

399. F:15:4   ACE IX, 98; XI, 93   '5–'6793   7:4:15
     B:IVB:2   ENG IX, none; XI, 89   '4860–'25   10:2:20X
                     HSR 97
                     SVIB WR'

"Pretty but not at all vain," this girl was "a motherly, family type who continued the excellent tradition of her mother after her death." She was "kind of farmerish" and a little uncomfortable in social situations, but she was nevertheless exceedingly active, hard working, and respected. She was in every way a leader and she won several scholarships and prizes. After graduation she continued her education at a teachers' college.

The father was interested in and proud of his children. A "driver" in his work, he got along well with other people and "had a big heart for his family." He was a firm disciplinarian, usually fair but sometimes rough about it. The mother died when the girl was in the ninth grade and the girl took over much of the responsibility for the family.

400. F:14:0	ACE IX, none; XI, 77	'5–'87	7:4:15
N:VII:3	ENG IX, none; XI, 96	'45689–2'0	4:1:23
	HSR 87		
	SVIB none		

This was "a pretty blue-eyed blonde who was carefully protected by her mother." "She liked to have her own way and had a fiery temper." Her schoolwork was good and she was especially active in music. During her first two years of high school she was popular and a leader in school activities. In her junior year she became pregnant, dropped out of school, and married. By home tutoring she was able to keep up with her class. She returned to school in her senior year and attempted to take up her former place of leadership, but her classmates tended to ignore her. With graduation she was also divorced. It was felt by many that she was the aggressor in her marriage. After graduation she went to work to support herself and her child and reportedly she was going with an older man. It was said that she had matured in the year following graduation.

The father, a "silent man," had had a long illness and the daughter had had to take over many home responsibilities. The mother, foreign born, was "volatile, quick, and emotional." She had been very upset over the girl's pregnancy and had insisted, along with the father, that the girl get married. It was a comfortable home, but the family was not well known in the community.

401. M:14:1	ACE IX, 53; XI, 76	'5–'9	4:0:17
N:III:1	ENG IX, none; XI, 78	'53–'9	2:1:16
	HSR 76	'523 49–6'	3:1:17
	SVIB none		

Mature and well liked by everyone, this boy was "a very fine chap." He was polite, friendly, dependable, good looking and well dressed, and "somewhat of a leader." He liked mathematics and hoped to go into some field that would emphasize this subject. He played in several sports and was a member of the band. He always accepted responsibility with an unassuming manner. Outside of school he worked at several jobs. He continued to a university, where he was reported to be maintaining a C average in a pre-law course.

The father's business was considered by the community to be somewhat shady and unethical. The father was strict with the boy, requiring that he keep up to his assignments.

402. F:14:4	IQ (centile) 55	'51–'47	9:2:18
N:III:3	HSR none	'0438–'9	4:1:20
	SVIB none		

The description of this girl said that she always appeared to be "very sad." A poor student, she seemed unable to get much from school. She did have a few friends, and she was a quiet member in certain activities.

403. F:14:5   ACE IX, 10; XI, 46   '51–'9   0:7:9
      N:VI:2   ENG IX, none; XI, 12
                   HSR 33
                   SVIB none

This girl attempted to overachieve, apparently under pressure from home. She was very popular and was in many activities. "Giggly, flighty, and a little scatter-brained," she seemed to lack self-confidence. She was often the center of minor disturbances.

404. F:14:1   ACE IX, none; XI, 79   '5194–'0   2:5:18
      N:III:1   ENG IX, none; XI, 74   '584–2'09   2:5:17
                   HSR 81
                   SVIB none

In both personality and appearance this girl was friendly and attractive. At school she appeared normal and stable, and she was well mannered and cooperative. Her primary school activities were music, girls' athletics, and the chess club.

405. F:15:4   ACE IX, none; XI, 29   '5108436–'7   4:7:10
      N:IVC:4   ENG IX, none; XI, 25
                   HSR 18
                   SVIB 'WR

This quiet and reserved farm girl was always polite, but she never took part in anything or made herself noticeable.

406. F:15:6   ACE IX, 17; XI, 46   '52–'379   9:7:17
      N:III:4   ENG IX, none; XI, 47   '283465–   9:9:22
                   HSR 57
                   SVIB '–

This girl was briefly described as pleasant, likable, and very quiet. She was no conduct problem and was an average student in school. A ninth-grade teacher thought that she might later develop emotional problems.

407. M:14:1   ACE IX, 59; XI, 71   '52–4'3781   3:2:10
      N:II:1   ENG IX, none; XI, 58   '437185–'9   3:1:21
                   HSR 99   '58234 71–'9   2:5:20
                   SVIB none

Equally well liked by pupils and teachers, this boy had many assets. He was an athletic star, and he was very much interested in outdoor activities. In academic work, he was not outstandingly capable, but he had great persistence that compensated for what he lacked in ability. He was termed "the finest boy in the whole class" by one teacher. "Girls would have been happy to go with him, but he was very busy and serious with his schoolwork and activities." His most noticeable fault was that he used poor grammar. Some school subjects caused him unusual difficulty. After graduation he went to college.

His was a very good home. The parents were both good, wholesome people, "much interested in the boy."

408. F:15:6	ACE IX, none; XI, 16	5′2347–′9	5:1:19
N:VI:3	ENG IX, none; XI, 20	′43<u>25</u>8–′0	7:2:18
	HSR 48		
	SVIB ′WR		

Coming from a large family with a poor standard of living, this girl was not able to dress as well as many of the other students and did not have money for extras. She was a quiet girl who got along fairly well in school but tended to be seclusive and not very friendly. After graduation she married and lived in the community.

The family had a low economic status. One of the siblings caused the family a great deal of trouble.

409. M:15:2	ACE IX, none; XI, 87	5″2′46<u>173</u>–9′	7:3:19
N:III:3	ENG IX, none; XI, 81	′6<u>54</u>–′0	4:0:19
	HSR 97	′50<u>46</u> <u>27</u>–	3:0:18
	SVIB ′5–		

A very effeminate youth who was thought of as a great overachiever through conscientiousness and application, this boy was at the "top of the class." He was in a few activities and had a few friends. He was well behaved and straightforward and did not present any conduct problem.

410. F:14:6	ACE IX, 30; XI, none	5′2<u>48</u>970–6′3	8:3:21
N:VI:3	ENG IX, 78; XI, none		
	HSR DO 10th gr.		
	SVIB none		

This American Indian girl dropped out of school in her sophomore year to be married. While she was in school she was a good worker; she studied hard and was cooperative, but she was very shy and needed encouragement.

The family was characterized by a long history of intermittent public assistance. The father had been hospitalized for alcoholism.

411. F:14:1 N:IVC:2

ACE IX, none; XI, 98
ENG IX, none; XI, 92
HSR 72
SVIB none

'526–'7   3:4:10

This was "a small girl with big hopes, dreams, and ideals." She was perhaps a little too self-consciously righteous at times. Her constant determination to do the right and sensible thing made her a little critical and she had the tendency to pick people apart. Generally, however, she was well liked and a good student with considerable common sense. Her teachers described her as "more interested in giving than in receiving." Outside the school she was tolerant, honest, and able to assume much responsibility. Her general attitude toward life was considered to be unusually mature. After graduation she hoped to go into nurses' training.

The family was strongly knit. The father had a chronic illness that limited his earning capacity to such an extent that both his wife and his children were compelled to work at jobs outside the home.

412. M:14:1 N:III:2

ACE IX, 65; XI, 71
ENG IX, none; XI, 85
HSR 64
SVIB –2

5"2'847130–   9:0:20

A teacher described this boy as "easygoing, a follower," and one who "needs to develop a more independent attitude." He wanted to have friends and tried hard to become part of the school's elite student clique. He was, however, merely accepted by this group to the extent that they could boss him around.

413. F:15:5 N:VI:4

ACE IX, 10; XI, none
ENG IX, none; XI, none
HSR DO 9th gr.
SVIB none

'520–'639   8:6:12

This girl was "sort of sweet and appealing," but she was shy and unassuming. She had "no will power," and she was easily led. There was no encouragement from her home to stay in school and she dropped out in the ninth grade. She took no part in school activities, and some of the teachers thought she would later develop emotional maladjustment. After dropping out of school she got married.

414. M:15:1 N:VI:1

ACE IX, 70; XI, 59
ENG IX, none; XI, 42
HSR 66
SVIB '–

'5203–4'86   9:3:14

This boy was absent quite a bit in his freshman year owing to a tumor that required hospitalization for a while. The operation left no permanent disability and he was able to participate in athletics during the rest of his high school years. He had "a strong natural interest in learning without being a bookworm." He was a little reserved and not inclined to speak up, but very serious in manner and purpose. He was unassuming, cooperative, dependable, and mature. He "set standards to live by and was not afraid to express them." Not a member of a gang, he got along well with all. His interests tended toward social service, and after graduation he went on to college.

The parents and an older sister always wanted the best for this boy. The sister, who was considerably older, had married and moved away. The boy was born when the parents were comparatively old.

415. F:14:1	ACE IX, 48; XI, 32	'5208746–'9	6:7:19
B:II:1	ENG IX, 68; XI, 81		
	HSR 33		
	SVIB none		

Very feminine and attractive, this girl was "a little mouthy." Apparently outside of talking all the time, her contributions in school were reasonably unobtrusive and without distinction. She was consistent in her grades and a little above average in application to her studies. She and her brother had been adopted by relatives.

416. M:14:0	ACE IX, none; XI, 24	52'0876–	7:9:10
B:III:1	ENG IX, none; XI, 11	'053–9'2	1:7:11
	HSR 03		
	SVIB '1–		

This boy had a pleasant disposition and was well liked. He "worked hard at being liked." He was guilty of some disturbances in class, mainly to attract attention. He went in for fads such as unusual haircuts. Schoolwork was hard for him but he tried and wanted to cooperate.

417. M:14:1	ACE IX, 97; XI, 92	'53–6'1	6:3:17
N:V:2	ENG IX, none; XI, 85	78'459 36–	3:4:19
	HSR 75		
	SVIB none		

"A boy's boy who was not much with girls," this was a "good, wholesome boy who might have been a little spoiled." He was cooperative and a hard worker, and he liked to be identified with the crowd. He considered himself better than the rest, however, and was occasionally a show-off with fancy clothes. Mature and serious-minded, he was somewhat of a leader, but not aggressively so. He was active in school sports. After graduation he went to college and hoped to become a teacher and possibly an athletic coach.

The father was active in the community. He was a hard worker but not a leader. The mother was hard working, good-looking, neat, and well dressed.

418. M:14:7	ACE IX, none; XI, 85	'53–6'7	5:6:8
B:V:3	ENG IX, none; XI, 51	9'734–20'	4:2:17
	HSR 26		
	SVIB none		

The most outstanding item about this boy was that he was always "very busy." He was enterprising and resourceful in the discovery of new activities when disappointed with any of his current ones. He was a good leader and "a fine boy." Some persons believed that his industrious activity was a compensation for a poor home situation. In spite of his busyness his academic achievement was inferior.

The boy's stepfather, who was foreign born, had resisted becoming completely Americanized. He had children by a former marriage and although the two sets of children lived together, they had almost nothing to do with one another.

419. M:14:2	ACE IX, 90; XI, 96	'53–9'	4:0:17
N:III:1	ENG IX, 95; XI, 89	'5–'4918	4:1:15
	HSR 86	'4368751–0'9	4:2:25
	SVIB '5–		

This student was "in everything and yet he was quiet about it." Shy and retiring, he was a very good student and he achieved top scholarship honors. He worked very hard at his schoolwork and always had the right attitude. He was popular among his fellow students and "a good boy." It was frequently mentioned that he was conscientious, reliable, and dependable. He made a good contribution in athletic and musical activities. It was said of him that "considering his parents, he was very well adjusted." After graduation he continued on to a university professional course and he subsequently received a large scholarship in recognition of his achievement and ability.

The father was described as stubborn and the mother was considered to be exceedingly unstable. At times the mother appeared to be wholly disoriented. She was always accusing others of doing her children an injustice or of expecting more of them than they could give. "She seemed as though she was always mad at somebody." She was more interested in her son's musical activities, while the father was more interested in the boy's athletic accomplishments.

420. F:14:6   ACE IX, none; XI, 41   '53–'90   4:5:18
     N:II:3   ENG IX, none; XI, 74
                     HSR 54
                     SVIB none

This attractive, popular girl was the freshman homecoming queen, a cheerleader, and a participant in many other class activities. At the end of her junior year she transferred to another school because the family moved, but she refused to make friends in her new school, and she was so unhappy about the change that she returned to her original high school to graduate with the rest of her class. After graduation she expected to go to college.

The father, a college graduate, was very interested in the progress of his sons, whose school careers he followed so closely that he sometimes annoyed school personnel. The boys were taught to work at an early age. The mother was described as an intelligent person who made a good home for her children. Her large family kept her close to her home. The family was well accepted and liked in the community.

421. F:15:2   ACE IX, none; XI, 34   '53<u>18</u>–'0   2:5:18
     N:VI:1   ENG IX, none; XI, 40   3'4<u>52</u>–9'   4:2:14
                     HSR 21
                     SVIB none

This girl was a below average student, but she was not a behavior problem. Occasionally she was slow and needed to be urged to work. She had a poor attendance record. This was said to be due to illness, but it was thought that, although some absences were justified, she frequently used illness as an excuse to avoid the demands of school. Her absences kept her from much school activity. However, it did not seem likely that she would have been active in any case, since she was more a follower than a leader. She was described as "a dreamer, unable to concentrate on her work." Her manner was friendly, her appearance neat. She readily responded to positive adult guidance with constant supervision. In church she took part in a few activities. After graduation she took a secretarial course and, subsequently, a full-time position.

The home was neat and adequately furnished. The family was respected even though its financial state was precarious because the father's income was not large and his employment was subject to seasonal variations. On several occasions illness and accidents forced the family to seek financial assistance from community agencies.

422. F:15:4   ACE IX, 94; XI, 82   5'3187–   3:2:14
     N:VII:1   ENG IX, none; XI, 70
                     HSR 70
                     SVIB WR'

Poor posture and a sullen expression put this girl at a disadvantage in her appearance. She also suffered from asthma, which, although not severe, was seen as a convenient excuse for escape from distasteful tasks. She was stubborn. One description referred to her as "the greedy, graspy type." She had minor clashes with teachers and was not very popular with other students, although she was not rejected by them. Her sincerity was doubted. There was an incident in which she was found to be taking credit for an honor that she had not won. In spite of all these drawbacks, she did fairly good work in school and was moderately active in some of the musical work. Her typical pattern was a promise to do better and a subsequent failure to carry out the promise.

The father did not have a regular job and he "seemed to be on the move all the time." Other children in the family were also considered to be stubborn.

423. F:14:0	ACE IX, none; XI, 90	5'348–'97	7:0:19
N:V:2	ENG IX, none; XI, 93		
	HSR 99		
	SVIB '–		

Everything seemed good about this girl. She was bright, dependable, and had a good sense of humor. She did everything well and was especially skillful in writing and artistic projects. "She was an only child, wholesome and well balanced and unspoiled."

424. F:14:1	ACE IX, none; XI, 99	5'3<u>61</u>–97'<u>428</u>	5:1:14
B:I:2	ENG IX, none; XI, 97	3'162–9'5	3:2:19
	HSR 100		
	SVIB none		

"Tops and outstanding in every way," this girl got the highest grades and was in many activities. "She was a real leader." In spite of her participation in activities, she was considered to be reserved in manner. She was very religious.

425. M:15:2	ACE IX, 100; XI, 100	5'38–4'6	4:2:15
N:V:3	ENG IX, 96; XI, 99	'54–'<u>26</u>	3:2:17
	HSR 94		
	SVIB 0'–		

Described as extremely mature during his junior high school years, this boy was also called selfish and cocky, and "he had an aloof and know-it-all attitude." He was a "very sturdy young man who had lots of ambition and drive and who knew what he wanted." Although his character and morals were high, his behavior aroused some resentment among both the students and the faculty. One person said that he was "tied to his mother's apron strings and should have been a little more independent and done more thinking for himself." His general ability and scholarship were consistent with his high opinion of himself. He had one traffic offense against him.

The father and mother were both very active in community affairs. The father was also said to be conceited, and the mother was described as aggressive and domineering.

426. F:15:2	ACE IX, 46; XI, 38	'54–'912	5:1:16
N:V:1	ENG IX, none; XI, 67	'59–2'6170	3:1:16
	HSR 39		
	SVIB none		

One of twin girls apparently very similar to one another, this girl was shy, timid, and not noticeable around school. [The twin's MMPI codes were, ninth grade, '09–1'83267 3:2:10, and, twelfth grade, '5439–'18 5:4:10. See p. 369 in this volume.] Both girls were attractive and neatly dressed, very interested in their appearance, and "boy crazy, with boys always around them." These were not among the better boys from the school. The girls were often "sassy and mean" with smaller children in their neighborhood. The twins were both married immediately upon graduation.

427. M:15:2	ACE IX, 59; XI, 64	'54–9'6	5:6:16
N:III:1	ENG IX, 64; XI, 31	'325178–9'46	1:7:13
	HSR 45		
	SVIB 4'89–		

This boy had great trouble with the study of English but wanted help so he could improve, for he expected to attend college after his military service. He wrote poetry — mostly "love stuff" — in his English class which, although poor in quality, showed real effort. He was a healthy, happy-go-lucky, extremely pleasant and enthusiastic boy. Particularly respectful toward his teachers and all adults, he was said to have "idolized his pastor." He was friendly, cooperative, and considerate. His main asset was his persuasiveness, and he hoped eventually to go into some form of sales work. Always willing to volunteer, and a good follower, he worked diligently in school programs to show his loyalty. During his senior year he was out at night a great deal with a younger girl of "questionable character." After graduation he entered the armed services.

The father was a skilled mechanic and the mother was said to "always feel sorry for the boy."

428. F:14:3	ACE IX, 94; XI, 100	5'437986–	3:5:15
N:V:5	ENG IX, 93; XI, 87	'47983562–	3:1:20
	HSR 95		
	SVIB none		

This girl was a good student who worked up to her capacity. Full of pep, she was rather well liked by other boys and girls. Her popularity, however, was limited by the fact that she had a sharp tongue and also was very aggressive. "If she didn't think a thing was right, she would tell you so." After graduation she attended a small college where she earned a place on the honor roll.

The father, a small businessman, was an aggressive person who was said to dominate the home. He became somewhat of a problem drinker but later "straightened out." He was fond of his daughter and she seemed to be closer to him than to her mother. The mother was pleasant, aggressive, and hard working—"perhaps a little distant and cold with her husband and her daughter." There was some tension in the home because of the father's not being religious and the mother's being devout.

429. M:14:5	ACE IX, none; XI, 99	'5467–2'9	7:2:17
N:III:4	ENG IX, none; XI, 99	'56974–'23	5:4:17
	HSR 100		
	SVIB none		

Athletic and psychologically mature, this boy was a leader and a very active participant in school affairs. He was considered "democratic, honest, and fair," and was the valedictorian of his class. There was some reason to believe he would enter the priesthood.

The family was a good one that was "well supervised." The father was described as "demanding and religious."

430. F:14:1	ACE IX, 91; XI, 67	'5478–	7:3:22
N:II:2	ENG IX, 83; XI, 84	'3579–	6:2:20
	HSR 68		
	SVIB WR'		

In the ninth grade this girl was shy and retiring, but as she continued in school these traits became less apparent. She was described as sweet in disposition, friendly, and popular with fellow students and teachers. She engaged in many social activities and projects; she was industrious, cooperative, and completely dependable. An above average student, she was, however, "bewildered" by any science class. It was suggested that the "social pushing" of the mother affected the girl so that she was "kind of stuck on herself and liked to think she was cuter than she really was." After graduation she attended a small college.

The father was very "extroverted and a real promoter." A brilliant man, he quickly climbed upward in the community. The mother was more shy but was described as a social pusher. The parents kept very close watch over the children. The family occupied a position in the upper social level of the community.

431. F:14:2   ACE IX, 30; XI, 43   5'487 31–'20   5:5:25
     N:IVC:3   ENG IX, 33; XI, 70   5'483 67–'92   7:5:24
                     HSR 69
                     SVIB WR'

The girl was "very sweet, well liked, and respectful of adults." Quiet and unobtrusive, she did not show much leadership and was in few activities, she was reliable and cooperative but difficult to know and to talk to. Although she took little part in school activities, she was active and talented in 4-H work.

The family lived on a marginal farm. They were sincere people, and there was a good relationship between parents and children.

432. M:15:4   ACE IX, 90; XI, 92   5"489'3671–'2   1:6:14
     B:V:1   ENG IX, none; XI, 93   5"9'873–'42   0:3:14
                     HSR 85   59'874–'1   1:3:18
                     SVIB none

Although this boy had severe acne in his early high school years, this had no ill effects on his social adjustment. He was mature for his age and was, in some ways, very competent. He "had to overcome effeminacy, but seemed to do well at it." His strong interests were drama and speech. His avocational interests were the collection of records and reading. He was very ambitious for recognition, and when he got low grades, he seemed very disappointed. He had occasional temper tantrums, and would pout and sulk. He was once sent out of a class because of insolence to the teacher, but he returned and apologized. There was suspicion that he had at one time been cheating. Outside of school he got into trouble a few times because of drinking and disorderly conduct. He was much bothered because his home was cluttered and disorderly, although his own room was neat at all times. He was generally considered to have much emotional instability.

The mother had been divorced from the boy's father, and the stepfather seemed to be on good terms with the boy. He was not a very adequate person, however, nor did he discipline the boy. The mother was friendly and likable enough. She supervised her son and took some interest in school and civic affairs. The house was messy and disorderly and the children felt they could not take friends home because of this.

433. F:15:2   ACE IX, 40; XI, 71   5'49–2'60   1:0:15
     N:VI:3   ENG IX, 45; XI, 66   9'54–127'   0:5:8
                     HSR 67
                     SVIB WR'

A dark, short, cute girl who was very clothes conscious, this student was well liked and generally well adjusted. However, she had a "so what" attitude and was considered somewhat moody. Inconsistent in temperament, at times she appeared earnest and concerned but at other times she was carefree. She was rebellious about her parents' attempts to discipline and control her. More a follower than a leader, she liked to have people around her and wished to do what others were doing. There was a suspicion that she was a member of a group of young people who broke into a store. After graduation she became a secretary.

Through hard work the father was able to provide fairly well for his family. It was suspected that the mother and father did not get along well together and that they clashed over the manner of controlling and disciplining the children.

434. M:14:2	ACE IX, none; XI, 44	'5490–72'	4:7:9
N:III:1	ENG IX, none; XI, 62		
	HSR 27 DO 11th gr.		
	SVIB none		

With a record of habitual truancy and frequent tardiness, this boy resented anything he was told and defied authority. He was a nonconformist and a disturber. The other pupils merely tolerated him and he had very few friends. At the end of his junior year he dropped out of school to join the armed forces. The police had no official record of delinquency for this boy, but he was known to them and on occasion had been warned for minor infractions.

435. F:16:2	ACE IX, 24; XI, 23	5'402–	7:4:10
N:III:1	ENG IX, none; XI, 15	'4370–	9:6:18
	HSR 34		
	SVIB none		

The first two years of high school were an especially unsatisfactory experience for this girl. She was unhappy because she could not keep pace either academically or socially. Hoping to find her place, she transferred to another school in her junior year. She was remembered at the first school as slow, quiet, shy, withdrawn, and, to some extent, a daydreamer. Not well known, she was one who "just came and went." She was described at one time as uninterested in school, a poor student without ambition or much ability who seemed not to resent low grades and who had a pleasant and accepting attitude. In contrast, at least one teacher in the school from which she graduated described her as intensely ambitious. She told of her crying because she was so worried about her grades, and that at times she worked late into the night in an effort to achieve an A or a B. In the twelfth grade she worked as a nurses' aide. She hoped to take nurses' training but failed to pass the qualifying entrance examinations. She then went into practical nursing after completing high school. She had a boy friend who was in trouble several times with the police. She stayed close to him through these troubles.

The father was a skilled tradesman who operated his own shop. He had been ill for several years but was apparently the dominant parent. The mother was considered to be somewhat unconcerned over the behavior of her girls, especially regarding their freedom with boys. An older sister was described as more outgoing and very interested in boys. The parents had provided the children with travel and camp experiences and both girls had a large wardrobe.

436. F:15:2	ACE IX, none; XI, 52	5'6–'237	6:1:17
N:III:3	ENG IX, none; XI, 65	4'7856–'92	3:2:24
	HSR 59		
	SVIB WR'		

Neat, tidy, and immaculate in appearance, this girl was very active in athletics and had many friends. The teachers enjoyed having her in their classes. She showed initiative and anticipated what was wanted and expected of her. After graduation she went to work as an airline hostess.

The family, a leading one in the neighborhood, had a comfortable home and a congenial relationship.

437. F:14:2	ACE IX, 38; XI, 64	'56–'90	4:0:18
N:V:1	ENG IX, none; XI, 84	— —	— —
	HSR 48	4'3859 167–'0	8:0:26
	SVIB none		

A girl with a good personality, this student was well liked, a good mixer, active, and a leader. She was soft-spoken, serious, and dependable. One person summed these qualities by saying she was "a good, average college type." The boys with whom she went did not have good reputations and were "noisy and boisterous." After graduation she attended college, where she developed more sparkle and seemed to have more social interests.

It was a middle-class family with good family ties. An older sister married very young and may have been a disciplinary problem.

438. M:14:2	ACE IX, none; XI, 89	'56–'09	4:3:20
N:IVC:1	ENG IX, none; XI, 93	'31–0'92	4:1:23
	HSR 91		
	SVIB none		

This boy was tall and big, but his mannerisms and behavior seemed effeminate. He had "esthetic values" and was rather immature. Although he conformed and was not a problem because of his conduct, he was "headstrong and determined, and he would get what he wanted at the expense of others." He had the ability to lead others but would never do anything to put himself into a "belligerent" situation.

439. M:15:3	ACE IX, none; XI, 92	5'64239–	5:2:15
N:V:1	ENG IX, none; XI, 88	— —	— —
	HSR 93	'9563–8'7	7:5:11
	SVIB none		

This was a good student who was conscientious and dependable. He was no problem, but "he had peculiar mannerisms." He was a "gifted musician."

440. M:14:2	ACE IX, none; XI, 100	'56439–1'20	0:4:10
N:V:1	ENG IX, none; XI, 94	–2178'063	2:3:7
	HSR 97		
	SVIB none		

"The brightest in the school," this boy was somewhat of a problem until his senior year, when his behavior improved. Earlier he had been in trouble for fighting and falsifications. "He knew his ability and was egotistical," and he was not well accepted by other students. A nonconformist, "he would try every situation to the 'hilt' if he thought he could benefit from it." One teacher said that "he had to learn to accept some of the limits set by society." He won a substantial scholarship in a national competition and enrolled in a large university following high school graduation.

441. F:14:5	ACE IX, 52; XI, 34	5'648–'93	4:6:14
B:V:1	ENG IX, 27; XI, 40	'8–	6:6:16
	HSR 53		
	SVIB none		

Although she did very poorly in the ninth grade, this girl's grades improved when she began to emphasize commercial subjects. She tried hard in school but lacked real drive. She was hurried and careless in her work. Her manner was pleasant and easygoing, but she was not active socially; she was "just around." She had, however, fewer opportunities for social contacts than most of her classmates. Her extracurricular activity was confined to membership in the band. After graduation she became a secretary and was reported to be doing well. Her work experience seemed to help her gain social poise. Small and slight in stature, she even looked more attractive after she began to work.

The father died when the girl was eleven years old. The mother worked and was "a typical poor man's wife, resentful toward the world." All the children had records of school absence without reason. The home was old and run-down; there was no known delinquency or severe health problems.

442. F:14:3   ACE IX, 54; XI, 61   '5678–'24   3:4:14
　　N:IVA:4   ENG IX, 40; XI, 59   '2387–　　　1:1:9
　　　　　　　HSR 74
　　　　　　　SVIB WR'

This large girl was described as loud, boisterous, and unable to speak quietly. An active leader in farm and church organizations, she was also a good student. She was usually pleasant, trustworthy, and dependable. She felt, however, that others had better breaks than she. After graduation she entered a university, where she majored in home economics.

　　The father was homely, outspoken, and friendly. He dominated everyone he could, including the daughter. The mother was not known to the school personnel. All the children were considered to be fine, and it was a satisfactory home.

443. M:14:5   ACE IX, none; XI, 89   56'78 03 214–   4:5:17
　　N:VI:3   ENG IX, none; XI, 78   '83759–　　　　2:5:16
　　　　　　　HSR 84
　　　　　　　SVIB none

The boy was "a he-man but very nice." He was described as a fine type of person, cooperative, ambitious, and sincere, who had never done wrong. He was good at taking responsibility and willingly shared service jobs. Realistic in his planning for the future, he worked hard to save money to go to college. In his junior year he had some trouble because of an accident. He was accused of careless driving, lectured, and released.

444. F:15:3   ACE IX, 81; XI, 93   56'9748–'2   4:5:13
　　N:VI:2   ENG IX, none; XI, 66   '057–4'21   4:1:15
　　　　　　　HSR 79
　　　　　　　SVIB WR'

Because she liked home economics this girl considered further education in order to become a home economics teacher. Her ability and marks were considered to be well above average. She was reliable and hard working, although not really a leader. She was quiet and minded her own business and had a mature and sensible outlook. Outside of school she worked part time as a receptionist. Her only school activity was in girls' athletics. After graduation she continued working.

　　The father was quiet, hard working, and home loving. He was warm and sensible with his children. The mother also stayed close to the home and was good in handling the children. The home was very modest but well cared for, and the family stood very well in the neighborhood.

445. M:15:7   ACE IX, 09; XI, none   56′9708–′1   2:7:8
     N:IVC:5   ENG IX, 02; XI, none
                        HSR DO 10th gr.
                        SVIB none

This introverted and passive boy was not likable and did not take part in any school activities. In the schoolroom he "rested and coasted" but gave no trouble. "He showed no interest in anyone or anything." One report said that he was "acceptable to a small group." The most positive thing said of him was that he was "trustworthy." He ultimately dropped out of school because of discouragement over his inability to learn. He seemed to feel somewhat ashamed and to become more reserved in his sophomore year when his mother developed a mental illness. After he left school, he went to work in a town some distance from his home.

The home situation was very poor. The mother was psychotic and the father, who was an alcoholic, was "cold, mean, and mentally retarded." The economic status of the family was low and its reputation in the community was poor. The mother's illness was characterized by depression and withdrawal. Only two of the siblings were known to the informants; they were described as "sincere, honest, and interested in farm work." They did well in spite of their "low mentality."

446. F:15:2   ACE IX, 81; XI, 55   ′57–   3:2:21
     B:III:1   ENG IX, 85; XI, 84   ′089–1′2463 1:3:14
                        HSR 71
                        SVIB none

Both this girl and her twin sister were very reserved and quiet. [The twin's MMPI codes were, ninth grade, ′98–′5 2:1:18, and, twelfth grade, ′07–′52 0:3:21.] They looked and acted much alike, seldom smiling and seldom appearing animated. They were no problem for the school and they were accepted by other students. This girl was somewhat more socially expressive than her twin and was somewhat better accepted socially by fellow students. Neither had many close friends, however. If they had ideas or opinions, one did not find out about them. Occasionally they could be seen to be arguing quietly between themselves.

447. M:14:1   ACE IX, 59; XI, 22   ′57–1′34   1:5:9
     B:II:2   ENG IX, none; XI, 25
                        HSR 33
                        SVIB none

This boy had many friends and "wanted to be a good guy." A little immature, he "bordered on wearing a leather jacket." Although he was sincere and tried hard in some classes, he acted bored and lazy when a class did not interest him. The police reported him to be mischievous. He "fought smaller kids and antagonized people."

The boy's father was dead and the mother had remarried. This marriage reportedly was a rather unhappy one.

448. F:14:1   ACE IX, 17; XI, 29   5'7–<u>90</u>   0:6:16
    N:V:3   ENG IX, 57; XI, 84
                    HSR 65
                    SVIB '–

This girl was an average student and relatively cooperative, but she hated to take orders. She put forth little effort on her own initiative; she needed to be pushed. She hoped for an education in music or the career of an airline hostess.

449. M:14:3   ACE IX, 90; XI, 99   '578<u>13</u>–'29   3:2:18
    N:I:1   ENG IX, none; XI, 88
                    HSR 97
                    SVIB '–

This was a boy who did not like to assume responsibility, although he was reliable and responsible when these qualities were demanded of him. A little retiring and quiet, he was also cooperative and a good student. It was said that he could have been a leader although he did not take the role.

450. F:16:9   ACE IX, 59; XI, 30   '579<u>43</u>–   8:4:17
    N:IVC:4   ENG IX, none; XI, 40   9'465–2'0 6:2:15
                    HSR 34
                    SVIB 'WR

This girl "would not say boo." She was very quiet, meek, and inconspicuous. In appearance she was "Germanic and buxom looking." Within her own class she was not particularly popular and she tended to go about with older boys.

451. F:14:2   ACE IX, none; XI, 36   5'79<u>80</u>4–'16 2:7:12
    N:III:2   ENG IX, none; XI, 28
                    HSR 34 DO 12th gr.
                    SVIB none

The main good point made about this girl was that she was pleasant when she wished to be and could be attractive and put up a "good front." She had many unexcused school absences; she was undependable and "never was where she was supposed to be." Outside of school she had "three or four fellows at one time." Her morals were questionable, and she went through several engagements before finally marrying. Her friends were of "low calibre." She was described as having many emotional problems and some of her school absences were due to her claimed "nervous breakdowns." She had a number of jobs, but lost them all. "Brazen" in manner, she nevertheless lacked self-confidence. Apparently some of her emotional reaction was a result of attempts at discipline by her father. She dropped out of school in the twelfth grade for no apparent reason.

452. M:15:0   ACE IX, none; XI, none   5′70<u>462</u>–   4:6:16
     N:III:1   ENG IX, none; XI, none
                HSR DO 10th gr.
                SVIB none

Other fellows called this boy a "fairy," so he became uninterested in school, dropping out in the tenth grade. He wanted to become a baker, and he planned on attending a vocational high school to complete his education. He had a "weak personality," and wasn't liked by others. He seemed to be goodhearted, willing, and helpful. In appearance, he was masculine-looking and always well groomed. He had his own car, and was guilty of at least one traffic violation. Outside of school, he liked to stay home to cook, bake, and keep house.

His father was a skilled workman. The mother was talkative and "boss of the family." She was very concerned about the boy. Both parents were slow to put the boy on his own. The mother also worked. It was thought that the parents sheltered the boy too much, giving him no responsibility. The home was described as a "nice, average, artistic home."

453. M:14:5   ACE IX, 79; XI, 82   '58–'2<u>63</u>   2:7:13
     N:VI:4   ENG IX, none; XI, 73   '8<u>3765</u>–   0:3:14
                HSR 55
                SVIB 4′–9

Quiet and serious for the most part, once in a while this boy could become stubborn. In the tenth grade he got into minor trouble because of fighting in the lunchroom, but generally he was fairly cooperative and seemed moderately well adjusted. He had a record of careless driving.

454. F:14:1   ACE IX, 68; XI, 72   '58–'<u>20</u>   3:1:19
     N:III:1   ENG IX, none; XI, 90   '94<u>685</u>–20′1   1:2:17
                HSR 94   9′–<u>02</u>′   2:2:18
                SVIB none

Bubbling over with eagerness and vim and vitality, this girl appeared older than she was. By some she was considered loud and boisterous and overenthusiastic. She had a good school record and was a leader in many activities. Although somewhat erratic, when she was given a job she got things done and done well. These virtues were somewhat balanced by the fact that she "lacked a lady-like discretion in personal matters." She was immodest, "almost exhibitionist at times." She seemed to wish to attract boys and was possibly overcompensating for a feeling that she lacked attention from them. She won a scholarship that was considered a distinct honor and went on to successful college work without making any definite decision about her ultimate vocation.

The parents were fine people and there seemed to be a good relationship between them and the girl.

455. F:15:3	ACE IX, none; XI, 99	'584–92'	7:2:21
N:IVA:6	ENG IX, none; XI, 99		
	HSR 75		
	SVIB none		

This girl was described as having many friends but no boy friend. Ambitious, she was a good worker and a leader. There was no conduct problem. "She was a girl with very good ideas — big ideas." She had an "innate sense of humor."

The father, a farmer, was very active, and the family was described as "splendid and religious."

456. F:14:10	IQ (centile) 50	5"8'406793–	4:11:13
B:III:3	HSR DO 11th gr.		
	SVIB none		

This girl "looked like she needed a meal, a bar of soap, and clothes." She missed many days of school, and, when she did attend, she was quiet and she kept to herself. She had few or no friends. Her conduct was acceptable, however, and she "seemed like a good girl." At least one of her teachers predicted that she would develop emotional maladjustment.

The father had abandoned the family, and the mother worked. The home was considered a poor one and the family was large.

457. M:14:1	ACE IX, 69; XI, 49	5'86–9'3	3:5:17
N:VI:2	ENG IX, 44; XI, 80	'867542–	2:6:18
	HSR 37		
	SVIB '8–		

The behavior of this boy became more unacceptable as he continued in school. In the ninth and tenth grades he was considered to be quite a good student, having a constructive attitude toward school; he was outgoing and friendly. However, he became a habitual absentee and offered false excuses for his truancy. He also became sullen and more narrow in his friendships. His record of scholastic achievement dropped markedly during his last two years in high school. He was caught cheating in a test but appeared unconcerned. He was interested in music and was a good performer. After high school graduation he enrolled in a junior college.

The family had a reasonably good reputation in the community. They lived in a rented apartment in a nonresidential area. Their income was thought to be below average despite the fact that both parents worked. The father was involved in an industrial accident during the boy's last year of school and this contributed to the family's financial stress.

458. M:15:3	ACE IX, 38; XI, none	58'6427–'1	2:13:2
N:I:5	ENG IX, 40; XI, none		
	HSR trans. 10th gr.		
	SVIB none		

"He could be a perfect gentleman when necessary" and yet this boy was also described as "a stinker — you name it, he did it." Shifty and underhanded, he was also nosy and discourteous, and he "picked on the smaller kids." In addition to these adverse traits, he was frequently absent from school, and four teachers predicted that he would become involved in some legal difficulty. One or two persons liked him, but most said that he "had Sunday manners at best." He would do anything to gain attention and liked to upset things in the schoolroom. Information about him was limited by the fact that he had left the region early in his high school years.

The home situation was characterized by a dominant father and an indifferent mother. The father was somewhat opinionated and was "the boss in his home and severe in discipline." The father had a chronic physical illness. An older brother of the boy, who was very much liked at school, was friendly though somewhat likely to withdraw from social contacts. It was believed that the children resented their father.

459. F:15:3	ACE IX, 65; XI, 34	'5867–	11:4:21X
N:VI:1	ENG IX, none; XI, 49		
	HSR 55		
	SVIB none		

This girl's mother worried about her because she was shy. The mother "went to parent-teacher meetings loaded." She expected a great deal of her daughter, wanting her to go to college even though the girl did not want to. She was a nice, average, and attractive girl, but too quiet and unaggressive. One ninth-grade teacher thought she would later develop emotional maladjustment.

460. F:15:2	ACE IX, none; XI, 50	'587–	5:2:18
N:II:3	ENG IX, none; XI, 28	46'317<u>28</u>9–	7:5:17
	HSR 66		
	SVIB 'WR		

Although she was very quiet in class, this girl liked to boss and was not tactful when she got an opportunity to dominate a situation. In appearance she was "a willowy blonde, attractive, well dressed, and gracious." She had no friends; possibly this was because of her "smug and self-righteous" attitude. When there was no opportunity for her to be dominant, she was contrastingly in the background. Her extracurricular interests were music and dramatics, in which activities she was competent. After graduation she went to a teachers' college.

The father was active in community affairs and a hard worker. He was not well liked and was apt to be "pushy and not very tactful." The mother, who was much overweight, was a poor conversationalist and was fanatically interested in card playing.

461. F:14:2	ACE IX, 46; XI, 59	'589–0'	5:2:23
N:V:1	ENG IX, 81; XI, 87	'95 <u>78</u>–0'6	3:1:20
	HSR 53		
	SVIB none		

This "sparkling" girl was very popular and active in school organizations. Definitely a part of things, she had moderate leadership ability and was exceedingly well liked, giving the impression of being truly interested in people rather than having only superficial interest. She was cheerful and optimistic and did things well, being very cooperative and willing. She was a hard worker. However, she felt that her teachers put too much emphasis on test scores, and, for their part, the teachers thought of her as not working up to her ability. After graduation she went to a small college.

462. M:14:9	IQ (centile) 53	58'<u>04</u> <u>679</u>–	1:5:6
B:VII:1	HSR DO 11th gr.		
	SVIB none		

Lazy, indifferent, lacking in energy, initiative, and motivation, this boy was a poor school investment. He was often truant, staying out of school for the slightest reasons. His mother tended to support him in these absences, and, in general, she exercised little control over him. He was easily led but was basically "not too bad a kid."

The father had died before the boy entered high school.

463. M:14:3
    B:V:3

ACE IX, none; XI, 92   '5806–1'423   2:5:10
ENG IX, none; XI, 72   '538–'92   2:4:16
HSR 79
SVIB none

An "uninteresting follower," this boy took little active interest in school and engaged in no activities. He was an excellent student and had no apparent problems. He was tidy and neat. His friends tended to be restricted to a small group.

464. F:14:2
    N:VI:2

ACE IX, 23; XI, 26   5'807–   3:2:10
ENG IX, none; XI, 31   4'78609–   2:9:12
HSR 70
SVIB WR'

Neat, confident, talkative, and a little of a tomboy, this girl was characterized as a nice, pleasant, happy student of average ability. In the ninth grade she was considered to be a little immature, but she matured considerably during her senior year. Although she took part in no school activities, she was neither meek nor retiring. She liked home economics and put in extra time on this subject. After graduation she took a part-time clerical job.

The father was a semiskilled workman, shy and retiring but acceptable. The mother, more outgoing, was dependable and thorough. Somewhat stronger than her husband, she handled the family discipline. It was a congenial family group.

465. F:14:1
    N:V:2

ACE IX, 97; XI, 95   '59–1'206   6:0:16
ENG IX, 94; XI, 93   '4935–21'867   3:1:12
HSR 92
SVIB '–

This girl, a twin, had many outstanding qualities. [The twin's MMPI codes were, ninth grade, '6–1'389 5:1:11, and, twelfth grade, '965834–'20 9:1:23.] She was in various activities and had a number of good friends. Her schoolwork was outstanding and she was highly regarded by her teachers. She did especially good work in science courses. She was altogether a fine person. After graduation she continued to a junior college.

The father was a small businessman, and the mother, although a little overprotective, was a very capable person. The twin sister was like this girl. Both girls had a great deal of respect for their parents and other adults.

466. F:14:2
    N:V:3

ACE IX, 44; XI, 43   '59–'6   6:3:14
ENG IX, 62; XI, 53   6'378–2'5   7:8:16
HSR 42
SVIB 'WR

This was a "big, clumsy girl who was clean and neat." Though many of her fellow students liked her, they made fun of her. She was very emotional and made desperate bids for attention, easily becoming depressed and elated. She often cried. "She was very maladjusted." She made a nuisance of herself seeking friendship and recognition, but she was always hurt because people didn't talk to her. She associated mainly with adults and "got terrific crushes on faculty men or other older men." Seemingly driven by feelings of inferiority she would "go off on tangents and would talk too much." She "walked alone at night," and when she was in the ninth grade she wrote letters to instructors in a nearby small college asking them about her possibilities of success in college. The police had a record citing her for "loitering at late hours." One teacher predicted emotional maladjustment for her.

The father, a small businessman, dominated the home. He was rigid in his ways but gave the girl a good deal of freedom. The mother was "weak in character." Both parents showed little interest in the children's activities.

467. M:14:1	ACE IX, none; XI, 86	'59–72 06	5:4:15
N:VI:3	ENG IX, none; XI, 69	'58436–02'	6:4:20
	HSR 36		
	SVIB 8'4–120		

This was a medium-sized, rather good-looking boy who was a member of the basketball team. He was said to have a high opinion of himself and to have a terrible temper, which he controlled pretty well, but "he would do small, spiteful things and mutter under his breath when corrected." His teachers described him as "foul-mouthed"; he wrote obscene words and phrases in his schoolbooks. In his sophomore year he was charged with racing a car in the street; he admitted his guilt at a hearing. He had hoped to receive a scholarship for college, but he failed in this and was very disappointed, expressing a wish to get away from home.

The family changed church affiliations frequently. The father was said to be like the boy in physique and temperament. People around him felt that he "must be handled with gloves." The mother, nervous and high-strung, had a nervous breakdown, which did not require hospitalization, when the boy was in his junior year. It was said that she alternately was indulgent and strict with the boy, causing him to be deceitful with her and with others.

468. F:14:1	ACE IX, 89; XI, 82	'594–21'37	2:5:10
N:IVB:3	ENG IX, 90; XI, 92	4'897–	1:4:14
	HSR 77		
	SVIB '–		

Described by ninth-grade teachers as "immature, giddy, giggly, flighty, and not well accepted by classmates," this girl improved somewhat so that she was better liked and had a wider circle of friends by the time she graduated from high school. She was responsive to boys, who liked to tease her. She had a close girl friend whom she was always with. They double dated often with "unsavory boys." She was apparently considered to be less intelligent than she was in fact, and it was mentioned that she contrasted with her best friend, who was very bright. Some persons saw her as a "winsome, attractive girl with a pretty smile." The relationship between the girl and her mother was "unhealthy." The mother put pressure on the girl to get high marks to go to college, and she attempted to keep boy friends away. After graduation the girl began teachers' training.

The mother was dominating and had a "peculiar personality." She was brusque, impecunious, and narrow-minded. By contrast, the father was "relatively invisible."

469. M:15:0	ACE IX, none; XI, 61	59'438–	1:5:13
B:V:2	ENG IX, none; XI, 57		
	HSR 57		
	SVIB 4'8–0		

Teachers were not in agreement about this boy. Apparently the disagreement was partly a result of whether the boy liked a teacher or not. If he liked a teacher there was no trouble. He was "sometimes friendly" but also often sullen. Occasionally he caused disturbances in study hall and classrooms. On the other hand, he was described as a very good worker. An only child whose mother had died when he was quite young, he had been reared by his father.

470. F:15:12	ACE IX, 26; XI, 37	'5948–0'2	5:5:16
N:VI:2	ENG IX, none; XI, 36	9"561–'20	3:6:10
	HSR 23		
	SVIB WR'		

One of the older of thirteen children, this girl was popular with boys, had frequent dates, and had a good moral reputation. Talkative, relaxed, and moderately well liked, she was not in many activities and not a leader. "Thoroughly extroverted" in grade school, she was less so in high school. She worked reasonably well but was a slow student; her schoolwork was "average." After graduation she worked in a clerical position.

The father was a day laborer who had some chronic physical illness. The mother was the dominant person in the family. She was inclined to be belligerent, even with her neighbors. The children were neat and clean, and although the home was located in a poor district, it was well kept up and fairly neat and clean inside.

471. M:14:2	ACE IX, none; XI, 82	'596–2'170	3:1:13
N:II:1	ENG IX, none; XI, 85	'958–02'	2:0:14
	HSR 100		
	SVIB none		

"A real politician," this boy planned his activities tactfully and purposefully to get just what he wanted. He was a nice-appearing, aggressive, and very active youth with athletic ability and a facility for capitalizing on his positive traits. Respected by many students, he was class president and captain of an athletic team; however, some of his teachers felt that he did not always use his leadership qualities in the best way. He was described as an alert, capable and interested student who expressed himself well and was "quite reliable." He obtained excellent grades in school. His teachers recognized that he ranked higher in achievement than in ability and yet they said that he tried to get out of as much work as possible and did just enough to get by. It was also said that "he wanted to go as far as possible" and yet "he did not meet a challenge"; he typically avoided competitive situations. He liked attention, and he frequently wore loud colors. His greatest concern was that he be accepted socially. His last three years of high school were marked by a number of traffic offenses, ending with an accident to which drinking might have been a contributing factor.

The father was a successful and wealthy businessman.

472. M:15:5	ACE IX, 44; XI, 33	'59<u>738</u>–6'4	3:3:13
N:VI:2	ENG IX, none; XI, 05	'943–20'6	6:0:18
	HSR 43		
	SVIB 4'8–0		

Although "on the quiet side," this was "a pretty good kid." He was unenthusiastic and lacked initiative. Keeping pretty much to himself, he had few, if any, friends. He was cooperative and "worked for C's" in school, but he exhibited little interest. He always appeared neat and well dressed. At some time after his graduation he was involved in a disorderly street fight, but it was ruled that he had been provoked by the other person and the complaint was dismissed.

473. M:16:1	ACE IX, 36; XI, 28	'59<u>84</u>–1'<u>302</u>	4:8:10
N:VI:2	ENG IX, none; XI, 14	7'98<u>564</u>–'<u>10</u>	3:2:14
	HSR 43		
	SVIB 8'49–		

One person said that this boy had a "weak personality," although he was thought of as a "good kid" on the whole. Several persons described him as temperamental, "inclined to be a little hotheaded," and if things did not go right, "he would not argue, he would just quit." He appeared to have been a fairly acceptable member of school groups. In academic work he was a C student and did rather well considering his measured intelligence. He was interested in music, art, and shop courses, and was active in outdoor sports such as basketball, track, football, and camping. In spite of these many activities he was described as "rather retiring except with his own group, tending to be self-conscious and shy." He "did not have much time for the girls." After high school he entered a small college with the hope of going into some form of athletic or vocational-educational activity. It was reported that he was having difficulty keeping up with the college work.

The mother and father, who both worked, were described as steady, reliable,

161

and frugal. They were apparently good persons who were very close to their children.

474. F:14:2	ACE IX, 98; XI, 82	59'84–0'21	6:0:15
N:V:5	ENG IX, 77; XI, 87	9'54–06'<u>271</u>	2:3:15
	HSR 67		
	SVIB 'WR		

It was said of this girl that she did everything too young. She entered the ninth grade from a parochial school and assumed a great deal of sophistication. She cheated and was "sneaky," but she was "smart enough to cover." She made herself conspicuous, chiefly in connection with sex behavior. She dressed provocatively and hung around with "black jackets," showing indiscriminate interest in boys and men. She "cheapened herself with makeup, wore tight sweaters, etc." Her immoral behavior commenced in the ninth grade. There were "sex parties" at her house. A number of the ninth-grade teachers predicted that she would have emotional difficulties and two expected her to get into legal difficulty. After graduation she married; it was reported that the marriage was unlikely to be a stable one.

Her home life was "nonexistent." The father was a poor contributor. He was dependable but weak. The mother was ambitious, full of energy, and active in numerous community affairs, to such an extent that her family was neglected and the children were left to care for themselves. The girl's older sister was said to follow the same promiscuous pattern.

475. F:15:6	ACE IX, 46; XI, 26	5'908–3'<u>12</u>	3:10:7
N:IVB:4	ENG IX, 21; XI, 37	6'7<u>94</u>–1'5	4:2:14
	HSR 41		
	SVIB 'WR		

This girl possessed more ambition than ability. She worked hard for everything in school, and she was a dependable and responsible leader in both church and school organizations. At times she became discouraged over her lack of scholastic achievement but gradually she learned to live with her limitations. Her personality was pleasant and she "gave people a lift." She expressed an interest in becoming a beauty operator after graduation.

The father, a farmer, was a good family man, pleasant and kind. The mother was similarly described, and the parents were termed "salt of the earth type."

476. F:15:2	ACE IX, 16; XI, 24	5'0–31'4	3:5:8
N:IVB:3	ENG IX, 33; XI, 50	0'54–<u>61'3</u> 289	7:6:9
	HSR 50		
	SVIB '–		

"She should be a good beauty parlor operator" was one of the statements characterizing this girl. She was described as vivacious and high-strung, a bundle of nervous energy. She was also called mature, good looking, and reserved. Generally, she seemed to be a very cooperative, reliable, attractive, and acceptable person. After graduation she went to a beauticians' school.

The father, a skilled workman, was cooperative and helpful. The mother was actively interested in home and community affairs. The children "really participated in activities at home." In all, it was a well-respected, close-knit family with good personal relationships.

477. M:14:1   ACE IX, none; XI, none   '50–'461   8:9:8
     N:VI:2   ENG IX, none; XI, none
                  HSR DO 10th gr.
                  SVIB none

Five teachers predicted that this boy would become emotionally maladjusted. He was described as withdrawn and lonely, and he had few friends. He dropped out of school before his junior year to begin working in a factory. The school records show that he was frequently absent from classes.

The family income was considerably below the community average.

478. M:15:4   ACE IX, 44; XI, 49   '502–1'639   1:6:9
     N:V:2   ENG IX, 41; XI, 27
                  HSR 21
                  SVIB none

The boy appeared lethargic, slow moving, and rather pale, although he was apparently healthy. He did not "put himself out" but was accepted by other students. He was pleasant, cheerful, and happy-go-lucky; in fact, he would rather "fool around than study." Music was his primary school interest.

479. M:14:1   ACE IX, 70; XI, none   5″02′7638–   2:6:5
     N:VI:5   ENG IX, 80; XI, none
                  HSR trans. 10th gr.
                  SVIB none

This boy was quiet and reserved, and, in one description, he was said to "walk and talk like a girl." He was very concerned about achieving good marks. He did not enter into any extracurricular activities and was very hard to know. He was faithful in church attendance and wanted to continue his schooling in theology.

The father was shiftless and unable to keep a job, appearing to have little intelligence. The mother was mentally ill for a period, and, as she became worse, she was unable to care for her children.

480. F:15:3   ACE IX, 67; XI, 79   '5048–'123   8:4:17
     N:V:5   ENG IX, 78; XI, 92   '90 38674–   5:4:19
                     HSR 82
                     SVIB '–

This was a friendly, responsive girl who was called an affectionate nickname by both faculty and students. She was always dependable and mature, and she was sought out by others in the school. She was described as being considerate and fair in her judgments.

The father was well thought of and a leader in active community work. He was described as rather easily offended, however, and he "appeared to lack depth." The mother was more interested in a career than in the home. Despite this she was a good manager, kind, generous, and interested in her children. Although the family seemed to be a compatible one, the members were rarely seen together and the children might have felt somewhat neglected.

481. F:14:1   ACE IX, 44; XI, 28   '506–'213   1:4:13
     N:VI:2   ENG IX, none; XI, 38   '03–9'451   3:6:10
                     HSR 73
                     SVIB WR'

This girl was overweight and appeared shy and self-conscious because of it. She could talk easily with acquaintances and friends, and she was a good, hard-working student. She was immature in some ways and did not show much leadership ability. She was interested in becoming a teacher and she received a scholarship for this education. She went to a teachers' college, then changed to business training, and then quit to work and be married.

The father was a hard worker, likable and outgoing. The mother also worked. She was described as quiet, well balanced, and affectionate. Both parents were interested in their children and were good at directing them.

482. M:14:2   ACE IX, 98; XI, 100   '506–'41279   1:2:13
     N:IVB:4   ENG IX, 100; XI, 99   '50–'129   2:1:15
                     HSR 100
                     SVIB none

This charming, outgoing, and personable boy had a slight speech impediment but was untroubled by it. He was referred to a speech clinic but was not interested. Full of "fun and curiosity," he demonstrated leadership qualities that his teachers said they wished they could develop in others. There was no information regarding his career after high school.

The father was a farmer and the mother was in a mental institution. There was little information about the family, but it appeared that they were reasonably well adjusted to the mother's absence.

483. F:14:1   ACE IX, 52; XI, 64   50'6489–31'2   0:20:7X
    N:III:3   ENG IX, 63; XI, 69
                HSR 75
                SVIB WR'

This girl was chubby, exuberant, and smiling. She seemed to be happy and well balanced, a very nice schoolgirl. In class she was well prepared, conscientious, and able to assume responsibility when necessary.

484. M:14:1   ACE IX, none; XI, 96   5'0684 972–1'3   6:8:8
    B:III:3   ENG IX, 81; XI, 93   '5649–   8:4:17
                HSR 74
                SVIB none

The terms used in the descriptions of this boy were mostly laudatory. He was well liked, had many friends, and was active in school affairs. He was able to take the initiative in interpersonal relations and was generally considered very capable. It was mentioned that in his early high school years he had not been so dependable but that he had developed stability as he continued in school. He had an active hobby in photography and was also a good public speaker.

The family background seemed to have been somewhat irregular. It was said that the father, who was dead, had been "no good." The stepfather, however, was a stronger person, and apparently the boy got along well with him.

485. M:14:4   ACE IX, none; XI, 33   '507–'463   3:1:14
    N:V:7   ENG IX, none; XI, 29   5'2–'84 913   4:3:14
                HSR 58
                SVIB none

This boy labored under the disadvantage of a tyrannous father and a chronic physical disability. Although he was sometimes hot-tempered and in some degree isolated in school relationships, he was, on the whole, a very good and sincere boy. Those who knew him well felt he showed a fine sense of humor and a great sincerity. Working at neighborhood jobs, he was considered one of the very best of workers. One teacher expected that this boy would become emotionally maladjusted.

486. F:14:5   ACE IX, none; XI, 12   '507983–   5:4:17
    N:VI:3   ENG IX, none; XI, 18
                HSR 27
                SVIB none

This girl could be "good fun." She was pleasant and she behaved herself; "she did not dare to be different." However, "she needed to be kept under control because she was a follower," somewhat moody, and untrustworthy.

487. F:15:1   ACE IX, 14; XI, 11   5′098–4′2   5:9:4
      B:VII:4   ENG IX, 30; XI, 31   ′08257–6′   9:3:16
                      HSR 43
                      SVIB ′–

This girl was quiet and mousy. She managed to do fairly well in school, although she was caught cheating on several occasions. She showed no resentment at being caught and reprimanded, but she continued to cheat. She was a follower and not very dependable. She made a poor social adjustment and was not well liked. A "plugger and prodder who minded her own business, she was hard to know and was too apprehensive to formulate her own plans." She was slow in motion and in schoolwork. She lacked both initiative and imagination. After graduation she went into practical nursing. She seemed to be gaining some independence, but nevertheless, she was seen more frequently with her mother than with people her own age.

The father was shiftless, surly, and not a dependable worker. The mother was more ambitious, capable, and aggressive. Often both parents were termed "slow thinkers." The community did not think well of the family.

488. M:14:7   ACE IX, 14; XI, none   ′6–1′3 40   4:2:15
      N:VI:4   ENG IX, 14; XI, none
                     HSR DO 10th gr.
                     SVIB none

About the only good thing said was that this boy was "a very dependable and pleasant paper boy." He was manifestly uninterested in school and, although not loud or noisy, he was annoying and frequently guilty of scuffling, fighting, hitting, and the like. He took no part in school activities and was often absent. In other moods he was quiet and did not talk. It was hard for him to conform and he was much and badly influenced by his older brothers and companions. After quitting school he joined the armed forces. Before he was old enough to go into the service he was in considerable trouble with the law. These difficulties included traffic offenses and stealing while in the company of two other boys. The offenses were severe enough to have sent him to a reform school had he not shortly been entering the armed services.

The family reputation was poor. Some of the family were "very fine and some were very bad." The home was "utterly deplorable and abominably dirty." The mother apparently was the stronger of the parents. The father worked hard but was inarticulate and made excuses for himself. The mother was aggressive and resented the "persecution" of her children. She was outspoken, "fat, coarse, and crude." She was so obnoxious that welfare people hated to visit the home, and she blocked all efforts to improve conditions, talking constantly and blaming everyone for the misbehavior of her children. There were no known physical problems but much emotional instability.

489. F:15:2	ACE IX, none; XI, 76	'6–<u>14</u>'59827	4:2:14
B:III:3	ENG IX, none; XI, 89	'0<u>36745</u>–'9	4:1:20
	HSR 98		
	SVIB '–		

A "slender blonde with a pleasing personality," this girl was popular with both boys and girls, and was a leader in her class. Her activities were broad in scope. Described as a perfectionist, she would stay home from school in order to get her work just right. "She would have to know exactly how to go about a thing before she would start it." She asked very intelligent questions and expected to be answered in the same way. She was particularly outstanding in English and art. Other students considered her "the most likely to succeed," and she was awarded scholarships and other honors. She hoped to become a teacher, and after graduation continued training in a small college.

The father, who had left the mother when the children were small, was described as a man with charm and good looks but "helter-skelter and irresponsible." The mother reared the children and she had a very close relationship with them. She was considered pleasant, hard working, and courageous.

490. F:14:2	ACE IX, 77; XI, 72	'6–'19	2:4:14
N:V:5	ENG IX, 86; XI, 82	7'<u>48321</u>–'5	2:6:19
	HSR 77		
	SVIB WR'		

Characterized as "cute as a bug's ear," this girl was attractive and had a nice personality. She was well liked by students and the faculty. Considered to be an extrovert, she was active and successful in a variety of ways. She was a well-behaved and capable student, and although not a leader in ideas and actions, she was respected. She had "fine, strong convictions and the courage to stand firmly." After graduation she went to a small religious college with the intention of becoming a teacher.

Both parents were considered to be fine persons with wide interests and many community activities. The mother, although not a "~~driver~~," was judged to be the stronger of the two parents.

491. M:14:1	ACE IX, none; XI, 67	'6–1'9	5:0:10
N:III:3	ENG IX, none; XI, 49		
	HSR 40		
	SVIB none		

A "smart aleck" who had no respect for traffic rules and who had been reported for drinking, this boy "took advantage of every situation." He had to be excluded from school assemblies because he created a rumpus. Although small he was a good baseball player. He was very neat and "had a wonderful personality at times." During a vacation period he worked and "did a fine job."

The boy's teachers said that the parents "tried to be cooperative," but that they were indulgent, not punishing the boy for such things as wrecking a car. A sister was described as a "very fine girl."

492. F:15:10	ACE IX, 82; XI, 98	'6–'24 18359	1:7:11
B:V:3	ENG IX, 95; XI, 93	'43 9578–'02	1:5:16
	HSR 92	'534–2'	1:3:16
	SVIB '–		

The descriptive word most frequently applied to this girl was "talkative," supplemented by "chatterbox, scatterbrained, and happy-go-lucky." In junior high school she was "bossy and headstrong." She "threw her weight around for no reason." At this time she was also considered to be an immature girl with "a poor attitude." Apparently she changed somewhat as she continued through high school, for in her senior year she was very active in both church and school, generally likable and always friendly. Although chronically tardy for school, her achievement was high. Most persons referred to her as "a fine girl"; however, one reported hearing rumors that she was "fast and wild and liked to chase around." She was a scholarship winner and entered a university to take technical training.

The family situation was good. There were many children, some of whom were very industrious and worked their way through college; it was said, however, that this girl had "everything given to her." The girl's father had died when she was only a few years old, but the mother remarried and the new marriage appeared to be good and stable.

493. F:14:2	ACE IX, 99; XI, 99	'6–5'231	2:4:10
N:III:1	ENG IX, none; XI, 99	'367–5'40	1:1:13
	HSR 92	–45'62	2:2:14
	SVIB none		

Described in laudatory terms by everyone, this student was very good looking and "an outstanding girl with many facets to her ability and talents." She was "an excellent person, sweet in manners and personality." She was friendly and active in school affairs, particularly in drama, speech, and journalism. Although she was very attractive, she had few or no dates, and her teachers felt this was because she was too busy. She was enthusiastically recommended for scholarships and was altogether a successful person, who was said to have remained humble despite her many successes. After graduation she went on to a university.

The family had a high income level and was described as "nice."

494. M:15:1   ACE IX, 48; XI, 84   '6–'5<u>71</u>   2:2:15
     B:VI:1   ENG IX, 59; XI, 28
                   HSR 54
                   SVIB none

This was a quiet, retiring boy with no evidence of leadership ability. He was not a discipline problem while in high school; however, when younger he was reported to have been a nuisance to his family's landlord because he treated the property carelessly and "ran wild" with a neighbor boy who was a bad influence. The mother was "overindulgent with him," illustrated by the fact that she would not allow the stepfather to discipline the boy in any way. It was said that the boy was "ruining their home." His school grades were poor. He hoped to continue in aircraft pilot training but was unable to fulfill the physical requirements. In his junior year his driver's license was suspended for a time. In the same year he transferred to another school.

The home situation was confused and there was no information about the boy's real father. The mother, who overprotected her son, had a very violent temper and quarreled constantly with the stepfather. She refused to discuss the family problems with a welfare agency or anyone else. In contrast, the stepfather was a fairly competent person who made efforts to clarify the family relationships and to obtain help from welfare agencies.

495. F:14:4   ACE IX, 57; XI, 56   '6–'7<u>23</u>   8:5:17
     N:IVC:6   ENG IX, 54; XI, 69
                   HSR 67
                   SVIB none

The strongest point made in describing this girl was that she was stubborn. Once her mind was made up she would not change it. In other ways she was a very acceptable person. She was neat, cooperative, and responsible. She was well liked by other students and was quite active in extracurricular affairs. Her forte was music.

There was little information about the family except for a notation that the parents were "shiftless."

496. M:14:1   ACE IX, none; XI, 29   '6–9<u>2</u>'75   5:5:14
     N:IVC:2   ENG IX, none; XI, 23
                   HSR 43
                   SVIB none

This boy would do just enough to get by; however, it was believed that he could have done better. Teachers described him as "an underachiever." Because he "stayed out all night," he was "sort of passive as a student and in no condition to study." He did not participate in school activities. His friends were described as a "fringe group — a fast crowd." He was often truant from school, and when he had an opportunity, he would "stretch school rules." He was easily led and not a leader. On several different occasions he was in trouble for careless driving and other "hot-rod" offenses.

497. M:15:1	ACE IX, 79; XI, 62	'6–'01578	5:2:16
N:III:3	ENG IX, 61; XI, 42		
	HSR 33		
	SVIB '14–		

Just "an ordinary student," this boy was retiring, indifferent, and lackadaisical; he "needed pushing." He was "car crazy" and it was only in this area that he showed any ambition. He got into difficulties with the law for speeding and reckless driving, and in another episode he "created a general disturbance at a girls' camp."

498. M:14:4	ACE IX, 11; XI, 25	'6134–	5:1:15
N:IVC:2	ENG IX, none; XI, 10	4"163978–	2:5:20
	HSR 53		
	SVIB '4–		

Described as "rather quiet, dependable, and cooperative," this boy "could talk with an individual but would clam up in a group." He was not a conduct problem but "lacked strength of character and did not have much ambition or drive." He "needed social skills and activity badly but could not participate in school activities because he took the bus to school." He did not date. As a student he was a hard worker and did A work in mechanical studies. He may have been an overachiever in the latter, or he may have had considerably more ability in mechanical than in verbal areas, for his other grades were only average. At the time of graduation he was managing two small farms with his father's help. He expressed some dissatisfaction with this work, stating that he would prefer to enter the armed services so that he could follow auto mechanics as a career.

Although the family was situated on marginal farm land and had very little to work with, the home situation was good. The father and mother seemed to be harmonious and affectionate, and they were interested in their children.

499. M:15:2	ACE IX, none; XI, 08	61'4837–	5:12:9
N:III:3	ENG IX, 15; XI, 34	84"72'36510–	3:16:12X
	HSR 26		
	SVIB none		

This boy was a little cocky and irritating but "not at all malicious." He was "very, very lazy" and lacked confidence in himself. He tended to be "a bit moody." He liked school and was active in athletics. He was not outstandingly popular although he had friends.

500. F:15:4   IQ (centile) 38   '624–9'   6:5:17
      N:VI:1   HSR DO 11th gr.
                      SVIB none

Although a neat and quiet girl, this student was undependable and deceptive. Her attendance record was poor and she finally dropped out of school because of lack of interest.

501. F:14:6   ACE IX, 26; XI, 29   6"2'809 74–   5:13:12
      N:IVB:5   ENG IX, 15; XI, 10   76'8902543–   2:12:6
                      HSR 11
                      SVIB 'WR

This girl was "pudgy" but had a perfect complexion. She was quiet and retiring, "the type who goes unnoticed." Although one teacher predicted that she would become emotionally maladjusted, others described her as well balanced. She was lacking in the "social niceties" and did not improve during her high school years. She did the ordinary work in class and teachers found her reliable, although she was merely tolerated by her classmates. After high school graduation she worked as a clerk but was unhappy with her job and eventually quit to stay at home.

The family was characterized by strong interpersonal ties and a satisfaction with their status. The mother was considered a hard-working woman who lacked personal warmth and social polish. Both the father and the mother were adequate but quiet and reserved.

502. M:14:3   ACE IX, 40; XI, 87   '63–'1   7:4:18
      N:IVA:4   ENG IX, 43; XI, 65   '564–'219 2:1:16
                      HSR 85
                      SVIB none

The chief interest of this boy, who was from a farm family, was his 4-H Club. He was friendly, well liked, and more mature than the average student. A "hard worker," he was considered one of the better all-around students. He had won statewide recognition in his agricultural accomplishments. At school his major activity was track. Although he had no steady girl friend, he did date. After graduation he worked on the family farm.

The family was described in superlative terms. These compliments referred to the personalities, the community activities, and the interrelationships of the family. The three other children were as socially and academically successful as their brother.

503. M:15:0	ACE IX, none; XI, 73	'63–2'094	3:3:16
B:V:1	ENG IX, none; XI, 57	'36–'207	5:5:17
	HSR 97	'365–'09	3:3:20
	SVIB none		

This boy was friendly, well liked, and not a disciplinary problem. He was a good student. He worked part time while going to school, and after graduation he enrolled at a university.

504. M:14:3	IQ (centile) 91	'63–5'29	8:3:15
B:III:1	HSR trans. 10th gr.		
	SVIB none		

This boy was likable, cooperative, and desirous to please. He seemed highly intelligent and he had a good record. His particular interest was in science. He played a musical instrument well and outside of school he was a golf caddy. In summary, he was a very good, quiet boy. At the end of his freshman year he transferred to another school, where he did well. In his first year at college he enrolled in an engineering course and earned a scholarship.

The father had died when the boy was very young. The mother did well holding the family together, although she was highly nervous and complaining.

505. M:15:4	ACE IX, 96; XI, none	6'3–'902	4:3:16
N:VII:2	ENG IX, none; XI, none		
	HSR trans. 10th gr.		
	SVIB none		

A naturalized American, this boy was described in very laudatory terms. He was "all business," a leader, and a very hard worker. He was bright and conscientious, and he learned the new language and customs quickly. In the tenth grade he transferred to a vocational school.

506. F:15:1	ACE IX, 05; XI, 08	6″3240'718–'5	6:12:8
N:V:1	ENG IX, none; XI, 24	3'4672180–'95	3:4:16
	HSR 23		
	SVIB none		

Bored all through grade and high school, this girl lacked initiative. She was restless, satisfied with inferior work and with being a follower. She had a marked tendency to "magnify small ailments." In high school, however, she was happy, honest, cooperative, neat, and reliable. She was interested in becoming a good homemaker. She liked sewing and art work, and she tried to help her mother all she could. Although she got married before graduation, she finished her senior year.

The mother suffered from migraine headaches and many illnesses. She was basically an inadequate, lethargic person, unwilling to accept much responsibility. The mother favored the son; the father favored the girl.

507. F:15:2	ACE IX, 100; XI, 100	'634–5'1	4:2:15
N:III:4	ENG IX, 100; XI, 100	'36–'<u>0529</u>	9:1:23
	HSR 100		
	SVIB 'WR		

Everyone attested to the good qualities of this girl. Almost nothing that could be said in praise of her was omitted. She was brilliant but humble, generous and sensitive, mature and realistic, democratic but a leader, and "had compassion for the underprivileged and a great charity in her heart." She ranked first in her class and was high on a national scholarship test. There was only one item reported that marred this description: On one occasion she attempted to step off her pedestal almost with deliberation and did some drinking. Although this incident was probably not very bad, the girl was terribly ashamed of it and rationalized it as best she could. She continued to college after graduation and there again her record was outstanding.

The family was described in terms as glowing as were those used for the girl. The children were all well mannered and well trained, and at least one of the other girls was very like the subject. It was suggested that the other sister, although called a "delightful rascal," may have felt the need to break off and establish herself as more of an individual against the competition of others in the family.

508. F:14:2	ACE IX, none; XI, 88	'63<u>478</u>–'02	4:3:20
N:II:2	ENG IX, none; XI, 90		
	HSR 50		
	SVIB 'WR		

Attractive and personable, this girl was a leader with many outside activities. High in moral standards, she had a strong sense of school spirit and was "a fine school citizen." She was also described as "fun, articulate, and easy to know and to like."

She came from a closely knit family with high moral standards, and it was considered a very good family in the community.

509. F:14:1	ACE IX, 84; XI, 65	'637–5'<u>129</u>	2:4:14
N:IVB:4	ENG IX, 90; XI, 69	'76<u>84310</u>–5'	3:3:16
	HSR 61		
	SVIB '–		

In spite of the fact that she participated in many activities, this girl was repeatedly described as somewhat shy, retiring, and self-effacing. She was called "pampered but not spoiled." She "appreciated lovely things, gravitating toward the good things in life." Although she was charming and loving, she did not seem to have many friends. It was believed this may have been due to her mother's interference rather than her own inability to make friends. She did have a boy friend and seemed to appreciate leaning on him for emotional support. She was reticent about revealing her plans for the future; she was in a college preparation course and had good ability. The girl was very much attached to her mother, although her attitude toward her mother was described by an informant as one of "indifference." The mother was self-centered and selfish, so that it was expected that the girl would have a better life if she were away from the mother. On the other hand, she was considered not emotionally ready to go to college. Upon graduation she did leave home to attend a small college, but returned shortly thereafter because of the illness of her father. She was dissatisfied and unhappy while away at school and continued to live at home even after the crisis of the father's illness had ended.

The reputation of the family was good and this appeared to be a result of the father's good qualities. However, he was handicapped by a serious physical limitation. Both parents worked outside the home. The mother continued to work even during the father's illness, although there was no real financial need. She was said to have placed too much responsibility upon her daughter. Some considered her to be self-centered and selfish, and believed she perhaps dramatized her husband's illness in order to gain pity for herself. She was apparently a nagger who was not always truthful in what she said, and she was unscrupulous in certain social relationships.

510. F:14:0	ACE IX, 100; XI, 100	63′98714–0′5	5:6:19
N:IVB:6	ENG IX, 100; XI, 99		
	HSR 90		
	SVIB ′–		

At one time this girl had a bad reputation as a "flirt" who liked boys but did not like girls. She claimed boys were more intelligent and that girls were silly. She preferred her father to her mother and always went steady, primarily with the same boy. She did not present a problem for the school; on the contrary, she was in many activities and was particularly interested in politics and government. Some teachers predicted that the girl would later become emotionally maladjusted; however, nothing particularly deviant was reported subsequent to these predictions.

511. F:14:0	ACE IX, 93; XI, none	64′39 87–5′20	3:6:16
N:III:1	ENG IX, 97; XI, none		
	HSR 84		
	SVIB none		

Although she was popular, socially strong, and well liked, this girl was also moody and "had some real problems." There were good and bad days, and on the bad days she sometimes had thoughts of suicide. In her schoolwork she was reliable and cooperative, and she actively engaged in school functions. She left the region in the spring of her junior year and transferred to a large West Coast school. In this new setting she was considered a better than average student, both scholastically and in terms of school citizenship. While still attending this school she was married and became pregnant. However, she continued her schooling and did graduate with her class.

512. M:15:4	ACE IX, 28; XI, 18	6'458-1'73	3:6:8
B:VI:4	ENG IX, 23; XI, 19	-7'928	5:2:13
	HSR 08		
	SVIB '4-5		

A boy with very little drive and initiative, this youth had a "negative personality; others liked him because there was nothing about him to particularly dislike." He never seemed to find anything that caught his interest. This was, however, supposition, since "he did not share his ideas with others." He was said to be introverted, serious, and difficult to know. When younger he was "ornery but never bad." On occasion in high school he would lose his temper when faced with a difficult task. His teachers said that he tried to get his schoolwork done but that he seemed to have less ability than his aptitude tests would indicate.

Illness forced him to leave school during his senior year. The school faculty and administration went to considerable trouble to make it possible for him to graduate with his class because this seemed to be very important to him. These efforts, as well as the solicitude expressed by his classmates, appeared to leave him unmoved, for he failed to acknowledge their help and expressions of concern.

He went steady with a classmate throughout high school. This affair was thought to have kept them both in school. After graduation they were married. Some persons expressed the belief that neither of them was mature and that they "lacked enough backbone" to establish a good marriage.

The family background was not a desirable one. Most of the children seemed to be at least on the fringe of delinquency. The father died when the boy was young and the stepfather was not a very strong person. The mother was physically thin and not healthy. Her personality was characterized by suspiciousness and ineffectuality. At times she was subject to overt demonstrations of hostility. She apparently tried hard to maintain "cleanliness and social standards," but she lacked the vitality and organization necessary to carry through.

513. M:15:1	ACE IX, none; XI, 99	6'47835-'9	7:3:15
B:III:3	ENG IX, none; XI, 100	'4368-2'	6:2:20
	HSR 99		
	SVIB '4-		

Occupied with many school activities such as chorus, yearbook, student council, and class offices, this boy, although industrious and hard working, often put off tending to details. He was, however, well liked, a fine boy, an excellent student, and a good organizer. A champion of the "underdog," he went out of his way to defend racial minorities and other "causes." After graduation he went to a small college on a scholarship where he majored in mathematics and was active in athletics and other campus affairs. In his second college year he transferred to a military academy to continue his education.

The family had good parent-child relationships. They lived in a middle-class neighborhood where they had somewhat above average income. The father was agreeable, cooperative, and popular with his co-workers. The mother had died early and the stepmother appeared kind and a real mother to the children.

514. F:15:2	ACE IX, none; XI, 84	6'4789–1'	1:6:10
N:III:1	ENG IX, none; XI, 87	'603–'9	0:3:14
	HSR 64		
	SVIB none		

The outstanding characteristic of this girl was that she was overcautious for fear she might be "out of order." She did not dare say anything to anyone and hated to get up in front of the class. If forced to recite, she did so very quietly; she would do almost anything to avoid public appearances. She liked singing and music and was socially accepted in the school's "upper set." The teachers thought of her as cooperative and dependable. Other than her musical interests she had no extracurricular activities. After graduation she married and took a clerical position.

The home and family were "above average." There were no known health or delinquency problems. The father was a small businessman.

515. F:15:1	ACE IX, 48; XI, 52	'648–9'2	3:3:14
N:III:1	ENG IX, 55; XI, 59	'<u>34857 16</u>–	5:1:25
	HSR 61	'<u>487</u>–'59	6:2:24
	SVIB none		

Teachers regarded this girl as "average in all personality traits except leadership, in which she was very low." Although she did not always carry through on the good ideas she might have, she was not a problem in class and was conscientious. She was very well liked by her peers and was considered "sweet." After graduation she attended a teachers' college.

The family appeared to be a good one with no known health or behavior problems. Although the father was somewhat of "the old school," he was an interesting and congenial person. The mother worked outside of the home.

516. M:15:5	ACE IX, 84; XI, 83	6"489'27–'15	0:15:6
N:V:2	ENG IX, none; XI, 92	'435–'02	0:1:20
	HSR 76		
	SVIB 8'4–		

This boy had a "neutral personality; he didn't stand out at all." Physically husky, he was interested in wrestling. At times he seemed mature and confident, but he was not a leader. A little lazy, he needed prodding to do his work. He was interested in music. Generally well behaved, at one time he got into trouble for careless driving. After graduation he went to a junior college.

The father was in business for himself, but was unambitious and a relaxed, "nice" fellow. The mother also worked. She appeared to dominate the family. The parents seemed interested in the boy and were affectionate toward him, but they did not push him to achieve.

517. F:14:2	ACE IX, none; XI, 93	64"89'371–'5	0:6:15
N:V:3	ENG IX, none; XI, 94	'94–5'2	4:3:15
	HSR 94		
	SVIB none		

Though considered "narrow in her religion," this girl was a "terrifically grand person," popular and active in the school. She had a fine sense of humor and was a top student. She wished to take training as a teacher.

The father was a small businessman; the mother a "very devoted teacher." It was described as a "grand family."

518. M:14:2	ACE IX, 74; XI, 76	'649–'7520	3:4:17
N:II:2	ENG IX, none; XI, 68	'524–'9	6:1:16
	HSR 79		
	SVIB 2'1–		

When younger, this boy had been considered "nervous, sensitive, and apt to quarrel." "Short and chunky," he preferred to play with older children. In high school he was not very popular outside of his own small group and was "a kind of know-it-all whose biggest problem was his lack of social activity and leadership ability." The most outstanding fact about his schoolwork was his aptitude in scientific, mechanical, and computational areas. He was very interested in electrical engineering, radio, and other similar activities, these being his sole interests. He was in trouble at one time because he was caught stealing some electrical parts. After graduation he registered at a university, intending to study engineering.

The family situation appeared good in all ways, and both parents had had some college training.

519. M:15:2	ACE IX, 77; XI, 89	'6498–'3	2:6:10
N:III:3	ENG IX, 67; XI, 71	'468 79–	3:4:21
	HSR 69		
	SVIB '8–		

Immaturity was the most prominent characteristic of this boy. He was quiet and intelligent, likable but very shy. His character was impressively good. He was playful in the halls and had a number of friends although none among girls. He was particularly shy with the latter. Although he was somewhat lazy and unmotivated in his studies, he worked hard at his family's place of business. Expecting to go into engineering, he attended a university after graduation.

The parents were described as fine, able leaders. It was a closely knit, stable family, one wanting to do things as a unit.

520. M:15:1	ACE IX, 34; XI, none	'6490-1'	1:12:3
N:V:1	ENG IX, 23; XI, none		
	HSR DO 12th gr.		
	SVIB none		

The counselor said that this boy was "very friendly and aggressive, and he used to come frequently to talk with me." Others described the boy as "an explosive kid and a fast talker who got into troubles because of this." He was "somewhat bitter on a lot of counts." "He had a lot of things bothering him, mostly related to his home and family." There was a repeated description of him as nervous, unhappy, and unstable. It was mentioned that he was one of the few boys who checked the item "considered suicide" on a personality check list. His school record was consistently poor and he often repeated subjects. He wanted to quit school and did so after his junior year. He had hoped to go to a trade school, but instead he joined the Navy.

The father was an alcoholic whose income was low, making it necessary for the mother to work outside the home. The father had also been in some trouble with the law. The parents were incompatible and the mother considered separation from her husband, but he managed to prevent any effective moves, often describing his wife as having "something psychologically wrong with her."

521. F:15:7	ACE IX, 44; XI, 52	6'409873-'52	3:7:11
N:IVB:4	ENG IX, 67; XI, 72	'07-'9	1:3:13
	HSR 55		
	SVIB WR'		

In spite of the fact that this girl was not considered "popular," she was accepted by everyone and was said to have "a million-dollar smile." She did well in her schoolwork, could hold her own, and was never forward. She was not shy, but neither did she "shine." She was unusually fastidious. There was one peculiar incident reported in which she brought some equipment from her home to be used temporarily in a class project. Although this equipment was usable, it was "utterly filthy." The girl was asked to return it to her home, but never did so. This incident attracted attention because of the contrast with her fastidiousness in most other things. While still in school, she worked in a professional office where she was very successful, and it was believed that after graduation she would continue in this position. She married shortly following graduation.

There was a fine relationship among the members of her family, and in general it was described as an acceptable and responsible family. The least personable was the father, who could be quite unfriendly and at times was thought of as "grasping." The mother, who was the dominant one in the family, was the main source of the good reputation that the family had. All the children were said to resemble their mother and to possess her efficiency and homemaking ability. They all tended to marry at an early age.

522. M:14:1	ACE IX, none; XI, 12	'65–2'3	2:16:8X
B:VII:2	ENG IX, none; XI, 03		
	HSR 14		
	SVIB none		

Except for the comment that he was cheerful and good-tempered, few praiseworthy things were said about this boy. He was neither well dressed nor clean. He appeared always to be in a hurry to get things done and was "a careless, sloppy workman." Requiring close supervision, he was "too dumb to know he was making a mistake." He was a slow reader, and his interests were "mechanical." He tended to worry some about his health. He was not a leader among his classmates yet he was talkative and got along reasonably well. It was mentioned that he was "kind of a butt of jokes," but this he took in his stride. In his freshman year he was caught in a minor offense that led to a police warning. Evenings and weekends he worked with his father. After high school graduation he worked in a low-level occupation.

The parents were divorced and the boy lived with the mother and an older sister, although he continued to see his father. The mother worked outside the home.

523. M:14:3	ACE IX, 88; XI, 92	'65–31'2	4:4:9
N:I:4	ENG IX, 92; XI, 95	459'73–'0	1:4:14
	HSR 93	9'457–'026	3:2:16
	SVIB '1–		

Throughout the majority of his high school years this boy was quiet and unable to take criticism; he was generally suspicious and inarticulate. He was "stubborn and materialistic, but a good thinker, serious about everything and unsatisfied except with the best." He seemed to feel superior to women teachers and did not lend himself to general school activities, although he did become a star athlete. In spite of his athletic success he "was no hero." He would sulk when his performance was not perfect. In his last months of high school he began to change markedly. He "threw away his paperback books" and began to read the books that were recommended in English class. He even offered to read parts of the assignment in front of the class, much to the surprise of other students. Although his earlier mercenary feelings did not disappear, he became far less cold and cynical; "he changed from being disagreeable to being warm and responsible." There was a minor episode in which he was questioned by the police, but he was not guilty of any severely delinquent behavior.

The father was a well-known professional man. He was protective of his son so that some of the boy's earlier attitudes were thought to be related to those of his father. The father was "inarticulate and reserved except with his few friends." The mother, talkative and self-centered, was strongly attached to her children. She would always conform to her husband's wishes and then turn to others to share her troubles. The family was not outgoing.

524. F:14:3	ACE IX, 95; XI, 96	'65–'91	4:6:12
N:IVC:5	ENG IX, 91; XI, 74	'4–	10:1:20X
	HSR 77		
	SVIB none		

Although this girl seemed to lack self-confidence and social grace, she was mature in many ways. A country girl who worked hard on her family's farm, she planned to become a missionary. She mixed fairly well with other students. At times she tended to be obstinate: "Sometimes she would do what she was told but she would not do things on her own." She could be "sneaky in some ways to avoid work."

525. M:15:4	ACE IX, none; XI, 93	'6537890–'1	3:5:10
N:II:1	ENG IX, 83; XI, 74	'938–2'0	1:5:13
	HSR 88	9'867–2'0	0:7:16
	SVIB 9'–		

"A well-rounded boy who worked very hard," this youth was considered pleasant, respectful, cooperative, and responsible. His grades improved as he progressed through high school and he "did okay in everything but math," where "he tried but could have worked a little harder." A polite and friendly person, he was liked by fellow students and teachers, although he did not have a wide circle of friends. "He was the kind of boy who would not visit or talk to you until he got to know you quite well." He was a member of a "hot-rod" club which was sponsored by a member of the police department. He seemed to have a sincere interest in automobiles rather than in the less desirable fringe activities sometimes associated with "hot-rod" groups. After graduation he continued his education at a university and was working to earn part of his expenses.

At one time when he was younger, this boy's mother was hospitalized for a serious illness. The father, who was "a very nervous man and under financial pressure," applied to a homemaker's service for help with the children. Two of the boy's younger brothers had minor brushes with the police.

526. F:15:1	ACE IX, 61; XI, 44	'654–	5:3:20
N:II:1	ENG IX, 77; XI, 68	'5–'20	1:0:22
	HSR 46		
	SVIB none		

"Terribly shy and quiet and a dreamer," this girl never responded and her facial expression did not seem to change much at any time. Nevertheless, she was considered "a real nice girl" and other pupils liked her. It was "nice to have her around." She had just enough interest to maintain a C average. She took part in a few extracurricular activities.

527. F:14:3	ACE IX, 32; XI, 03	6'57–'13	3:7:11
N:V:2	ENG IX, 64; XI, 53	'697–15'	3:3:10
	HSR 29		
	SVIB WR'		

This girl, who had a contagious smile, was full of pep, active, and attractive. She was motivated by a great desire to learn and was very cooperative in class. However, she was unassuming, rarely volunteered, and showed no inclination to take a position of leadership. She was relatively inactive in extracurricular affairs, but did take an average interest in church activities. After graduation she went on to a junior college, working part time to help meet the expenses.

The family circumstances and their personalities were average and were not noteworthy in any way.

528. M:16:4	ACE IX, 46; XI, 56	6'5789 21304–	6:11:9
N:V:2	ENG IX, none; XI, 33	3'6785291–	3:5:16
	HSR 82		
	SVIB '–		

Handicapped by poor eyesight, a "reading block, and a lisp at the sixth-grade level," this boy began to improve with special attention from his teachers and changed from a poor achiever to an honor society member. Although unaggressive and a follower without much initiative, he was not weak. Mature and well adjusted, he kept to himself and was rather reserved. Some teachers said, however, that he "mixed well," and he participated in school sports, winning letters. After graduation he registered in a university, where he began training as an engineer. There was some suggestion that he had always felt inferior to his sister, who had not had difficulty in school.

529. M:15:3	ACE IX, 100; XI, 100	6'5780 1249–	3:5:9
N:I:5	ENG IX, 100; XI, 97	74"236'581–	2:4:14
	HSR 100		
	SVIB 1'–58		

The phrase "quite a kid" was applied to this boy, who, in addition to being an outstanding student, was well liked and admired by all. He had the combination of intelligence, common sense, and a good personality. He "appeared to have everything and to do everything well." Far above the others in his class, he was one of the most creative writers that the school had ever had. He was outgoing and active in band, chorus, dramatics, and journalism. After graduation he attended a small sectarian college.

The community respected this family. The father, who was a professional man, was sympathetic and understanding toward education, community, and church. A man with strong prejudices, however, on occasion he could be stubborn, vindictive, and dictatorial. The mother was highly educated, musical, charming, and gracious. The parents were strict but fair with their children, who responded by respecting them and by being excellent school and community citizens.

530. M:15:1   ACE IX, none; XI, 14   '650–'37   1:6:9
     N:V:1   ENG IX, none; XI, 03
                     HSR 11
                     SVIB '–

One teacher predicted delinquency for this boy, and the prediction was correct. He was indifferent toward school and his ability was low. Guilty of at least petty larceny, he was also suspended from school for hitting a classmate. Outside of school he associated with "a tough bunch of hoods."

531. F:15:8   ACE IX, none; XI, 05   '6509–'437   8:9:10
     N:VII:1   ENG IX, none; XI, 03
                     HSR 07
                     SVIB none

This girl was slow but even-tempered, well mannered, and had a good sense of humor. She was referred to as a "solid citizen." In her schoolwork she was generally cooperative and dependable. However, she was a follower and found school very difficult. Her emotional adjustment seemed satisfactory, and she was friendly and considerate of others.

532. F:15:2   ACE IX, 48; XI, 78   '67–'1   5:4:13
     N:I:1   ENG IX, none; XI, 74
                     HSR 80
                     SVIB '–

In her early high school years this girl was only interested in getting married and she expected to drop out of school at any time. As she continued she changed her mind, and in her senior year she had hopes of going on to college. She took part in few activities and had a poor school attendance record. The teachers considered her above average in reliability and cooperation.

533. M:14:1 ACE IX, 84; XI, 95 '6724 59–'01 2:4:14
    N:III:2 ENG IX, 81; XI, 50 9'65–2'10 1:4:12
               HSR 49
               SVIB 45'–

"Not scholastically outstanding," this boy "made up for it with his social graces." He was popular, a good athlete, and a leader. The teachers considered him dependable, cooperative, and "an average personality who stayed in line well." In one grade he did have trouble because he "clashed" with a teacher. Following high school he entered a small college.

Both parents seemed concerned about the boy's grades and other achievements. They were described in laudatory terms, and both were rather active in civic and church affairs. Because of ill health the father was partially retired and the mother ran their business. The boy had a close relationship with his father.

534. F:14:1 ACE IX, 84; XI, 95 6'7280 43– 3:10:7
    N:V:3 ENG IX, 90; XI, 84
               HSR 69
               SVIB '–

This active, hard-working girl was considered an extrovert. She was pleasant and met people easily. Particular emphasis was given to the fact that she was ambitious, in addition to being well balanced, creative, and poised.

535. F:14:7 ACE IX, 67; XI, 68 '673948–5' 3:5:14
    N:V:3 ENG IX, 77; XI, 78 '6–85'94 4:3:14
               HSR 49
               SVIB none

This girl's school attendance was poor and she was described as an underachiever, although she apparently did well in some subjects. She wanted "just to get by" in school and needed occasional prodding. She had a job outside of school and did very well in it. This position required her to meet people and capitalized upon the fact that she had a nice personality and many friends. One person described her as "the happy-go-lucky type."

536. M:14:1 ACE IX, none; XI, 91 '6758–2'9 4:2:17
    N:I:3 ENG IX, none; XI, 82
               HSR 92
               SVIB none

Quiet and reserved as a ninth-grader, this boy became more friendly as he approached his senior year, developing a fine personality. He was a good student, and by the time he finished high school he had engaged in many extracurricular activities. Throughout high school he participated in athletics, although he never quite made a varsity team. His hobby was photography and he became quite good at it. He expected to continue in either photography or science after graduation.

537. M:13:3   ACE IX, 84; XI, 81   '675834–'1   3:5:14
     N:IVB:5   ENG IX, 80; XI, 72   67'4502831–'9   3:2:15
                HSR 98
                SVIB 4'2–90

As a freshman this boy was quiet, reserved, withdrawn, and hard working. By the time he was a senior he "had broken out of his shell"; he belonged to many groups and was well adjusted.

538. M:16:4   ACE IX, none; XI, 14   6'782341–   10:8:19X
     N:III:3   ENG IX, none; XI, 02   '672 84 31–   6:4:20
                HSR 48
                SVIB 24'1–5

This listless boy was careless of his personal appearance. His teachers wondered if he got proper food and rest at home. He "puttered" when he worked and he was not careful of details. His companions were considered undesirable. He did not, however, get into any known trouble. He was proud of his mother, who was a capable person with artistic interests. He himself had no interest in anything except photography, at which hobby he was a hard worker.

The father was a quiet, hard-working man. The mother, although creative and artistic, was not a good housekeeper. Some of her behavior and ideas were a little unconventional.

539. F:15:6   ACE IX, 34; XI, 37   6'7894–   7:3:17
     N:IVA:3   ENG IX, 22; XI, 30   '4653–   5:0:21
                HSR 15
                SVIB WR'

Described by her minister as "winsome," this girl was quiet and retiring. One person said that she had a "blank" personality. A point was made of the fact that she was "innocent." In school she was reliable, cooperative, and helpful although relatively inactive. She sometimes "carried a chip on her shoulder," a trait that may have been related to the fact that she was sensitive because her mother was mentally ill and because she herself had low ability and was conscious of her low achievement.

The home situation was described as "good." The parents were reliable people who pushed themselves hard and expected the children to "do anything."

The father was called "trouble prone" and was an alcoholic problem. He was a superior farmer but was retiring and inarticulate in social relationships. The mother, who was very nervous and eccentric, had received occasional psychiatric treatment. She was a hard worker.

540. F:14:1	ACE IX, 50; XI, 65	'67042–'95	6:1:17
N:V:1	ENG IX, 86; XI, 74	'062–5'1	4:2:14
	HSR 89		
	SVIB none		

One teacher said of this girl that "she really thirsts for knowledge and is not satisfied to know without understanding." She was too serious and could not relax or smile. Quite mature and realistic, she was not one of a school crowd, but she was frequently described as being "a real nice girl." Although she was shy, she was poised and interested in everything. She was president of a girls' sorority in high school and was interested in dramatics and music. It was mentioned that she "had the attitude that society does not do enough for the poor" and showed sincere concern for the underprivileged. After graduation this girl went on to attend a university.

The parents were first-generation Americans and spoke with an obviously foreign accent. The father was a skilled worker.

541. M:15:2	ACE IX, none; XI, 92	6'70854–	3:5:10
N:V:3	ENG IX, none; XI, 53	'879 23–0'	3:3:24
	HSR none		
	SVIB 4'–0		

This boy was a fairly hard worker, although he was careless and sloppy about his work. He posed no conduct problem and appeared to like school; however, he engaged in few school activities. He had an average number of friends. He liked automobiles and got into some difficulty because he was "wild with a car." This difficulty did not result in any official police record.

542. F:15:3	ACE IX, 05; XI, 33	'68245 79–'1	4:10:13
N:V:2	ENG IX, none; XI, 19	9'68 7452–'3	6:9:11
	HSR 03		
	SVIB '–		

This was a neat, cooperative, and sensitive girl of low mental ability. Average in appearance, she was a "nice child" who was quiet, pleasant, and accepted by other students. She had poor vision. Her school attendance was excellent, although she was a D student and ultimately ranked at the bottom of a large graduating class. In spite of the fact that her strongest interest was in home economics, she occasionally failed even this course. She did manage to graduate from high school and soon married a "responsible, mature fellow." The couple built their own home before they married.

The girl's father was a quiet but adequate person. The mother had a chronic physical illness which limited her activities. The relationship between the girl and her parents was considered to be a good one.

543. F:14:1   ACE IX, 63; XI, 78   6'837–'25   5:7:19
     N:VII:1   ENG IX, none; XI, 87
                   HSR 65
                   SVIB '–

A rather dramatic change in attitudes and behavior occurring near the middle of her high school career was reported of this "very pretty girl." She was described as being "a little devil" during the ninth and tenth grades. She was caught skipping school, and she associated with a tough bunch of girls who "ran around a lot nights." Quite "the gal about town, she began to use too much makeup and look kind of cheap." During her last two years of school she was said to have been a "nice girl with a pleasant personality." She became "quiet, sincere, and desirous to improve." She was well behaved in study hall, reliable, and conscientious to the point that she was considered to be somewhat of an overachiever. She began to associate with a new group of friends, who were a stabilizing influence. She showed considerable ambition, working at part-time jobs whenever she had the opportunity. She became very religious, and by her senior year religion had become the center of her life; she even considered entering mission work. Her schoolwork, like her general behavior, seemed to be responsive to emotional stresses resulting from relationships with her boy friend and with her family.

The girl's parents moved to this community when she was in the ninth grade. She had been going with a boy in her former home town and for a time she returned to visit this boy. Later she became very much involved with another boy who shared her religious interests. After graduation they married and entered a college where they both took religious training.

The father, an alcoholic, was frequently in trouble because of irresponsible acts. He was particularly unreliable in his treatment of the children, sometimes involving them emotionally in his irresponsible behavior. It was said that he had been earlier a more steady person but that he had been unable to adjust to the move from farm to city. The mother, a college graduate, was strongly opposed to the use of alcohol. When the girl was still in high school the family broke up and the girl remained with her mother.

544. F:14:2   ACE IX, 26; XI, 33   6'8374 021–5'   5:5:15
     N:III:1   ENG IX, none; XI, 17
                   HSR 42
                   SVIB none

The school had a difficult time with this girl when she was a tenth-grader. She habitually skipped school; she was a problem to discipline and resented any corrective measures that were attempted. This phase passed after the tenth grade and she became just about "perfect," carrying out the demands of school in a quiet, pleasant manner. An attractive and popular girl, she associated with a group of girls who maintained a pretty fast social pace. They seemed to be involved in a continuous round of parties or plans for activities that kept them on the go. It was said that she was "boy crazy" and had a way with boys. During the latter part of her high school career she showed considerable concern for a seriously maladjusted younger sister who was receiving psychiatric care. A minor traffic violation was on record against her: she had permitted a boy friend, an unlicensed driver, to use the family car and he was involved in an accident. The girl entered a university after completing high school, but at last reports was preparing to marry.

The family had a fairly high income and lived in a good neighborhood. Reportedly there was marital discord between the parents. The father took no part in school conferences relating to his daughter's early difficulties. The mother was said to have worked hard to keep her family together and to have set high standards for them; but she was "neurotic, full of excuses, and not too cooperative."

545. M:15:0   ACE IX, 70; XI, 73   68′4713952–   0:6:19
     B:VII:2   ENG IX, 68; XI, 54   ′42–1′3   1:2:11
                HSR 42
                SVIB 4′–

"A capable, friendly, and well-adjusted kid," this boy was a good student. School reports revealed he was cooperative and well behaved but that he did need occasional prodding. Just before his senior year he got into trouble over a traffic violation and was warned. He was later involved in a gang fight and was again warned after being charged with disorderly conduct. After graduation he went on to attend a small college.

The boy lived with his mother and there was doubt about the paternity. The mother used her maiden name, but the boy used the name of the man assumed to be his father. This man permitted the boy to visit him but always refused to enter into any agreement that would establish the paternity. The putative father was not a very stable person and had difficulty with alcoholism. The mother was more stable but suffered from guilt over her earlier behavior.

546. F:14:2   ACE IX, 34; XI, 41   6′″″84′″″7″239′01–   2:21:7X
     N:III:2   ENG IX, none; XI, 56   9′847–20′1   2:5:11
                HSR 40
                SVIB ′–

The words "undependable," "sneaky," and "untrustworthy" were repeatedly applied to this girl. She seemed insecure socially, wanting to be with the best crowd but never accepted by them. There was nothing she would not do to get what she wanted, including the use of underhanded methods. When she was caught at cheating or lying, she was brazen. She often felt everyone was against her and she seemed sorry for herself. She was "emotional" and easily depressed or elated. When depressed she acted "crabby." She was absent from school often, complaining of ill health. Rather attractive in appearance, she was a little boy crazy, but the boys did not like her.

547. M:14:3   ACE IX, 52; XI, 24   6'849–'25   3:5:18
     N:V:2   ENG IX, none; XI, 06
                      HSR 08 DO 12th gr.
                      SVIB none

School authorities thought of this boy as "a problem kid; always mischievous, into everything, always doing something out of order, always making trouble." It was said that he was bright enough but that he was uninterested and indifferent toward his schoolwork. He finally dropped out of school during his senior year. The school attributed his difficulties to the fact that he was easily led and "got in with bad company," that he had a "desperate need for attention," causing him to be "very active and always doing something."

During his high school years the boy had been in considerable trouble. Offenses ranged from traffic violations to burglary, for which he was placed on probation along with one of his classmates. His probation officer described him as an immature boy, but, nevertheless, one with a good prognosis.

The parents accepted responsibility for the misdeeds of their son and made no alibis. The family had an above average income, with both parents working. Both were interested in their children.

548. M:14:3   ACE IX, 34; XI, 28   6'8490–'53   7:16:8X
     N:VII:2   ENG IX, none; XI, 04   0'84216–5'3   10:3:20X
                      HSR 04
                      SVIB none

This boy was childish and immature — "a lone wolf who seemed to be against anyone and everything." Sullen, stubborn, and truculent in personality, he had no desire to achieve and was a continual problem in the school. He would become very frustrated and one could see him holding in his rage. At such times he became withdrawn, not answering, and was uncooperative in every way. At other times he was a malicious show-off. He did everything he could to stir people up. Apparently his worst behavior occurred in connection with school. He had a police record of minor offenses. After graduating from school he enlisted in the Navy.

The father was an alcoholic and in constant conflict with the boy. The parents were divorced while the boy was in high school; the father had threatened the mother with physical harm. The boy lived with his mother after the divorce. She was neurotic and cried in response to problems. She was overprotective of the boy, and her own reputation was not good.

549. F:14:3   ACE IX, 21; XI, 47   6'854709–'3   3:14:4
     N:IVC:5   ENG IX, 24; XI, 38
                     HSR 37
                     SVIB none

A little on the defensive in her sophomore year, this girl seemed to lose this defensiveness in her later high school years. She was pleasant and nice in appearance. A hard worker, she got average grades and "after beginning a thing, she would take the initiative."

550. M:14:8   ACE IX, 84; XI, 84   685'9740–   3:11:10
     N:IVA:5   ENG IX, 42; XI, 40   '896345–   4:4:16
                     HSR 55
                     SVIB '2–5

Admired by students and teachers, this boy was socially well adjusted and was courteous and respectful to all. He was "outspoken but never impetuous." As a student he was a steady and cooperative worker, but he was considered "a good thinker and a good leader." He did not engage in any sports, nor was he outstandingly active in other extracurricular affairs. He was very active in the Future Farmers of America movement, but after graduation he enrolled in a small college with the hope of becoming an engineer.

The home was considered "splendid." There was a strong religious influence and regular family and church devotions. The father was considered somewhat stubborn and resistant to learning new ways of farming. His erratic discipline of the children was believed to be a hindrance to the development of the boy. In spite of these somewhat critical observations, he was a very respected man and a leader in the community. The mother was "one of the finest." Although a worrier, she "depended upon faith to see things through."

551. F:15:2   ACE IX, none; XI, 77   '68740–'1   2:5:15
     N:II:2   ENG IX, none; XI, 92
                     HSR 94
                     SVIB WR'

A desire to do "perfectly in everything and to know what's going on" was the primary characteristic of this girl. She was a responsible, fine person, quite independent, and very active in the school. After graduation she hoped to take training as a teacher.

552. F:16:0   IQ (centile) 17   68'94753–   7:16:11X
    N:III:1   HSR DO 10th gr.
                SVIB none

Although this girl was rather friendly and cheerful and had some friends, she was certainly not popular. Her school grades were poor to failing and she seemed uninterested in school or any of its activities. Her only interests were in sports and art. Her school difficulties mounted until she dropped out in the tenth grade. The best that was said of her was that she could be very helpful if she was asked to do anything.

553. M:15:4   ACE IX, 21; XI, 21   68'9740–'1   3:13:8
    N:IVB:4   ENG IX, 01; XI, 02   '489–'02   4:6:15
                HSR 04
                SVIB '4–

This boy was "mean on the playground, a bully, erratic, and loud." He had a low tolerance for frustration. When thwarted in his attempt to dominate situations, he would lose his temper. He "matured early and has not developed since." He could be "very obnoxious" and he "had a mean facial expression which indicated that he might take a poke at you." These traits were more apparent when he was with other students than when he was with adults. The boy did enter into some church activities and, with his family, attended church regularly. He was neat in appearance. He was capable of doing practical, mechanical work. During his high school years he gradually improved and was expecting to marry a "nice girl." However, after graduation he broke up with this girl and took a job as a clerk.

The family was a relatively wealthy one in the community and both parents were praiseworthy. They seemed to be stable and interested in their children. The children, however, appeared "unstable, slow mentally, and inferior in their feelings."

554. F:14:0   ACE IX, 50; XI, 18   68'9027–   5:10:11
    N:VI:2   ENG IX, none; XI, 55   '398–'2   8:4:21
                HSR 75
                SVIB WR'

"A peach," this girl had a pleasant, outgoing personality. "Kids loved her" and she was "the life of the party." Although not a leader, she was active in many things. She was a serious and hard-working student, and was considered an overachiever. It was mentioned that this girl was "sickly and always taking pills for anemia." She was active in church work and had a part-time job in an office during her school years. She was talented musically and a good office worker. After graduation she decided to enter college — a decision that reflected her father's wishes.

The parents were active socially. The mother was possibly a somewhat stronger person than the father.

555. M:15:8	ACE IX, 34; XI, 52	68'0794–'5	1:6:10
N:IVC:4	ENG IX, 27; XI, 58	'09–4'2<u>13</u>	2:6:12
	HSR 27		
	SVIB 4'8–		

This boy was well liked, "not outgoing, but friendly." He was emotionally well balanced and seemed unembarrassed by the fact that his father was mentally ill. His schoolwork was average and he actively participated in school affairs. All his fellow students liked him. He married after graduation and continued his education at a small college.

The family was socially isolated, although the mother was a "very nice, hospitable woman." The father was frequently hospitalized because of mental illness. The mother seemed to lack the stability and force to guide the family adequately. The children appeared to lack training and to have poor ability to plan, although they were generally polite, cooperative, and pleasant.

556. M:15:2	ACE IX, none; XI, 71	'69–<u>02</u>'7	6:4:19
N:III:1	ENG IX, none; XI, 54		
	HSR 46		
	SVIB 4'–		

A record of a few truancies, "a few scrapes," and occasional periods when he would not work in class got this boy into slight trouble with some teachers. In general, he had an excellent personality, was well liked, and was an average student. He was "a real fine athlete."

557. M:16:1	IQ (centile) 15	6'94–2'13	4:5:10
N:VI:3	HSR DO 9th gr.		
	SVIB none		

"Vulgar, coarse, and indecent," this boy was "a hot-rodder who wore the typical leather jacket and boots." He kept poor company, being a follower rather than a leader in this group. One person called him shy and retiring. Until he dropped out of school in the ninth grade he was a poor student and a careless worker who showed no interest and prepared no assignments. He apparently caused no trouble in school, however.

558. F:14:1	ACE IX, 99; XI, 92	'6947–<u>5</u>'2	2:8:9
N:V:1	ENG IX, 98; XI, 72	'94<u>36</u>–<u>20</u>'7	5:2:16
	HSR 55		
	SVIB none		

"Reaction-wise, this girl seemed older than the other students" and dated older boys while in high school. She tended to remain aloof from school activities except for a girls' small social group, in which she held an elective office. Frank and straightforward in manner, she quite openly stated, for example, that she hoped to enter a college where none of her present classmates would be in attendance. One teacher described her as "boy crazy — a girl who had good ability but did not use it because she was too much of a daydreamer." However, it was also said that she was "quite realistic." She attended, but was not active in, a church other than that of her parents. Her driver's license was suspended at one time for a speeding offense. She attended a small liberal arts college after graduation.

559. M:14:1	ACE IX, none; XI, 21	69'4782–	6:10:14
N:VI:1	ENG IX, none; XI, 18	9'846–5'	7:6:17
	HSR 64		
	SVIB none		

This boy "never stood out, and did nothing terrific." He engaged in no school activities, although he did work outside of school. He was not a conduct problem. He hoped to go into a trade after his graduation. His interests definitely did not emphasize schoolwork, although test data seem to indicate that he was overachieving.

560. F:14:2	ACE IX, none; XI, 49	'695–'137	3:4:11
B:VI:3	ENG IX, none; XI, 51		
	HSR 31 DO 11th gr.		
	SVIB none		

One teacher predicted that this girl would have legal difficulties later in her school years, although there was no evidence that this prediction came true. However, she did drop out of school for an unknown reason near the end of her junior year. She was an average student with good ability to write and speak, but as she went through high school she "slipped." It was said of her that she was "rather forward and had to be kept at a distance or she would get too familiar."

This girl was living with a relative because her home was a broken one.

561. M:14:1	ACE IX, 11; XI, 47	69'7345–'2	3:9:11
N:IVB:7	ENG IX, 09; XI, 05		
	HSR 11		
	SVIB '8–		

Some of the descriptions of this boy reflect good qualities. He had a fine sense of humor, was personable, and possessed "unlimited physical resources." His manner was kind and friendly, and he was interested in others; he seemed to appreciate favors. "He meant well." In activities he was "a big wheel" and followed right after the leader. "A real ladies' man and heartbreaker," he was called. When he was in the fourth or fifth grade he had a nervous breakdown with "jerking and twitching," for which he received psychiatric care. He remained easily excitable through the years and always found it hard to accept new situations. He talked too much and was "high-strung." During his high school years he got into repeated difficulty for reckless driving and irresponsible behavior. Warnings did not seem to deter him from repeating these acts.

Much of the time the boy lived with his grandparents. The mother and grandmother were said to be dominant in the home. All members of the family were said to be high-strung, easily excited persons who "would scream to get results."

562. F:15:2	ACE IX, 23; XI, 11	6″9′784–5′0	3:5:15
N:V:1	ENG IX, 72; XI, 68		
	HSR 78		
	SVIB none		

This girl matured physically and socially at an early age. As a result, older boys tended to become familiar with her, and, as their advances became more obvious, she reported them to school officials. She seemed to be upset and confused over these advances. As she continued in school, she was very popular, showed good development, and was well adjusted. Active in extracurricular activities, she hoped to become a nurse. She had a steady boy friend who wanted to go to a professional school. After graduation she got a full-time position as a receptionist and secretary.

563. F:14:0	ACE IX, 54; XI, 65	'6970–'3425	4:5:10
N:V:4	ENG IX, 79; XI, 70	'7806 29–'5	0:4:16
	HSR 72		
	SVIB '–		

The first contacts her teachers had with this girl when she was a freshman resulted in descriptions of her as "cold, unresponsive, and indifferent." However, she changed, and by her senior year she was extremely poised, self-confident, and "happily adjusted to growing up," although it was still claimed that she "suffered pangs of immaturity." A possible factor in the change was that she had a steady boy friend with whom she was exceedingly close and on whom she depended to aid her in overcoming her feeling of insecurity. She was "lovely looking, nice-mannered, and perfectly groomed." She was credited with having greatly helped the internal adjustment of her family so that there was less quarreling and unpleasantness. After graduation she went to a small college and subsequently announced her engagement to the boy.

The father was apparently a fairly adequate man, engrossed in his business. He was "charming and outgoing." He was very much criticized by his wife, who in public could be "excellent company, gracious and fun." However, in more restricted company she was highly critical of everyone, including her husband, and loud in her statements of how much she had done for others. "She complained without thought or reason." She "doted on her daughter" and "mourned the day her daughter would go away to school." On the other hand, she encouraged her daughter to go with one boy before she had an opportunity to go out with other boys.

564. M:15:1   ACE IX, 98; XI, 95   '6984–25'3   3:7:12
     N:III:5   ENG IX, 87; XI, 83   '84796 53–'0   2:2:22
             HSR 82
             SVIB 12'–

This boy was "small, dark, handsome, and vivacious." He once exchanged impertinent words with a teacher and was disciplined for it. He accepted criticism well enough; in fact, other boys thought of him as an "apple polisher." His classmates were antagonistic toward him, feeling that he was egotistical and that he "put himself on a higher plane, thinking he had more maturity than he really did." He had "an excellent opinion of himself and flaunted his money and possessions." He was never popular; however, he could show great charm, poise, and a good sense of humor. In spite of the fact that he accepted criticism, he was stubborn and did not try to understand others. He was an excellent musician. After graduation he went into the armed services, where he was known as a "lone wolf." After his discharge he continued his education at a small university.

The father was also described as egotistical and opinionated, although he was a steady person and a relatively successful small businessman. He felt his children "could do no wrong because they were his." The mother was a "petite, attractive dynamo who did everything well." She was sociable and always busy. It was suggested that she probably encouraged the boy to "show off."

565. F:15:3   ACE IX, none; XI, 14   '6985–'231   3:6:9
     B:III:3   ENG IX, none; XI, 35
             HSR 39 DO 11th gr.
             SVIB none

Described as "a rather brassy blonde with a mannish haircut," this girl was considered a "toughy" by other students. She wore boy's blue jeans and rode a motorcycle about town. During the eleventh grade she became pregnant and was forced to drop out of school to get married.

The girl's mother died when the girl was young and the father, a "good, steady man," continued to care for the children as well as he could. His main concern about the children was that they become self-supporting. This girl was thought to have been left "pretty much to her own devices."

566. F:14:3   ACE IX, 32; XI, 59   6'9078–2'13   0:5:8
     N:IVA:4   ENG IX, 58; XI, 77   '46–1'59   3:5:11
             HSR 60
             SVIB WR'

A good student but quiet in class, this girl appeared to lack self-confidence. One person felt this lack might be better called social reserve. Described as "loyal to her own rural group," she was considered an "average, nice girl who was liked by many." After graduation she went to a larger city to work as a secretary.

The reputation of the family in the community was good; however, the father was considered "penurious, domineering, and strict." He "kept the children under his thumb and watched them too closely, and they appeared to be carrying a load on their shoulders." The girl seemed to resent this discipline less than the other children. The mother was a more stable person, a good manager, and a "gracious farm wife." It was doubted that she had enough influence over the children.

567. F:15:1	ACE IX, 94; XI, 99	'60–85'1973	3:1:7
N:I:1	ENG IX, none; XI, 99	96'8047–51'23	0:4:9
	HSR 68		
	SVIB none		

Very conscious of the fact that she was obviously overweight, this girl may have felt inferior, and she seemed to seek out companions who were also large. She had a quick, sharp temper and could say bitter, satirical things, sometimes being a disruptive influence. In spite of this trait, she was well accepted and generally thought of as "friendly, happy, and cheerful." The teachers regarded her as an underachiever, although she was active, reliable, and cooperative in her school-work. She hoped to continue to some sort of teachers' or nurses' training, and after high school went on to college. One person commented that if she married, she was the type who would "give her husband a rough time."

The parents expected a good deal from their children. The father, although a professional man, did not practice in his field. He was thought of as "vicious and negative." The mother worked in an administrative position and was regarded as the dominant person in the family. Both she and the father were considered very intelligent.

568. M:14:3	ACE IX, 50; XI, 68	'60–'91384	6:2:13
B:IVB:4	ENG IX, 58; XI, 71	'65–9'	6:2:18
	HSR 60		
	SVIB 4'–		

When this boy was in the eighth grade his mother died and he was lonely afterward. As a result he "never wished to be a bachelor." While he was still in high school his father also died. The boy seemed to adjust well to this added problem. He was a "big blond boy" who spoke with a strong Scandinavian accent and was affectionately teased for this. He had a fine sense of humor and was, in a quiet way, a leader in school and church activities. He was a good athlete and was chosen co-captain of one of the school teams. Although he was mature and poised in many ways, he was particularly shy around girls and would "get so upset around them that he broke out in eczema." He was especially mentioned for his high moral standards and his good acceptance of responsibility.

The family lived on a farm and the boy and his brother continued farming after the death of their parents. The parents had been very "worthwhile people."

569. F:15:0	ACE IX, 30; XI, 40	6'0<u>2874</u>–'9	5:8:8
N:VI:3	ENG IX, 50; XI, 65	0'<u>74</u> <u>286</u>–	5:8:13
	HSR 71		
	SVIB WR'		

This girl was so quiet that she was unknown to the counselor and was generally considered inarticulate and hard to know. One person claimed she had "a very fine personality," but she never exhibited animation or intense interest. Although moderately active in church, she engaged in only a few school activities. She never exerted herself or took a leader's role. During high school she thought she wanted to be a religious worker. After graduation she went into teachers' training, but became homesick and abandoned it to return home.

The family was considered a stable one and they did many things together. The father was a semiskilled workman and the mother was very active in church affairs. The minister thought that perhaps because of the mother's very outgoing personality, she was dominant in the home and was more responsible than the father for the girl's somewhat suppressed behavior.

570. F:14:2	ACE IX, 08; XI, 25	'605–1'<u>2379</u>	4:6:6
N:IVB:3	ENG IX, 24; XI, 42	'0546–'<u>2719</u>	0:6:10
	HSR 18		
	SVIB WR'		

This girl was "a bundle of energy with her own crowd and with those she trusted; she would joke and tease with this group but would withdraw from others." In general she was cooperative, pleasant, helpful, considerate, and reliable. In the classroom she was extremely quiet and well behaved but was not a leader. She worked very hard, although she had no special achievements. She was further characterized as "a small kid" and "a poor little girl."

The home was dilapidated and unkempt. The parents, although nice, were slow and somewhat eccentric.

571. M:14:1	ACE IX, none; XI, 69	'6075–'19	3:5:10
N:III:3	ENG IX, none; XI, 70	'085–'<u>49</u>	1:3:17
	HSR 80		
	SVIB none		

Although this boy was very small in stature, his size was thought not to be a handicap to him. He was interested in school activities and was a fairly good student. His main interests were in music. Pleasant and courteous, he was "a nice boy," but he "might pull something if not watched."

572. M:15:6   ACE IX, none; XI, 73   '6085–1'<u>39</u>   1:11:7
    B:IVB:1   ENG IX, none; XI, 28   '0<u>78</u>–'<u>139</u>   1:1:15
             HSR 35
             SVIB none

"In spite of the family background, this boy did well." He made a good adjustment in school and was not a conduct problem. He engaged in most school activities, including some athletics, and he was socially well adjusted. He had a slight speech impediment and a few students thought of him as a sissy. "He was interested more in esthetic things."

The home situation was called "unusual," in that his mother was dead and he lived with a great aunt and uncle.

573. F:14:3   ACE IX, 38; XI, 41   '6087–'3   2:3:15
    N:V:3   ENG IX, 88; XI, 77
             HSR 86
             SVIB WR'

This girl was anxious to succeed and did well in school, although she lacked initiative and spark. She was shy and "could get emotional," and one person said that she needed help in growing up.

574. M:14:8   ACE IX, 59; XI, 52   6'0<u>87</u> <u>94</u>–'31   5:7:13
    N:III:5   ENG IX, 18; XI, 17   74'80<u>965</u>–   4:4:15
             HSR 26 DO 12th gr.
             SVIB none

Physically small and not very neat, this boy was quiet and yet gave the impression of having a chip on his shoulder. He was hot-tempered, was said to have "a persecution complex," liked to "let people know he was around," and was antagonistic, yet he did not get into real trouble. Although he was considered lazy in school, there was a report that he worked very hard at home. He skipped school often and resisted discipline. Described as "a loner," he had few friends. During his senior year he dropped out of school to join the armed forces.

The family caused the school much trouble, for all the children seemed to have difficulties. The children claimed that their father was a college graduate. Vocationally he was a skilled workman who was "slovenly and often needed a shave." He was further described as a passive individual, disinclined to discipline his children. The mother, a hard-working woman, assumed a man's role to support the family. She "ran the show." Even when they were wrong, she defended the children, and her personality seemed to dominate their behavior.

575. M:14:2 ACE IX, 21; XI, 25 '6094 825– 4:7:11
     N:IVC:4 ENG IX, 10; XI, 22 486'312 075– 6:7:20
              HSR 44
              SVIB 4'–50

Saying "I ain't got no problems," this boy refused treatment for a bad lisp which was a real handicap to him. He was described as opinionated, narrow in concepts, and self-sufficient in his personal life. "He knew what he was going to do and would not be told." These qualities made it difficult for him to participate in group activities. He was accepted by one small "farm group." He took no active part in school, and whenever a teacher visited his home, he would absent himself and never enter into the discussion. He assumed no responsibilities and was undependable and inarticulate. At least one person described him as "having a very sharp mind which showed up in written tests only. He could have been a fine scientist." After graduation he worked on his father's farm.

The family lived in considerable social isolation and were "personally untidy." The children wore the same clothes to school that they wore to do chores. One person said of the children as a group that they were "honest, dull, and serious." The father did not want interference with his ways of doing things and tended to stick to the old methods of farming, claiming, "No city feller can tell me how to farm." Apparently the father was dominant in the family, which was organized in a patriarchal pattern.

576. F:14:2 ACE IX, 87; XI, 84 6'0985–1'34 2:8:6
     N:VI:2 ENG IX, 87; XI, 93 '59 687– 1:5:15
             HSR 66
             SVIB WR'

This very pretty, wholesome girl had a great deal of energy and was pleasant and well liked. Although she had quite a few friends, she was also described as being "on the quiet side." One person described her as "a very fine salesman." She was "socially inclined," and appeared in local talent shows in which she played a musical instrument. After finishing high school she continued on to take professional training.

The family appeared to be without any particular deviant or outstanding characteristics. On the whole it was a good, solid family. The girl's brother was considered very nervous: "he just shakes" and was retarded in school.

577. F:14:3 ACE IX, 90; XI, 85 '7–1'4932 3:2:12
     B:II:1 ENG IX, 96; XI, 95 '78–'1 4:5:17
             HSR 65
             SVIB none

Although she did many things very well, it was agreed that this girl could do things better than she did. She was overly interested in sex and boy friends, and she was moody and subject to extreme ups and downs. She "had bothersome traits which probably only served to hinder her; she would please when convenient." Her judgment was considered to be immature, and at times she would try to attract attention by smoking where she should not or other such behavior. She liked to talk rather than to listen and was outspoken. Although she was more often against than for things, she was easily led. In spite of these somewhat undesirable traits she was considered very likable. Her parents were divorced during her early high school years and she was openly ashamed and troubled about this. After graduation she went to a small university.

The father was also described as immature, with little interest in family life. He was, however, a steady worker and he had a good income. The mother, an attractive woman, was a social climber and considered herself exotic. The parents had not been speaking to one another for a year or so before the divorce, and the mother's actions in the affair were somewhat childish. Both parents were considered to be nice persons in spite of their marital difficulties.

578. F:15:6	ACE IX, 16; XI, 68	'7-1'5<u>3</u>89	3:3:13
N:V:2	ENG IX, none; XI, 82		
	HSR DO 11th gr.		
	SVIB none		

This girl was large for her age and she was careless in her dress. In manner she was self-conscious and withdrawn. In the classroom she "just filled a seat." She seemed to realize she was a poor student, but she made no effort to improve. It was possible that she was lazy or a daydreamer. She dropped out of school in her junior year and was married soon afterward.

579. M:15:4	ACE IX, 48; XI, 73	'7-'2<u>16</u>	1:3:9
N:V:3	ENG IX, 57; XI, 71	'5-1<u>486</u>'3	5:3:6
	HSR 46		
	SVIB '4–		

This boy was tall and strong; he tried athletics but was awkward and not very successful. He was neat and well dressed. Although highly ambitious, he seemed unable to work hard and did not strive to realize his ambitions. He was an "absent-minded character" who frequently complained and found excuses to avoid schoolwork; however, he was well liked and had some leadership ability. Teachers considered him to be potentially a good citizen. He had a "wonderful singing voice." Very interested in girls, he went with one steadily in his senior year. A teacher on one occasion tried to advise him against such steady dating and "he blew up." He "had the car bug" and got into minor trouble because of traffic offenses. After graduation it was believed that he went to work with his father.

The father was a cheerful small businessman who was well accepted by the community. The mother was similarly personable and active. It was a closely knit, highly respected family.

580. F:14:3	ACE IX, 100; XI, 98	'7-<u>21</u>'60	2:2:15
N:I:2	ENG IX, 100; XI, 98	-24'<u>671</u>	2:1:15
	HSR 99		
	SVIB 'WR		

With an abundance of maturity, sophistication, and poise, this girl was an outstanding student, an aggressive leader, and a "fine club worker." She had an inquiring mind and a variety of interests, and she was in many activities. A National Honor Society student, she received a scholarship to a small university where she majored in business and languages.

The father was a man of very strong moral beliefs who was at one time forced to resign from his job because he would not yield to political pressures. He was well educated and competent. The mother was attractive and pleasant. It was a close-knit family that worked together, and the children were well disciplined.

581. M:14:6	ACE IX, 50; XI, 33	'7-<u>25</u>'69	3:6:16
N:IVB:5	ENG IX, 33; XI, 30		
	HSR 41		
	SVIB none		

This boy was his mother's pet and "she backed him up." He tended to be spoiled and a little resentful of rules and regulations, although he caused no great trouble in school. His general attitude toward school was not good and he was considered an underachiever. His only activity was in the Future Farmers of America. His sisters who had preceded him in school had achieved outstanding academic records.

582. M:15:0	ACE IX, 48; XI, 61	'7-5'	5:2:18
B:III:1	ENG IX, 27; XI, 47	9'42-'<u>560</u>	4:3:18
	HSR 50		
	SVIB none		

His fellow students, particularly the boys, especially liked this youth, as evidenced by the fact that they helped pay his tuition at one time during an emergency when he might otherwise have had to change schools. A big boy and a good football player, he was pleasant, conscientious, and seemed to like school. Although his schoolwork was not strong, he was considered an overachiever by most teachers. In some contrast, one teacher said he was consistently lazy and liked to get out of things if he could. He was a follower and not a leader. He made his own way financially, owned a car, and was a hard worker outside of school. He appeared to be stable and took the loss of his parents with unusual stability. After graduation he had a steady job but was reported to be dissatisfied with it.

The boy's own father died early and the mother remarried before the boy entered the ninth grade. The mother then died and the stepfather tried to hold the home together.

583. F:15:3   ACE IX, none; XI, 89   '7–5'19   3:7:10
     N:V:2   ENG IX, none; XI, 92
                     HSR 87
                     SVIB WR'

A hard worker, well liked and gifted, this girl was considered very well adjusted, although she was in "too many" activities. She had many friends. A "stickler for detail," she could not easily accept getting a B; her reaction was to sulk for a while. The parents were "nice, quiet, retiring people." Both of them worked.

584. M:14:1   ACE IX, none; XI, 55   '7–69'38<u>5</u>   2:5:14
     N:V:1   ENG IX, none; XI, 74   '9–1'64<u>2</u>   1:1:10
                    HSR 90   9'76–'1<u>32</u>   1:3:13
                    SVIB none

This boy was retiring and lacking in many leadership qualities. He was a good student and no problem in class. His teachers described him as "a gentleman." His interests were wide, extending from music to athletics, and he was accepted well in groups in spite of his retiring manner. He did well in whatever he attempted and showed evidence of good planning.

585. F:15:6   ACE IX, none; XI, 47   '7–9'   7:1:20
     N:VI:2   ENG IX, none; XI, 78   '543–2'6   4:2:20
                    HSR 59
                    SVIB none

This girl was the "home economics type." Reliable and cooperative, she was well liked. She had a friendly, outgoing, and pleasing personality. A fair student, she worked up to her capacity.

586. M:14:2   ACE IX, 75; XI, 37   '7–0'<u>26</u>   5:4:16
     N:III:4   ENG IX, 66; XI, 57   '483 <u>17</u>–'90   10:1:25X
                    HSR 83
                    SVIB none

This boy was mature, friendly, and well liked. He made a good appearance in public; he was businesslike and much admired. He could be babyish, however, if he did not get his own way. No conduct problem, he was a good student and a hard worker both in and out of school.

587. F:14:2   ACE IX, none; XI, 84   '71<u>20</u> <u>5843</u>–'9   2:5:18
    N:II:3   ENG IX, none; XI, 75   '53–'4<u>29</u>   4:1:20
                 HSR 90   '<u>35678</u>–'9   2:4:21
                 SVIB '–

Attractive in appearance, this girl was a good student and one of the school leaders. She worked hard, "minded her own business, and was very helpful." She sometimes became quite "disgruntled" if things did not go her way, but she was never sulky or nasty. She was active in several different extracurricular areas. After graduation she continued on to a university.

The father, a white collar worker, was considered a serious person and much given to study. In some contrast to the seriousness of the father, the mother was described as "flighty and social." One older child had been forced into marriage shortly after his graduation from high school and this was a great disappointment to his parents, who had hoped that he would further his education. This son suffered an ulcer attack shortly after his marriage.

588. M:14:4   ACE IX, none; XI, 84   '710<u>84</u>–   3:1:10
    B:VI:3   ENG IX, none; XI, 60
                 HSR 55
                 SVIB none

This boy was a "terrific competitor" to the point of being obnoxious. Never satisfied with his success, he became easily discouraged and often threatened to quit school. He was very defensive and caused trouble by "scuffling in the hall when in a defensive mood." He felt that the other students were not friendly. He often got angry at himself and others, only to level off again and be pleasant and stable for long periods. He got into some trouble because of careless driving.

The father had been killed in the war and the boy had a stepfather. He and the mother were reported to be happily married.

589. M:14:3   ACE IX, 88; XI, 68   7'2<u>305</u> <u>184</u>–   1:5:5
    B:III:1   ENG IX, none; XI, 88
                 HSR 38 DO 11th gr.
                 SVIB none

This boy had a poor complexion and was not very attractive in appearance. He was, however, well liked by his fellow students. Indifferent toward school, he skipped whenever possible and needed prodding to achieve what he did. When his younger brother ran away to join the service, this boy dropped out of school and followed his brother to bring him back. He sent him back instead and joined up himself. The younger brother was lazy and shiftless.

In this family both parents had been previously married. Each of the parents had two children before the present marriage. A younger sister of the boy became illegitimately pregnant and was forced to get married.

590. M:14:10   ACE IX, 57; XI, 72   '724–5'0   2:2:16

N:IVC:3   ENG IX, 55; XI, 51   4"972'186305– 5:7:14

HSR 71

SVIB none

The brief description of this boy emphasized that he was well liked, quiet, and serious, but with a good sense of humor. He was also described as helpful and industrious.

591. F:14:6   ACE IX, none; XI, 53   '72834–'9   8:2:23

N:IVB:5   ENG IX, none; XI, 59 '49–12'5   3:3:11

HSR 38

SVIB none

This girl, who was shy and retiring, was not a conduct problem. She worked very hard and had a pleasant manner, although she had trouble getting her schoolwork. She did not engage in any school activities and it was not known what became of her after high school graduation.

There were no notes about the family aside from the fact that the father apparently committed suicide when the girl was still in high school.

592. M:15:5   ACE IX, none; XI, 62 7'2840136–9'5 5:6:16

B:V:2   ENG IX, none; XI, 12 '57 2390–'6   2:5:10

HSR 03

SVIB none

This student was quiet to the point of being described as "slow." He had little motivation and merely occupied a place in the classroom. He was reliable and fairly cooperative, although he seemed to be a definite underachiever.

593. M:15:3   ACE IX, 34; XI, 41   7'2854–'9   5:6:16

N:V:1   ENG IX, 37; XI, 43 758'024639–   1:6:7

HSR 37

SVIB '89–2

A high voice and effeminate mannerisms were this tall, slim boy's most distinguishing characteristics. Throughout his high school career he was the only boy on the school's cheerleading squad. He was self-conscious when he entered into feminine activities and felt that he was rejected by boys. He always appeared shy and not quite sure of himself. Although he participated in many activities, he was always on the edge, never in the midst of them. He was never really accepted by any student group. His teachers were of the opinion that he was so troubled by inferiority feelings that he probably would have dropped out of school had he not been involved in even this limited way in activities. During his senior year he finally gained a degree of acceptance from the boys in the school by adopting some of their rather extreme fads in dress. He was mentioned by his ninth-grade teachers as probably headed for later difficulties in emotional adjustment. After graduation he enrolled in a junior college.

The father, although apparently a fairly good provider, was described as a physically rugged and somewhat crude man. Occasionally he drank too much and he never assumed any responsibility in community affairs.

594. M:15:1   ACE IX, 57; XI, 53   '720859–   0:7:10
     N:III:1   ENG IX, none; XI, 42
               HSR 21
               SVIB none

When he was in the ninth grade this boy was "very girl crazy — thought of himself as a kind of pretty boy and combed his hair at all angles." He had a sullen, sneering attitude at times, and he felt that he was too mature to be disciplined or controlled by school rules. A lazy and poor student, he smoked in school and slept in class. He was never openly rebellious, however, and was, in fact, quiet around school. He had several jobs outside of school at which he worked very hard, appearing to be more interested in them and in his car than in school achievement. By the twelfth grade he had "gone to pot" and it was thought he would probably not graduate. His ninth-grade teachers expected him to have difficulty in his emotional adjustment.

595. F:14:4   ACE IX, none; XI, 47   '72098–'531   7:6:11
     N:IVB:1   ENG IX, none; XI, 60   47'68239–   4:5:9
               HSR 90
               SVIB WR'

Although shy when in the tenth grade, this girl later became more outgoing and "blossomed into a leadership role." Always thoughtful of other people, she was courteous, kind, and cooperative.

596. M:15:3   ACE IX, 54; XI, 22   '73–20'   3:10:17
     N:IVB:5   ENG IX, 29; XI, 10
               HSR 25
               SVIB 9'–

It was difficult to describe this boy because one could not predict his behavior; he was "sometimes a gentleman and sometimes a terror." On occasion he was reliable and dependable, but generally he was indifferent and undependable. He had poor work habits and was not motivated toward good school behavior. Nothing seemed to affect him. He was "a smart aleck," and he smoked and was usually out at night in his car with no place to go. He had an accident that was said to be a result of his fast driving. A number of his ninth-grade teachers expected that he would get into emotional or legal difficulties.

597. M:14:1   ACE IX, none; XI, 25   '73–'0   7:1:19
    N:IVB:6   ENG IX, none; XI, 33
                   HSR 08
                   SVIB '4–

"You could see this boy's personality in his swagger." He was "a master at deception" and would go as far as he dared. He was "a sneaky prevaricator." He did not participate in any activities and was a "lone wolf," although apparently polite in his contacts with others. He would not study in school and was untrustworthy. He was guilty of a number of offenses, including drunken driving and stealing. A probation officer said that the boy was "more sorry to be caught than to have broken the law." The police described him as "a bad actor who seemed to profit by a stay at a correctional school." Two ninth-grade teachers expected that he would have difficulty with the law.

The father was an excellent farmer and businessman. The home was described as clean and fine. People claimed that "the easiness of the parents" was the cause of the boy's behavior.

598. F:14:0   ACE IX, 100; XI, 97   '731468–5'   1:2:14
    N:V:4   ENG IX, none; XI, 97   '6937–45'   0:5:7
                   HSR 91
                   SVIB none

This girl was "dependable, cooperative, well liked, and happy." She engaged in all types of school activities and was interested in continuing on to professional training at a university. In appearance she was described as "plump."

599. M:14:2   ACE IX, none; XI, none   7'326184–'9   3:3:17
    B:VII:3   ENG IX, none; XI, none
                   HSR trans 10th gr.
                   SVIB none

This boy was not a conduct problem in the school, and was friendly and likable, but he did not take part in any activities. He enjoyed school, was willing and eager to learn, and was considered bright.

600. M:14:1   ACE IX, 61; XI, 72   '734258–'96   5:2:20
    B:VI:1   ENG IX, 64; XI, 36   '5–1'280   2:3:11
                   HSR 45   '39–0'857   4:1:17
                   SVIB 9'0–

This boy's interest was dramatics. Although he was not especially talented, he had good imagination and clever ideas. A likable boy, he was accepted by his fellow students and respected by his teachers, although some of the latter complained that he was a minor troublemaker who was at times belligerent in attitude. After graduation he went to a university.

His father was dead and the mother had remarried. The stepfather was an unskilled worker. Neither parent took an active part in school, church, or community.

601. F:14:4	ACE IX, 91; XI, 93	'73<u>4062</u>–'5	5:1:17
N:VI:1	ENG IX, none; XI, 78	'34–'<u>297</u>	6:1:17
	HSR 86		
	SVIB WR'		

"Well liked and emotionally well balanced," this girl showed qualities of average leadership. She was considered reliable and moderately mature in her judgment.

602. F:14:0	ACE IX, 65; XI, 59	'73548–0'<u>92</u>	6:0:20
N:V:2	ENG IX, none; XI, 89		
	HSR 84		
	SVIB '–		

Described as an A student, this girl was trustworthy and capable. She did everything well, and she was "a sensible school leader." Well liked and popular, she had many friends. In school activities she "made a careful choice and participated well."

603. M:14:1	ACE IX, none; XI, 89	73'<u>501</u> 846–	2:1:14
N:II:1	ENG IX, none; XI, 82	47'398<u>02</u>–	0:5:12
	HSR 96		
	SVIB 4'2–5		

There was almost no information regarding this boy. It was said that he got along well with other students and that he was not a conduct problem. An introvert, he entered into no activities, but he was characterized as "popular and responsible."

604. M:14:4	ACE IX, 96; XI, 98	'7398–2'	1:5:16
B:III:1	ENG IX, none; XI, 92	— —	— —
	HSR 86	9'76<u>384</u>–	0:1:18
	SVIB 4'–		

This boy liked to bluff and would, if he had the chance, take advantage of teachers. He had sporadic bursts of antagonism which got him into minor difficulties. In his last year of school his behavior improved. His teachers felt he was an underachiever. After graduation he continued on to a university.

The father was a businessman. The boy's mother had died sometime before he entered the ninth grade and the father had remarried. A great deal of resentment arose between the boy and his stepmother.

605. F:15:3	ACE IX, none; XI, 29	'74–'9	3:1:20
N:III:3	ENG IX, none; XI, 41	'4<u>36789</u>–5'0	7:2:22
	HSR 48		
	SVIB WR'		

This quiet, shy girl had a few close friends but no large circle of friends. She was dreamy and indecisive, seemingly unaware of time. Physically she was frail. Easily discouraged, she found her schoolwork very hard. She had one friend whom she stopped seeing when the other girl developed a close friendship with a boy. Later in high school the girl herself found a boy friend. She had a persistent desire to became a missionary which amounted to a feeling of obligation that she was unable to explain. The teachers felt this choice of occupation a poor one because she seemed too antisocial and too limited in the ability to talk to others.

The father, pleasant and affable, provided a steady middle-class income which was lower than might have been expected for his level of education. He was also described as "slow and lazy." The mother, an intelligent woman, was active in community affairs; she was, however, described as "quiet, slow, and almost lazy" because her housekeeping was so poor.

606. M:14:1	ACE IX, none; XI, 91	'74<u>16</u> 0<u>358</u>–'9	4:5:21
N:V:3	ENG IX, none; XI, 85	'4876–	0:2:20
	HSR 93		
	SVIB none		

Every comment about this boy was favorable. He was liked by teachers and fellow students, and he got good grades. He was active in athletics and he became president of his class. "Solid in physique and personality, he was a hero to the boys in the school." His teachers described him as a friendly, fair, clear-thinking boy with a fine droll sense of humor.

607. M:15:9	ACE IX, 18; XI, 28	7'42<u>81</u>–	5:9:17
N:VI:1	ENG IX, none; XI, 16		
	HSR 38		
	SVIB none		

Although he was "a little breezy," this boy was generally well thought of. He was nice looking, a fine athlete, and "the friendly type." In school he was very cooperative and reliable and a hard worker. He had repeated difficulty with the law because of traffic offenses.

7'43<u>218</u>–

The boy came from a large family which was not very highly regarded in the community. An older sister had been in considerable difficulty.

608. M:14:1   ACE IX, 79; XI, 84   7'43<u>218</u>–   6:2:24
     N:V:1   ENG IX, 79; XI, 78   — —   — —
                   HSR 10   '4<u>1378</u>6–'05   5:3:25
                   SVIB '9–

When this boy was not with his friends, he was quiet and not troublesome, but there were minor discipline problems whenever he and his friends got together. He always had excuses for any trouble he got into. At least one ninth-grade teacher thought that he might develop later emotional problems. He seemed to be a gross underachiever and to be poorly motivated. After high school he enrolled in a university.

609. M:14:3   ACE IX, 53; XI, 36   '7<u>4689</u>–5'   2:3:20
     N:I:1   ENG IX, none; XI, 47
                   HSR 50
                   SVIB none

This very tall, thin boy was not particularly attractive. He was, however, well accepted and well adjusted socially. He suffered badly from acne. He had few friends, and the most recurrent description of him emphasized that he was a "lone wolf," quiet but not shy. One person also described him as "tired." He was deliberate in manner, honest, and responsible. At school he worked hard and achieved C's and B's. His teachers believed that he suffered from constant comparison with an older brother who had been a most capable student. Although good in athletics, he was never very close to the other team members. It was said that he was under strict parental supervision. In his junior year his driver's license was suspended for a period because of a traffic violation. After graduation he went on to attend college.

The boy's parents were intelligent, highly educated persons who held positions of social and economic prominence in the community, as had their families before them. The father had few real friends and was a quiet and dignified person. He was particularly proud of the achievements of this boy's brother and occasionally became objectively defensive and protective of him. The mother was outspoken and argumentative, but she was considered to mean well. She was ostentatious in denying that she was demanding of her children, but there did seem to be evidence that she controlled them closely. Religion and church were said to hold a central position in this family's life. It was considered that the parents were open to some criticism because they tended to be narrow and intolerant of those whose beliefs differed from theirs.

610. F:15:2   ACE IX, none; XI, 38   '748569–   3:2:16
     N:III:3   ENG IX, none; XI, 83
                 HSR 84
                 SVIB none

Called "vibrant, charming, and much fun," this girl could be the life of the party. She had a fine sense of humor but she would "never hurt anyone with her wit." In another instance she was described as resembling "a friendly puppy." She was always dependable and responsible, and she was considered more mature than the average student. She was in most of the school's extracurricular activities and "contributed generously of herself."

611. F:14:1   ACE IX, 93; XI, 92   74'863912–   1:7:12
     N:II:1   ENG IX, none; XI, 87   '87349–'05   4:1:19
                 HSR 69
                 SVIB none

Although this girl wore glasses and "was not really pretty," she was voted the best all-around girl in the senior class and was popular in many ways. She was a leader and "worked at being popular." As this implies, she seemed a little artificial. She impressed her teachers as an outstanding student academically and as excellent in almost every way. It was mentioned that although she had an older and prettier sister, this did not present a problem. Her interests included music, dogs, and sports. After graduation she went to college, where she received a leadership award for all-around outstanding qualities.

The home was a nice one in a nice neighborhood, and the parents were "most attractive, outgoing people." The father, who was described as "a dynamo of energy — yet always calm," was devoted to his daughters. The mother was not mentioned. The older sister was said to be even more pleasing in personality and accomplishments than was the subject.

612. F:15:2   ACE IX, 52; XI, 44   '7480–'51   3:5:13
     N:VI:2   ENG IX, none; XI, 31
                 HSR 46
                 SVIB WR'

Described as "big and a little loud," this girl was an average student with average adjustment. She dressed neatly, was courteous, and participated in many school activities. She was also described as reliable, cooperative, and mature. She was happy and enthusiastic. She wanted to go on to a trade school, and in her senior year she worked part time in a job where she was regarded as very satisfactory. In her senior year she won a national award in a literary competition. Her expectation of further schooling was changed when she became engaged before graduation and married shortly thereafter.

This girl's family had moved often but no other significant item was reported about the family.

613. F:14:4   ACE IX, 77; XI, 73   7'493680–'5   2:5:10
     B:V:3   ENG IX, 86; XI, 63
                     HSR 31
                     SVIB WR'

"Sincere and friendly," "never stepping out of line," this girl was pleasant to have around and saw the best in everyone. She had her own group of friends. Her schoolwork suffered from many absences for which the cause was not known.

614. M:14:1   ACE IX, none; XI, 11   '74980–5'63   7:7:16
     N:VII:4   ENG IX, none; XI, 34   '872 109–   3:9:9
                    HSR 10
                    SVIB none

The boy was sickly, dull, and unaggressive. He was socially introverted and he caused no difficulty in school. He showed no leadership and made few friends.

615. F:15:3   ACE IX, 59; XI, 69   '75–'2   4:2:18
     N:III:1   ENG IX, 69; XI, 48   '46372–   1:3:18
                    HSR 50
                    SVIB none

The chief thing emphasized about this girl was that she was "engaged and disengaged to the same boy" a number of times. She was personable and friendly, but not especially outgoing or much of a leader. She was very mature for a high school student. "Thoughtful, kind, and sympathetic, she was the kind one is always glad to meet." She liked to do extra schoolwork, especially in creative dramatics. She was in a number of activities and was fairly successful in social affairs. After graduation she went to work in a local department store.

616. M:15:4   ACE IX, 42; XI, 28   '751082 34–9'   4:4:16
     N:IVC:5   ENG IX, 52; XI, 62   5"07'62–9'   4:4:12
                    HSR 85
                    SVIB none

Because he lived on a farm this boy was somewhat limited in his social contacts. He mingled nicely with classmates, however, and was no school problem. He was considered "average, nice, very cooperative, and well adjusted." He was sincere, did his work well, and possibly achieved above his intelligence level.

617. F:14:3   IQ (centile) 99   '756–'120   3:3:14
     B:III:3   HSR trans. 10th gr.
                    SVIB none

Very bright and pretty, this girl was "boy crazy," scatterbrained, and flighty. Described as "the type who will marry young," she had many boy friends, was "feminine," and "a clothes horse." However, she took pride in her schoolwork and was not a conduct problem. One teacher predicted that she would later become emotionally maladjusted. She moved to another state during the tenth grade and was lost from the follow-up study.

618. F:15:2	ACE IX, 41; XI, 43	'758–'1	3:2:15
N:III:1	ENG IX, none; XI, 77	'35–'69	5:1:14
	HSR 61		
	SVIB none		

Although not outstanding in scholastic activities, this "very normal" girl was a leader and a good organizer. She engaged in social activities as an active participant and was particularly active in girls' groups and church work. It was also mentioned that she spent a considerable amount of time training her dog. One of her teachers predicted that she would become emotionally maladjusted. After graduation she went to a small college.

The father was unemployed and the mother had started working. The mother was reported as a "nice, pleasant person" of whom the girl was noticeably proud.

619. F:14:2	ACE IX, 84; XI, 77	'7624098–5'	3:3:16
B:VI:1	ENG IX, none; XI, 92		
	HSR 77		
	SVIB none		

A blonde, ruddy, Nordic-appearing girl, this student had many friends and was a leader among her classmates. Although one person spoke of her as "slightly timid," she participated in many activities and, when a junior, went abroad with a group of high school students.

Both her parents had died before she entered high school; she and her two sisters lived with their stepfather.

620. M:14:1	ACE IX, 34; XI, 56	'7658–1'	6:5:11
B:V:4	ENG IX, 63; XI, 80		
	HSR 22		
	SVIB none		

This boy was adopted as an infant and the adoptive father died when the boy was a sophomore. He was considered mentally alert, although physically lazy. At one time he was overweight and, on the suggestion of a teacher, he dieted very effectively. He was well liked by his classmates. In his schoolwork he was dependable and a good thinker, especially in problem solving, and his teachers felt he would go far. He had a fine sense of humor and was mature, so that the problems he experienced in the death of his father and in other phases of his family situation were apparently easily adjusted to. He expressed a desire to be either a minister or a journalist.

The father had been a successful businessman who was highly thought of by the community. The mother was described as self-centered and shallow, without appreciation of anything except beautiful clothes, an orderly home, and social status. She was not well regarded by the community; she lacked judgment and was censored for some of her behavior after her husband's death. A younger sister, also adopted, was "unattractive and slow."

621.	F:15:1	ACE IX, 38; XI, 25	'76820–'5	2:9:12
	N:V:1	ENG IX, none; XI, 56	'59 478–'0	1:4:17
		HSR 57		
		SVIB none		

This girl, who was a "better than average dresser," frequently avoided examinations by getting "sick." Her teachers felt that she was not to be trusted and perhaps cheated in the exams that she did take. Descriptions of her varied from such negative items as "sly," "apt to be a nuisance," "distractible and immature" to comments of a much more positive sort in which she was called pleasant, lively, and never moody. She was apparently well liked by fellow students and her teachers. One report, in claiming that she had a lot of courage, followed the word "courage" with "or nerve." She showed no special interest in boys. During her junior year she was caught shoplifting and was warned and released. There were two other such episodes recorded in her senior year. She wanted to become a "technician."

622.	M:14:5	ACE IX, 07; XI, 13	'7684–	2:8:13
	N:VI:5	ENG IX, 10; XI, 21		
		HSR 16		
		SVIB none		

This shy, quiet, withdrawn boy was not a conduct problem, but he never did anything more than was necessary. When urged, he would be cooperative, but he never went beyond the task in hand.

623.	M:14:2	ACE IX, 61; XI, 72	7'684–	3:5:17
	N:IVA:2	ENG IX, none; XI, 78		
		HSR 59		
		SVIB 4'8–50		

Active in the Future Farmers of America, this boy was selected as outstanding for his care of livestock. He was independent, had some friends, and, in general, was friendly and cooperative, although he was said to be lacking in self-confidence. He liked school and was not a conduct problem.

The boy's parents both had some college training. They ran an excellent farm and home.

624. F:14:3	ACE IX, 100; XI, 96	'76<u>85</u> <u>42</u>–	5:3:22
N:III:1	ENG IX, 100; XI, 99	'6<u>02</u>–94'<u>15</u>	3:2:13
	HSR 85	'6–'5<u>29</u>	3:2:21
	SVIB none		

Not especially attractive, this girl was unassuming, shy, and an "introvert." She was not particularly popular but was well liked, pleasant, and "a wonderful girl when you got to know her." In school she was conscientious, dependable, and generally a desirable student. She had a deep-seated interest in becoming a professional woman and everything she did was geared toward this goal. The teachers considered her "solid" and thought that she would probably be successful. She continued on to a university.

The family was termed "good" and the children were under great pressure to go into professions. The father was a skilled worker.

625. M:15:1	ACE IX, 08; XI, 30	'76<u>80</u>–'59	7:10:17
N:IVA:4	ENG IX, 07; XI, 22	'7<u>86</u>–'1<u>20</u>	4:4:15
	HSR 31		
	SVIB '4–5		

This boy was aggressive and full of fun. His hobbies were hunting and cars. He took part in many activities and "tried hard to be all boy." He had no particular girl friend but was liked by fellow students and teachers. He had a fine sense of humor, and he was cheerful, dependable, and trustworthy. In his junior year he had his driver's license revoked for a period because of a traffic offense. After graduation he went to work with his father on the family farm. During his high school years the boy had accumulated considerable savings through farm work.

The father was a superior person, influential and respected. He was a fine father and it was felt that his encouragement had helped make the boy a hard worker and a good person. The mother, although more retiring and quiet, was regarded as the more capable of the parents. She was an excellent mother. A brother was considered to be very feminine in manner, but in general the children and family were highly regarded in the community.

626. M:15:3	ACE IX, 20; XI, 17	7'68<u>09</u>–'2	3:8:6
N:V:4	ENG IX, 14; XI, 04		
	HSR 26		
	SVIB none		

When this boy lived some distance from the school he had a record of many absences and poor cooperation. As soon as he moved closer to the school "all situations improved greatly." He tried to work hard and to please. His teachers believed he was covering up his feelings concerning a marital difficulty that existed in his home. Two of his teachers expected he would later develop emotional maladjustment and legal difficulties.

627. F:14:1	ACE IX, 94; XI, 84	7'6948–5'	1:0:16
B:III:2	ENG IX, 94; XI, 90	'7862–'59	2:4:17
	HSR 58		
	SVIB '–		

Described as a "pretty, doll-like blonde," this girl was very popular with the boys. She "had a timid appearance," was shy, and blushed easily, but several informants felt that this shyness was put on and she was also described as "socially experienced and sophisticated." Although she had little interest in academic work, she did what was asked of her. Some teachers considered her low in ability. About the time of graduation she became engaged and left the locality to live with relatives.

This girl's real father died sometime before she entered the ninth grade, and she lived with her mother and stepfather. There seemed to be tension in the relation of the girl with her stepfather, and there was also rivalry between her full brother and her stepbrother, who were the same age. The mother was a hard-working person of good character.

628. F:14:3	ACE IX, none; XI, 29	'76048–3'1	4:9:10
N:III:2	ENG IX, none; XI, 42	'7–'319	6:4:17
	HSR 51		
	SVIB none		

A very positive, responsible, conscientious girl, this youngster was thought by her teachers to be serious and sincere. "Petite and well groomed," she made all her own clothes. Although she was absent from school occasionally, she would make up even a week's absence of work. After graduation she entered a university liberal arts course.

629. M:14:4	ACE IX, 59; XI, 56	'78246–9'	3:5:15
N:V:2	ENG IX, none; XI, 47	78'13 42659–	2:5:11
	HSR 65		
	SVIB '4–5		

This boy seemed to be especially "cocky" while he was in the tenth grade. Throughout high school he was an erratic worker, doing well at what he liked and what was easiest for him and letting the rest slide. He never worked up to his ability. A "small, fat kid," he was unpopular and he did not mix well with other students. He had some "rather rowdy fellows" as friends and he was described as a follower rather than a leader. He was interested in music and it was reported that he often played for beer at dance halls. In spite of all these negative comments, he was considered a rather steady and reliable boy outside of the school setting. He earned his board and room working on a farm all the time he was going to school. He had a number of contacts with the police because of reckless driving and inadequate equipment on his car. After he graduated he was fined for drunken driving. It was reported that following completion of high school he was not working.

The father, although a good provider, was neither warm nor close in his relations with his children. The mother had an even disposition and she got along well with her husband. Although better than he, she too was unable to be very affectionate with the children. The whole family was said to be uninterested in the school achievement of the children; they concentrated instead on earning money to buy material things.

630. M:14:3	ACE IX, 72; XI, 53	'784–23'65	2:5:12
N:IVC:5	ENG IX, 48; XI, 27.	'46813–'0	7:4:23
	HSR 15		
	SVIB 4'–		

Although this boy was considered attractive, likable, and a good boy if away from bad companions (his associates were called "hoodlums"), he was, in general, not well thought of. He seemed resentful of authority and could be unpleasant. "mouthy," and at times a "wise guy." His abilities seemed dormant; school was a joke for him and if not watched, he would "goof off." He could not be trusted and always wanted attention. The one steadying effect seemed to be his activity in the choir. In his sophomore year he got into trouble because of stealing and was placed on probation. This seemed to have a stabilizing effect on him. His parents provided him with a car, which he drove recklessly. At least one teacher predicted that he would have emotional maladjustment. He went into the Navy after completing high school.

The father, a shiftless and lazy man, had a poor reputation. He protected his child even when the boy admitted being wrong. The mother, a friendly woman, was the stronger parent. But, though appreciative of the boy's problem, she also was inclined toward overprotection.

631. F:14:1	ACE IX, 28; XI, 25	'784–'31<u>25</u>	3:7:13
N:V:3	ENG IX, 46; XI, 64		
	HSR 72		
	SVIB WR'		

"Cute and lively," this girl "cut up" in her earlier high school years and was sometimes "snippy." As she continued in school she became more mature, and by her senior year she showed very good personality development. She was loved by her classmates and teachers, although some believed she was too talkative in class discussions. She was a good student but not very industrious. She did get her work done and was able to express herself well.

632. M:14:2   ACE IX, 79; XI, 68   7'84<u>23</u> <u>16</u>–'5   1:8:20
      N:VI:4   ENG IX, none; XI, 60
               HSR 12
               SVIB '140–

This boy had been "mature ever since the eighth grade," but he was "a cocky show-off, acting as a grown-up man of the world." Along with this uneven maturity he was always complaining of sickness and pain. He was a gross underachiever and he needed constant prodding in his classwork. His classmates merely tolerated him. He was said to be "in love."

633. M:15:1   ACE IX, 50; XI, 65   78'<u>45</u> <u>13</u> <u>96</u>–   6:10:16
      N:III:1   ENG IX, 68; XI, 56   '6<u>48</u>710–9'   5:3:22
               HSR 30
               SVIB '4–

"About as nice a kid as you'll ever find," this boy was slow in reading and comprehension. He tried hard but had difficulty in maintaining even a C average. He was nice looking, nicely dressed, and respected by fellow students. Shy and retiring, he was "a quiet leader." After graduation he continued his education at a small college.

     Both the father and mother worked at skilled jobs. The boy was said to have had a good home background.

634. M:14:3   ACE IX, none; XI, 41   7'84<u>59</u> <u>62</u>–'1   4:6:9
      N:IVA:7   ENG IX, none; XI, 19   8'769<u>143</u>–   1:10:14
               HSR 29
               SVIB none

Described as "very nervous," this boy was modest and lacking in poise. He often became red in the face and fidgety, especially when reprimanded. He wanted to be a good athlete but he had poor coordination and fell easily. He was often "in the wrong place at the wrong time"; he would, for example, sneak off to play ping-pong during class hours. He was, however, said to be likable. Emotional problems were anticipated for him by one of his ninth-grade teachers.

635. M:15:2   ACE IX, 70; XI, 62   7'8<u>46</u>–   3:6:13
      N:III:3   ENG IX, none; XI, 43
               HSR 18 DO 12th gr.
               SVIB none

A member of the "leather-jacket crowd," this boy was always tardy to school and unreliable and erratic in his behavior. Seemingly always tired and indifferent, he had to be pushed to get him to do anything. He was unusually close to his two sisters. Shortly before graduation he suddenly quit, left the state, and got married. He had a record of several traffic violations.

636. M:14:7   ACE IX, none; XI, 22   78'493620–   4:10:7
     N:III:1   ENG IX, none; XI, none
                     HSR 04
                     SVIB none

Although it was said that this boy was sincere and that he took part in activities, especially audiovisual work, he showed a sour attitude and had a chip on his shoulder when under pressure. He did just enough work to get by. In class he engaged in "horseplay." He tended to be by himself a great deal, having only a few friends. He was accepted but not sought out by the larger group.

637. F:15:8   IQ (centile) 35   7863'29041– 3:9:3
     N:VI:1   HSR DO 9th gr.
                     SVIB none

Physically overmature for her age, this girl dropped out of school at the end of the ninth grade in order to be married. Before she quit school she had clearly been more interested in marriage than in academic pursuits. Although descriptive statements given in retrospect characterized her as happy and well adjusted, three teachers predicted that she would become involved in legal difficulties, and one expected her to become emotionally maladjusted. Incomplete follow-up information did not support these expectations.

638. M:15:1   ACE IX, 08; XI, 14   '789–2'354   4:5:15
     B:IVC:5   ENG IX, 18; XI, 11   97'68–'312   2:10:8
                     HSR 29
                     SVIB 48'–0

This boy "smoked and tore around." He was lazy and only went to school because he had to. He did not cause trouble in classes but he seemed to lack self-confidence. He took no part in social functions. He was an orphan and lived with a bachelor uncle, who was a hard-working, good man.

639. M:14:6   ACE IX, none; XI, 65   '7891–5'6   5:6:17
     N:II:5   ENG IX, none; XI, none   5'978–0'2   4:3:10
                     HSR 64
                     SVIB none

This boy was dignified but effeminate in manner. He was interested in music and fine arts and he liked to dance. He was a hard, conscientious worker, often volunteering to help the teacher. He was gregarious, a little gossipy, and was well liked. He did not engage in sports but he was a cheerleader and a reporter for the school paper. He liked science.

640. M:15:1   ACE IX, none; XI, 71   78'9140– 2:5:17
   N:VI:3   ENG IX, none; XI, 72
         HSR 69
         SVIB none

"An extra extrovert," this boy talked all the time and was the center of attention. He was always "jazzing it up"; he could talk anywhere and at any time. Playful and immature, he seemed full of fun and starved for attention. Physically large and strong, he was a football "hero." After graduation he hoped to study medicine. He had a record of several traffic offenses.

641. F:14:4   ACE IX, 67; XI, 98   7'896 42–5' 2:2:16
   N:III:1   ENG IX, 95; XI, 97   '726–5'4 2:6:11
         HSR 79
         SVIB none

Described as efficient, pleasant, cooperative, and never known to scowl, this girl was well liked by her classmates. She was an outstanding student, particularly in dramatics. She was also talented in creative writing and was active in school affairs where such talents were appropriate. Though relatively active, she was not aggressive, nor did she offer much of herself in social gatherings. One incident was described in which she showed great persistence in continuing an academic task until its satisfactory completion. After graduation she went on to a small college, having won a scholarship grant to help her continue in her schoolwork.

  The girl's family was briefly described in very acceptable terms and did not appear to be deviant in any known way.

642. M:15:5   ACE IX, none; XI, 84 78"9'6423– 2:12:8
   N:III:1   ENG IX, none; XI, 51 4'3862715– 1:9:9
         HSR 76
         SVIB '890–

This boy's speech was "rapid-fire and he stuttered." He was co-captain of an athletic team but he seemed to lack confidence and would often "choke up" during a game. He was described as "well disciplined but eccentric — he seemed to have some emotional problem." He had a steady girl friend. An older brother was "a great star in all things" while he attended school.

643. M:15:2　　　　ACE IX, none; XI, 85　　　78'9045 63–　　0:7:10
　　　N:VI:2　　　　ENG IX, none; XI, 45　　　879 46'523–　　2:7:8
　　　　　　　　　　HSR 23
　　　　　　　　　　SVIB none

When this boy felt good he was likable enough, but he had a short temper and occasionally clashed with teachers at school. He cooperated when he felt it was convenient. He was described as "flighty" and unsure of himself. He was active in the band. Outside of school he sometimes associated with a rough crowd.

644. M:13:2　　　　ACE IX, 38; XI, none　　　7'80–'6123　　1:8:8
　　　N:V:3　　　　 ENG IX, 41; XI, none
　　　　　　　　　　HSR trans. 10th gr.
　　　　　　　　　　SVIB none

This shy boy had nice manners. He was soft-spoken and anxious to please. Slow and always behind schedule, he seemed to lack confidence in himself. He transferred to another school when in the tenth grade and further information could not be obtained about him.

645. F:14:2　　　　ACE IX, 82; XI, 95　　　'78023–'95　　2:3:15
　　　N:V:1　　　　 ENG IX, 82; XI, 82　　　'947–5'6　　　0:3:14
　　　　　　　　　　HSR 63　　　　　　　　　'9843–2'05　　2:5:22
　　　　　　　　　　SVIB none

Neat in appearance, this girl was well liked, although she was described as shy and an introvert. She was considered "tops as a student," volunteered for reports, and generally knew the answers when questions were put to her. Her chief activity was a church youth group. After high school graduation she entered a university, but it was believed that she later dropped out to take full-time work.

　This family had limited social contacts and both parents were described as shy and lacking in initiative; they were not leaders in the community. All the children had pleasing personalities and were well accepted socially. The family was described as "just basically little people."

646. M:16:1　　　　ACE IX, 34; XI, none　　　'78052–'1　　1:7:10
　　　N:III:1　　　　ENG IX, 46; XI, none
　　　　　　　　　　HSR DO 11th gr.
　　　　　　　　　　SVIB none

This boy was sensitive about having to get extra help because he was "dumb." He was a hard worker who lacked confidence. He repeated the fourth grade after failing English and, except for shop courses, found schoolwork difficult. When he dropped out of school following the tenth grade, he and his parents agreed that he should learn a trade. This plan apparently worked out well.

647. F:15:2   ACE IX, 82; XI, 78   '78059–   0:5:8
     N:III:1   ENG IX, none; XI, 88
                     HSR 54
                     SVIB none

This was "a kind of unnoticed girl who was ordinarily quiet." Although she was irresponsible in most of her schoolwork, she did well in commercial courses. When reprimanded for truancy, she became stubborn and belligerent, appearing to be high-strung and excitable. She liked music; she sang and played a horn.

648. M:14:1   ACE IX, 36; XI, 49   '79–1'26   4:8:5
     N:IVB:5   ENG IX, 33; XI, 24
                     HSR 37
                     SVIB none

This boy was "very sickly — something was always wrong with him." These illnesses caused him to miss a great deal of school, especially in his ninth and tenth grades. In school he was indifferent and lazy at times, and he was considered to be an underachiever. His main interest was in girls and he seemed to have no definite goals in life. He was considered "quite negative." According to reports he had a "fine family."

649. F:15:0   ACE IX, 95; XI, 72   '79364–'5   4:0:16
     B:II:2   ENG IX, none; XI, 98
                     HSR 100
                     SVIB 'WR

Described as "a hyperthyroid individual," this girl was overactive, excitable, and a little "scatterbrained." To balance these qualities, she had "lots of drive" and was in many school activities. She was respected as a leader and had "a lot of verbal talent." She never became a conduct problem.

650. F:15:1   ACE IX, 69; XI, 84   '7965–'2   5:2:15
     N:II:5   ENG IX, 86; XI, 77   '374 96 81–'50   5:2:23
                     HSR 89
                     SVIB WR'

Considered "immaculate in home, dress, and in everything," this girl was also "very persnickety, a definite perfectionist like her mother." She was active in church affairs and was a leader in the church choir. In general, she was described as friendly, outgoing, and popular although her "self-righteousness" evoked a little resentment among other students. She was particularly well liked by her teachers because she would go to the limit to please, and she was so reliable that they would ask her to help in the teaching. Considered the hardest working student in the entire school, she always did more than was expected of her. After graduation she continued on to university work with the aid of a small scholarship. She added to this by earning her room and board working in a private home. She seemed willing to miss out on campus affairs in order to obtain this financial help.

The family situation was good, with "a balance between the parents," who were very compatible. The girl was "the light of her father's life." The father himself was a teacher and was described in many fine ways. He was very proud of his daughter. In some contrast, the mother was sharper of tongue and more critical, "a perfectionist with much drive and determination." She was also described as "tense and nervous."

651. M:15:1	ACE IX, 95; XI, 94	'79680–13'4	2:3:6
N:III:1	ENG IX, none; XI, 77	9'4586–0'12	2:2:13
	HSR 42	4'9568 73–'20	2:2:19
	SVIB none		

Descriptions of this boy varied from good to rather adverse. He was pleasant, well liked, and friendly in his general social relationships, but he was also called a "liar" and "glib." He could not be trusted and he seemed to lack respect for the rights of others. Never a leader, he was easily led into trouble and he went around with groups of boys who were likely to get into trouble. He had good ability but was an indifferent, unreliable student. In his senior year he was often involved in drinking bouts and he forged an identification card to purchase liquor for himself and others. Out of school he had numerous part-time jobs. He got into trouble because of careless driving and "malicious mischief." Some blame was put on his home, where he was "somewhat overprivileged and allowed freedom that others did not have." He was active in a number of school clubs and he went with a well-respected girl. After graduation he continued on to university work but was reported to be achieving only mediocre grades.

The father was a successful small businessman. Despite the fact that the parents were somewhat lenient, the family was said to be "fine, homey, and close-knit."

652. F:14:2	ACE IX, 52; XI, 62	7'98456–	3:5:16
N:II:1	ENG IX, 77; XI, 62	43'98167–	2:6:14
	HSR 71		
	SVIB none		

Having an older sister who was outstanding in schoolwork and who was popular may have adversely affected this girl. Although she was well dressed and well liked, she sometimes appeared quiet and a bit withdrawn. She was considered a little rebellious and easily led by undesirable companions. In the tenth grade she received some therapeutic help for her peculiar way of speaking. In her senior year she was caught in an episode that involved a kind of sexual promiscuity. Before this she had gone around with a fringe group of youngsters, who had involved her in behavior that probably built up to this more severe episode. After graduation she went on to attend a university.

The home and family seemed unusually good. The mother was considered the more domineering parent. The parents took a great deal of interest in their children, did things with them, and were very cooperative. They attended not only school functions in which their children were involved, but also those their own children did not take an active part in.

653. F:14:1   ACE IX, none; XI, 26   7'98564–   4:10:15
     N:III:1   ENG IX, none; XI, 57
                   HSR trans. 11th gr.
                   SVIB none

According to her teachers, this girl gave the impression of being quiet but not withdrawn. She seemed to lack initiative and she did not stand out in school or in groups. Considering her ability, her teachers generally thought she had done well at school. The girl's mother, however, who was said to have high aspirations for her children, was dissatisfied with her daughter's performance. There were some who suggested that the girl did not work to capacity because of rebelliousness toward the mother. She enrolled at a private school after completing the tenth grade. This change reflected the mother's wishes and was contrary to the girl's expressed desires.

654. M:14:1   ACE IX, none; XI, 72   79'8506–   3:4:10
     N:V:1   ENG IX, none; XI, 43   7"02'581–'3   0:7:5
                   HSR 58
                   SVIB none

Satisfied with himself and simply coasting along in school, this boy was nevertheless "nice to have in class." He did his work and was moderately popular and quiet in class. Although he never volunteered, he did his written work well. He was active in sports. It was mentioned that he was not easily led by others.

655. M:14:3   ACE IX, none; XI, 38   '798062–'4   3:12:10
     N:IVB:6   ENG IX, none; XI, 12
                   HSR none
                   SVIB none

Described as "erratically reliable," this boy was occasionally moody and often neglectful so that he needed to be prodded even on small projects. He was well accepted by other students although he could be "snippy." His judgment was "fair to poor." He did not actively participate in schoolwork, and when he was in the ninth grade several teachers ranked him as likely in later years to have emotional or legal difficulty.

656. M:16:3   ACE IX, 17; XI, 32   '790126–'3   3:7:10
     N:III:1   ENG IX, 17; XI, 11
                  HSR 07
                  SVIB 4'–0

Although apathetic and a nonparticipant, this boy caused no real disturbance or difficulty in school. He was not belligerent, but rather a "submerged person." He was absent a great deal, but, despite the excuses he gave, he was not known to have any severe illnesses. In appearance he was sloppy and in manner he was withdrawn, tending to have no connection with anyone. The few times he did participate in activities, he seemed fairly capable.

657. F:14:2   ACE IX, none; XI, 78   '7905–'1   2:5:7
     N:II:3   ENG IX, 83; XI, 71   '49–2'05   2:2:15
                  HSR 69   '94–2'85   4:3:14
                  SVIB none

This girl was very neat and well groomed. She was "smart," not a conduct problem, and well liked. She participated in many school activities, and she was particularly good in music. She had a steady boy friend. She hoped to teach English and after graduation continued on to a university.

658. F:15:1   ACE IX, 57; XI, 47   '70234 58–'16 7:2:13
     N:II:5   ENG IX, 54; XI, 43
                  HSR 76
                  SVIB none

A fair student, this girl worked hard and was cooperative in class. She took part in some activities and was very well accepted by other students. She was a drum majorette with the band and was in the choir.

659. M:16:8   IQ (centile) 10   7"02'684–9'5   4:7:12
     N:VII:3   HSR DO 9th gr.
                  SVIB none

This boy was interested in hot-rods and liked to make over old cars and race them. Very poor in his schoolwork, he dropped out in the ninth grade.

The father, a farmer, was "always going to make money on ideas," but the ideas never materialized. The mother was nice and anxious to please. The family all worked hard but they never seemed to get anywhere.

660. F:15:3   ACE IX, none; XI, 26   '70342–   2:5:9
     N:IVB:3   ENG IX, none; XI, 76   9876'2 3405–   3:6:7
                   HSR 42
                   SVIB none

This farm girl stayed in town in order to work while she attended high school. She appeared to have some ability in artistic work but lacked the interest and drive to take advantage of this ability. She was not shy and she had many friends. One report claimed that she had a tendency to use too much makeup.

661. F:15:2   ACE IX, 52; XI, 87   '7045–9'   7:6:13
     N:VI:2   ENG IX, none; XI, 75   6'78043952–   3:7:10
                   HSR 59
                   SVIB 'WR

Although a little shy, this girl would relax and become more free after she knew people. Described as a "nice kid," she was courteous, mature, dependable, and well adjusted. She had a good many friends but did not engage in school activities. She apparently doubted her own ability, because she wanted to go on to professional training and yet questioned her acceptability as a candidate. After graduation she completed a subprofessional training course.

     Both parents were interested in their children, and the home and family seemed very acceptable.

662. F:15:5   ACE IX, none; XI, 98   7'068 34–9'   5:4:20
     N:VI:2   ENG IX, none; XI, 89   4'270816–'9   5:4:26
                   HSR 92
                   SVIB none

An attractive, pleasant, and friendly girl, this student was thought of as a fine worker. However, she was "not very wise in the selection of her boy friends" and at one time was said to have made a fool of herself in the school hall with a boy. Another person said she "ran with bad company."

663. M:14:4   ACE IX, 63; XI, 37   7'0846–'235   3:6:9
     N:IVA:5   ENG IX, 60; XI, 25   '0–3615'2   2:11:8
                   HSR 28
                   SVIB 4'9–5

With male teachers this boy was respectful and not much of a problem; with female teachers he threw books and was a "smart aleck." He was immature and belonged to a group who were shy and considered not good for him. He did average school-work, and he was cooperative in class projects. During high school he improved somewhat, but he never became a very good school citizen. He got into some minor difficulties with the police because of "hot-rod" activities. After graduation he went into the armed services.

The father was described as friendly, honest, and sincere, very well liked but ineffectual. He was apparently a successful man in business relationships. The mother was a schoolteacher, the "salt of the earth type." She dominated the home. She expected much of her children and tended to get it because of her quiet and warm control over them.

664. F:15:1	ACE IX, 94; XI, 83	7'08641259–	8:3:24
N:II:1	ENG IX, 97; XI, 93	'6483 701–'5	10:3:24X
	HSR 86		
	SVIB none		

Described as "a little overprotected at home," this girl was, nevertheless, considered one of the more mature and dependable girls in her high school. She was president of a girls' club in which there were problem girls, and she handled them very well. In other areas, however, she was not much of a leader. She did very good work in school and would always do extra assignments, so that she was recommended for several scholarships, though there is no record that she received any of these. In the beginning of her senior year she was involved in some trouble with the traffic court, but she did not appear to be much at fault and the case was dismissed. After graduation she went on to a small college, and there she became a member of a sorority.

The parents were described as average, friendly people with neither health nor other obvious problems. The home was very well kept and the family was both socially and financially strong.

665. M:14:1	ACE IX, 77; XI, 79	'7089–'13	1:5:11
N:I:2	ENG IX, 87; XI, 74	'8679–5'3	1:1:11
	HSR 69		
	SVIB '4–90		

This tall, well-built boy was in many activities and was characterized by good ambition and goals. He was conscientious; he "knew exactly where he was going" and "had lots of push." He had a part-time job outside of school. Eventually he hoped to become a physician, and his teachers felt that with his drive he would probably succeed. When he was younger it was said that he had often been neglected by his parents, who spent much time in taverns. After graduation the boy went to a junior college.

The mother and father were both college graduates. The mother was particularly characterized as "a very brilliant woman." She had taught school for several years. The father was a professional man in political work. Both parents had some problem with alcoholism.

666. M:15:2   ACE IX, none; XI, 67   '7094–6'   5:3:10
     N:VII:3   ENG IX, none; XI, 61   '50–41'98   3:6:11
     HSR 20
     SVIB 4'8–9

Although this boy could have been a good student, he tended to get by with as little work as possible. Uninterested either in academic studies or in extracurricular activities, he stayed away from school whenever he could. He did have a part-time job outside of school, and it seemed that he was physically tired; this may have influenced his poor showing. After graduation he married and became a tradesman.

The parents were hard workers and the family was well liked and stable. Both parents worked outside the home.

667. M:14:0   ACE IX, none; XI, 49   '8–125'06   3:3:12
     N:IVA:5   ENG IX, none; XI, none   '869–'02   1:3:17
     HSR 60
     SVIB none

This was an unobtrusive boy who was well liked and not a troublemaker. He was a hard worker and he took part in some school activities, although he was a little shy. One ninth-grade teacher expected that he might develop emotional maladjustment.

668. F:15:2   ACE IX, 86; XI, 88   '8–1'20 35   1:1:17
     N:VI:4   ENG IX, 93; XI, 80   9'487–5'2 10   3:3:17
     HSR 90
     SVIB none

"The mother possibly spoiled this girl," who was haughty in attitude, and felt very self-important. "Sassy," sometimes mean and malicious, she gave the teachers a hard time although she was considered only a slight conduct problem. She had a small clique of friends.

669. M:15:2   ACE IX, 21; XI, 09   '8–'13   3:2:16
     N:VI:4   ENG IX, none; XI, 14
     HSR 04
     SVIB '9–5

This boy "wanted to be kicked out of school but his parents kept him in." He was negative, lazy, and untrustworthy. Most of the time he passively resisted authority;

occasionally he exhibited outward resentment. He wished to get out of school in order to take a steady job.

670. F:14:3   ACE IX, none; XI, 65   '8–'2   6:4:17
     N:III:2   ENG IX, none; XI, 82
                    HSR 62
                    SVIB none

This nicely dressed — even immaculate — girl was outstanding and had high morals. She was well liked by everyone. Fun loving, she had a fine sense of humor. Generally a leader and fine citizen, she was in many activities. She went on to attend a junior college after her graduation.

671. F:14:0   ACE IX, 28; XI, 30   '8–'4659   5:2:16
     N:V:1   ENG IX, none; XI, 47   '64–15'2 90 4:3:16
                    HSR 29
                    SVIB none

This girl was overweight and not very attractive, and her classmates made jokes about her. She was not a disciplinary problem. Although she was not accepted by her classmates, she had one special friend. Her interests were in cooking, sports, and music, but she was not very successful in any of these. She hoped to become a practical nurse. She was easily satisfied with average or poor grades and she would do her work wrong rather than take the trouble to find out the correct way. The reason for her poor achievement was sometimes given as timidity, lack of interest, or laziness. She worked as a baby sitter and provided part of her school expenses from the money she earned. After graduation she became a clerk in a store where she was fairly satisfactory. From early childhood she suffered from a chronic illness which needed constant treatment.

The father was a hard worker who was nervous and worried over bills. The mother was pleasant, active, and well enough liked, although she was condescending and unwilling to recognize her daughter's academic limitations.

672. M:15:2   ACE IX, 21; XI, none   '8–5'26   5:5:19
     N:IVB:6   ENG IX, none; XI, none
                    HSR DO 12th gr.
                    SVIB none

This boy dropped out of school probably from lack of motivation. He showed considerable interest at times and "demonstrated that he was able to think," but his grades were poor. He seemed to become depressed often and he tended to condemn himself. He was rather well liked and he had a good sense of humor. Although he was neither particularly active in school affairs nor a leader, he did become student manager of athletics.

673. M:15:0	ACE IX, 84; XI, 81	'8–562'3	2:5:16
N:V:3	ENG IX, 57; XI, 33	'87431–'965	3:0:22
	HSR 36		
	SVIB 4'–0		

In the ninth grade this boy was accepted only by a marginal group. He was always "smarting off," and taking an "I don't give a damn attitude." As he continued in school his general behavior improved, although he still went about with the rough gang. His interest in school vacillated, varying from enthusiasm to irresponsibility. By the twelfth grade he was likable, dependable, and relatively mature. He was interested in the theater and he liked to read. He was also interested in mechanics and automobiles. Although he was an underachiever, his teachers expected he would do well in college. He enrolled in a sectarian college.

"Average, hard-working people who try their best to raise a good family," the parents were "plodders, not leaders."

674. F:14:2	ACE IX, 38; XI, 36	'8–5'91	3:4:20
N:V:1	ENG IX, none; XI, 64		
	HSR 53		
	SVIB none		

This girl was a problem pupil when she was in the tenth grade, but she improved greatly as she continued through school. During her ninth and tenth grades she ran with a tough crowd and apparently followed its ways. Later she made a good adjustment and became conscientious, pleasant, and mature.

675. M:14:4	ACE IX, none; XI, 90	'8–6'9	3:5:15
N:IVB:6	ENG IX, none; XI, 36	— —	— —
	HSR 64	70'26485–3'	1:11:12
	SVIB '8–		

This boy was a little timid and shy, and he was "quiet nearly all the time — you had to dig it out of him." He was a hard worker in school and his most prominent activity was in the field of sports. Somewhat contrastingly, his teachers also described him as easygoing, pleasing, and well liked. He had several friends. He went to a university after graduation.

676. M:15:1 ACE IX, none; XI, 65 '8–'75 3:6:11
    N:VI:3 ENG IX, none; XI, 21 '964–'372 3:5:9
            HSR 04
            SVIB none

Although clean and tidy, this boy was the "blue-jeans type." He was friendly but he took no active part in school and showed no interest or ability in athletics. He was interested in hunting and fishing, and he worked part time outside of school. In his schoolwork he achieved barely passing grades. In his senior year he was fined for theft and was placed on probation.

677. M:15:9 ACE IX, none; XI, 14 8'''124 709–'5 3:23:16X
    N:IVB:3 ENG IX, none; XI, 06 '8967 04–2'513 3:5:14
            HSR 25
            SVIB '4–5

Because he had to commute to classes and had to work at home on the farm, this boy had little time for school activities, but he was well liked in and out of school. He came from a very religious family. After graduation he went into the armed services.

The father, a farmer, was a "big, quiet, slow-thinking man dominated by his wife." The mother was somewhat eccentric. She often interfered in school policy, being "a person who wrote letters to the editor." A strong worker for "causes," she was earnest and outspoken, sometimes to the extent of neglecting her children.

678. F:16:3 ACE IX, 08; XI, 10 8''1'263 45 709– 5:10:22
    N:IVB:2 ENG IX, none; XI, 06
            HSR 11 DO 12th gr.
            SVIB none

Although not a conduct problem in school, this girl was mentally slow and had trouble understanding. She was pleasant and conscientious, but she did not mix well and had just a few friends. She dropped out of school at the beginning of her senior year.

679. F:15:3 ACE IX, 05; XI, none 81''27'409365– 4:14:8
    N:VI:1 ENG IX, none; XI, none
            HSR DO 10th gr.
            SVIB none

A girl who appeared sloppy and had a "squatty" physique, this student was very self-conscious and would never look a person straight in the eye. Quiet, withdrawn, and not accepted in school, she became discouraged and dropped out in her sophomore year. After she quit school she reportedly turned into a "skid row type" who went around with older persons and was "all painted up." She was satisfied to work as a waitress until she was married.

An older sister was quite the opposite of this girl and had "a great deal on the ball."

680. M:15:5   ACE IX, none; XI, 07   8‴1″6729′350–   6:30:13X
     N:IVC:2   ENG IX, none; XI, 01
                 HSR 17 DO 12th gr.
                 SVIB none

This boy's main interest was in boxing rather than school. He was discourteous and his school attendance was irregular. He felt he was "always being picked on" by the teachers and other students. Uncooperative and resentful of authority, he finally quit school during his senior year. Two offenses occurring during his junior year, one for fighting and one for intoxication, were found in police records. One ninth-grade teacher had anticipated emotional difficulties in later life for him.

681. M:14:11   ACE IX, none; XI, 19   81′674029–   3:15:16
     N:IVB:5   ENG IX, none; XI, 13
                 HSR 02
                 SVIB none

Except for his senior year this boy was a conduct problem. He caused trouble to his teachers and to the school bus drivers. His teachers described him as "one of the worst." Not a good student, he seemed to have no motivation to try. His activities in the school were limited to some athletics. He had a few friends in a limited circle. Then in his senior year his behavior improved, and by the end of this year, he was a much more acceptable boy. The family did not have much money and the boy worked very hard outside of school. The police reported him as one who drank and who was "a maniac with a car." Several of his ninth-grade teachers expected that he would have legal difficulties and one predicted emotional problems.

682. M:14:3   ACE IX, 02; XI, 04   8″17′234069–   9:10:17
     N:VI:3   ENG IX, 15; XI, 03   7′4806239–   7:7:18
                 HSR 02
                 SVIB '4–

"Too negative for anyone to know him reliably," this boy "just filled a seat" in the classroom. He was a "definite introvert" and passively resistant to anything academic. He was frequently absent from school and eventually failed to graduate because of his inability to pass courses in social studies and in mathematics. One person claimed that he was "manually inclined but had very low mentality." Another said, "Maybe he could run with a fast crowd." The only difficulty that he was known to have had in connection with the law was a minor traffic offense.

The family was little known, but there were reports that the boy had a poor home background.

683. M:14:2   ACE IX, 63; XI, 69   8179′4063–5′2   3:13:18
      N:V:4   ENG IX, 61; XI, 51   ′319–2′50   5:3:20
                      HSR 54
                      SVIB 4′–

Very few good things were said about this boy, although he was described as well coordinated and likable and one informant reported that he wished to learn a trade. Most other persons did not have such positive things to say about him. He was sullen and bitter regarding the authority of teachers. Both he and an older brother, who was in the same class, would threaten people, using their father's influence as a weapon. This older brother was even more of a problem than was the boy, and he greatly influenced him. The boy created an extreme problem in the classroom. One day he could be controlled, but the next day he would be likely to be worse than ever before. He was active in athletics but had to be punished for breaking training rules by smoking and drinking. There were many absences from school that he attributed to "minor aches and pains." He embarrassed others by his public behavior with his girl friends. He openly used obscene and profane language. The other students merely tolerated him. The school nurse said that she felt sorry for him, but that he always made her feel inferior. He appeared unappreciative of any effort by the teachers on his behalf. He made much show of bravado and was in repeated trouble for speeding in his car. Ultimately his driver's license was revoked. When he was a freshman, he and two other boys were involved in an escapade in which they behaved "improperly" with a girl. As a result of that incident the boy was placed on probation. There was one report that he had at one time been troublesome at a camp and had gone on a starvation diet in an effort to get his way with the counselors. When he was a senior he got into a drunken fight. After graduation he went into the armed services and became engaged to be married.

There was a great deal of information about the father, who was a small businessman. He was described as being emotionally unstable and was characterized by brutal bursts of temper, sullenness, and an aggressive need to excel, a trait that was also common in his sons. He was ambitious for his boys to excel in athletics, and he seemed to take a vicarious interest in their athletic achievements, forcing them beyond their capabilities. He "bullied the way for his boys all through school." He resented the school principal and any attempt made to help the boys. Although the boys disliked their father's interference, they regarded him with hero worship. Apparently his nature was ambiguous, since he was also described as generous and a fine organizer. The mother was dominated by the father she was described as "sweet, dependable, and wholesome."

231

684. M:15:0   ACE IX, 95; XI, 96   '819375–0'   4:2:21
    N:III:1   ENG IX, 92; XI, 73   48 31'27 695–0'   2:6:20
                HSR 63   '231 78495–0'   1:1:22
                SVIB '8–

Self-confident, pleasant, and happy-go-lucky, this boy was occasionally a little too loud for the other students. He was described as a procrastinator and his school-work oscillated in quality. In over-all evaluation, he was believed to be an under-achiever. His teachers suggested, however, that he was apt to think he had more ability than was actually the case. He was also described as easily influenced, and he and another boy got into some trouble over skipping school. He had a little trouble with the police because of curfew violations and "hot-rod" activities. After graduation he continued on to a university with engineering as his goal.

The entire family, including aunts and uncles, was "emotional and striving for social position." There appeared to be tension among family members, with one trying to outdo the other. Although the father's vocational achievement was mod-erately good, the family was considered to be living above the level appropriate to the father's position.

685. F:14:5   ACE IX, none; XI, 62   8'1976 40–5'   6:6:16
    B:N:3   ENG IX, none; XI, 86
                HSR 86
                SVIB none

Although this girl was not a conduct problem in school, she kept late hours and was known to have undesirable companions outside of the school. She also worked outside of the school. In school she was very satisfactory; she got good grades and was quiet and mature. She planned to be married as soon as she graduated.

686. M:14:2   ACE IX, none; XI, 76   '810–'6   4:4:11
    N:V:1   ENG IX, none; XI, 77   '9–7'82 563   2:1:13
                HSR 76
                SVIB none

This boy was "the retiring type," but he had some qualities of leadership and was well liked by others. Consistent in his schoolwork but never spectacular, he made good use of his ability. "A good student to have in class," he was not a conduct problem. He was honest and conscientious, and he had strong religious convictions.

687. M:14:8   ACE IX, 03; XI, 22   82'13 7046–   7:9:17
    N:IVB:5   ENG IX, 11; XI, 15
                HSR 12
                SVIB 9'–5

This boy changed schools before much information was accumulated about him. It was said that he lacked initiative and industry; he "was lazy and worked only when necessary." His conduct was "poor," and two of his ninth-grade teachers expected that he would later have emotional difficulty.

688. M:15:6   ACE IX, none; XI, 19   8‴2175′49360–   5:16:20X
     B:IVB:5   ENG IX, none; XI, 06   8′6941573–   5:6:16
                 HSR 04
                 SVIB none

Low in ability, poor in achievement, and afflicted with a slight speech impediment, this boy probably stayed in school because of his athletic interests. He "carried a chip on his shoulder" and felt oppressed and picked on. When things went wrong he could be mean. He was somewhat extroverted and was, despite his disposition, popular with his classmates. His closest companions, however, were a "rough crowd." He was known to have lied, and it was occasionally necessary to send him to the principal's office for discipline. As he progressed through school he seemed to gain a better understanding of some of his problems and his behavior improved. At one time he stole gasoline and was forced to make restitution. There was also an incident in which he vandalized a police car.

The boy lived on a farm and worked very hard there. His mother had been dead for some time before he entered high school.

689. F:14:3   ACE IX, 09; XI, 33   ′8240–   9:8:16
     N:IVB:4   ENG IX, none; XI, 56   ′0962–′14 6:6:10
                 HSR 55
                 SVIB ′–

Immature and "kiddish," this girl was a minor conduct problem. She could, however, do fair work if she wished. She had several good friends. She was neither a leader nor a participant in school activities, although she was a "bouncy, peppy girl."

690. M:17:4   ACE IX, 18; XI, 04   8″261′70543–′9 3:14:14
     N:IVC:4   ENG IX, none; XI, 03   ′7958063124–   6:8:15
                 HSR 02
                 SVIB ′8–

This boy was frail, short, and slender, having a thin face, large ears, and beautiful dark eyes. He spoke with a decided lisp and his physical coordination was poor. He missed a great deal of school because of illness. Other students teased him when they had an opportunity. He appeared "physically and mentally incapable of making his own living." He was feminine in many ways: he "loved and needed flowers," and he was a good baker and cook. It disappointed him that other students did not like him and he tried to buy popularity. He wanted to impress people that he was a regular fellow. He worshipped one teacher and this teacher was amazed at the improvement of the boy over four years of high school. Excited and thrilled over graduation, he hated to leave. One teacher predicted emotional maladjustment for him.

The father was very proud of even the minor accomplishments of his son. He was hard working, friendly, easygoing, and articulate. The mother was friendly and was particularly mentioned as a good cook. She was affectionate and sincere with the children. The home was dirty and disorderly. Several of the children were mentally defective.

691. M:15:2	ACE IX, 06; XI, 03	82′74130̲6̲9̲–′5	6:14:17
N:IVC:1	ENG IX, 04; XI, 07		
	HSR 24		
	SVIB 4′–90		

Indifferent and inconspicuous, this boy wasted time in school and had very few friends. He "just filled a seat." Several of the teachers expected that he would become emotionally maladjusted.

692. M:15:5	ACE IX, 46; XI, 28	′829̲6̲7̲ 5̲4̲3̲0̲–	6:4:13
B:N:2	ENG IX, none; XI, 17		
	HSR 01		
	SVIB ′89–		

Although this boy had a record of some tardiness he was not a major conduct problem in school. He was not a bright student, although when he liked things, he could do them well; for example, he was interested in and did good work in the subject of electricity. He took part in few activities and was generally seen as an immature boy. He got into some minor trouble because of a traffic offense in his junior year. He was the youngest child in his family and his father died sometime before he entered high school.

693. M:15:3	ACE IX, 23; XI, 29	82′079̲3̲5̲–′1	3:10:5
N:III:1	ENG IX, none; XI, 27		
	HSR 24		
	SVIB none		

This boy "had courage in athletics but nothing else." He was nice appearing but seemed to be in poor health, both physically and mentally. He tried to work in class, but he was very slow and he never volunteered. He was always a follower.

He tried a lot of things, including athletics, but he could not achieve and seemed to have great insecurity and a lack of self-confidence. He had a period of mental breakdown, during which he was briefly in an institution. After this, he adjusted fairly well again. In all, he was a very "different" boy.

The father seemed to be a great deal like the boy. He also was different; he was slow in achievement and slow in movement. The father was, however, a moderately successful businessman and provided a good home for his family. The mother had taken teachers' training and was considered a nice person. She was quiet like the boy.

694. M:14:2	ACE IX, 74; XI, 59	'83165–0'9	7:9:19
N:III:1	ENG IX, none; XI, 56	— —	— —
	HSR 63	'584–2'10	4:7:16
	SVIB '–		

This boy was egotistical and had a "know-it-all" attitude. He seemed not to care to associate much with classmates because he considered himself above them. When in their presence he always acted "distant." He created a disturbance in and around the school by smoking, occasional absence without permission, abuse of pass privileges, and other forms of disorderly conduct.

695. M:15:8	ACE IX, none; XI, 02	'8310694–	2:7:12
N:VI:9	ENG IX, none; XI, 02	'17 3420–6'9	5:4:14
	HSR none		
	SVIB '14–		

Fellow students tended to make fun of this boy, who was feminine in his behavior. He hated physical education courses but cooperated fairly well in other classes. Because of his poor scholastic record he had to repeat the ninth grade. He was described as "reliable but emotional and fickle."

696. M:15:2	ACE IX, none; XI, 10	'834–'509	7:5:18
B:VI:1	ENG IX, none; XI, 04	'31–'29	5:0:18
	HSR 34		
	SVIB none		

A good worker with a nice personality, this boy was described as a poor producer. In his junior year he was involved in a gang fight. A pleasant youth, he was moderately successful in social connections. During his senior year he became very interested in girls.

697. M:15:5   ACE IX, 11; XI, 15   8''3'5971 604–   7:10:10
     N:VII:2   ENG IX, none; XI, 04
                    HSR 03 DO 12th gr.
                    SVIB '89–5

This boy was limited in many ways. He had poor hearing, poor teeth, poor eye-sight, and not much mental ability. He did not keep himself clean and neat, and he had a "weak personality." Although his attitude was not negative, he was in-different in school and let everything slide. His greatest interest was in shop work, but even here he did not do well. His school attendance was irregular, and he finally quit in his senior year to take a full-time job. His actual behavior in school was not bad, but outside of school he got into occasional trouble. He had a steady girl friend and was described as a "lover."

Both parents were heavy drinkers, and they "kicked him out of the home when he complained about not having decent clothes." A younger brother also had trouble at home and left to live with relatives. It was a "lousy home situation."

698. M:15:2   ACE IX, 14; XI, 17   '8361457–   6:7:16
     N:N:5   ENG IX, 17; XI, 06   '635–'780   11:5:15X
                    HSR 44
                    SVIB '8–

This hard-working and cooperative boy presented no conduct problem. He was a "clean-cut, very fine boy." Interested in the Boy Scouts, he was very dependable if given a specific task to complete.

699. F:14:1   ACE IX, 86; XI, 96   836'70142–'5   1:4:14
     N:IVB:3   ENG IX, 94; XI, 93   870'16324–'59 0:7:13
                    HSR 95
                    SVIB WR'

This was a good-natured and exuberant girl, well adjusted, intelligent, and easy to get along with.

The father was a substantial and highly respected citizen in the community, and the family lived on a good farm. It was an excellent home situation with good economic and community status.

700. F:14:7   ACE IX, none; XI, 100   83'7416 90–'5   1:14:11
     N:VI:5   ENG IX, 100; XI, 100.
                    HSR 94
                    SVIB none

The description of this girl was inadequate in detail. She was considered to be extremely bright and she had a good student record. She was, however, sexually promiscuous and in her junior year was involved in an episode that resulted in two men receiving prison sentences. The girl later ran away with a boy in a car stolen from her family. There was one illegitimate child from these escapades. It appeared that she returned to school later and began to make a good adjustment, intending to marry as soon as she graduated. One ninth-grade teacher thought she would have future emotional problems.

701. M:15:3   ACE IX, 86; XI, 95   '837459–'2   2:3:12
     N:VI:1   ENG IX, none; XI, 51
                   HSR 60
                   SVIB none

This boy dressed neatly and had a nice appearance. He participated in school activities and was "a likable kid." In general, he "completely minded his own business" and seemed willing to learn, to listen, and to try.

702. F:14:3   ACE IX, 75; XI, 77   8"3'064 97 12–   0:13:10
     N:V:1   ENG IX, none; XI, 87
                   HSR 43
                   SVIB WR'

Although this girl was apparently no behavior problem, she had a poor attendance record in school. She seemed to lack motivation and purpose, and her teachers believed this was the cause of her poor scholastic achievement.

703. M:14:2   ACE IX, 100; XI, 97   '84–'9   3:1:20
     N:III:2   ENG IX, none; XI, 93   '8179 34–2'0   2:1:23
                   HSR 89
                   SVIB '49–0

This boy was depicted by some as big, slow moving, and slow talking and by others as energetic and hard working. Courteous, "very adult in manner," always neat and well dressed, he was popular with his classmates and generally well thought of by adults. Elected to class offices throughout high school, he was characterized as "a good politician" because he was respected by all and was able to work with everyone including the "tough boys." He had always evinced a wide-ranging curiosity, reading extensively and earning awards for achievements in scholarship, athletics, and other activities. His teachers described him as being personally and socially well adjusted during his senior year. He had been a "sensitive child" when younger. Just before entering high school, he was arrested for stealing a car, and early in his high school career he associated with an undesirable group of boys until his father took firm measures to stop this. His ability to adjust improved as he progressed through school. After graduation he entered college.

The father was not particularly outgoing; however, he was active in community affairs and well thought of, despite the fact that he was a little "cocky." He was said to be a good businessman, a firm disciplinarian, and the kind of person who demands perfection. Although described as even-tempered, he suffered a severe "nervous breakdown" in the year following the boy's graduation. The mother, well balanced, very serious, and an avid reader, was professionally trained. Her method of controlling the children emphasized persuasion, while the father's was more stern but somewhat erratic.

704. F:15:0	ACE IX, 70; XI, 52	'84–'92	3:2:22
N:III:1	ENG IX, none; XI, 88	'0–21'34569	1:1:15
	HSR 75		
	SVIB none		

In appearance this student was a "chubby, homely girl with very poor figure and posture." She was also congenitally somewhat lame. Other boys and girls considered her as "odd." With all these handicaps, the girl's obvious wish to be a part of the socially active student groups was frustrated. A summer trip with her mother helped her considerably, and she gained greater self-confidence. In her schoolwork she was a good student, working alone in a quiet, conscientious manner. Outside of school she had a job as a clerk. She wished to go to an exclusive girls' college after graduation but she was not accepted; she compromised by going to a junior college.

The father and mother were immigrants. They both worked and were relatively inactive in community affairs.

705. M:16:8	ACE IX, 01; XI, none	841'37256–	9:9:21
N:IVB:5	ENG IX, 01; XI, none		
	HSR DO 10th gr.		
	SVIB none		

Although this boy was not a problem in or out of school, he "went to school only to occupy his time." He was "not even a good physical education student," doing minimum work in everything and avoiding that if he could. It was believed that he not only lacked interest but also had poor ability. He had been held back in a grade, so that a younger brother was in the same class with him.

The parents did not seem to take much interest in their children, allowing them to go their own way. The father had a "strong personality" and "ruled the roost." He was described as an honest, hard-working farmer who was a good provider for his family. He was thought to be difficult to live with, however, since he was "loud, domineering, slovenly, and nearly illiterate." The mother was also described as slovenly; she was large and not too bright.

706. M:14:6   ACE IX, 48; XI, 62   8'4592016–   6:12:10
     N:VII:1   ENG IX, none; XI, 31
                     HSR 01
                     SVIB none

This boy "looked more like a waif than a high school student." He was unkempt
and sometimes dirty, with shabby clothes and missing front teeth. He seemed to
be unaware that he did not fit into the high school pattern. The girls in school were
very protective toward him and thought of him as a "cute little brother." He seemed
to enjoy this protective attitude and became "frisky," a nuisance, and a scatterbrain
but not a real conduct problem. He could be described as a "pleasant, happy,
immature boy." The librarian thought of him as a nice and helpful boy, pleasant
to have around — "but he never got his books in on time." Always needing to be
directed and prodded, he was irresponsible. Two ninth-grade teachers thought he
would have future legal trouble.

The father was rigid and strict with his children. Although he drank a lot, his
wife did not object because of the improvement in his behavior during these
periods. The mother "seemed lost and beaten down." She was a hard worker.
Several of the children were delinquent.

707. F:16:3   ACE IX, 01; XI, 02   8"46'13725–'9   7:16:20X
     N:IVC:4   ENG XI, 04; XI, 03   '82 47630–'9   9:13:15
                     HSR 01 DO 12th gr.
                     SVIB none

This girl was neat in appearance and interested in making herself attractive.
Neither shy nor retiring, she gave the impression of being pleasant, interested, and
dependable. Generally, her appearance and ordinary behavior did not indicate as
low a level of ability as did her schoolwork, reading level, and other intellectual
activities. During her high school years, she got a job for a while in the home
of a doctor, where she had to be taught to take baths, wash her hands, brush her
teeth, and do other routine self-care activities. She chose not to eat with this family
at mealtime and she ate odd things and mixtures. Her work habits were poor and
she did not finish projects. Her friends ridiculed her because of her lackadaisical
approach to things. Her friends were much younger than she, and when she was
given responsibility for the care of children, she tended to behave much like a
preschool child. She hated school and her achievement was exceedingly poor,
especially in reading. She finally quit and took a job as a housemaid.

The father was a pleasant, hard-working man. He was slow although willing
to learn. The mother also seemed very slow in thinking, but articulate and able
to cover up many of her own intellectual deficiencies. She was apparently unconcerned about her daughter's peculiarities. She was "much too impressed with
her own importance to realize the girl's inability to learn." With all these handicaps, the home was clean and neat, and the family appeared unusually happy.

708. M:16:9   ACE IX, 40; XI, 33   84″61′7932 50–   6:22:16X
     N:VI:2   ENG IX, none; XI, 11   34′851 9672–′0   1:5:16
                 HSR 21
                 SVIB ′0–5

Neat, clean, and well dressed, this boy did not present a conduct problem in the school. He was an active, lively boy who could not sit still for long and who was "quite a talker." He needed to be pushed in his schoolwork but was considered to do well enough in relation to his ability. Outside of school he was guilty of a long list of offenses. Both he and his twin brother were offenders and the brother was finally sent to a reform school. This boy's offenses were relatively minor in nature. They were generally characterized by defiance of authority in throwing rocks, fighting, and the like. He did not seem to think for himself but followed the crowd. He let his hair grow long, wore sideburns, and was "the Elvis Presley type."

The father was much older than would be expected in a family with children the age of this boy. He was a pleasant, cheerful person with a good sense of humor. He was described as "affectionate but ineffective." The mother, who was chronically ill, was "inert and resigned." In summary, the parents were considered to be morally straight enough but were lacking in discipline.

709. F:15:9   ACE IX, none; XI, 15   8″4639′7120–   2:16:15X
     N:IVC:3   ENG IX, none; XI, 15   96′48 57–′21   2:14:7
                  HSR 15
                  SVIB WR′

This was "the kind of girl you would never notice twice." If she had problems, she kept them to herself. Not a good student and very quiet, she was in danger of not graduating. She was "a bus student," never entering into school activities and merely coming from and going back to the farm where she lived with her large family. She became a waitress after graduation.

The father was a farmer and did odd jobs to supplement his income. He was an older man who had had a previous marriage. He was said to have a pleasing personality. It was also said that he had spent a short time in prison. The family was on periodic relief. The mother was a fairly adequate person, genuinely concerned about the children and the general running of her home. A number of the children had physical defects and at least one of the boys was delinquent.

710. F:15:9   ACE IX, 67; XI, 19   8″46′0279–′1   2:9:8
     B:VI:5   ENG IX, 67; XI, 51   ′704 2869–′5   4:5:13
                 HSR 15
                 SVIB none

This girl was untidy and unclean in appearance. She lacked confidence, and although she had one or two close friends, for the most part she kept to herself. She was friendly and smiled a good deal, but in attitude she seemed "fatalistic and passive." She carried a lot of responsibility at home, and seemed to be a thoughtful youngster. One ninth-grade teacher predicted emotional maladjustment for her.

The father had died when the girl was young. The mother had a poor reputation and was "beaten down, indifferent, and slow in reaction." The home was dirty, poorly heated, and badly kept. The family, however, was closely knit and acted only after conferences to make decisions.

711. M:15:6 ACE IX, none; XI, 05 84'7105–   7:11:20
   N:VI:3 ENG IX, none; XI, 14 8'421 397–'6 10:4:24X
        HSR 25
        SVIB none

This boy was unattractive; he was thin and he had a pointed head with big ears. Never a problem to the school or to his parents, he "could be trusted any place." He was neither disliked nor popular, and he was mediocre in all things. One ninth-grade teacher predicted that he would develop emotional maladjustment.

712. M:14:1 ACE IX, 93; XI, 99 84'723–   1:2:15
   N:V:1 ENG IX, 94; XI, 96 '58 41 37–'0 1:5:17
       HSR 41
       SVIB 45'8–

In his early high school years this boy was disrespectful to teachers and authorities. He was active in athletics, but even in this area he seemed unable to do anything right. As he continued in school his behavior improved and he was considered to be more dependable, although he still needed prodding to get schoolwork done. He was always somewhat retiring in manner. A lazy student with very poor penmanship, he tried to use his older sister's themes as his own. His interests shifted toward dramatics when he was a senior. He had always been fairly well liked by other students and his activities in community projects for the school led to his being moderately well accepted by the upper social group. After graduation he went into the armed services.

The boy's father had a police record and was considered unstable. The mother had a job, but the family was on relief part of the time and was considered lower class.

713. M:17:4 ACE IX, 04; XI, none 8"472610–'95 8:15:18
   N:V:1 ENG IX, none; XI, none
       HSR DO 11th gr.
       SVIB none

When he quit school after the tenth grade, this boy talked of enrolling at a trade school, but this plan did not work out. He later enlisted in the Army. After a short period he was discharged for going AWOL. He was subsequently committed to a mental hospital. The reason for this commitment could not be determined; however, the family reported that he was "fine now and would soon return home." School reports, while recognizing his limited intellectual ability, were generally favorable until his final year. Elementary school reports stated that his attendance, deportment, health, and appearance were all good and that his work was "satisfactory for his ability." He was once considered for placement in a special class. At this time one of his teachers said that "he tried so hard; he was such a serious boy; he seemed to be worried much of the time." In high school he was described as a nice-looking boy, always neat and friendly although quiet and reserved. The school report for his final year indicated that "academic subjects were beyond his capacity and he was starting to become a behavior problem." One teacher said that "he could be made or ruined by his associates, for he was naturally a follower." Another teacher said he was a "prevaricator." He had a reading difficulty and received special help from time to time while he attended school. His best school performance was in gym, where he had "excellent muscular coordination"; he participated in some school athletics. He also worked during summers and after school hours.

The boy was much younger than his brothers and sisters, who had much of the responsibility of rearing him. Both parents had spent time in mental hospitals, and other members of the family had also been hospitalized for mental breakdowns. When at home, the father was always dissatisfied and he seemed to hold a deep resentment toward his wife. The mother was described as constantly nervous and upset. The social agencies who occasionally gave the parents assistance thought, nevertheless, of them as "clean-living, sober, and reliable people."

714. M:14:6	ACE IX, none; XI, 36	'8473–	6:2:24
B:V:1	ENG IX, none; XI, 31	9'786–	3:3:14
	HSR 84		
	SVIB none		

Quiet, cheerful, and helpful, this boy was no problem in class and he had a good attitude toward school. He had an excellent sense of responsibility and was active in school affairs.

The father was a skilled workman. The parents divorced sometime before the boy entered the ninth grade. The boy lived with his mother.

715. M:16:6	ACE IX, 08; XI, 07	8'473196–'5	3:12:13
N:IVC:2	ENG IX, none; XI, 14		
	HSR 01 DO 11th gr.		
	SVIB none		

This boy dropped out of school in his junior year because he was failing and at the bottom of his class in grades. He neither liked nor did well in academic subjects; his best marks were in mechanics. He was not belligerent, but he was indifferent and lacking in enthusiasm, drive, and leadership qualities. The only thing he showed any particular interest in was baseball. His friends tended to be like him, and although none was a troublemaker, all were below average students. After school he had to go home and do heavy chores; when he dropped out of school he continued to work on the family farm. He was not known to have had any dates with girls.

The father was an unprogressive, unambitious farmer, a hard worker but inefficient and physically not strong. He encouraged his children to stay home and work on the farm rather than to go to school. He was a fairly firm disciplinarian. The mother was more capable and had more drive than her husband. Apparently she was more interested in getting the children to continue in school. The farm was a run-down and unattractive place.

716. M:15:2	ACE IX, 28; XI, 28	84'76 391–	9:9:23
N:V:4	ENG IX, 30; XI, 25	'473861–'0	8:1:26
	HSR 57		
	SVIB '489–		

This boy was characterized as having a flair for good clothes. It was said that he would have liked to be more daring in his dress but was governed by conformity. His desire to conform and be accepted was also evident in his earlier years. He was willing to work, to do more than his share; sometimes he seemed almost too willing — "the type to whom you can give any job and know it will be done." In manner he was easy to talk with, modest, charming, and tolerant. He was a good leader who was liked by both teachers and students. He was able to talk comfortably on many subjects, and although somewhat opinionated, he was not intolerant of others' opinions. He impressed others with his seemingly broad knowledge of distinguished writings and paintings and his good taste in art and literature. He was active in athletics and in other school activities. Outside of school he was particularly interested in automobiles. He was once arrested for speeding. After graduation he went to a small college.

The father owned a small business. He was described as dogmatic and stubborn about his opinions, always looking out for himself. The mother caused neighborhood talk because of her indulgence of the children. She seemed to have a great need to feel important, but did not outwardly seek recognition. In her contacts with others she was meek and reserved.

717. F:14:1	ACE IX, 88; XI, 96	84'796–31'25	0:6:13
N:V:3	ENG IX, 91; XI, 89	'59 78–0'2	0:0:17
	HSR 87		
	SVIB 'WR		

Beautiful, but "flippant, giddy, and immature," this girl was said to be "madly in love" in the tenth grade. She "had a weakness some place" and could get very antagonistic and snippy, becoming belligerent when someone tried to advise her.

She didn't get along well with other students but liked parties and liked to get around. She took part in a great many activities. Always helpful and courteous, she seemed more capable than she showed in her schoolwork, for many of her teachers considered her an underachiever. In the latter part of her senior year she appeared to stabilize and was described as a mature, gay, and lighthearted girl. After graduation she went into nurses' training, where she did well.

Her father was a "gay blade" and rather shiftless. The mother was hard working and made a good home for her children. It was thought that she stayed with the father because of the children.

718. M:14:1	ACE IX, 30; XI, 37	84'913–'2	4:14:16
N:V:2	ENG IX, 33; XI, 59		
	HSR 33		
	SVIB '24–5		

"Clean and tidy," this boy was average in most respects; he was well liked but not sought out. He simply did not stand out in any way and he engaged in no extracurricular activities. There was some doubt about his being completely honest.

719. M:15:2	ACE IX, 32; XI, 55	8"493 6'712–'5	2:6:9
N:V:1	ENG IX, 33; XI, 40		
	HSR 08		
	SVIB '0–5		

This good-looking boy was always very courteous in personal relationships with adults and he was well liked by other students. His motivation for schoolwork was poor; he talked out of turn in class, he was lazy, and he showed no ability or real interest. He was apprehended by the authorities because of participation in a fight where several boys fought several men; this boy used a tool as a weapon.

720. M:14:2	ACE IX, 28; XI, none	84"9'620–'53	5:17:11X
N:VII:3	ENG IX, 42; XI, none		
	HSR DO 11th gr.		
	SVIB none		

This was a tall and healthy boy. He disliked school; he was truant and passively resistant to authority. Finally he dropped out in his junior year. He was relatively quiet and he engaged in no extracurricular activities. After leaving school, he developed "hood" tendencies and was guilty of many petty disturbances such as drinking, thievery, and association with a tough group. He was put on probation but the probation was revoked to permit him to go into the armed services, where he established a good record.

The father was chronically ill and had been an invalid for a long time. The mother had to work. She was very slovenly and the home was "a rat's nest." She was also very emotional, often laughing and crying simultaneously.

721. F:14:0	ACE IX, 48; XI, 13	8'''49''67301'25–	4:15:8
N:VI:4	ENG IX, 36; XI, 36	47 06'235891–	1:6:7
	HSR 22		
	SVIB '–		

This girl was unusually physically mature for her age. She was "a picture of health, but a chronic complainer." She often missed school because of illness, and she gave the appearance of being erratic and discouraged. She "fussed and fretted constantly" over symptoms. School records did not provide any evidence of definite physical difficulty. She was described as a "big blow" who was "anxious to get married and finally did" shortly after graduation. She was uninteresting and had few friends. A continuous talker, she seemed to be unrealistic and to be living in a world of phantasy. She had the tendency to blame the teacher for poor grades. Two teachers thought she would have future legal problems.

The father, a skilled workman, was dominated by his overly talkative wife. The mother was almost incoherent because of her constant talking. She also lived in a world of phantasy. She was overanxious, and in general behavior she was "peculiar, nervous, and high-strung." The home situation was not a good one. The whole family seemed to lack strength.

722. M:14:1	ACE IX, none; XI, 52	8''4'9605173–	0:11:11
N:V:1	ENG IX, none; XI, 41	9'8453–'0	0:5:16
	HSR 13		
	SVIB none		

"The boy never grew up — he was a child and on the defensive." Always doubting, he would push a point, thinking he was right. He "made annoying facial expressions" and was a "very irritating boy." Although he did not apply himself in schoolwork, he managed to get by. One teacher expected he would get into legal difficulties, and there was a record of minor offenses.

723. M:15:1	ACE IX, 69; XI, 91	8'497 2365–	3:7:9
N:V:1	ENG IX, 33; XI, 42	7'29408–'6	6:9:13
	HSR 49		
	SVIB none		

In classes this boy did what was expected but was not really socially outgoing. To compensate for an early history of stuttering, he talked so rapidly that he made errors in forming the sounds. He was a good worker who tried hard and was objective about the fact that he had a speech problem. But his grades were not very good and he was dropped from speech class because he did not have a good attendance record. After graduation he joined the armed forces.

724. M:14:5   ACE IX, 38; XI, 50   84′976–5′12   2:9:15
     N:III:1   ENG IX, none; XI, 23
                  HSR DO 11th gr.
                  SVIB none

As an individual this boy was "okay and would take mandates well"; when alone he was withdrawn and quiet. He was, however, easily led, and with others he became a disruptive influence in class and created disciplinary problems. He dropped out of school to join the armed forces when he was a junior. Two of his teachers expected that he would get into trouble with the law.

725. M:15:1   ACE IX, 63; XI, 49   84′0–   5:8:16
     B:V:1   ENG IX, none; XI, 22   134‴287″65–   8:15:24
                  HSR 19
                  SVIB none

Although this boy was friendly and basically well behaved, he did not mix socially and he was uninterested in school because it did not fit into the pattern he had set for his life. He wanted practical training and had his own ideas about what he would do for a living. His interests were motorcycling, woodworking, and other of the more masculine activities. His English teacher said that when he was bored he could be very belligerent. He sometimes got that way when he couldn't do just as he wanted. After graduation he went into the Army.

726. F:14:2   ACE IX, 36; XI, none   8′40567 31–   3:8:18
     N:IVC:3   ENG IX, 26; XI, none   ′49730–   2:5:19
                  HSR 23
                  SVIB WR′

"A very fine, uncomplicated, and stable girl," this student was quiet, capable, and worked up to her ability in school. She was shy and rather mousy in social relations, had few friends, and was in a minimum of school activities. After graduation she went to a business college and from that into a secretarial job.

An only daughter, the girl was favored by the family. The father, a farmer, was easygoing and "philosophical." In some contrast, the mother was "a nagger, straight-laced, and a bit of a chronic whiner." She gave her children little freedom of decision. A son was poor in schoolwork and "overly interested in girls." Not clearly delinquent, he was, nevertheless, a behavior problem. The family lacked sufficient money a great part of the time because of illness.

727. M:15:2   ACE IX, 100; XI, 99   '85–'279   2:0:16
     N:I:2   ENG IX, 99; XI, 98
                 HSR 100
                 SVIB 1'2–

Although almost a "literary snob" — he favored the best literature and used the largest vocabulary in the school — this boy was popular and often elected to class offices, the only nonathlete to be so honored. Popular with teachers and students, he was a hard worker, putting his schoolwork ahead of any extracurricular activities. He had a good sense of humor and frequently made complicated puns.

728. M:14:3   ACE IX, none; XI, 95   '85349–   5:3:17
     N:III:2   ENG IX, none; XI, 91   819'432–'0 6:7:20
                 HSR 87
                 SVIB none

A good, industrious, and ambitious student whose interests tended toward science, this boy would assume leadership in some social situations. He was abrupt but well mannered and neat in appearance.

729. F:15:0   ACE IX, 84; XI, none   '8530–4'69   5:1:18
     N:VI:5   ENG IX, 65; XI, none
                 HSR 80
                 SVIB none

A large, somewhat clumsy, and poorly coordinated girl, this student dressed well and had an attractive personality. An only child, she "was babied" by her parents. She worked slowly and sloppily in school, and she was often absent. She was, however, in some activities in and out of school. More a follower than a leader, she was cooperative, hard working, and, in the view of the school, mature. After graduation she went into nurses' training.

The father had a weak personality and appeared delicate and in poor health. He was not often around the home. The mother was much stronger, a stable, outgoing person who made an excellent impression; she controlled the home. She was much interested in her daughter, and both parents had higher aspirations for her than she could fulfill.

730. F:14:2   ACE IX, none; XI, 64   '854367–   4:3:19
     N:III:3   ENG IX, none; XI, 74
                 HSR 88
                 SVIB none

This girl had a good deal of pep; she was very popular and always doing something. She had high motivation and was a fine student. She was considered very well adjusted.

247

731. M:15:1   ACE IX, 44; XI, 46   8'56017–'4   2:12:7
    N:V:2   ENG IX, 60; XI, 66
                   HSR 13
                   SVIB none

Responsive to any interest shown in him, this boy could come right back after his failures. He was immature, but during his school years he became more mature and likable. However, he still seemed unsure and afraid of being rebuffed. It was believed he missed his father, a traveling man. He became attached to a male teacher. In his junior year he got into trouble because of a traffic offense.

732. M:15:4   ACE IX, none; XI, 97   '8574–'916   2:5:15
    N:VI:3   ENG IX, none; XI, 91
                   HSR 97
                   SVIB none

When younger this boy had felt inferior because of the low economic status of his home. As he went through high school he became more open and outgoing. By his senior year he was popular and was described as a "wonderful boy — one of the nicest in the class." Stable and persevering, he took responsibility well, and in tasks he was creative and imaginative.

The home was described as "messy" but full of love and affection. The mother spent her time writing books, working to supplement the family income, and taking college courses. The children were all characterized as "uninhibited, happy, and ingenious."

733. M:14:5   ACE IX, 17; XI, 30   8'57614–   6:11:19
    N:IVB:2   ENG IX, none; XI, 32
                   HSR 08
                   SVIB none

This boy was friendly, sincere, and cooperative as a student. Very quiet, he had few friends and did not take part in any extracurricular activities. He was a slow student with little ambition, but he was not a conduct problem. One ninth-grade teacher predicted future legal difficulty for him.

734. F:14:9   ACE IX, 34; XI, 37   8'''5''764'9120–   5:18:19X
    B:IVB:5   ENG IX, 26; XI, 13   47''68'092–   5:10:12
                   HSR 25
                   SVIB WR'

This "large and awkward" girl was "too big for the boys to like." She was untidy in dress, socially inadequate, and ill at ease. She seemed to try to be pleasant; she accepted her rejection by others without apparently feeling much resentment. She was known by few, but she had two or three friends. After graduation she took a steady job.

The father had died when the girl was young. The mother continued on the family farm and was much hampered by financial problems. She was retiring and inarticulate. Several of the other children were defective and had social difficulties similar to this girl's.

735. F:14:1   ACE IX, 91; XI, 78   '8594–'2   3:1:16
     N:III:1   ENG IX, none; XI, 93   '836–0'   1:1:18
               HSR trans. 11th gr.
               SVIB none

Although when this girl was a ninth-grader one teacher expected future maladjustment, the somewhat limited information available did not support this prediction. Before she transferred to another school in her junior year, she seemed to be a very good student with high motivation, completely reliable and cooperative.

736. M:15:3   ACE IX, 61; XI, none   8'597 3624–   2:7:8
     B:I:3   ENG IX, 63; XI, none
               HSR trans. 11th gr.
               SVIB none

There was not much information about this boy, who transferred to another school after his sophomore year. He was described as "having a mind of his own" and as having a lot of confidence in himself. His was a wholesome character, and he was reliable and cooperative.

The father was a professional man, and the parents were divorced before the time of testing.

737. F:14:5   ACE IX, 05; XI, 04   '8507–'92   5:5:7
     N:IVB:3   ENG IX, 05; XI, 11   '5046–'91   4:1:13
               HSR 10
               SVIB WR'

This girl had bad teeth but "blossomed out" after she got them fixed. She was a nice, sweet little girl who was cooperative, reliable, and pleasant. She worked hard and did all her assignments to the peak of her ability. She had a "smiling" personality and always had a smile for everyone. During the summer she worked and earned enough for her room and board during the school year. The employer found her very satisfactory.

The father was moody and a real "griper." He did not get along well with his neighbors. He deserted the family when their house burned down. The mother, a pleasing person, had greater influence on the family. She was much interested in the girl. The children of the family were allowed a great deal of freedom and one brother was said to be quite wild.

738. F:14:5   ACE IX, 10; XI, 52   8'50794–   4:7:10
    N:III:3   ENG IX, 38; XI, 76
    HSR 21
    SVIB WR'

This girl was attractive and had more drive than the other members of her family. She wanted to get ahead but felt that her family could not help her. She had a "terrific temper," over which she had fair control, but she could not take criticism and her reaction was to "clam up." She was a quitter when things got tough.

The mother was reputed to be coarse and also to have a bad temper.

739. M:14:1   ACE IX, 90; XI, 78   '86–   6:3:14
    N:II:4   ENG IX, 72; XI, 61   '87̲3–   5:1:18
    HSR 80
    SVIB '49–

Descriptions of this boy showed contrasts. He was seen by some as a "goody-goody and stuffed shirt" who "acted like it hurt him to have a sense of humor" and who "had a terrible, jazzy, chatty manner." However, at least one teacher who first saw him in these less good ways later came to think of him as the opposite; apparently he was hard to know and evaluate. Many saw him as pleasant and outgoing, cooperative and unusually steady, even accepting of tasks that were drudgery. His interests were in engineering and he worked late at night on projects in this field. He was not well liked by other students; he had a superior air and resisted being told things. It was suggested that he was indulged by his parents and spoiled by having everything he wanted. After graduation he went to a small college.

The father was a businessman much engrossed in his work. He was highly respected for his business output, but he seemed self-centered and hard to know. The mother tried to rear her children well and was very unhappy when an older boy had an unsuccessful marital experience.

740. F:15:6   ACE IX, 42; XI, 16   8'6179402–   5:7:8
    N:III:4   ENG IX, 27; XI, 31   462'79830–5'   6:16:8X
    HSR 18
    SVIB WR'

Teachers thought of this girl as shy and retiring. However, she worked every day after school hours, she went steady throughout her high school years, and she was engaged in extracurricular activities to the extent that her grades suffered. In spite of all these activities she was only moderately well accepted by students. She had had an illness that was the basis for much excuse-making by her and her mother. The illness had forced the girl to miss a considerable amount of school and this subject came up in many conversations. Upon graduation she married the boy with whom she had gone steady.

The home was described in good terms. The parents were compatible and their reputation was good. The father was ambitious, always working, friendly, dependable, but "dull." The mother was an emotional person who felt superior to her husband. Definitely she was the boss of the family. She found it hard to accept critical items relative to her children and had a tendency to blame the school.

741. M:14:1	ACE IX, 07; XI, 02	8″6′10937–′45	4:10:12
N:VI:1	ENG IX, none; XI, 12	— —	— —
	HSR 11	′9678–14′325	3:15:4
	SVIB none		

There was great contrast between this boy's athletic and social accomplishments and his intellectual achievement in school. He was captain of athletic teams and a cooperative and interested student in many ways. He presented no problem of discipline and was liked by teachers and students. He dated an outstanding girl in the school. It was expected that he would ultimately be successful in the field of business, possibly in selling. His academic achievement, however, was very low. He was poor in reading and in study habits. He lacked initiative in schoolwork and did not hesitate to cheat when it became easy and necessary for him to do so in order to remain eligible for athletics. After graduation he enrolled in a university.

The father, a workman, was steady and acceptable. The parents, although in a lower income group, seemed to be good people and much interested in their children.

742. M:15:0	ACE IX, 05; XI, 30	86‴2″413′79–	6:19:20X
N:III:5	ENG IX, 01; XI, 03	′473915–	4:5:12
	HSR 04		
	SVIB ′–		

This boy had trouble with reading. He was a poor student except for shop courses. At times he was a discipline problem, becoming resentful and truculent toward some of the teachers. He liked attention and was considered to be spoiled by getting his own way at home. He was resentful of punishment, even when he had obviously done wrong. His behavior outside of school was somewhat better than that in school, and it was thought that he was compensating in classes for inferiority feelings. He wanted to quit high school, but his mother would not permit it. After graduation he went to work for his father. Two teachers expected that he would have future legal difficulties.

The father was a skilled workman who was, in the main, self-employed. He was unaggressive and considerably older than the mother. The mother was "neat and precise," and she "doted on the boy." She had come from a poor family and was determined that her boy should rise higher in the world.

743. M:15:3   ACE IX, 26; XI, none   86'294703–   4:15:12
    N:II:2   ENG IX, 38; XI, none
                 HSR DO 10th gr.
                 SVIB none

Described as "a complete stinker who could not be trusted with anything," this boy dropped out of school at the end of his tenth grade. He had failed the ninth grade and was repeating it at the time of testing. He was irresponsible, and with a gang of boys — of whom he was considered the leader — he committed a series of acts of vandalism. He was guilty of many other misdeeds. The neighborhood considered him a nuisance, although none of his activities constituted a serious offense. In manner he was quiet, tricky, and sullen when reprimanded. After leaving school he joined the armed services; but he deserted, stole a car, and was imprisoned.

The parents were educated people. The father was described as a fine man, and the mother as a good homemaker. The parents could not accept the boy's behavior and did not believe he did the things of which he was accused. A younger brother was also a troublemaker guilty of many misdeeds. In general, it seemed to be a good home. The parents gave the children a moderate allowance and were very embarrassed by the behavior of the boys.

744. M:14:3   ACE IX, none; XI, 92   '8634715–'0   4:2:19
    N:VI:2   ENG IX, none; XI, 83   '78421–'6   1:4:15
                 HSR 53   '489573–0'   2:2:22
                 SVIB none

Although this boy had a "sort of retiring disposition," he was a permanent nuisance. He had few friends and took part in no school activities. He told dirty stories out loud in class, made disturbing noises, was irritating and belligerently noncooperative. He was unreliable and would not do any schoolwork; consequently, he was a serious underachiever. In his freshman year he was warned for a minor traffic violation and in succeeding years he was in several other scrapes which came to the attention of the police. None of these was very bad, however.

745. M:14:5   ACE IX, 05; XI, none   86'''42'731 90–   8:23:12X
    N:IVA:5   ENG IX, 04; XI, none
                 HSR DO 9th gr.
                 SVIB none

One of identical twins who were so much alike that they could hardly be distinguished, this boy was honest, dependable, and a fairly good student, although he dropped out of school in his freshman year. He seemed almost completely lacking in a sense of humor. The twins were "taught nothing but work"; there was no time for social life or the development of hobbies. They were "friendly but seldom seen, and they had no girl friends."

The father, a farmer, was domineering, critical, and uneducated. The mother was strong-willed and held the family together with her warm and generous nature. The family was proud and characterized as "dull moneymakers."

746. F:14:2   ACE IX, 23; XI, none   86′″47″93′205–   3:28:9X
    B:III:4   ENG IX, none; XI, none
                 HSR trans. 10th gr.
                 SVIB none

This girl, who was deserted by her parents, lived with her grandmother. She was described as insecure, scatterbrained, and unpredictable. "She acted flighty" and was "very slippery and erratic." She was not accepted by others, she had no friends, and she did not take part in any activities. A majority of her teachers expected that she would develop emotional and legal difficulties.

747. M:14:4   IQ (centile) 83   8″64709′25–′3   1:13:7
    B:VII:3   HSR none   4′8956–   2:4:16
                 SVIB ′48–

This boy's biggest problem was to get enough money to run his car, which was his "pride and joy." He was "very much on his own financially." His schoolwork was satisfactory, and he was not a discipline problem. In manner he seemed adult and mature. Outside of school he had a job, and upon graduation from school he went into the armed forces.

The boy's father, an immigrant, had been married before he married the boy's mother. At the same time he was involved in an irregular relationship with still another woman. The mother was "well-meaning, with the best interests of her children in mind." Several of the children had been in varying amounts of trouble. The family's reputation was not good.

748. F:15:9   ACE IX, 20; XI, 07   8′″64″937′0521– 7:28:7X
    N:IVB:3   ENG IX, 04; XI, 19   68″″4′″9″7′05 231– 0:23:7X
                 HSR 19
                 SVIB WR′

This quiet and somewhat withdrawn girl was well enough liked, but she participated in no activities and showed no leadership abilty. In schoolwork she was cooperative, reliable, and helpful, impressing others as working up to her capacity.

The father was a good farmer and the family was much respected. It was felt that none of the family had much ability.

749. F:16:4   ACE IX, 09; XI, 03   8′640 357–   8:10:9
    N:V:3   ENG IX, 08; XI, 02
                 HSR 01 DO 12th gr.
                 SVIB none

With "a lot of personality and personal attraction," this girl was outgoing, talkative, vivacious. She had a good disposition and was well liked by her own group. She was uninterested in school, was often truant, and generally made a poor adjustment to schoolwork. She was often petulant and at other times was withdrawn in manner. At the end of her junior year she dropped out of school to be married.

The father was a skilled laborer and a heavy drinker. The mother was thin and sickly appearing. She also worked. The children were considerably influenced by a small religious sect and were stanch "witnesses" in this sect. All the children had at times an arrogant manner that was irritating to teachers. Although the parents were interested in the children and seemed to try to do well by them, discipline was considered lax.

750. M:15:2	ACE IX, none; XI, 36	8''''6'''5274'1093–	1:37:6X
N:V:3	ENG IX, none; XI, 14	8'475 62–	5:14:16
	HSR 20		
	SVIB '8–		

Clinical study of this tall, blond, well-built boy suggested that he had suffered brain damage. He was epileptic from childhood. There was some evidence that his condition was progressive and that he was losing intellectual efficiency. His worst behavior occurred in the middle school grades and in the ninth grade he was a great problem to the school and to the neighborhood. He associated with younger children, who tolerated him but with whom he was selfish and hostile. He was interested in girls, although they rejected him. He wrote several obscene letters to girls. Uninhibited, talkative, and distractible, he got great satisfaction in public performances and was a constant source of amusement to his classmates. As he continued in school, an intelligent acceptance by the school and neighborhood of the fact that he was handicapped tended to minimize the problem that he created. Apparently he had some musical aptitude: he was able to hum a tune before he could talk and his ambition was to be a disc jockey. During a conversation he was likely to break into song, which might then develop into "senseless jibber-jabber." He had marked inferiority feelings, often expressing the desire to become famous which was frequently mixed with the delusion that he was becoming more and more famous.

The father was a good, steadily employed worker. The mother, who worked outside the home, was aggressive and outgoing. Both parents were genuinely concerned about the boy and tried in every way to get help for him.

751. F:14:3	ACE IX, 99; XI, 98	'8657–1'2	2:1:7
N:V:1	ENG IX, 100; XI, 94	'9478–'5126	1:2:13
	HSR 75		
	SVIB none		

This girl did not work up to her ability. Around school she appeared to be bashful and quiet. Her oral recitation was especially poor. Frequently absent from school, she was always looking for excuses. Truancy, supported by the mother, was suspected. During her sophomore year she had been very friendly with her teachers and willing to do extra work. This pattern changed, however, perhaps in part because she clerked at a store after school and on weekends. At least one teacher expected her to become emotionally maladjusted later. After graduation she registered at a university for teachers' training.

The mother was "too lenient about the aches and pains that kept her daughters out of school."

752. M:15:7	ACE IX, 05; XI, 03	86''''7''19'32405–	5:27:14X
N:IVB:5	ENG IX, 04; XI, 14	'08 97–5'	6:8:6
	HSR 10		
	SVIB –5		

This boy was serious, reserved, and "a definite introvert." He was not interested in people and "gave very little of himself." He never volunteered to recite or to give any service, but he was willing to do what he was told. Liked by other students, he did not, however, identify with any group. Later in his high school years he played football, which helped him some in his social contacts.

The father, a farmer, was quiet, hard working, and dependable. The mother, more quiet still than her husband, was considered an excellent homemaker and a good neighbor. The parents and children were compatible and the home was free of tension.

753. M:16:6	ACE IX, 26; XI, none	8''''6'''74''20195–	1:25:11X
N:VII:2	ENG IX, none; XI, none		
	HSR DO 10th gr.		
	SVIB none		

In earlier grades this boy was a "hoodlum" and did all sorts of attention-getting things. In the ninth grade he seemed emotionally unstable and tended to "go far off the deep end." By the tenth grade he had quieted down somewhat and was no real problem in the school. "He seemed to want to do right but felt compelled to do otherwise." In general, he was very hard working, but he had little ability or interest in school and he was a poor reader. He finally quit school in the tenth grade and began working full time while living at home. He had a record of minor traffic offenses.

The father was a workman with an above average income. The mother "had good principles and was a good church member." There was another brother who had got into repeated trouble and who was a member of a gang that was identified as guilty of sexual molestation and other serious offenses. The home discipline was weak; the parents gave no companionship to their children.

754. F:15:1	ACE IX, 74; XI, 83	'86749–	1:6:14
N:V:1	ENG IX, 78; XI, 77	6'0283714–'5	4:14:14
	HSR 32		
	SVIB none		

Physically large and mature looking, this girl dressed nicely. Pleasing and co-operative, she always did more than was expected of her, and she was very sensible and dependable. Despite her high measured intelligence, some teachers considered her to be working above her ability; others, however, thought that she had the ability but that "she probably had too many social activities outside the school." She was not snobbish but her teachers thought she had tendencies in that direction. It was said that she got by on "social know-how." Her behavior was erratic. Despite her social activities she was not popular with the majority of the other students. She became engaged to "a very fine boy" in her senior year and her schoolwork, which had been somewhat low, improved to A's and B's. After graduation she was married. Her husband began university study, and the couple "appeared mature beyond their age."

755. M:15:3	ACE IX, 24; XI, 25	8″679′130 254–	2:9:10
N:V:2	ENG IX, none; XI, 02	8‴7″69′250413–	1:21:9X
	HSR 02		
	SVIB 4′–		

This boy was average in dress and physical appearance. His activities seemed to be slightly immature. He cooperated when prodded, and he was inattentive and irresponsible in school tasks. He was, however, not a disciplinary problem, although his school attendance record was poor. He seemed to be well enough liked by a group of rural boys. In manner he was pleasant but somewhat withdrawn. He was kept busy after school by the chores that he had to do.

756. M:15:5	ACE IX, none; XI, 07	8‴6794′13502–	6:20:16X
N:VII:3	ENG IX, none; XI, 14	8″570 296–′1	4:14:8
	HSR 20	′930 56–′2	3:5:10
	SVIB 4′–		

This boy was a superior athlete who was likable and popular with his classmates. His schoolwork was poor, however, and his English was "horrible." When he was corrected, he would insist that the correct English usage sounded wrong to him. He was willing and kind, and he could have had an athletic scholarship to college, but "knowing his limitations," he did not accept. After graduation he took a job as a recreation director.

The father was very good to his children. He was kindhearted, slow, and easygoing. The mother worked as a cook, and, though coarse and loud, she was a friendly person. The parents lavished all their income on the home and children.

757. F:14:3	ACE IX, none; XI, 13	8′695–′23	1:6:5
N:V:1	ENG IX, none; XI, 34	′8906–′325	2:11:5
	HSR 04		
	SVIB none		

The interesting thing about this girl was that teachers considered her higher in ability and creativity than appeared to be the case either by measurement or by school achievement. She had "an affected accent" and acted more mature than the average high school student. "She analyzed things well." She wanted a great deal of personal freedom, and it was thought that she was rebelling against a strict father. In attitude she was cynical and frank, and, although she had a good deal of social poise, the other students did not like her. She seemed unaffected by her lack of popularity.

758. F:14:6	ACE IX, none; XI, 24	8'6̲9̲5̲3̲1̲2̲–	9:12:14
N:IVC:2	ENG IX, none; XI, 20	'5̲4̲8̲3̲9̲7̲–'21	6:7:10
	HSR 35		
	SVIB none		

Heavy-set in appearance, this girl was quiet and unassuming. She was slow in schoolwork, where she was too shy, trying to work and cooperate but lacking in ability.

759. F:15:1	ACE IX, 08; XI, none	8'''69''74'2105–	6:24:20X
N:VI:5	ENG IX, 08; XI, none		
	HSR DO 11th gr.		
	SVIB none		

This girl had been physically handicapped since birth with crippling that affected one hand and one leg. She also suffered from strabismus and seizures of an unknown origin. It was believed that she had undergone a brain operation. In class she was dull and nervous and crowds bothered her. She frequently asked favors and made herself a pest. Apparently she was babied at home and she was not well liked by fellow students. Both she and her mother were considered loquacious. She dropped out of school when in the eleventh grade. Several of her teachers had predicted emotional problems for her.

760. M:14:1	ACE IX, 08; XI, 17	8'6̲0̲9̲ 7̲5̲–'2	4:11:8
N:IVA:5	ENG IX, 12; XI, 15	94'87̲6̲3̲5̲–'1	6:10:10
	HSR 06		
	SVIB '49–		

A daydreamer and shy when a ninth-grader, this boy became more forward as he continued in school. His more successful relationships were in church groups, where he was a leader and held responsible positions. In school he was "detested by the teachers and students—a stinker." His manner was unpleasant and fault-finding. His high opinion of himself and his inability to take criticism kept him from being a star in athletics. After he got a car he used it to secure entree to various groups. Although he was never caught, he was a reckless driver, and drank and smoked. He seemed merely to want to graduate without seeking distinction in any way. After graduation he went into the service for a few months and then returned to farming.

The father was much like the boy — outspoken, forward, and full of advice that was not always sound. In general, he was a rather strong person. The mother was the most socially acceptable of the family and was described as friendly, placid, easy, and a good homemaker. She was a capable woman, always available to her children. She was considered overprotective of the children in that she gave the boy everything he wanted whenever he asked.

761. M:14:9	IQ (centile) 16	8′″″71″32′64<u>59</u>–	6:25:14X
B:VII:3	HSR DO 10th gr.		
	SVIB none		

This boy was completely indifferent and stubborn. He would put his head on his desk and not raise it until forced to do so. Dull and obstinate, he could not or would not follow instructions. He seemed to have no respect for anyone and was always trying to outsmart his teachers. He stole from lockers and "seemed to have criminal tendencies." Just before he was to be expelled, in the tenth grade, he dropped out of school to join the Navy. Several of his ninth-grade teachers predicted delinquent behavior for him.

762. M:14:4	ACE IX, 59; XI, 61	8′7<u>146325</u>–	7:8:19
B:VI:5	ENG IX, 56; XI, 16	8″<u>947</u> <u>163</u>–	2:8:20
	HSR 21		
	SVIB ′–		

This boy was very thin and he had a poor complexion. He was not clean or neat about his person or dress. Tall and awkward, he seemed tired in school, possibly from working nights. Although he was not considered a leader, he had many friends among the boys in school. With teachers he seemed to be self-conscious and, in general, his relationship with the school indicated low motivation. He lacked initiative and self-confidence in academic work and did his best work in shop courses. He was not a conduct problem.

The father was something like the boy in appearance — tall and thin — and he rarely shaved. He was "sharp-tongued and he liked to throw his weight around," but he was good to the children and in many ways a friendly man and a good worker. The mother was dead. One of the sisters was described as outspoken and tactless, but she was not a severe school problem. The home was in a bad location and was not well kept, but the family had a good moral reputation. The children all worked outside of school.

763. F:15:4   ACE IX, none; XI, none   '871563–2'9   4:4:17
     N:VI:1   ENG IX, none; XI, none
                     HSR trans. 9th gr.
                     SVIB none

Information about this girl was restricted to her ninth-grade year because the family moved away before she entered the tenth grade. She was described as happy, well liked, peppy, and a good mixer. These reports came from the school and from the church, where she was especially active. She was interested in science and piano. She got along well at school but her marks were mostly D's. It was noted that she took great pride in her own room and possessions, caring for them unusually well. Sensitive to teasing, she cried easily. There was much quarreling between her and a brother. Some of the teachers expected her to become emotionally maladjusted.

The home situation was very unsatisfactory. The father had been in repeated difficulties with authorities. He was unfaithful to his wife and had been an alcoholic. The mother seemed the stronger of the parents; however, she made a nuisance of herself with the teacher of one of her sons, insisting that the boy should be passed even though he did not work. She showed a marked preference for the girl over her other children. Another boy in the family was a very severe behavior problem; he was characterized by temper tantrums and violence toward his home and siblings.

764. M:15:2   ACE IX, 74; XI, 84   8"72'356094–   5:10:12
     N:II:1   ENG IX, none; XI, none   48'720–'6   2:5:16
                     HSR 66   '8–5'92   3:1:17
                     SVIB none

This boy was friendly and cooperative, well balanced, and of very fine temperament. A little shy, especially with girls, he was serious in doing his assignments and competent in music, but he never volunteered to perform before others. He participated in athletics, played chess, and worked after school. Occasionally he was mischievous. After graduation he went to a university and took engineering.

The mother was interested in her son and in school activities. She was pleasant, friendly, and cooperative, but her health was poor. The parents lived apart much of the time because the father's job kept him out of town.

765. M:15:4   ACE IX, none; XI, 25   8"7'246153–   4:9:23
     N:IVC:3   ENG IX, none; XI, 08   '0–5'913 68   1:7:14
                     HSR 03
                     SVIB none

"A very big, husky, St. Bernardish type boy," this youth was playful but never mean. He was irritating in the classroom and needed frequent discipline. He accepted discipline well enough and came in time to respect it. He was good-natured, unimaginative, unambitious, and immature. Slow and capable of short-time projects only, he was weak in his schoolwork. "He will be a farmer — a good one" was the prediction made for him.

766. F:15:8   ACE IX, 10; XI, 06   8'7<u>25</u>–'<u>1369</u>   2:6:12
    N:IVB:3   ENG IX, 33; XI, 24   7'<u>89</u> <u>654</u> <u>02</u>–   3:6:12
             HSR 26
             SVIB WR'

The description of this girl emphasized that she was average and acceptable. Pleasant and good looking, she handled social situations well; she was reliable and dependable. Her activities were restricted to the 4-H Club.

    The family was well respected in the community — "a good, solid family."

767. M:18:11   IQ (centile) 05   8''''72''<u>51</u>'<u>96</u>430–   7:22:18X
    N:III:3   HSR DO 10th gr.
             SVIB none

Older than most of his classmates, this boy seemed to be correspondingly more mature and to have better judgment. He was a steady worker and was very well liked, always agreeable and pleasant. He quit school in the tenth grade to go to another state and take a full-time job.

    The father was described as "an almost childlike person." He seemed to have poor judgment about money and discipline of the children. The family had a comfortable home and an average income. The mother was the mainstay of the family, but she was chronically ill and continually in a crisis with one or another of the children. She was a hard-working person. Several of the children got into trouble in the school and community.

768. M:14:2   ACE IX, none; XI, 50   8'''7''20'4135–   6:14:14
    N:V:3   ENG IX, none; XI, 56
             HSR 56
             SVIB '4–9

There were not many items reported about this boy's earlier high school years, but in his junior and senior years he was repeatedly suspected of drinking. As a senior he began to slump obviously in his schoolwork and to show signs of nervousness. This nervousness appeared in part as a deterioration in his writing. It was reported that "he had something bothering him, something on his mind."

769. M:15:0	ACE IX, none; XI, 85	8'7209–'346	1:4:6
N:V:3	ENG IX, none; XI, 54	78129'453–'6	0:7:9
	HSR 80		
	SVIB none		

This very nice boy had many friends, but he lacked confidence and was indecisive and "unable to face up to pressure." His teachers characterized him as emotionally immature. He was a good student.

770. M:15:1	ACE IX, none; XI, 94	8'734–'50	2:4:16
N:III:1	ENG IX, none; XI, 76	——	——
	HSR 32	71'48935–	2:4:11
	SVIB 9'0–		

This boy was said to be ashamed of the fact that he was an underachiever. He had no specific goals established for himself. In manner he was outgoing with a good sense of humor and he got along well with his classmates. He got into trouble because of careless driving that led to an accident during his junior year. After graduation he continued on to university work.

771. M:15:9	ACE IX, none; XI, 32	8'7493106–5'	3:15:11
N:VI:1	ENG IX, none; XI, 10		
	HSR DO 11th gr.		
	SVIB none		

Shy and reserved, this boy needed friends. He was "lacking in all-round development." His only extracurricular interest was chess. He left school during his junior year. He was convicted of driving without a license.

772. F:14:2	ACE IX, 21; XI, 43	8'749 361–'5	9:5:17
N:VI:2	ENG IX, 66; XI, 67	4'768103–'2	4:5:14
	HSR 46	'6837–'40	3:3:15
	SVIB WR'		

Small and rather attractive, this girl was shy and reticent. She suffered from migraine headaches and was extremely unhappy in her home. She planned to leave home as soon as she could. She had few friends, was socially slow, and lacked social graces. Her school conduct was unobtrusive; she was no problem and just filled a seat. She married shortly after graduation.

The mother was a highly nervous woman who was feared by her husband and children. When in a temper she would physically abuse her children and would break up furniture. One of the children was mentally retarded and another was handicapped from birth by a physical defect.

773. M:15:6   ACE IX, 14; XI, 15   8″7′490513-   5:15:10
     N:VI:4   ENG IX, 04; XI, 01   ′648-′3   3:11:10
                  HSR 07
                  SVIB 4′–0

This boy emphasized his physical prowess and physical disabilities. "He always thought of his illnesses as the worst." Though he went out for all athletics, he did not do well. He had matured early physically but his skills were not correspondingly great. He expected to go into the armed services for the opportunity of further physical development. His relationship with others varied, so that he was not very popular although some thought him likable and he had a small number of friends. He could be very irritating in his manner and he was a braggart about his sexual conquests. There was doubt about the veracity of his claims. "His high school graduation was simply social, not the result of application to work." He was suspected of stealing and of violating game laws but there was no official record. One teacher predicted that he would have later emotional problems.

The father was a relaxed person who could not take any pressure. When pressures built up he drank. He was proud of his son, but his own behavior was neither stable nor dependable. He deserted his family for a year when the boy was in the ninth grade. The mother was strict in religious matters and was emotionally unstable. She dominated the children, who resented her but never rebelled. Within the family there was "no hope for individual development."

774. M:14:3   ACE IX, none; XI, 62   87″402′96 31–′5   1:15:9
     N:VI:2   ENG IX, none; XI, 21
                  HSR 57
                  SVIB 4′–5

Outside of school this boy was a good worker with a pleasant personality. In school he was "a smart aleck" and he was guilty of minor infractions of school rules. He was below average in initiative and leadership, and he did not take part in school activities. His interest was in mechanics.

775. M:14:8   ACE IX, none; XI, 69   87′61304 25–   0:11:10
     B:N:1   ENG IX, none; XI, 35   ′984–′61   1:4:8
                  HSR 59
                  SVIB none

This was a big, shy, friendly boy who had very little drive. He was artistic. Although he played basketball, he did not develop as much as it seemed he should. One of his ninth-grade teachers anticipated that he might become delinquent; however, no offenses were found in official records.

776. M:14:6   ACE IX, none; XI, 59   '8762–5'9<u>13</u>   2:8:11
     N:III:3   ENG IX, none; XI, 09
                  HSR 31
                  SVIB none

Descriptions of this boy centered around his health and his home life. He seemed mostly to be reacting against his home, where he was one of a large family and had working parents. It was said that he "needed privacy at home and never had a place alone." He became sassy and obstinate when his home problems were pressing. A chronic physical disorder, discovered in his sophomore year, caused him to have "an intense emotional upheaval." It was also said that he "needed someone to talk with, was not able to understand his own problems, and was very friendly and appreciative when he talked them over with someone." He was outspoken and liked attention. When he was punished he seemed to take it well, but he appeared inhibited on the subject and would avoid talking about it.

777. M:14:3   ACE IX, 11; XI, 19   8'''762'43190–'5   7:12:13
     N:III:2   ENG IX, none; XI, 07   9'3<u>76</u>–20'   2:5:10
                  HSR 17
                  SVIB none

This boy's family moved frequently and he was often forced to adjust to a new school. He had a speech difficulty, and was described as lazy, contrary, negative, and obnoxious. He was also termed immature, irresponsible, and as having "no staying power." In classes he was noisy and "a clown" and, at other times, a daydreamer. As he went through high school he tended to settle down. In his senior year he became popular and was elected to the student council. In general, however, he was not active in extracurricular affairs. Although he wanted to take part in athletics, he had little ability and did not exert himself. One of his teachers predicted that he would have emotional problems.

    The father was a very good person who made a fine impression. The boy admired his father and worked for him after school hours. He returned his son's admiration by wanting to be "a pal."

778. M:15:8   ACE IX, 14; XI, 07   8''7'6<u>490</u>–'2   0:11:7
     B:VII:2   ENG IX, none; XI, 21   8'''6'4<u>719</u>305– 3:9:13
                  HSR 24
                  SVIB '–

"Very cocky and mouthy," this boy was lazy, indifferent, and negative in school. He liked to be one of a group, but he did not lead. He always tried to show off. When he got low grades he complained, although he did not apply himself. He did not get into bad trouble but he had "a sneaky, antisocial manner" and he "liked to get even with people." He was irresponsible and often untruthful. His strongest contribution was in athletics, where he excelled. He was not widely liked, and he tended to go with "the wrong crowd." There were a few minor episodes of vandalism. After graduation he joined the Army.

The father was "a no-good who deserted the family." The mother, although not particularly warm or affectionate, was hard working. She appeared to be calm and likable but was not a strong personality. She did a good job of rearing the children. There was little money and the home was only fairly well kept.

779. M:14:1 N:IVB:2	ACE IX, none; XI, 68 ENG IX, none; XI, 22 HSR 42 SVIB –5	87″692′0453– 3:8:14

This boy was indifferent to school and needed prodding. His behavior was unacceptable; he was a "show-off" and he did things to attract attention in class. Outside of class he was also a show-off; he drove recklessly and made U-turns at high speed. He was erratic in reliability. He did take an interest in the 4-H and Future Farmers clubs. His father expected him to do chores when he got home from school.

780. M:16:1 N:IVC:3	ACE IX, 18; XI, none ENG IX, 15; XI, none HSR DO 10th gr. SVIB none	87′690–5′ 5:12:16

This boy was sullen, quiet, and "completely negative." He had no friends and contributed nothing to school activities. Apparently he only marked time until his sixteenth birthday when he could drop out of school and become a full-time farmer, which was his only interest.

The father was "nonexistent as a factor in the home." The mother had had numerous children by numerous men. The whereabouts of these children was unknown. None of them finished school. The home was a poor one on submarginal land.

781. M:14:4 B:IVB:4	ACE IX, 54; XI, 22 ENG IX, 28; XI, 19 HSR 25 SVIB 4′–5	8″76′904– 5:11:15 ′9132–5′6 7:5:17

The mother of this boy died in an accident shortly before he entered the ninth grade. Others did not know how he reacted to this loss because he did not talk about himself or his feelings. Apparently he was likable and fairly popular with his own small group of friends, but he contributed nothing to the school. His behavior became worse after he got a car and began to go with boys who cared for nothing but their automobiles. He became a braggart, telling of his great conquests, but it was felt that he exaggerated his deeds. In his school relationships he was "obnoxious without half trying," and on one occasion he was "mouthy" to a teacher. After a reprimand he behaved himself. One report said that he suffered from his mother's death and that his loudness and other behavior represented a compensation for the loss of her attention and devotion. He joined the Marines after graduation and he expected to become a farmer after his discharge.

The father, an immigrant, was quiet and reserved. He may have been cold and hard to live with, although when people got to know him, he seemed neighborly. The relationship between the father and the boy was a close one. The mother had been nervous, tense, and unable to make friends. It was possible that her death was suicidal.

782. F:15:5	ACE IX, 02; XI, 04	8'''7'601 593–	7:18:12X
N:IVC:4	ENG IX, none; XI, 01	5'608947–'3	3:13:9
	HSR 07		
	SVIB WR'		

Although not a conduct problem in school, this girl was a poor student. She simply did not apply herself and she seemed to have trouble "getting things." She had few friends and was in no activities. Outside of school she was a conduct problem. Both the police and sheriff had had contact with her because of curfew violations and promiscuous behavior.

The father was an Indian, and the mother was described as "brilliant." In the home there was very poor discipline and it was considered to be "a problem home."

783. M:15:7	IQ (centile) 15	87"60 21–'9	2:11:12
N:IVB:2	HSR DO 11th gr.		
	SVIB none		

This boy was most interested in farming and his school record showed many absences. He was indifferent and slow in school, and he took part in no activities. Finally he dropped out of school without any notice — he just didn't return. He most likely went into farming.

784. F:15:2	ACE IX, 75; XI, 43	87'603492–5'	5:5:10
N:IVB:4	ENG IX, 61; XI, 40	'9786 042–'135	2:5:11
	HSR 46		
	SVIB WR'		

A "nice, quiet, petite girl," this student was likable and cooperative, working up to her capacity. There were no personality difficulties. She had a small group of intimate friends and she was an active contributor to church affairs.

The father, a farmer, was considered clannish and retiring — a person who stayed within his own family church group. The mother was even more reserved in manner than the father. All the children were quiet, mousy, and seclusive. The reputation of the family was good.

---

785. M:15:6　　　ACE IX, 85; XI, none　　　87″9′1<u>40263</u>–　　3:12:9
　　　B:VI:1　　　ENG IX, none; XI, none
　　　　　　　　　HSR DO 10th gr.
　　　　　　　　　SVIB none

This boy was involved in a number of episodes of misbehavior during his early high school years. He was guilty of burglary. He was also caught in a gang fight. At one time, after considerable truancy, he was put out of school. He later quit because he felt he could not make up the work. After a year's absence he returned to school, at which time he was polite and seemed relatively well adjusted. He was also described as a "bright boy." Several teachers expected him to be involved in legal difficulties. Part American Indian by birth, he was said to have had a poor economic background.

---

786. M:15:2　　　ACE IX, none; XI, 21　　　8′7940–5′3　　1:8:10
　　　N:VI:1　　　ENG IX, none; XI, 11　　　8<u>79</u>″04<u>21</u>–′5　3:10:10
　　　　　　　　　HSR 33
　　　　　　　　　SVIB 4′–

This boy had a pleasing personality and was very quiet, but he did not like school-work. His teachers attributed his indifference and reluctance to participate in school activities to laziness. "He tended to take the path of least effort." He was put on probation late in his high school years when he was apprehended twice for possession of liquor and intoxication.

---

787. M:14:3　　　ACE IX, 81; XI, 85　　　87′90–1′32　　0:10:8
　　　B:III:2　　　ENG IX, 93; XI, 80　　　′4–5′<u>81</u> 37　3:3:10
　　　　　　　　　HSR 26
　　　　　　　　　SVIB 4′8–5

A "bum around school," this boy had a chip on his shoulder all the time. He was uncooperative, unreliable, and indifferent. He blamed his poor grades and difficulties in conduct on the teachers. Indifferent toward the school, he was a show-off and tried to attract attention by his misbehavior. This misbehavior occurred when he had an audience, at which time he was impudent, ill-mannered, and arrogant.

He had a great interest in girls and was a good dancer. In his freshman year he was guilty of drunken driving and of leaving the scene of an accident. In the succeeding years he had other difficulties, being charged with disorderly conduct and other driving offenses. After graduation he went into the Navy.

The father, who was a partial invalid, was a hard worker who tried to support his family. The mother, a heavy drinker and promiscuous, deserted the family. The father remarried and the children resented this. An older brother also experienced a good deal of conflict in school because of competition with a relative who was an outstanding student.

788. F:15:3   ACE IX, 87; XI, 55   8'7906–   4:8:7
     N:V:2   ENG IX, none; XI, 68   39'6874–5'0   6:4:12
                  HSR 84
                  SVIB '–

A homecoming queen, this girl was "sweet and very popular." She was poised and mature, unaggressive, and without much initiative. She had been sheltered and doted upon by her mother, but she did not seem spoiled. Although she worked fairly hard in school, she was never outstanding. Not a leader, she was inconspicuous in school activities. After graduation she went to a vocational school.

The father had been a fairly adequate person until he suddenly quit his job and family and went away for a while. He was considered weak but kindhearted and honest. His behavior led to a divorce, which occurred when the girl was about sixteen years old. The mother was self-sufficient and quiet. She was a follower and had to be drawn out. She had a number of physical complaints and seemed to crave attention and sympathy. The girl, who was much younger than her siblings, was very close to the mother.

789. M:16:5   IQ (centile) 23   87'09264–   3:9:12
     N:III:3   HSR DO 9th gr.
                  SVIB none

When a ninth-grade student, this boy became interested in wrestling, and for a time it looked as though he would continue in school because of this interest. Soon, however, he began to skip practice and to fall behind in his schoolwork, so that he became discouraged and dropped out of school. His manner was usually irritating; he seemed always ready for a fight. He was a surly, crude, and unaccepted roughneck. Most of his companions were "rowdies." Several of his ninth-grade teachers expected that he would have problems in adjustment and that he would become delinquent.

The father, who was an alcoholic, was described as being similar to the boy in temperament. The mother worked full time.

790. M:15:2   ACE IX, none; XI, 43   8″7′09$\underline{42163}$–   2:21:9X
     N:VII:3 ENG IX, none; XI, 23   98$\underline{6″7}$204–31′   3:10:8
              HSR 14
              SVIB 4′–5

During his early high school years this boy went with a group that had a bad reputation. He had little interest in school. Later he joined the school band, which did him a great deal of good, he attempted to develop new friends, and he became a better student. After graduation he took a steady job to help support his family after his father's death.

The father, who had been a laborer, died suddenly when this boy was a senior. After his death, the mother showed herself to be a very strong person. With the help of the children, she kept a good home.

791. M:14:2   ACE IX, 72; XI, none   87′$\underline{096}$ $\underline{54}$–   1:9:7
     N:IVB:4 ENG IX, 61; XI, none   7′92$\underline{840}$–   2:3:13
              HSR 41
              SVIB ′9–5

Although this boy had an irresistible smile, a keen mind, and a nice appearance, he was not well liked by fellow students. He seemed to be a lonely boy who was rejected for reasons that were unclear. He bordered on being impudent with teachers, but he knew how to limit himself so that he didn't get into real trouble. Capable of being an outstanding student, he was regular in his school attendance but was satisfied with mediocre achievement. He seemed to have a chip on his shoulder — "like his father" — and was agreeable only when things went his way. He became sullen and cross when frustrated. Outside of the school he worked with his father. He was a good worker and got along well with others on the job. He got into considerable trouble as a careless driver and on occasional alcoholic bouts. As he continued in high school he settled down somewhat and became "more of a gentleman." After graduation he joined the Marines.

The father was friendly, easygoing, and a good person. The mother was respected and likable, although she was more reserved than her husband. They were "not aggressive but loyal, fine people."

792. F:14:2   ACE IX, 66; XI, 53   ′89–′2$\underline{41}$ 0:5:12
     N:V:1   ENG IX, none; XI, 80   ′98$\underline{3}$–2′0   5:4:18
              HSR 51
              SVIB none

As a student this girl was only average and was relatively uninterested and inactive. In extracurricular activities she was, by contrast, active and successful. Very much interested in boys, "she threw her sex charm around." She was artistic but did not develop her talents. She seemed to be basically quite sensitive but reluctant to show this aspect of her personality. Usually her personality was pleasant, but she became hostile when she could not have her own way and she was at times moody. By her senior year she became a little more steady, and the school tardiness, which had been prominent in her earlier record, was less of a problem. She continued on to university study and worked part time, getting a B average in her schoolwork.

793. M:14:3	ACE IX, 48; XI, 44	'89–5'1	4:5:12
N:V:1	ENG IX, none; XI, 45	'130–98'56	4:3:13
	HSR 23	'3–98'7526	4:1:14
	SVIB none		

Although this boy never got into any severe trouble, his school attitude was poor. He was sulky, uncooperative, stubborn, and at times rude. He knew just how far he could go without getting into real trouble: he was a "shady character never convicted." He was friendly with persons he liked, but he was not so popular as he apparently wanted to be. He was active in athletics, where he showed promise, but he never met his own expectations, which seemed to make him sad and to give him a feeling of failure. His teachers thought he had approached athletics with too confident and cocky a manner.

The father and mother were divorced when the boy was in the tenth grade. The father seemed interested in the boy's activities but the mother didn't care about anything but her own enjoyment. She was described as a "daffy-down-dilly."

794. M:14:10	ACE IX, none; XI, 20	'8924–'3	6:12:9
N:V:3	ENG IX, none; XI, 05		
	HSR 05 DO 12th gr.		
	SVIB none		

This boy was not a good student and he did not take part in school activities. He left school in the twelfth grade to work with his father. His home life was unhappy because of constant friction between his parents.

The father had never been able to support the family because of alcoholism and other problems. He was an unskilled worker and he expected the boys in the family, on a rotating basis, to leave school in order to help with the work in the home. The mother was young and attractive. She was unhappy about the children's being absent from school but there seemed to be nothing she could do about it. Among the many children there was a close family bond and they were very interested and solicitous about their mother, showing her great affection.

795. F:14:1	ACE IX, 70; XI, 64	'89347–'205	1:1:16
N:V:2	ENG IX, 83; XI, 91	'36–'25	3:6:12
	HSR 65		
	SVIB WR'		

This girl did better in the nonacademic subjects but was generally an average and consistent student who was a good worker, earnest, and eager to do well. Very

269

quiet, she seldom smiled, but she always had friends, among them a steady boy friend whom she expected to marry. It was said that she was rather unpredictable and could not always be depended on to carry out promises. She became a secretary after her graduation. Apparently she wanted to follow in the footsteps of her sister, who was professionally trained and very well thought of.

Both the father and mother worked and were respected in the community.

796. M:14:1	ACE IX, 94; XI, 96	'894–'725	1:1:14
N:II:2	ENG IX, none; XI, 73	9'6438–127'0	0:4:8
	HSR 63		
	SVIB '489–5		

This boy was neat in appearance, he had high ability, and he was liked by the other students. In some contrast, he was also described as erratic and "a smart aleck who wisecracked in class." He seemed to lack confidence, and some of his behavior may have been compensating for this. He was dominated by his parents, especially his father, and would not admit to any wrongdoing because he feared parental punishment. During his senior year he fell very much in love. He was good in mathematics and had mechanical aptitude. He owned a car and was "a maniac behind the wheel." Toward other students he could be possessive and dictatorial. He was a leader among "the semi-hoods," and he was in numerous troubles with the police because of traffic offenses and because he was caught in a drinking party. After graduation he entered a school of business administration.

The father was arrogant and egotistical. A "smooth talker," he was "very sure of himself or at least he put up a good front." Because he had two full-time jobs, he spent little time with the family. The mother had poor health, but she was intelligent and generally a good mother.

797. M:15:0	ACE IX, 87; XI, 91	'89436–'02	1:3:19
N:V:1	ENG IX, none; XI, 84	'984371–'20 65	2:2:19
	HSR 37	'43687 915–'0	3:1:21
	SVIB none		

This boy was "a pretty good kid." He was, for the most part, cheerful and easygoing. In his schoolwork he got poor marks and appeared to be not strongly motivated. He could be "strong-headed, shrugging off discipline after obeying." Outside of school he had varied interests; he both read a great deal and worked in a part-time position with much responsibility. He had a steady girl friend. He took part in sports and other sorts of competitive events. Severe allergies may have contributed to the fact that he was absent frequently from school. After graduation he went to a university for engineering study.

The parents, although fine people who were concerned about their son, did not give him much guidance. They tended to baby him.

798. M:15:3   ACE IX, 67; XI, 91   8'945673–2'0   1:1:18
       N:IVC:5   ENG IX, 68; XI, 43   '4398–2'506   2:3:20
                        HSR 74
                        SVIB 4'8–0

This boy was very neat and dressed nicely, but was reserved and often withdrawn in manner. "A person could be talking to this boy and all of a sudden he would seem to be someplace else — like he was in a trance." He had a good, quick mind and seemed to feel superior to the school, often being stubborn and too independent. He worked hard and was a good student. He did get into some minor trouble in junior high school, but later he settled down. He was responsible and steady, and at one time he took care of his whole family while the parents were away for several months. After graduation he continued to work on his parents' farm.

The father was a hard worker with "a fairly strong personality." The mother was quiet and stable but a little difficult to talk to and not very friendly. She was interested in and concerned over her children.

799. M:15:0   ACE IX, 58; XI, 62   8'94673–'0   2:2:16
       N:III:1   ENG IX, none; XI, 68   58"3'74961–   5:5:19
                        HSR 64
                        SVIB none

This boy was shy and expressionless, making little impression of any sort on his teachers. He was friendly, willing, very serious, and cooperative, with no apparent time for "horseplay." He took better advantage of his opportunities than did most boys. A competent musician, he was well accepted by others. His polite and unselfish behavior was especially mentioned. After graduation he went to a university, where he was a C+ student. In college his interests were in religion, band, and athletics.

The parents were good, intelligent, and sincere. They were interested in the activities of the boy and they were proud of him.

800. M:15:4   ACE IX, 28; XI, none   8'''9"467'5013–   1:22:7X
       B:VI:2   ENG IX, none; XI, none
                        HSR DO 10th gr.
                        SVIB none

This was "a complete no-good who was easily led." His attitude toward school was negative and indifferent, and he was described as "impudent, smarty, and small but noisy." He dropped out of school in his sophomore year after he had failed several courses. His behavior outside of school was not much better. Described in the community as lazy, he ran with "the motorcycle crowd." In his earlier school years he suffered from a minor speech defect. Before he quit school he had a record of truancy and traffic offenses. He enlisted in the Navy. One teacher expected he would have future emotional maladjustment.

The father had died, after an intermittent long illness, shortly before the boy began high school. He had been a hard-working, conscientious man. The mother remarried. She was an attractive woman with a fairly strong personality. She was somewhat negligent in the care of her children.

801. M:15:3	ACE IX, 10; XI, none	89'460–5'	2:15:12
N:III:4"	ENG IX, 12; XI, none		
	HSR DO 10th gr.		
	SVIB none		

Very little good was said of this boy, whose bad record had begun early. He was a "shiftless little sneaker" who was at times openly hostile, always sullen, moody, and disrespectful. Although at least one teacher felt that the school had failed miserably and had not helped the boy as much as it should have, there was little evidence to support this view. The boy was guilty of immoral relations with girls, he had stolen automobile parts, he began drinking when very young, and he was known in his neighborhood as a tough boy. He was physically attractive. After accumulating a long record of offenses, he was sent to a reform school; when released he seemed improved and expressed the intention of "going straight." He bore no resentment toward the police and seemed more friendly and talkative than before. One ninth-grade teacher had predicted that he would have emotional problems.

The father's record was bad. He had few friends and spent his time drinking and playing cards. He did not seem interested in his son's welfare. The mother seemed to be the brighter of the two and the dominant member of the family.

802. F:14:1	ACE IX, 70; XI, 68	8'947 60–'1	1:11:6
B:III:1	ENG IX, none; XI, 90	7'4823 69–	3:5:13
	HSR 33		
	SVIB none		

Teachers considered this girl to be intelligent and capable but unable to concentrate and work up to her ability. This inability to achieve well was blamed upon her unsatisfactory home life. She seemed to have several phases in her personality development. Until she got to the ninth grade she was highly rated as happy, well balanced, and an all-around girl; but by the ninth grade these ratings had changed and she became erratic, annoying, and disturbing to others. Later in high school she seemed to enter another phase where she was "in a daze at times" — flighty, not responsible, immature, childish, and excusing herself with the statement "I forget." She did a great deal of nonacademic work outside of school and was very self-conscious about her family. She hoped to go into secretarial work after graduation.

The father had died before the girl entered the ninth grade and the stepfather was not very likable. Both parents went with a "fast crowd." Neither spent time with the children and both felt that their having a good time was more important than the children.

803. M:14:1	ACE IX, 59; XI, 50	'895–6'2	3:7:13
N:V:2	ENG IX, 42; XI, 53	9'34 75826–0'	4:4:21
	HSR 15		
	SVIB '–		

This boy failed English in the eleventh year and was much embarrassed by this. He was rather lazy and had a poor school attitude. Occasionally truant, he once wrote his own excuse. In his junior year he was involved with a group that was guilty of vandalism. In manner he was pleasant and unusually courteous. He was good looking, very popular with girls, but not a "mixer." He went with one girl all through high school, but the relationship broke off after graduation. He was an all-around athlete. After graduation he went to a small junior college where he was reported to be doing well.

The father was partially disabled. He was very proud of the boy and tended to criticize the school for any action he considered reflecting adversely on his son. He gave the boy everything he wanted. The mother was not conspicuous and nothing was said of her. A sister was described as a good student, beautifully dressed. The family was generally characterized as very happy.

804. F:14:0	ACE IX, 54; XI, none	89"64'13 07–	2:24:4X
N:VI:3	ENG IX, 49; XI, none		
	HSR DO 11th gr.		
	SVIB none		

This girl was repeatedly described as "saucy and impudent toward school authorities." Her antagonism was expressed by truancy from school. Finally, after the tenth grade, she dropped out and was married. She had "run around quite a bit outside of school" and several of the teachers expected that she might get into legal or emotional difficulties.

805. M:14:2	ACE IX, 42; XI, 58	89'642–'3	4:12:10
N:V:1	ENG IX, none; XI, 16		
	HSR 27		
	SVIB none		

This boy's main school interests were in manual arts and electricity. He had a good personality, a good sense of humor, and a feeling of responsibility, and he was well liked. Active in church affairs, he was a religious boy. It was felt that the church affiliation had done a good deal for him.

806. M:14:3	ACE IX, 67; XI, 91	8″9′67<u>14</u>–′5	2:9:9
N:IVC:4	ENG IX, 51; XI, 45	9′864–2′<u>51</u>	2:4:13
	HSR 29		
	SVIB 4′8–		

The appearance of this boy was marred by a greasy and erupted skin, giving the impression of possible uncleanliness. His manner was unpolished and rude, but at times he could put on a good front and act like a good citizen. He seemed to value himself highly and to resent criticism. He was never a severe problem in the schoolroom and he did a moderate amount of schoolwork. However, he associated with companions of doubtful reputation and was sometimes guilty of borderline or unacceptable behavior around the school. He was boastful of his sexual conquests and he was often guilty of speaking or writing pornographically in and out of school. He also boasted of his drinking, and on one occasion was caught with whisky in his car. The teachers thought it likely that his talk about sex and drinking was exaggerated, and it was noted that he was never seen with a girl. He was a bully around smaller children. He was also guilty of stealing small articles. Once when he was caught he seemed to feel very bad about it and exhibited uncharacteristic emotion. A number of persons tried to help him because he seemed to them to have possibilities of better behavior. These efforts were not well rewarded because he never confided in anyone. His only close friend was a boy with whom he exchanged smutty talk. He was often kept out of school to work at home.

The father seemed to be much like the boy. He was known to be dependent upon alcohol for support and social prestige. He was not a good provider and the family lived in a small, unclean home. Little was known about the mother, one report noting that she was discourteous and "lacking in social conscience." The family was not well accepted in the community; they appeared to place emphasis upon alcoholic conviviality to establish themselves. Neither parent was interested in having the children go to school.

807. F:14:4	ACE IX, none; XI, 22	8″9′6<u>74</u>–′5<u>20</u>	1:7:13
B:V:2	ENG IX, none; XI, 81		
	HSR 45 DO 12th gr.		
	SVIB none		

Although attractive and well groomed, this girl appeared to lack the social graces. She "wore a bored expression, was unresponsive and inarticulate, and was so quiet that you would almost suspect shyness — she closed up." Boys were her primary interest and school ran second to them. Although considered difficult to know, she seemed honest. Before her senior year, she ran away from school and was found some distance away in a larger city. Later she was forced to drop out of school because of pregnancy.

The parents were separated, and the mother, who was considered friendly and understanding, worked to support the family.

808. F:14:0	ACE IX, none; XI, 94	8''''96'''743'15–	2:22:8X
N:III:3	ENG IX, none; XI, 64	9'8<u>64</u>370–'5	4:12:6
	HSR 88	9'''486'<u>73</u>–	1:15:7
	SVIB '–		

"Like a cork on water," this girl was a small, red-haired dynamo of energy that seemed always bobbing about. There was never a dull moment when she was around. Nervous, high-strung, and ambitious, she frequently seemed about to explode. She was fairly popular, but she lost friends at times because she was too frank. In organizations she tended to take over too much responsibility. Her steady boy friend was a class leader, but she dominated him as she did others. Her opinions were rigidly held. She was in many activities and after graduation went to a university.

The father, a skilled workman, was well liked and respected. The mother seemed similar to the girl and was likewise excitable and talkative. It was obvious that the mother and daughter dominated the family.

809. M:14:4	ACE IX, 40; XI, 30	8'96<u>70</u>–'4	2:12:9
N:II:1	ENG IX, none; XI, 36	'731<u>564</u>–'0	6:4:17
	HSR 34	'7<u>384</u>–5'02	7:4:20
	SVIB none		

Although he was never malicious or rude, this boy was mischievous and in trouble a great deal of the time. He was the youngest in his family and it was felt that he was babied and spoiled at home. He could be charming and likable, but most of the time he was indolent, negative, and immature in attitude. In a discussion he would make satirical remarks when he was at a loss for a more solid position. Although he was gregarious with boys, he seemed to lack the courage to date girls. One teacher felt that he was insecure because he did not know what he wanted to do with himself and because he was not dating. He was especially interested in mathematics although his grades in this subject were poor. In his senior year he got into difficulty because of disorderly conduct when he was caught urinating in a public place. He was also jailed one night for a bad traffic offense. After graduation he continued his education at a university.

The home was a good middle-class one. It was said that the mother dominated the family. The father was away from home a great deal when the children were growing up.

810. F:15:3   ACE IX, 21; XI, none   896′70325–   5:10:4
     B:V:2   ENG IX, 40; XI, none
                     HSR DO 10th gr.
                     SVIB none

This girl was aware that she was illegitimate. In manner she was quiet and somewhat shy, never taking a leader's position. Her behavior was erratic; she was
indifferent, unresponsive, and tended to drive about town rather ostentatiously.
Occasionally she was "up all night." Her schoolwork was very poor and she had no
enthusiasm for school. Finally she dropped out in the tenth grade.

Both parents were hot-tempered and while they did not believe in striking the
children they were likely to do so in anger. Gradually they came to the point of
considering divorce because of their disagreements. The father was once arrested
for threatening his wife during a drunken spell. The mother, who worked, was
likely to be sloppily dressed. She had a doubtful reputation. She had married her
husband when the girl was about three years old.

811. M:14:0   ACE IX, none; XI, 37   8′96704–   0:15:5
     B:II:4   ENG IX, none; XI, 36   —— ——   —— ——
                     HSR 45   9′487–′13   1:9:10
                     SVIB 4′89–

Although the principal said of this boy that "he was no problem, really," there
were indications that there was "more here than the principal would admit." Others
reported that he was cocky and obstinate and that he "had been babied all of his
life." In his junior year he was caught with liquor in his possession and was warned
and released. One of his teachers predicted that he would become emotionally
maladjusted.

The boy lived with a relative who was influential in the school system. His real
parents were separated.

812. M:14:5   ACE IX, 50; XI, 55   8′972450–′6   2:10:11
     N:IVB:3   ENG IX, 26; XI, 09   ′420 587–   6:1:17
                     HSR 10
                     SVIB none

This boy had a speech impediment and was exceedingly stubborn. He was indifferent to schoolwork and school rules, and he was discourteous to his teachers. He had
to be prodded and he was unreliable. He was a follower and readily patterned his
behavior after undesirable models among the other students. Two teachers expected that he would later have emotional or legal difficulties.

813. M:14:7   ACE IX, 52; XI, 40   897'46<u>02</u> <u>35</u>–   2:11:10
    N:V:2   ENG IX, none; XI, 20
                HSR 25
                SVIB none

Very pimply and self-conscious, this boy was late in development, both physically and in his personality. In an immature way he engaged in horseplay, although he was not a conduct problem in class. He did not apply himself to schoolwork, and in his social life he had few friends.

814. M:14:4   ACE IX, 50; XI, 50   8'976–'5   5:12:11
    N:III:1   ENG IX, 34; XI, 43
                HSR 24
                SVIB 9'0–5

This boy was immature but pleasant, friendly, and smiling most of the time. He needed constant prodding in his schoolwork. He was some trouble in class, where he would talk when he was not supposed to. He was always willing to help with things other than classwork.

815. M:14:2   ACE IX, none; XI, 55   89"<u>76</u>'3–'1   0:11:7
    N:V:3   ENG IX, none; XI, 19   7'"<u>820</u>"64'9– 1:15:6
                HSR 10
                SVIB '8–5

Although undistinguished in his schoolwork, this boy was quiet and obedient. Because he had the ability to do better work, his teachers tried to inspire him, but he never did more than was needed to get by. He also never showed much interest in school activities or in a vocational future. In his junior year he got into minor trouble because of a traffic violation. After graduation he joined the armed services and was said to have become more outgoing and mature.

The father was a small businessman in the town and the boy expected to take over his father's business. The father was described as a fine man, honest and a "square shooter." In the boy's sophomore year the father was seriously injured and for some time refused therapy. The mother, who helped in the family business, was also a hard-working and conscientious person. The income and situation of the family were above average, but it was felt that the parents neglected family life in favor of their vocational activities.

816. F:14:0   ACE IX, 63; XI, 34   8'9760–<u>21</u>'45   0:0:9
    N:VI:2   ENG IX, none; XI, 39   '0678–1'3   4:4:10
                HSR 62
                SVIB WR'

"Fine, quiet, and dependable," this girl was not a strong student and she was not a leader. Although considered mature, she seemed to lack confidence and she

277

tended to worry about her health. She had a part-time job and did not engage in any extracurricular activities. After graduation she began secretarial training and hoped later to enter a teachers' college.

817. M:14:3   ACE IX, 09; XI, 29   '8970–'6135   2:9:8
     N:VI:5   ENG IX, 09; XI, 29   9"8476'5–'2   2:11:9
                  HSR 32
                  SVIB 4'1–9

"An outdoor type," this boy's primary interests were athletics, hunting, and fishing. In school he did poor work but was likable, "genuine, and a fine boy." Both teachers and fellow students liked him. He had no dates in high school, but after graduation he started going with a girl. He joined the Air Force.

The father was an alcoholic. When sober, he was an extremely interesting man with a good attitude toward his children. When drunk he was noisy and obnoxious, causing embarrassment to his wife and his children. The mother was a stronger person who did very well in controlling her husband. She seemed to do a good job with the children, although she was possibly somewhat overindulgent.

818. M:15:5   ACE IX, 32; XI, 37   897'062–   0:15:11
     N:VI:2   ENG IX, none; XI, 12   6'''8"72'49103– 3:16:11X
                  HSR 23
                  SVIB '4–

Reports on this boy were not always consistent. Good looking and strong, he apparently could make a good impression. There was general agreement that he was "quiet and almost meek" in manner in the school setting. Polite and pleasant, he never caused trouble. Some teachers said that "he used what mental ability he had to good advantage"; others were not impressed and felt that "he never worked too hard." While agreeing that the boy was pleasant and "nice to talk to," some teachers saw in him something of the "young hood type." To others he was "a nice kid," very friendly, cooperative, and well behaved. There was even some disagreement over his appearance. He was described as "not too neat but fairly clean — his hair was long and uncombed." Another report indicated that he was neat and well groomed and that "he did not dress like a 'hood.'" A good athlete, "he cut quite a swath with the women." After graduation he worked as a day laborer.

In his sophomore year this boy was picked up by the police for being in an undesirable house and for drinking. The following year he was again caught drinking. At the time of the second MMPI testing, during his senior year, he was being investigated for participating in a series of burglaries, for which he was subsequently convicted. Some persons were surprised and shocked by this conviction: "I would never have thought of him as a bad actor." In a somewhat different vein was this view: "A lot of his thievery may never have been detected; he drove a car and always had money."

The father gave the appearance of being self-satisfied and shiftless. He was ineffectual with his children and unable to keep them in check. Apparently he was relatively unconcerned about them. The mother worried about the family, and the boy's behavior particularly troubled her. She was, herself, rather "slovenly and beaten down." The house and surroundings were untidy and very run down.

819. M:15:3 N:V:2	ACE IX, 77; XI, 69 ENG IX, none; XI, 75 HSR 70 SVIB 4′8–0	8′90<u>67</u>–2′31 ′97–6′5<u>23</u>	1:8:6 2:3:12

Quiet, hard working, and serious, this boy was well liked by fellow students and teachers. He was not a leader but he mixed well and was outgoing with his own group. Teachers also described him as businesslike and mature. He went to a small college after graduation, planning to become a teacher.

Both the parents were rather reserved persons, but they were considered to be good with the children.

820. M:15:2 B:VI:3	ACE IX, 42; XI, 53 ENG IX, 59; XI, 39 HSR 15 DO 12th gr. SVIB none	′80–′2	3:4:9

This "big, easygoing, lazy kid" had a chip on his shoulder, was sullen, indifferent, and negative. He had always disliked school, would "only sit and warm a seat," and was contemptuous of any authority. Considered "a great underachiever," he accomplished nothing academically and dropped out of school in his senior year. He accumulated a police record that included convictions for careless driving, drunken driving, and stealing gasoline. The delinquencies occurred, for the most part, in his junior year and in that portion of his senior year that he remained in school. Eventually he joined the armed services.

The family situation was considered "poor" and little could be found out about the parents. Apparently the mother had died before the boy started school and the father had remarried.

821. F:14:2 B:V:1	ACE IX, 19; XI, 30 ENG IX, none; XI, 55 HSR 36 SVIB none	8″02<u>47</u>′631–′9 78′623<u>904</u>–5′1	3:17:10X 2:8:16

This girl was always neatly dressed. "Plain and clean," she wore little makeup. She paid no attention to boys and entered into few school activities. When she did undertake a job, she did it dependably and efficiently. She was exceedingly quiet and shy, giving the impression of being unhappy. Her shyness kept her from being part of a group. Her social contacts in school were further limited by the fact that she came and went to school by bus. There was "an interesting stubborn streak" in her that would at times almost make her forget her shyness. It took a great deal of persuasion to get her to admit any fault. She was often kept out of school by her father for minor or false illnesses. After graduation she went to a business college. One of the ninth-grade teachers predicted she would have emotional maladjustment.

The father and mother were incompatible and were divorced while the girl was still in grade school. The father seemed to make excuses for the girl and in general was exceedingly protective of her. The girl was ashamed of the problem that she had in her home. She particularly objected to the promiscuous behavior of her mother and seemed to compensate for it by accepting her father as law and giving in to his obvious overprotectiveness. A sibling had been referred to a mental health clinic as a sullen, unhappy boy.

822. F:14:3	ACE IX, 79; XI, 69	'80273̲1̲–'5̲9̲	7:3:16
N:IVB:4	ENG IX, none; XI, 80	'724̲03̲–'5	4:3:12
	HSR 72		
	SVIB '–		

Relatively few items were reported about this girl. She was not a conduct problem, she was faithful and cooperative, and she seemed well balanced. Although she was a fairly good student, she was more a listener and did not enter into many class activities.

823. F:15:7	ACE IX, none; XI, 23	'80475–9'1	3:8:17
N:VII:3	ENG IX, none; XI, 10	4'637–'05	3:7:14
	HSR 09		
	SVIB WR'		

This "small, red-headed girl" had a "negative personality" and was a poor student, indifferent toward schoolwork and school functions. Her teachers thought she could not be trusted; they reported that she cheated whenever she had an opportunity. For the most part she was ignored by the other students in her class. She was a "busybody" and was often found wandering in the halls peering into lockers during the hours she should have been in class. After graduation she went to a subprofessional training school but did not finish the course. She remained home for a while and then joined a troupe of traveling salesmen for a short time. After quitting this job, she found another, again for a short time. She then suffered a "nervous breakdown" and was admitted to a hospital. Her mother felt that "something was bothering her," but the girl would not discuss it with anyone.

The neighbors reported that the mother was "odd." She was a poor housekeeper and often left her washing hanging out for weeks at a time. She was almost a fanatically religious person. Although a good worker, she seemed to be "mentally slow." The father, much older than his wife, was a common laborer. The income level of the family was below average. It was reported that the parents tried to do their best for the children.

824. F:13:0   ACE IX, none; XI, 100   '80476–'2   2:10:6
     N:V:2   ENG IX, none; XI, 100   '640–'9   0:4:14
                HSR 44
                SVIB none

A girl who had never learned to study and could not apply herself, this student was a troublemaker in class, "constantly horsing around." Although she was an active girl, she had no interest in the extracurricular activities of the school since none held any appeal for her. She was bored with everything and was difficult to reach. She seemed to have no feeling of social responsibility.

825. M:14:2   ACE IX, none; XI, 56   8'0561943–   2:7:9
     N:VI:2   ENG IX, none; XI, 57
                HSR 26
                SVIB 4'8–

This boy was a conduct problem. While in school he had trouble with the librarian because he would not conform to rules and the teacher felt that he had a "persecution complex." Later he was suspended for several days because of truancy. There was one episode in which he was taken to juvenile court for using a car without permission.

826. M:14:1   ACE IX, none; XI, 55   8062'7549–   5:12:6
     N:III:1   ENG IX, 49; XI, 33   8"709'465–'1   2:16:6X
                HSR 13
                SVIB none

Slender and small in stature, this boy appeared unhealthy and nervous. When he entered the ninth grade he had a severe speech disorder and even after extensive speech therapy, he was unable to speak very clearly. He "looked as though he had been beaten down" and was a "frightened kid." He was sloppy in his dress. He seemed indifferent most of the time, and, unless specifically asked, he did nothing in school. Quiet and unaggressive, he was always in the background, and one teacher said he was the type who "impresses you as one who might drown himself one day." This general picture persisted into the tenth grade. Toward the end of his high school years he began to associate with an undesirable group of boys. He wore sideburns and dressed and acted in accord with the manners of these boys.

It was thought that this was the only group in school with whom he could gain recognition, although he himself was not considered the "motorcycle type."

The father was domineering and the mother was extremely passive. The mother's own family was characterized by violence and instability.

827. M:15:8	ACE IX, 40; XI, 19	'8065–'3	3:7:15
N:IVB:6	ENG IX, 22; XI, 19		
	HSR 15		
	SVIB '4–		

This boy was likable, very sincere, and trustworthy, but he had few friends and "led a colorless life." In school he was not a conduct problem. He tried very hard, although he was slow and apparently not very capable. Two of his ninth-grade teachers predicted the possibility of future emotional maladjustment. He engaged in few or no activities.

The family was poor and the boy had to work very hard at home.

828. F:15:2	ACE IX, none; XI, 11	8'065 972–'1	4:15:8
N:VI:3	ENG IX, none; XI, 24	0'97285–1'3	2:6:5
	HSR 33		
	SVIB WR'		

This blonde girl was quiet, soft-spoken, and unaggressive. In school she was considered trustworthy and dependable and may have been somewhat of an overachiever. She liked small children and had a good reputation as a baby sitter. She had never appealed to boys and was too shy to make any advances. Because of this she aroused curiosity in her senior year, when she abandoned her close girl friends and began to go steady with a boy who was not in her school. It was said that she "took a back seat in her family." After graduation she went to work as a clerk.

Her family was well respected and active in community affairs. The father was apparently very conscientious but of meager intellectual ability.

829. F:14:1	ACE IX, none; XI, 99	'80679–'5	0:4:6
N:III:3	ENG IX, 98; XI, 93		
	HSR 91		
	SVIB none		

This was a nervous, oversensitive, worrisome girl who was lacking in self-confidence. She had good academic ability and won a scholarship for college. Her only extracurricular activity was band.

830. M:16:3   ACE IX, 40; XI, 32   '807459–'3   1:15:11
     B:IVA:4   ENG IX, 27; XI, 41   8"792'4650–   3:16:11X
                      HSR 35
                      SVIB '59–2

The family of this boy was unknown since he was adopted from an orphan home during his later childhood. After some initial difficulty, he adjusted to his new home and became a popular, relatively happy boy. One person reported that "he created a shell about himself when he talked to some adults." He was also described as lacking confidence and as not very "verbal." He was active in school wrestling and he "loved music." He also participated in acting, and he was described as a good mimic. He had hoped to attend a trade school after high school graduation but instead he went to work on his adoptive parents' farm.

The many good things that were said about the home may be summarized in the phrase "an excellent home situation." There was much cheerfulness and love among the members of the family.

831. M:15:1   ACE IX, 46; XI, none   80'74926–'51   2:6:16
     N:V:2   ENG IX, none; XI, none   '438–'659   5:4:19
                     HSR 27
                     SVIB 4'–

Gangling and awkward in appearance, this boy was generally described as "odd," although he did participate in some athletics. Quiet, pleasant, congenial, and courteous in his manner, he was fairly well liked but was not a leader and had little scholastic motivation. Characteristic of him was the fact that he did nothing on time and only cooperated "sometimes." Despite his lack of motivation for school, he did not pose a problem for the teachers. After graduation he went to work as a laborer.

The family had moved from place to place. When the boy was a senior the father had a serious illness and the mother was forced to go to work during the hospitalization of the father.

832. F:14:3   ACE IX, none; XI, 46   '8095–36'4   3:11:9
     N:IVB:3   ENG IX, none; XI, 51   '7–'13   5:2:14
                     HSR 74
                     SVIB none

Although she was characterized as "quite average in every respect," this girl was more lively and full of spirits "than most of the farm girls in the school." She had a good sense of humor and felt herself a part of the school life. With a good circle of friends, she "promised both good emotional and social development."

833. F:14:10   ACE IX, 84; XI, 65   '9–1'   1:6:7
     N:V:2   ENG IX, none; XI, 92   70'846923– 6:7:11
                      HSR 96
                      SVIB WR'

This girl was enthusiastic, active, and popular. She was well liked by both fellow students and teachers and was no discipline problem, although "she liked to talk in study hall." Her manner was pleasant and friendly; however, she showed some social awkwardness. Neither a follower nor an active leader, she was an average school citizen. Her aptitude was good but her initiative only average. She went on to teachers' training and worked part time during the summers to help with expenses. She was "the deserving recipient" of a scholarship that assisted her in her further college work.

The father was "quite a drinker," unkempt in appearance but friendly enough. The mother also seemed unkempt; she was quiet and withdrawn, possibly a little stronger than was her husband. Two of the siblings were irresponsible and lazy but never in any real trouble. There was no evidence of home conflict and the family was fairly well accepted.

834. F:14:2   ACE IX, 61; XI, 37   9'–<u>12</u>'086357 3:2:10
     N:V:1   ENG IX, 83; XI, 83   '9–<u>71</u>'84205 2:3:12
                      HSR 76
                      SVIB none

"Cute, sweet, and well liked by the other students," this girl was never a problem. She was capable, conscientious, and thorough in her work. She never recited in class and was lacking in imagination, but her responsiveness and thoroughness made her easy to work with. After graduation she took a clerking job.

835. M:15:0   ACE IX, 92; XI, 53   9'–<u>231</u>'50   1:2:10
     N:VI:3   ENG IX, 47; XI, 88   '93–<u>20</u>'   2:2:16
                      HSR 82   2'59–7'4<u>1680</u> 3:4:12
                      SVIB 59'0–12

This boy was the ringleader of a well-organized ninth-grade rebellion against the school principal. During his first high school year he was an indifferent student. Lacking initiative, he worked only when convenient or when a course appealed to him. He was also caught cheating. There was, however, "tremendous improvement" in his behavior over the next three years. Always considered a leader, by his senior year he was also regarded as a top student and one of the outstanding boys in his class. He was then described as friendly, reliable, cooperative, and very mature. His teachers said that he was sometimes a little reserved in manner and that when teased he became defensive. A capable public speaker, he was active in politics and student discussion groups, winning awards in these activities. He read a good deal and his classwork improved to the point of his taking on extra assignments. A rumor that he drank on occasion was the only adverse report made on him during his later school years. He attended a university after graduation.

The boy came from "a laboring family with not too much money." The home was nice and the father was a steady worker.

836. M:15:4	ACE IX, none; XI, 38	9''–2'35	7:7:14
B:VII:3	ENG IX, none; XI, 17	9'3148–0'56	6:3:18
	HSR 45		
	SVIB 4'8–5		

A large boy with poor eyesight, this youth was popular with the other students. He had a good attendance record, and was concerned about his schoolwork. After graduation he went to a trade school. He had a record of several traffic offenses.

The father died when the boy was quite young. He had been a thrifty man who had accumulated property and who was popular in the community. The stepfather was not such a desirable person. He had a record of drunkenness and disorderly conduct. The mother was unstable, a poor housekeeper, and extravagant.

837. F:14:5	ACE IX, 38; XI, none	'9–2'670 31	8:5:11
N:VI:2	ENG IX, none; XI, none		
	HSR DO 10th gr.		
	SVIB none		

This quiet girl had an even disposition; she was likable and healthy, but she did not mix much in social activities. Although self-possessed, she was not a leader, and her main activity was church work. After dropping out of high school, she attended a Bible school for a short while until her marriage. She was later described as "a good mother and homemaker."

838. F:14:1	ACE IX, 67; XI, 83	9'–2'01	4:3:13
N:IVB:3	ENG IX, 78; XI, 89	'798–'26	1:1:17
	HSR 81		
	SVIB '–		

Attractive, chubby, and vivacious, this student was dependable and well liked. "A brilliant, fine girl," she was a better than average worker in school, and outside of school she "never loitered but worked to make further education possible." She had a fine sense of humor. After graduation she expected to go into nurses' training.

It was a "wonderful home." The family was close and the parents tried to give their daughters everything that would be good for them. They were much interested in the welfare of the children, and the family had fun together.

839. M:16:5   ACE IX, 26; XI, none   '9–516'23   5:8:12
     B:VII:2   ENG IX, none; XI, none
                  HSR DO 10th gr.
                  SVIB none

Physically small but healthy, this boy "dressed like a hood and was filthy and unkempt." Defiant and antagonistic, he always had a chip on his shoulder, although he exhibited his bold and bullying tendencies only when backed up by other boys. In school he was very poor in achievement. "He sat in class and looked angry all the time." When his classmates ignored him, he became surly, difficult, and often sullen, and he made many facial grimaces and contortions. He accumulated a long list of offenses involving stealing, creating public disturbances, drinking, and traffic violations, both before and after entering high school.

The home was "a glorified shack, not very clean." The father had divorced the mother and the children lived with their mother and a stepfather.

840. M:14:0   ACE IX, 94; XI, 91   '9–5'367   6:9:15
     N:III:2   ENG IX, 95; XI, 77   '9–7'218   3:1:11
                  HSR 58
                  SVIB '14–

Ruddy-faced, clean-cut, and quiet, this boy was "never a leader." His teachers thought him pleasant and socially well adjusted, although a little shy. He was cooperative in school but he seemed to lack motivation. After graduation he went to a college where he began to study technology.

The father, an engineer, was a good provider. The mother had a nervous breakdown which had "made it very difficult for the boy." Both parents were interested in their son and his education and, except for the mother's illness, there was a good family relationship.

841. M:14:2   ACE IX, 43; XI, 49   '9–'6   4:4:16
     B:I:1   ENG IX, none; XI, 36   '389–'056   3:3:21
                  HSR 40
                  SVIB none

The success of the father and an older brother seemed to be an important influence on this boy's behavior. He was overly concerned with grades and he worked hard at his studies, occasionally obtaining B's "by sheer effort rather than by ability." His wish to succeed seemed due to family expectations rather than his own interests and satisfactions. In personality he was quiet, almost shy, very polite, and generally well behaved. "He wanted to be liked," and he was liked and popular with his classmates. He was exceedingly interested in motorcycles and was in trouble on several occasions for traffic violations. His teachers felt that he was the kind of boy who "would conquer life's problems and do well at whatever he chose to do." He went on to college after graduation.

The father, a professional man, was a leader in civic affairs. He set high goals for his family. The brother, because he was better looking and more intelligent, somewhat overshadowed this boy. The mother had died when the boy was quite young.

842. M:14:6	ACE IX, 85; XI, 67	9'–7'0	1:6:11
N:VI:1	ENG IX, 57; XI, 50	'9864–'2	2:5:13
	HSR 71	'6–0̲'71	4:3:14
	SVIB '4–		

This boy labored under some handicaps because his older brother had been very successful in school. The boy felt that people expected him to be outstanding also, but he seemed to lack his brother's ability. Apparently his concern over this conflict became less marked as he continued in high school. His manner expressed a degree of resentment and he liked to argue. From first being described as a "brat," he came to be pleasant, "a good kid and a good student." Earlier, he seemed to have a chip on his shoulder, but later he relaxed, and after graduation went on to a university where he did very well. He wanted to become an attorney. Outside of school studies, he was interested chiefly in sports and recreation and in his senior year he was chosen captain of one of the school teams.

843. M:14:1	ACE IX, 77; XI, 64	'9–'7̲0̲1̲5̲	7:2:16
N:VI:2	ENG IX, 69; XI, 79	'69–0'8	1:3:14
	HSR 42		
	SVIB '5–		

With good ability and a "real fine personality plus," this boy was considered a "very fine kid." He was popular and had a good sense of humor. He was handicapped, however, by a kind of restlessness that made it difficult for him to adjust to class-rooms, where he was disorderly and often rude. He seemed to try hard to be funny and he talked up all the time. He was a good musician. He "did a lot of partying and drinking outside of school." This activity was not hidden from teachers and he would brag to other students about it. After graduation he went to junior college, where he reportedly did well.

The father came from a family that was not well respected; he, however, seemed to be one of its better members. The mother was a good woman who was interested in the welfare of the boy.

844. M:14:2	ACE IX, 59; XI, 32	'9–8̲3̲2̲'1̅6̅5	2:2:11
N:IVB:4	ENG IX, 41; XI, 36	9'784–2'53	1:7:12
	HSR 70		
	SVIB 4'12–5		

This boy was pleasant and did his work even when he might have been able to "slip through" without effort. Nevertheless he impressed teachers as having more ability than he bothered to use. He showed no leadership ability, but he was fairly well accepted by several groups in the school because of his cheerfulness and neatness. He was generally cooperative if it caused him no trouble. He was ordinarily very articulate and not at all on the defensive, but he seemed unable to discuss problems with the school counselor. His family had difficulties that he appeared to accept in a self-reliant way, although one teacher felt that he enjoyed the attention he received because of these difficulties and that he used them as an excuse to miss school. His driver's license was suspended at one time for a serious traffic violation. After graduation he got married and went to work on a farm.

845. F:14:0	ACE IX, none; XI, 61	'9–'0	9:0:16
N:III:3	ENG IX, none; XI, 78	'3–4'8<u>71</u>	3:1:11
	HSR 84		
	SVIB WR'		

Coming into the ninth grade from another school, this girl tried hard to achieve admittance into one of the better groups in the school. In spite of these efforts, she always remained on the fringe. She had more money to spend and better clothes than the average student, and she wanted to be in everything. She was lively, cheerful, peppy, and aggressive. A good student and a hard worker, she was active in a number of student organizations. As a junior she became engaged; this relationship seemed to be very satisfying to her. After graduation, however, the engagement was broken and the girl went to work. She continued to seem rather lonely. Her father had hoped she would go to college.

The father was a very active person with a drinking problem. He tended to be bitter and critical; he was not personally well liked in spite of his good standing as a small businessman. The mother seemed to be an adequate person. She worked but was a good housekeeper. In the girl's junior year the mother became seriously ill and the girl had to spend much time helping to care for her.

846. F:14:4	IQ (centile) 87	'9–'01	4:3:18
N:II:2	HSR trans. 9th gr.		
	SVIB none		

Outstanding in every way, including athletics, this girl was "well groomed, well mannered, and much fun." She was interesting and poised in social situations, and her teachers described her as a leader. After her freshman year she transferred to a girls' school.

847. M:15:0	ACE IX, 84; XI, 96	'91<u>34</u>–	6:6:24
N:VI:3	ENG IX, 74; XI, 68	'94 <u>873</u>–'<u>52</u>	4:3:22
	HSR 65		
	SVIB '4–9		

This boy was always boasting and bragging; he tried to get by on bluff. He gave the impression of having an "inferiority complex." Although he was considered to have a great deal of ability, he was "so lazy it was ridiculous." He let his hair grow long and he went with a rough crowd who wore boots and sideburns. He always made excuses for himself and was incapable of sustained concentration. He enlisted in the Navy after completing high school.

Little was known of the family. They had moved to the community shortly before the boy entered high school and moved out at the time he graduated: "When the family came to town they had nothing — not even furniture."

848. M:15:1	ACE IX, 46; XI, 79	'9134–52'06	1:9:15
N:III:4	ENG IX, 35; XI, 51	'98–'12	3:0:16
	HSR 46		
	SVIB 4'–		

This boy was loud, "wise acting," and obnoxious in manner, believing himself an authority on almost everything and seeming to want to write his own rules. He was "a hot-rodder." He dressed expensively but sloppily. He was so energetic that he was always in some sort of mischief. Though not generally popular, he had a car and those who liked to ride with him seemed to get along with him. He was in repeated trouble because of traffic offenses. His pastor thought that he would "settle down in time." He had good mechanical ability and after graduation he enrolled in a four-year engineering course.

The father was a prosperous businessman. He was described as a quiet, effective, well-respected man who directed much of his energies to community and humanitarian service. The mother was energetic, talkative, and outspoken. She, too, was a community leader. Their other son was said to be quiet and more like his father. The parents were said to indulge their children.

849. M:15:4	ACE IX, none; XI, 84	'9148 73–5'0	5:8:14
B:N:1	ENG IX, none; XI, 16		
	HSR 07		
	SVIB none		

This student was moody and depressed, and there were bizarre elements in his thinking. At times he appeared unkempt. He seemed to be unable to function at his best level and he was often truant from school. He got into trouble because of speeding, and his driver's license was suspended during his junior year. In his senior year he was placed in a technical school to learn auto mechanics.

850. F:15:2	ACE IX, 70; XI, 96	9″163847–	3:8:10
N:V:4	ENG IX, 90; XI, 86	'39–5'20	3:3:15
	HSR 78		
	SVIB WR'		

"Bubbling with ideas, wit, and plans," this girl was "100% alive, living and enjoying every minute of each day." She could be "loud in her enthusiasms but also equally awed by beauty or touched and moved to thought and action by life's sterner realities." Exceedingly responsive to people, she was sad and happy with them; she was a dynamic part of her society. Her participation in numerous activities seemed to be motivated not only by her enthusiasm and love of people but also by her constant striving to broaden herself and learn more about better ways of life. She was a leader without being domineering and was always perceptive and understanding of the problems and feelings of both teachers and classmates. Efficient and reliable, obedient without being subservient, she was conscientious about her social responsibilities, and yet working with her was always fun. At times she was frank to the point of shocking an overly sensitive person, but her basic kindness always limited any hurt that came from her actions. "She had a keen appreciation of home life, but was normal enough to enjoy sisterly scraps, too," one teacher reported. Her minister described her as "delightfully witty, wholesome; charming in appearance, dress, and actions." She was proud of her parents and was uninhibited in their presence. After graduation she continued her education at a university and later became engaged to be married.

The father was in a political position, which he filled competently. He had many friends and dealt with people well. The mother was also well thought of, articulate, and witty. Like the girl, she often spoke her mind freely, but she too was consistently considerate of others. Both parents came from humble origins and they felt responsible in their position, teaching this also to their children.

851. M:15:2	IQ (centile) 58	'9183–5'026	1:10:15
N:IVB:3	HSR trans. 10th gr.		
	SVIB none		

Although this boy appeared to have fair ability, his schoolwork was poor. He was not very cooperative and gave the impression of not being "well balanced." He was "erratic." He was accepted by other students but was not a leader. He got into trouble by speeding and he was found guilty of breaking and entering. His plan was to go into the Navy. One teacher predicted emotional maladjustment for him.

852. M:14:1	ACE IX, 89; XI, 58	9'10–2'	3:7:10
N:VI:2	ENG IX, 79; XI, 47	'62 58–'0	1:3:10
	HSR 28		
	SVIB '8–120		

In extracurricular activities this boy was a good worker, but he was a poor student. He tried to get excuses so that he could do only what he pleased. He caused disturbances in the classroom. His chief interest was in dramatics, where he was fairly successful. He was also athletically inclined and showed an interest in coaching. In general conduct he was described as "loud, a show-off, a big blow." Once after he was absent from school he forged an excuse to be readmitted. His appearance was marred by severe acne and he suffered from allergic conditions. After graduation he went to a junior college.

853. F:14:1 ACE IX, 34; XI, 56 '92–1' 8:4:15
    N:III:1 ENG IX, none; XI, 51 — — — —
                    HSR 82 '9–'<u>467</u> 10:2:15X
                    SVIB none

Serious but cheerful, this girl was somewhat unsure of herself and tended to underrate her abilities. She was very dependable and, in general, had a good achievement record, although she never stood out among her classmates. An excellent, conscientious, almost compulsive worker, she was ambitious and held a part-time job outside of the school. She was very close to her father, confiding in him on many details and often referring to him in school contacts. By contrast, she never mentioned her mother. After graduation she began taking training in a university two-year course but dropped out of school because of poor grades and went to work.

The father was a skilled workman. The family was very closely knit and interested in the girl.

854. M:15:2 ACE IX, none; XI, 26 '92–'<u>571</u> 3:0:14
    N:VI:3 ENG IX, none; XI, 04
                    HSR 21
                    SVIB none

Always big for his age, this boy used his weight to push the smaller boys around. His size was a basis for a generally overbearing manner. In spite of his size he engaged in no athletic activities because of a "cry-baby attitude." He used brass knuckles in a fight with one boy, and he had numerous difficulties and was warned by the police for misconduct. At times he displayed an incontrollable temper. He was untrustworthy and dishonest. As he progressed through high school he became more self-controlled and appeared to be more respectful of authority. There were traffic offenses on his record and at one time he was charged with disturbing the peace.

Both parents worked at unskilled jobs and there was much quarreling in the home.

855. M:14:2 ACE IX, none; XI, 92 92'4<u>760</u>–'3 1:5:9
    N:III:3 ENG IX, none; XI, 85
                    HSR 76
                    SVIB 4'8–

This boy worked and "did all right." He was reliable and dependable, and had a nice disposition. In the ninth grade he was a male soprano and sang in the chorus. He also was on one of the athletic teams.

856. M:15:8	ACE IX, none; XI, 02	'925–'7381	4:6:10
N:VII:2	ENG IX, none; XI, 12		
	HSR 26		
	SVIB none		

This boy got into repeated trouble with the law before and around the time of the ninth-grade testing. Offenses included petty larceny, shoplifting, and prowling cars. By the time he was a sophomore, he had had sixteen recorded contacts with the authorities. In school he was unruly and often tardy. In general, he was irresponsible. In spite of the unusually bad early behavior, he had a fairly successful senior year. He showed a great improvement and his reputation was then considered to be good. Several of his ninth-grade teachers predicted emotional and legal problems for him.

857. M:15:4	ACE IX, 01; XI, none	9'''2''68'13–7'05	9:6:15
N:IVB:4	ENG IX, 02; XI, none		
	HSR DO 9th gr.		
	SVIB none		

As soon as he was old enough, this boy quit school because he was interested in farming. His scholastic ability was poor and he was often truant. His lack of friends did not seem to bother him. His teachers remembered him as having matured early and as having "looked and acted like an adult." However, two of his ninth-grade teachers anticipated difficulties for him of both an emotional and a legal nature.

858. M:14:1	ACE IX, 44; XI, 28	'927–'1	2:3:11
N:III:1	ENG IX, none; XI, 31	'3791 45–'0	2:0:19
	HSR 32	9''638–02'	3:3:17
	SVIB none		

Clean, neat, well dressed, respectful, mannerly, and self-controlled, this boy was never a discipline problem. He had little drive and energy, however, and was so quiet that others did not bother to join him in casual activities. He was unconcerned about his studies and his teachers thought that he did not work up to his capacity. He was frequently absent from school, presumably because of health problems, but he may have been following his main interests of hunting, fishing, and sports. After graduation he went to a university, from which he dropped out after a short time because of low grades. He re-entered the school later and started another line of studies where he hoped to be more successful.

859. F:14:1	ACE IX, 61; XI, 67	'93–'2410	6:3:15
B:V:4	ENG IX, 80; XI, 91	'34–2'09	5:1:21
	HSR 97		
	SVIB WR'		

Many good things were said of this girl. "She was capable of deep, fine love that bubbled out of her chubby body." It was natural and easy for her to show love and affection, especially for children. The girl had lived with her grandparents all her life and never spoke of her father. The grandparents were a very good influence on her and it was felt that they kept her from missing her own parents, whose absence from her life was never well explained. It was said that there was a time when she was sensitive and unable to take criticism but that she changed completely. Her sense of humor helped her hold a good balance and lifted her above routine discouragements. She was generally active in school and community and received a number of honors because of her popularity and her musical talent. "She critically evaluated life about her and lived a good life fully and generously." After graduation she continued on to college.

The family was described as reserved and quiet but able to provide security and inspiring models of behavior.

860. F:15:1	ACE IX, 82; XI, 89	9'31468–'25	2:4:13
N:III:3	ENG IX, 83; XI, 88		
	HSR 65		
	SVIB '–		

Exuberant yet mature, this girl was popular and able to assume responsibility. She was socially active. She was neat and courteous and had a particular interest in music. She had a steady boy friend.

861. M:14:3	ACE IX, 72; XI, 55	'934–2'50	5:5:16
N:N:1	ENG IX, none; XI, 38		
	HSR 32		
	SVIB none		

This boy could have been a good student but "his associates were his downfall." Apparently he was easily led and he got into a number of scrapes such as skipping school, turning in false fire alarms, and violating traffic regulations. When not in the company of his friends, he was considered dependable and agreeable, and he could be a good student. His teachers were optimistic about him, for they said his older brothers had followed the same pattern but eventually turned out well.

862. F:15:7	ACE IX, 63; XI, none	'93416–27	4:4:13
B:VI:1	ENG IX, none; XI, none		
	HSR DO 10th gr.		
	SVIB none		

This girl dropped out of school after her freshman year in order to go to work. She had been thought of as making a fine adjustment, as cooperative and willing to make up her schoolwork when she missed it. On the other hand, she had been absent a great deal and was once truant with a group of boys. Constant complaints of being sick were considered psychosomatic by a physician.

863. F:15:4 ACE IX, 72; XI, none 93'468–'2 0:2:6
    N:VII:4 ENG IX, none; XI, none
    HSR 56
    SVIB 'WR

This girl was well liked, always cheerful and smiling. Although she was a little self-conscious, she was frank and outspoken. One of her ninth-grade teachers felt that she might develop emotional difficulties.

864. M:14:1 ACE IX, 100; XI, 100 9'3468–'7 2:3:17
    N:V:2 ENG IX, none; XI, 92 — — — —
    HSR 95 '946–0'52 3:4:19
    SVIB '4–

In the ninth grade this boy was conceited with a "superior attitude." He had few friends and participated in few activities. Much of his spare time was spent working at home. As he continued in high school he seemed to improve and lost some of his conceited manner. He was described as "a big, bright fellow." After graduation he entered engineering training.

865. F:15:9 ACE IX, none; XI, 44 '938–2'05 5:1:15
    N:IVB:3 ENG IX, none; XI, 63 '738–'659 2:4:16
    HSR 57
    SVIB none

A minor speech difficulty made this girl very self-conscious and quiet. She was not outstanding, but she was dependable and rather well accepted by her classmates. Teachers felt that she was a good girl from a good home, and at least one thought that the school should have given her more help.

866. M:15:1 ACE IX, 08; XI, 28 '938–'65 3:3:16
    N:III:1 ENG IX, 24; XI, 47 9'8513– 5:5:19
    HSR 37
    SVIB '–

This student was "strictly a yes-man, a follower," and he seemed to feel defeated. He was a slow-thinking, plodding sort of boy who was a little lazy. Physically he was big and "overgrown." He had to work hard to achieve average grades. In his early high school years there was a good deal of pressure from his home, where other members seemed to have more ability than he. He got along well with his fellow students, although he was not outstandingly popular. He was interested in music. Others sometimes were amused at his "childish antics." He continued on to university work in the field of agriculture.

The mother was "very nice but overprotective and concerned over details." She was aggressive and could not understand why the boy did not do better. The family had a good income and high cultural interests and standards.

867. M:15:2	ACE IX, none; XI, 77	9'3814–'06	1:5:15
B:III:1	ENG IX, none; XI, 76	9'834–'27	3:9:13
	HSR 26		
	SVIB none		

Teachers differed in their comments on this boy, although most agreed that around school he was quiet and almost always off by himself. He was rarely seen talking to anyone; he seemed to prefer to be alone and "let the rest of the world go by." He had no enthusiasms and participated in none of the school activities, although he did express a preference for the outdoors. Academically he was a poor student with poor study habits. Nevertheless he cooperated when asked. His schoolwork was usually neat but late. He was careless, however, about his dress. One teacher described him as "thin and shy and possibly insecure," while another said he was "juvenile and needed to grow up." "He needed firm management and help in seeing the importance of acknowledging his wrong deeds." He got into minor trouble on several occasions because he was caught smoking, and once he left school without permission. He planned to join the Navy after graduation.

The parents were divorced, and the boy lived with his mother, who worked. He liked and respected his father, whom he frequently saw.

868. F:14:1	ACE IX, none; XI, 91	'94–'167	2:3:12
N:V:3	ENG IX, none; XI, 89	'7980–1'3	1:2:8
	HSR 66		
	SVIB '–		

This girl was rather attractive in appearance and pleasant in manner. She had few close friends, and it required more than passing acquaintance to perceive her attractiveness and capabilities. Although she was a National Honor Society student her teachers felt that she could have done better in schoolwork. Active in both school and outside social affairs, she participated especially in numerous music and journalism organizations. In the family social life also there was much gathering of relatives and other activity of which she was a part. After graduation she attended a junior college.

The father, a skilled workman, was known as "a sour individual, a worry-wort." The mother, on the other hand, was friendly and outgoing, actively interested in church and school affairs. She also worked outside the home. The family seemed to be a good one with healthy relationships between parents and children.

869. M:15:2	ACE IX, none; XI, 50	9'4–52'	3:10:15
N:III:3	ENG IX, none; XI, 07		
	HSR 01 DO 12th gr.		
	SVIB '4–5		

This much overweight boy was teased by both family and friends because of his size. The teachers felt that he was to be pitied because of this teasing from his family. "He wanted to be friendly and funny but did not succeed" and he did not mix well with the other students. In school he was uncooperative, disobedient, and discourteous. He had little respect for his elders. He probably would not have been graduated because of his poor achievement, but in any case he left school before the end of his senior year. He then joined the Navy.

The father was "a typical hillbilly, rough and uncouth." The mother was seclusive, taking no part in church or community activities. The family's house was "rough" and not well kept, and the family was of low repute in the locality.

870. M:14:3	ACE IX, 54; XI, 36	9′41<u>73</u>–5′62	3:5:13
N:IVA:5	ENG IX, 15; XI, 13	4″9<u>81</u>′6372–′0	4:9:18
	HSR 41		
	SVIB –5		

Although he was very popular with teachers and students, this boy did not excel in anything and he was not a leader. Dependable and sincere, he was able to carry things through. He was well behaved; he seemed to enjoy life and had a subtle, well-timed sense of humor. Interested in farming, he limited his extracurricular activities to hunting and fishing.

The father and mother were pleasant, very good persons. The father was relatively reserved and left the mother to be the leader and to make most of the outside social contacts. The family had a good reputation and the parents were interested and helpful in their children's lives.

871. M:15:1	ACE IX, 20; XI, 82	9′42–′0	5:6:14
B:III:1	ENG IX, 96; XI, 49	′5468<u>93</u>–20′	1:3:17
	HSR 14		
	SVIB 12′–		

Tall and husky, this boy gave the impression of being athletic, but he showed little interest in sports and was actually awkward and uncoordinated. He suffered from severe acne. His teachers described him as "a strange boy — unpredictable and unreliable." He had good ability but he did not use it. He dropped out of a mathematics course during his junior year after having done very inadequate work. "He was always making excuses for himself and he tried to give the appearance of being self-confident when he really wasn't," one teacher reported. Frequently he "fabricated stories to get out of things; he lied with a straight face and did not give truthful information about even inconsequential matters." On one occasion he forged a teacher's name to a pass. He seemed to be a "lone wolf" and his few associates were "undesirable characters." He was easily led and he always seemed to be on the fringe of trouble with the law. He was known to the police for stealing once and for several traffic violations. His difficulties were apparently long-standing, for there were reports that even as a young child he had been "a nuisance and a behavior problem." The school reported, however, that there was a discernible change for the better in his senior year. Outside of school his only known activity was participation with his father in a religious organization. His father had been an active member of this group for many years. The boy planned to take special training and to make a career for himself within this group. It was not known if he carried out these plans after graduation.

The home life was one of marked instability. The father had poor health and was not very competent. He was considered to be somewhat of a fanatic about religion. He deserted the family when the boy was quite young. However, the boy continued to see his father. The mother was large, raw-boned, and coarse in dress and manner. She did domestic work, and the care of the children was largely entrusted to the grandmother. The mother remarried twice: the first marriage, a brief but disastrous affair, was followed by a more stable one which occurred about the time the boy entered high school. The boy did not get along well with either of his stepfathers.

872. M:15:2   IQ (centile) 55   '943–'20   10:3:21X
     N:V:2   HSR DO 11th gr.
                   SVIB none

When in junior high school this boy struck one of his male teachers. He was described as physically mature but socially immature. Frequent truancy and insubordination were coupled with his chronic neglect of schoolwork. His police record showed a long list of violations, including numerous traffic and stealing offenses, breaking and entering, and disorderly conduct. Finally in his junior year he dropped out of school to join the armed services. At the time of the ninth-grade testing several teachers predicted he would subsequently become emotionally disturbed.

The parents were characterized as "very emotional people." There was constant bickering and conflict in the home. The parents had emigrated from Europe, where the father had held a professional position. In the United States he was employed as a skilled tradesman.

873. F:15:9   ACE IX, 93; XI, 67   '94538–2'1   1:2:16
     N:III:2   ENG IX, 98; XI, 98   '94 30–2'1   1:4:13
                 HSR 76
                 SVIB '–

This very pretty girl was always happy and having a good time. She was well liked and had "a lot of personality." She did not seem to concentrate very well; a little "flighty," she occasionally "talked out of turn." After graduation she went to work in a local retail shop.

The father and mother were fine people, well respected in the community. Although the boys in the family tended to be problem children in school, the over-all evaluation of the family life, from the standpoint of the community, was good.

874. F:14:1   ACE IX, 79; XI, 69   94'56087–'3   5:16:4X
    N:IVB:5   ENG IX, 58; XI, 82
                  HSR 63
                  SVIB none

In school this girl was a good student, hard working and relatively well mannered. She was quiet and engaged in no group activities. Her teachers considered her withdrawn and she had very few friends. Outside of school she was a problem in the community. The police considered her to be "too free with her affections" and she was repeatedly identified in "joints" in violation of laws concerning minors.

875. F:14:2   ACE IX, 84; XI, 82   9'458–'2   0:9:11
    N:II:1   ENG IX, none; XI, 95   '46 7893–'2   1:2:13
                  HSR 48   19'874–'05   3:2:20
                  SVIB none

This girl's reputation was better in school than outside of school. Although some teachers saw her as quiet, relatively well adjusted, and mature, others saw her differently. She was erratic in her schoolwork, and once when caught cheating, she attempted to make light of the fact and to be critical of the penalty. She did only what she had to do and did not accept leadership. Her school attendance was poor and outside of school she went around with boys who were "a little fast." She was very interested in activities outside of the school, particularly sports. After graduation she went to a university and her grades were so poor that she was put on probation. She managed to do a little better later.

Both parents were college graduates. Together they operated a prosperous business that seemed to occupy most of their time.

876. M:14:2   ACE IX, none; XI, 81   9'458–'2   3:3:14
    N:I:3   ENG IX none; XI, 71   '958 24–1'3   1:0:11
                  HSR 87   9'45–'13   2:2:14
                  SVIB 48'–0

A fellow student aptly described this boy: "Not a bookworm or a social hound; just a nice guy to have around." He was good looking and well liked by boys and girls, taking part in class plays and being elected to class offices. He did not have much motivation, however, and although he did what was expected of him, he never went out of his way to do more. He was self-reliant and worked in the summers so that he could save to pay for most of his college education. He was arrested once for a traffic offense. After graduation he entered college to study engineering.

The father was a professional man — a "silent, deep man" with set ideas and opinions. The mother was "dark and vivacious." She did a great deal of entertaining. There seemed to be a good parent-child relationship and it was a desirable home.

877. F:15:4   ACE IX, 32; XI, none   9'45867–   1:8:11
     B:VII:2   ENG IX, none; XI, none
                     HSR DO 10th gr.
                     SVIB none

This girl dropped out of school after completing the ninth grade. No clear reason was given. She had been getting average grades and had not appeared obviously uninterested in school. She was an outdoor girl, interested in horseback riding and other sports. Although there was no other confirmation for her statement, she claimed she had poor vision and was hard of hearing. Soon after she dropped out of school the family moved from the community and it was believed she had taken a steady job.

The father died when the girl was nine years old. The mother, an unstable person, exercised little control over her children, who were always in trouble. She expected the daughter to do much better in school than she actually did. The family did not stand well in the community.

878. F:14:5   ACE IX, none; XI, 49   9'46–'2   2:4:15
     N:III:3   ENG IX, none; XI, 70
                     HSR 42 DO 12th gr.
                     SVIB none

This was a dark-complexioned girl who was not very pretty. While she was in school she had very little fun because she had to work so hard at home. During summers she had jobs both in the day and at night. In her junior year she became pregnant, and she left school at the end of the year to be married. One of the teachers predicted in the ninth grade that the girl would later have legal difficulties.

The father, who was a skilled workman, was considered "high-strung." The mother spent considerable time in a mental hospital, and the girl had to be "the mother of the family."

879. M:14:1   ACE IX, 54; XI, 74   '946–2'13   2:7:13
     N:III:4   ENG IX, 11; XI, 31   '49–21'38 570 3:7:9
                     HSR 27
                     SVIB 8'9–2

The descriptions of this boy were at great variance with each other. On the one hand it was said that although he had been an aggressive bully, he had grown out of this and become gentlemanly, courteous, and well liked: "a jolly boy who got along well with people." In great contrast, others called him noisy, boisterous, and unpredictable. More extremely he was described as "spoiled, rotten, and low in moral standards." Still another view of him was that he was "nervous and erratic." He was active in athletics and was in the school chorus. There were a number of traffic offenses recorded against him. After graduation he went to a small college. One ninth-grade teacher predicted emotional maladjustment for him.

The family was noted for "money, unhappiness, bickering, and drinking." The father was, however, a pleasant enough and successful businessman who was a "lone wolf." The mother moved with a "fast group" and drank with the husband, often becoming quarrelsome. On the other hand, she was "generous, unselfish, and likable." A sister of the boy was described as "wild."

880. F:14:2	ACE IX, 67; XI, 81	'946378–0'521	7:0:19
N:I:4	ENG IX, 86; XI, 93	'6349–0'5	3:3:13
	HSR 77		
	SVIB none		

Forward and aggressive, this girl "liked to talk too much." She was in many activities and had many friends. Altogether, she was extroverted and gregarious. In her studies she was a good enough student, but her teachers felt that she could have done better. She was guilty of a number of traffic offenses and the police considered her "a little wild."

881. F:14:2	ACE IX, 38; XI, 89	9"4'6780–2'13	3:5:11
N:iII:3	ENG IX, 85; XI, 95		
	HSR 81		
	SVIB 'WR		

Although she was a good student with good ability, this girl was moody and "handicapped by emotionalism." She was usually friendly and pleasant, and she was well accepted by the other students. She was "boy crazy."

882. F:15:2	ACE IX, none; XI, 73	94'68–21'3	1:11:11
N:III:1	ENG IX, none; XI, 87	9'45 68–20'	5:0:17
	HSR 81		
	SVIB WR'		

This girl was not a conduct problem in classes, but she was occasionally a little rude and headstrong. She had strong likes and dislikes and was assertive about them. After others got used to her, they accepted her well enough, and she was a moderate participant in school activities.

883. M:15:4	ACE IX, 95; XI, 98	9'4683 75–2'	4:1:15
N:V:2	ENG IX, none; XI, 69	'964–'15	1:4:13
	HSR 33		
	SVIB 8'4–1		

Socially and emotionally immature, this was a competent but daydreaming boy who never worked up to his capacity. He was neat and clean in appearance, but he had bad teeth and impaired hearing. Never in serious difficulty, he was, however, a dawdler who cooperated only when it was convenient. The one area of fairly successful achievement for him was athletics: he was on several of the school teams. At one time he was absent from school for nine days without his parents knowing it and without any apparent reason. Evidently he missed the first day and then was unable to face the problem of returning. After graduation he went into the armed services.

The father, although hard working, earned little and seemed to lack ambition. The mother was somewhat more aggressive, yet quiet and ill at ease with strangers. Both parents were warm, and they were interested in the children. It was a close-knit family suffering often from not having enough money.

884. F:14:0	ACE IX, none; XI, 34	9'46<u>87</u>–1'<u>35</u>	4:6:11
N:V:3	ENG IX, none; XI, 54	'9<u>35</u> <u>48</u>–'02	2:4:11
	HSR 78		
	SVIB WR'		

This was a tall, dark, attractive girl who immediately impressed others with her poise and maturity. She was very active in school affairs and also worked part time as a clerk outside of school. Although one of the leaders in school activities, she was not popular. Boys did not seem to like her and she had few close girl friends. After graduation she went to a professional school.

The father had a very close relationship with the girl. He was easygoing, relaxed, and fond of outdoor activities. The mother, a high-strung person, was active in community affairs. The girl did not get along well with her mother and would not take her word on anything unless the father agreed.

885. F:14:3	ACE IX, 88; XI, 97	9'47–'<u>01</u>	1:2:16
B:IVC:5	ENG IX, 94; XI, 89	9'4<u>53</u>–2'01	1:2:19
	HSR 93		
	SVIB none		

This girl appeared poised and comfortable in relationships with other students. She was described as effervescent and high-strung; she thought and talked fast and was ambitious. Although sensitive, she took criticism well; she was, however, occasionally capable of a crying spell. She could be "very affected, silly, and giggly." Definitely a leader in school activities, she won a scholarship to cover part of her college expenses. A relative who was domineering and who had much influence on her wanted to help with the balance of her college expenses. She, however, did not go to college, taking a job instead.

The father, who had been mentally ill, was dead. The stepfather was quiet and well thought of. The mother was conscientious and concerned about her children, controlling them closely. She had strong moral opinions.

886. F:14:1   ACE IX, 59; XI, 61   9'4758–   5:8:17
     N:III:2   ENG IX, none; XI, 68
                 HSR 30
                 SVIB WR'

This overweight girl was always eating and making no attempt to reduce. Her manners were crude, rough, and rather forward. She was a nuisance, a show-off — irritating, loud, and boisterous — "a big, fat pain in the neck." She was not very dependable and she had a tendency to childish deceptions. Under ordinary conditions she was indifferent to schoolwork and would merely talk in class or make clumsy efforts to gain attention. When given attention and praise, however, she responded well and did her best work. She could be good-natured and jolly at times. She tried to participate in activities but was frustrated in this.

The father, a marginally successful businessman, was ineffectual although loquacious and outgoing. The mother's health was not good. She had professional training and was close and affectionate with her children.

887. M:15:6   ACE IX, 70; XI, 72   9"4'7685–'01   1:7:14
     N:VI:2   ENG IX, none; XI, 46
                 HSR 37
                 SVIB 89'4–120

A real discipline problem, this boy "needed isolation." He was loud and boisterous, and on occasion he had to be excluded from class. He instigated fights and participated in drunken brawls. He "forsook good judgment for popularity." He was a football player. In spite of his erratic sense of values, he was leader in a church youth group.

888. M:16:7   ACE IX, 05; XI, 02   9'478–'12 35   5:2:13
     N:VI:2   ENG IX, 16; XI, 04
                 HSR 13
                 SVIB none

This boy was happy and friendly for the most part, but his teachers considered him to have "basically a weak personality." At school he was frequently involved in "horseplay." Easily led, he was exceedingly anxious to be liked and he quickly conformed when criticized. He was nervous and he stuttered badly. One person said he "thought he was better than he was." He participated little in extracurricular activities. He had a record of several traffic offenses.

889. M:14:3   ACE IX, 87; XI, 43   '9478–5'316   6:4:13
     N:V:2   ENG IX, 70; XI, 32
                 HSR DO 11th gr.
                 SVIB none

A dramatic series of acts, which became increasingly violent and destructive, were committed by this boy over a two-year period. This behavior began, seemingly without warning, about a year after the ninth-grade MMPI testing. In rapid succession occurred a number of thefts, burglaries, tire slashings, and other acts of serious vandalism that came to the attention of police. The youth was arrested for drunkenness on several occasions during this period. He was placed on probation and later, after repeated and more serious offenses, committed to a correctional school. In the early years at high school he had not been a behavior problem and nothing noteworthy was recorded in school reports. Apparently he was not a particularly good student. Typically, his grades went up and down from one report period to another. Frequently he would start off well but begin to slip before the end of the period. His school conduct remained good even during the first year of the period when he was seriously delinquent outside of school. During his junior year both his classwork and his school deportment rapidly deteriorated. He fell further and further behind in his classwork; he was bold; he caused disturbances and became completely irresponsible and untrustworthy. During this period he seemed unable to stand any routine. Finally losing all interest, he quit school. Shortly after leaving high school he was committed to the correctional school.

At the institution he was described as "nice looking, of average height and build, quiet, friendly, well mannered, and at least superficially well adjusted and accepted by others; a good sport who never complains." Closer examination, however, revealed him to be impulsive and nonconforming, with poor inner controls and defective practical judgment. At the time he entered the institution he reported that he had been "angry with everything." Nevertheless, during his eight-month stay when he had no alcohol and was under close supervision his behavior was acceptable. It was reported that he was now more "mature in his thinking." Because of his good record in this setting he was released under parole supervision.

After release from detention he went back to live at home. Somewhat later, following a very minor frustration, he killed several members of his family. Reportedly he had been drinking. There was little direct evidence that these killings were especially directed at the victims. One of these, a younger sister, was shot "because she was screaming all the time." The boy stated that he had originally intended to kill himself. He was sentenced to prison for life.

There was nothing particularly noteworthy about the family. The father was a skilled worker and well accepted in the community. The whole family had a good reputation. The mother occupied herself with the home. There were good recreational facilities, with the whole family working together on projects such as a lake cottage.

890. M:14:3	ACE IX, none; XI, 59	9′4781–′2	3:4:16
N:IVB:3	ENG IX, none; XI, 19	4′9–′2	0:11:10
	HSR 24		
	SVIB none		

The boy had little respect for authority. He was belligerent and moody. He readily lost his temper, and if corrected, he held a grudge. He was a ringleader of a gang; he would urge his friends to cause trouble but he himself would stop on the fringe.

9'47<u>83</u> <u>162</u>–

He lied to help himself, and he was a "sneaky, untrustworthy person." He accumulated a police record of traffic offenses, gang activities, and, finally, strong-arm tactics.

891.	F:14:3	ACE IX, 94; XI, 91	9'47<u>83</u> <u>162</u>–	2:4:18
	B:VI:2	ENG IX, 95; XI, 98	743'<u>281</u>690–	2:10:11
		HSR 63		
		SVIB '–		

This girl could do schoolwork if she wanted to and could get good grades on tests, but she was very erratic and undependable and only tried now and then. She followed her own interests to the neglect of other work. She had a continuous record of infractions of rules such as sleeping in class, truancy, disrespect, and forging excuses. Socially she was outgoing and exuberant, seeming bright and able to do more than she actually did. After graduation she went to a small college, where she was a failure; she then transferred to another college.

The girl was "the apple of her mother's eye." The mother was very talkative and apt to criticize the school and everything in it. The father had died when the girl was very young and the mother remarried shortly thereafter. The stepfather was well respected and good to the family.

892.	F:14:1	ACE IX, 99; XI, 98	'948–'<u>105</u>	1:2:16
	N:I:2	ENG IX, 100; XI, 95	9'<u>46</u>–'<u>712</u>	2:2:15
		HSR 96	'94–7'52	2:2:14
		SVIB '–		

With "flaming red hair and much beauty," this girl was very adult, sophisticated, and poised. She was "a little cocky," and had the attitude of "I can get along by myself." Sometimes she seemed bored. If pushed, she was likely to be rebellious. There were minor difficulties in some classes and occasionally she was truant and uncooperative. Her art teachers considered her exceedingly talented. "School was never a challenge to this girl." She was quite popular with boys and went with a boy that her parents objected to. This caused friction between her and her parents, who, in general, gave her a great deal of freedom and did not know what to do with her. After graduation she became pregnant and married the boy. The husband, a drifter and a drinker, and unstable when younger, seemed to mature after the marriage. The girl went on to a university and maintained a high scholastic standing.

The father and mother were professional people, both ambitious for their children. The mother, like the girl, was stubborn. The family was well thought of in the community.

893. M:16:3	ACE IX, 07; XI, 36	'948–2'73	4:8:6
N:IVC:3	ENG IX, 18; XI, 23	'491658–2'	2:10:9
	HSR 13		
	SVIB none		

A "law unto himself," this boy was boisterous and loud. He seemed always to have a chip on his shoulder. He was also described as arrogant, contemptuous of authority, and so uncooperative and uninterested that "he should have been kicked out of school." He had some traits of leadership and he was an extrovert. Two of his teachers expected that he would get into legal difficulties.

The father was a "dull braggart." He was domineering and a poor credit risk. He also was an alcoholic for a time. The mother was, contrastingly, responsible and dependable, the strength of the family.

894. M:15:1	ACE IX, 09; XI, 20	9'4827130–5'6	3:11:12
N:IVB:3	ENG IX, 06; XI, 06	'13248–'5	8:4:18
	HSR 29		
	SVIB 4'12–		

Because of a heart defect this boy was unable to do many things and he had had to spend considerable time in the hospital before entering high school. Although he was said to be a little unreliable at times, he was usually thought of as a very fine boy. He gave no trouble in school and seemed to be fairly well motivated. He was quiet and retiring in manner and he had "good common sense." Musically talented, he considered teaching music. There was a record of a traffic offense.

He came from a good, hard-working farm family of above average means. The relationships among the family were good and they enjoyed many activities together. The parents were pleasant and they had good control over their children.

895. F:14:2	ACE IX, 94; XI, 86	94"8'3765–'0	3:9:14
N:VI:2	ENG IX, none; XI, 95		
	HSR none		
	SVIB none		

A "bright, smart person," this pleasant and nice-appearing girl was actively "anti-school" and was the leader of a "revolution." Snappy and tart in manner, she seemed to have no conscience. She was sexually promiscuous: "she put out for everything that walked." She went out with married men and was the cause of several dramatic triangles. Expelled from school on three occasions, she had an illegitimate child during one of these periods. She "finally married a bum."

896. F:15:3   ACE IX, none; XI, 17   9'4851–   5:5:13
     N:VI:3   ENG IX, none; XI, 43   '349–'26   1:5:10
                     HSR 31
                     SVIB none

A description of this girl called her "a scatterbrained, flighty, peroxided blonde." Her school written work was poor but she was faithful in doing her assignments. In spite of her "cheap" appearance, she was characterized by high morals and regular church attendance. She also helped at home. Although not widely popular, she had a few close friends.

Two siblings had incurable diseases that led to the family's spending everything in searching for a cure.

897. M:14:3   ACE IX, 53; XI, 67   9'4863–'5   4:12:14
     N:V:1   ENG IX, none; XI, 41
                     HSR 09 DO 12th gr.
                     SVIB none

This student was small for his age and acted in an immature manner. Around teachers he was shy and he took no part in school activities. As a student he was lazy and needed watching or he would get into trouble since he was easily persuaded by his undesirable associates. He seemed to have poor ability to concentrate. He wanted to become a pilot and he may have joined the Air Force. The family moved from the community after he completed the eleventh grade. The school did not receive a request for the transfer of his school records.

898. M:14:3   ACE IX, 52; XI, 34   9486'70–'351   1:7:10
     N:IVB:3   ENG IX, 32; XI, 28
                     HSR 05 DO 11th gr.
                     SVIB none

This small boy was uninterested in school and he finally dropped out altogether. While he was in school he was quiet and nondescript, engaging in no extracurricular activities. With other students he was belligerent and obstreperous; he did not have many friends. Teachers thought of him as lazy, sullen, and having a "know-it-all attitude." Outside of school he was "a wild kid," engaging in "a lot of drinking and tearing around." The mother described him as "tired and scared of school." He was guilty of several traffic violations. After dropping out of school he went to work on a farm and soon had almost complete control of its operation.

899. M:15:2   ACE IX, 59; XI, 77   94'87 263–   0:7:8
     N:V:1   ENG IX, 80; XI, 60   '19342–5'6   1:7:13
                     HSR 26
                     SVIB none

This boy had had rheumatic fever and had been a partial invalid for some years. It was thought that the family had babied him because of this condition. He was not well liked and he seemed resentful of school and authority in general. He never had an opinion but "just sat in class." His attitude toward school seemed to be "what's the use?" He did not follow directions in industrial classes and refused to take safety precautions. He seemed to feel that he could do anything he pleased in the way he wanted to do it. He was one of a "black-leather-jacket group" and he was interested in cars. He had to be disciplined for wearing inappropriate clothes in school. After graduation he went to work in a garage.

The father was a skilled mechanic. The mother worked outside the home. She was unsympathetic with school authorities, feeling they picked on her son.

900. M:15:3	ACE IX, 23; XI, 50	94'873–2'0	2:10:15
N:V:1	ENG IX, none; XI, 35	'49–5'<u>23</u>	0:0:14
	HSR 17		
	SVIB none		

This boy was quiet. He was usually in the background and not much was heard about or from him. He was by no means a leader. His attitude was frequently "nasty," and he was immature and hard to reason with. He had his own car and was often truant with a group of younger boys. He got some recognition because of his musical ability. In his senior year he ran away with a younger girl and at about the same time he was guilty of petty larceny. The parents were very defensive about the trouble the boy got into, and they were uncooperative with school authorities.

901. F:15:3	ACE IX, 69; XI, 72	94'87<u>65</u>–21'0	1:6:15
N:I:3	ENG IX, 87; XI, 99	'348–'5	9:1:23
	HSR 98	'4<u>38</u> <u>75</u>–	6:1:27
	SVIB '–		

This girl was attractive, poised, and very popular. Co-valedictorian of her class, she held a number of school offices and was strongly motivated toward school and other activities. A leader in church work, she was thought of as charming, articulate, and outstanding in every way. It was suggested that her parents may have put considerable pressure on her to achieve. After graduation she went on to a university.

It was a "wonderful family," very civic-minded, close, and possessing high morals. Both parents gave generously of their time and talent to community affairs.

902. F:15:3	ACE IX, 58; XI, 67	'94<u>80</u>–'23	4:2:15
B:III:1	ENG IX, none; XI, 92	'3–'5<u>29</u>	3:2:18
	HSR 79		
	SVIB none		

Although this girl was a superior student, careful in meeting her assignments, her teachers felt that she did not extend herself to the limits of her capabilities. She was a little temperamental and would sometimes "get up on her high horse to resist criticism." Apparently these episodes were quickly over. She "radiated personality." She had many girl friends and a steady boy friend. She was described as dependable, cooperative, conscientious, mannerly, and adaptable. After graduation she worked as a secretary.

Her parents had been divorced and she had a stepmother. The home discipline was said to be very good.

903. M:14:3	ACE IX, none; XI, 65	9'480–'63	6:9:10
N:VII:1	ENG IX, none; XI, 43	4'7839–5'2	5:4:17
	HSR 52		
	SVIB '48–		

"A big, clumsy guy," this boy was polite and well mannered. He was retiring and he did not associate with girls. Toward school he was indifferent and he was frequently absent. He was "a dreamer."

904. M:14:5	ACE IX, 81; XI, 92	9'5–'123	3:4:11
N:IVB:4	ENG IX, 78; XI, 68		
	HSR DO 11th gr.		
	SVIB none		

A "wise guy" of the "typical motorcycle, black-jacket type," this boy was undependable and a smart aleck who picked on others. His talking and scuffling were a constant source of irritation to his teachers. When corrected he would become sassy and pout. Although small in stature, he was a muscular, well-developed, and handsome youth. He was, however, possibly sensitive about his size. He was an underachiever. He could have excelled in school and in athletics but he wasted his ability. He was unable to conform and lived by his own rules. He dropped out of school in the eleventh grade and later joined the armed services. While attending school he was guilty of several traffic offenses and was once caught stealing. One teacher expressed some optimism, predicting an eventual normal adjustment for him.

The father was an alcoholic who had frequently been in jail. He was described as dirty, disheveled, and unpleasant — a coarse, foul-mouthed, and vulgar man. Reports on the mother varied. Some described her as self-righteous, evil-tempered, unreasonable in her demands, unrealistic in her plans, a poor homemaker and mother. Others spoke of her as attractive and pleasant, a not immaculate but good housekeeper, a woman with high ideals. The paternal grandmother was said to have dominated the home. There was a great amount of fighting in the home. The children were said to hate each other. They were often used as pawns in family struggles. The parents were finally divorced and the father died a short time later.

905. M:15:2   ACE IX, 86; XI, 58   '95–270'6   4:2:16
    N:I:1   ENG IX, 83; XI, 68   '59 36–0'   6:0:21
                 HSR 74
                 SVIB 0'12–5

This boy, nervous and emotional, "attempted to 'clown' to cover up his feelings of inadequacy." He came from a family that had a high income, and both his father and brother were successful professional persons. The boy had money and an expensive car. He went to shows and other places when he was supposed to be in school. In manner he was aggressive, bluffing, and oversolicitous, "always buttering up someone." He idolized his brother and had a great desire to make good marks and ultimately to take professional training. In his efforts to accomplish this he was overbearing and egotistical, and he treated teachers as though they were something he had to put up with. He talked at great length about his knowledge of the university and of his acquaintance with professors. Concerning his achievement one informant said that "he did not have the ability to get by or to take professional training, but he was determined on this course and did not care how he made progress, whether it took cheating or apple-polishing." His associates tended to be older boys and he did not get along well with other students. He was repeatedly guilty of such offenses as writing bad checks for expensive things, prowling cars, shoplifting, and burglary. Someone said of him that "he might really be off base." It was also said that his behavior might be compensation for pressure from home.

The mother was "nervous and high-strung." She took the attitude "that the boy was something that she had to put up with." The father's profession took him away from home a good deal and the boy was left to shift for himself.

906. F:14:1   ACE IX, none; XI, 56   '954–'6   0:5:16
    B:V:2   ENG IX, none; XI, 69   4'9385–   5:6:15
                 HSR 64
                 SVIB 'WR

Described both as "attractive and well groomed" and "without any shape at all except for the prunes she swallowed — very thin," this girl was poised, decisive, and "a lot of fun." She was an "extrovert." Perceptive and possessing a fine sense of humor, she was an excellent mimic. She was in some extracurricular activities but was not really a leader. She appeared sophisticated and went with older boys. Some thought of her as somewhat conceited. She was hard working and responsible. After graduation she went to a teachers' college for a short time but then quit to go to work.

The father of the girl, who had been a heavy drinker, had disappeared before she was born. The stepfather was a good enough person although not very competent. He legally adopted the girl. The mother was mentally rather dull but was a devoted mother and good housekeeper.

907. F:15:6   ACE IX, 90; XI, 97   '954–631'2   3:4:16
     N:VI:2   ENG IX, 99; XI, 99   –4'58   2:4:8
                     HSR 86
                     SVIB 'WR

Before she entered the ninth grade this girl ran away from home with a boy to look for work in a neighboring town. They returned home the same night. After graduation she married this boy. She seemed to "pick at" every boy around her. In most ways she was a good girl; she was cooperative, attempting to please and do things right. She was a hard worker both in school and outside. A very active church member, she was dignified and acceptable although not a leader.

908. F:13:3   ACE IX, 86; XI, 50   9'546807–312'   2:5:5
     N:IVA:5   ENG IX, 73; XI, 78   '945–1'6   1:3:10
                     HSR 96
                     SVIB 'WR

This girl had considerable strength of character. Although she was attractive and well mannered, she was somewhat arrogant. This quality affected her relationships with other students. She was dropped by her associates for a while because she became very friendly with a boy who was not liked and who was considered "a physical and moral mess." Her friends could not understand this association. As the school years went on, the girl became much more attractive and "developed into a real lady." The boy also seemed to become a better person. Credit was given to the girl for her influence on him. After graduation she went to a teachers' college.

The father, conservative and frugal, was apparently a well-accepted person. At times he was overly critical. The mother seemed to be similar to her husband. The family was generally in good standing with the community.

909. F:16:0   ACE IX, 09; XI, 05   9'54738021–   4:20:10X
     B:N:4   ENG IX, 04; XI, 06   8"2'90 43561–   6:11:11
                     HSR 03
                     SVIB '–

One or two persons considered this girl to be agreeable, friendly, well dressed, and attractive, but these positive statements were contradicted by the description from the majority of informants, who considered her "clean but not very attractive, and her dullness showed through — she was negative." She had a speech defect and was giggly and silly. She could not graduate because she could not read or speak well enough. In general, she was "dull and slow." "School was just a place for her to pass time." Apparently her main interest was boys. She was so immature that it seemed she would not grow up, and her behavior was termed "immoral like that of her mother." The girl was found guilty of shoplifting, and after leaving school she was fired from a job because of immorality and dishonesty. Two of her teachers thought she would have later emotional difficulties.

The mother, attractive and outgoing, was "fast" and had low morals. She said that the girl did not know her own father, and she left the girl to be brought up with a relative. The relative attempted to protect the girl from censure.

910. F:15:2	ACE IX, 63; XI, 46	9′548–21′3	3:1:12
N:III:2	ENG IX, none; XI, 63	′64379–′20	2:1:10
	HSR 75		
	SVIB WR′		

Joyful, happy-go-lucky, personable, friendly, talkative, and outgoing were among the terms used to describe this somewhat masculine girl. She mixed well and was popular. However, she was not a leader nor did she participate in extracurricular activities. Both at school and on a part-time job, which she held after school hours, she demonstrated that she was neat, cooperative, dependable, and hard working. She had a "fairly strong" yet "open and warm personality." A well-adjusted girl, there was never a hint of nervousness or tension in her makeup. After completing high school she took a clerical job.

The girl was considerably younger than her brother and sister. The father was a skilled craftsman and the mother did part-time work outside the home.

911. F:14:4	ACE IX, none; XI, 91	9′5483–′012	4:2:18
N:III:3	ENG IX, none; XI, none	′5670–31′49	1:1:13
	HSR 65		
	SVIB ′–		

This girl was intelligent, well balanced, and mature. She was a hard worker and not a conduct problem. Active in student activities, she had many friends. She worked part time outside of school, and after graduation she hoped to become a nurse.

912. F:15:1	ACE IX, 54; XI, 47	9″5′487–23′10	1:9:12
N:III:4	ENG IX, 48; XI, 67	9′45–1′326	3:3:10
	HSR 59		
	SVIB WR′		

With a special talent in dressmaking, this girl was creative as well as able to follow direction. She was attractive and friendly. Her main problem seemed to be that she was always active, that she was never happy in one place and seemed never to stay at home. She was moody and impudent, and could flare out with an explosive temper, staying angry and sullen for long periods of time. Although she was well accepted among her friends, she was often short with people and was inclined to be critical. She would tell of family affairs and the behavior of others without much regard either to privacy or to accuracy. She spent her money carelessly and was not considered to be dependable. She took a full-time job after graduation and seemed to do good work and to make a good adjustment. There was a record of a traffic offense for which her driver's license was revoked.

The father was a "procrastinator" who ran a small business but did not fulfill the obligations of the business. The mother also worked full time. The parents took no community responsibility and were thought to "coddle" their son more than was proper. The girl also was loyal to her brother, always defending and protecting him.

913. F:16:9	ACE IX, 44; XI, none	9′54087–′13	2:9:7
N:VII:3	ENG IX, 75; XI, none		
	HSR DO 9th gr.		
	SVIB none		

Habitually truant, this girl never got her work done. She was indifferent to school, engaging in no activities and getting poor grades. She was sometimes impudent and stubborn. After dropping out of school in her freshman year she was married. The marriage did not progress well; the husband drank and the girl herself was reprimanded by the police because of intoxication. Several of her teachers had predicted that she would have legal difficulties and one teacher thought she would have future emotional maladjustment.

The girl's home situation had been poor. Her family lived in a shack and not one of them graduated from high school.

914. M:15:0	ACE IX, 67; XI, 83	9′573–2′4	1:8:11
N:V:3	ENG IX, 57; XI, 63	′5896–0′	5:7:22
	HSR 25		
	SVIB none		

A speech impediment did not seem to bother this boy, who was "a tremendous kid," active in Scouts, and a very hard worker. With "marvelous morals and a charming personality," he had poise and "excellent friends and companions." He was a male cheerleader. His relationship with his mother was especially close. After graduation he completed a course of technical training in a subprofessional field ancillary to medicine.

The father died while the boy was in high school. During the father's long chronic illness the boy helped with his physical care. The mother continued with the small business they owned. She was described as an aggressive person who was proud of her son and taught him to think as an individual and to stand on his own two feet.

915: F:15:3   ACE IX, 82; XI, 73   9'58467–2'01   2:5:10
    N:III:3   ENG IX, 82; XI, 82   9'4873–'65   3:5:13
                  HSR 80
                  SVIB 'WR

This was a very mature girl who was outgoing and well liked. She had high character traits and was reliable, doing more work than was required of her. She had
leadership ability and was popular in school affairs. After graduation she went into
teachers' training.

The family was well-to-do, fine, and well respected in the community.

916. F:14:8   ACE IX, 24; XI, none   95'87–'3   4:10:12
     N:VII:4   ENG IX, 20; XI, none
                  HSR DO 10th gr.
                  SVIB none

Most of the children in this family were handicapped in one way or another. This
girl had a deformed leg, and in spite of surgical help, she remained handicapped.
She had taken care of a younger sister who was mentally retarded and deaf and
who eventually died. The death caused considerable grief to the girl. Competing
with the other children in the family, she had to fight hard to get what she wanted.
She had few friends; she was always alone and seemed not to fit into any group.
Her appearance was somewhat against her: she was large, unattractive, and poorly
groomed. In school she was a poor student, but she was industrious, and she might
have graduated if she had stayed on.

The father was unstable and a heavy drinker, although he was pleasant and
easygoing. The mother worked. She was ineffectual, crude, and vulgar. She was
"incapable of managing her large family." The reputation of the family was poor
and the community was much concerned over the problems caused by the children.

917. M:14:0   ACE IX, 96; XI, 64   9'587–312'6   1:4:7
     N:V:2   ENG IX, 98; XI, 70   '983416–0'   5:3:17
                  HSR 69
                  SVIB 90'5–2

This was a big, fat boy "who was unpopular with other students." He was a "sissy"
and was often overbearing and too obviously interested in getting grades. He was,
however, fairly well accepted by some groups and, in general, was cooperative and
reliable, using reasonably good judgment and appearing always neat and well
mannered. "He had goals in mind and he shot for them with much ambition."
At one time he falsified a pass to leave the school building, and he was also charged
with careless driving. After graduation he went to a junior college where he became very active in dramatics, wanting "to run the whole thing." His behavior

tended to be dramatic both on and off the stage. He was once again fairly successful but not liked by others.

The parents were characterized as vying with each other to give the boy everything he wanted. The family lived in a middle-class, well-kept home.

918. F:14:3	ACE IX, 67; XI, 64	'950–3<u>2</u>1'	4:9:8
N:IVB:4	ENG IX, 62; XI, 61	'7–'<u>41</u>3	2:1:14
	HSR 84		
	SVIB WR'		

The smallest girl in her class, this youngster was attractive and bright as well as
petite. Although she was very quiet, she got along with people and appeared to
have no problems. She was a good student and was active in farm and church activities. After graduation she began doing office work.

The father and mother were described as excellent. The father was conservative and somewhat reserved. He seemed wary and mistrusting of people at first,
but he warmed up and became more pleasant with time. The mother was neater,
more polished, and less skeptical than her husband. The parents set high standards
and were interested in the children and their school.

919. M:14:3	ACE IX, 86; XI, 91	'950–'42	0:1:12
N:VI:2	ENG IX, 88; XI, 59	'871<u>39</u>–2'4	1:3:16
	HSR 74		
	SVIB '2–		

A small boy with a deep, mature voice, this youth was quiet, pleasant, and reliable.
Studying was a pleasure for him and much of his extra time was spent on chemistry.
"He has a lot of determination and a will to succeed." After graduation he went to
a junior college to begin training for engineering. He had a record of one minor
traffic violation.

The father was described as a hard worker. The boy's older brothers had good
ability but, in some contrast to this boy, they lost interest in school during their
later years.

920. M:14:0	ACE IX, 18; XI, none	9'6–'<u>41</u>3	4:6:10
N:IVB:3	ENG IX, 17; XI, none	'7<u>89</u>–25'<u>14</u>3	1:7:11
	HSR 03		
	SVIB –5		

This boy was not well accepted by his classmates. He was irritating in his sneering,
smirking, and swaggering. His hair was long and he had sideburns. He seemed to
adopt these peculiarities for recognition. He was indifferent in his attitude toward
school but appeared to be ambitious in his wish to be a farmer.

The father was a farmer and the family reputation was good. Although the
parents were not leaders in the community, they were the "salt of the earth" type.

921. F:15:2　　　　ACE IX, 51; XI, 78　　　9'6<u>28</u>473–5'0　1:3:13
　　　N:V:1　　　　ENG IX, none; XI, 89
　　　　　　　　　　HSR 87 DO 11th gr.
　　　　　　　　　　SVIB none

This girl felt somewhat insecure because of her family's lack of money but she did not seem to be extremely unhappy about it. She was a "good average student," quiet, well mannered, and unobtrusive. She was helpful to the teachers and enjoyed helping all she could. Although her classmates were friendly toward her, she did not mix with them outside the classroom. She "loved music" and took part in various singing groups. After completing her junior year she dropped out of school to get married. She had a child a year later and became "a sensible little mother."

922. F:15:2　　　　ACE IX, 99; XI, 100　　9'63–2'　　5:2:18
　　　N:V:1　　　　ENG IX, 98; XI, 98　　'6–4'71<u>25</u>　4:4:16
　　　　　　　　　　HSR 92　　　　　　　'43<u>69</u>–0'5<u>27</u>　6:3:22
　　　　　　　　　　SVIB none

This girl had a father who was alcoholic and had additional qualities that made him a very grave problem to the community and to her. Seemingly in response to this situation, the girl, as universally described, was mature and had an adult approach to problems. She worked outside of school and went with a boy who was also "on his own." This relationship was referred to as "an adult type." The girl was an A student, quiet but able to speak up when she had something to say. She was "a top personality, an outstanding student, always pleasant and reliable." She was moderately active in school affairs and was well liked by teachers and students. During her high school years she expected to continue working at her job without going to college, in spite of the encouragement of some of her teachers. After graduation, however, she did begin work at a university.

　　The father was in repeated difficulties because of his alcoholism. He was unable to stop drinking, and during the periods of drunkenness he became violent and exceedingly irresponsible. On these occasions the police were called and he spent several periods in jail. The mother was a "very set person" who stayed with the father because "he was such a pitiful mess." She was also described as "hostile and controlling." The difficulty in the home tended to bring the mother and girl into a very close relationship. The parents were foreign and uneducated. The community tended to feel that they needed protection or people would take advantage of them.

923. F:14:3　　　　ACE IX, 84; XI, 73　　9'64–<u>21</u>'8<u>03</u>　3:6:9
　　　N:III:5　　　ENG IX, 83; XI, 77　　'6<u>79</u>–<u>20</u>'18　5:1:17
　　　　　　　　　　HSR 92
　　　　　　　　　　SVIB none

This girl was mature and "without self-consciousness." She was reliable and dependable, seeking additional things to do. Altogether, she was a good, well-balanced student and a good leader. She was well liked by fellow students and adults. She did have a high temper, but she cooled off just as fast as she got angry. After graduation she went out of the community to work and continued in school by taking night courses.

The father was devoted, warm, and interested in the children. The mother was similar to her husband, and the family had a high standing in the community.

924. M:15:4   ACE IX, 38; XI, none   9'64-71325'   3:10:7
     B:III:2   ENG IX, none; XI, none
                  HSR trans. 10th gr.
                  SVIB none

This boy was nervous, overactive, and somewhat underweight. He bit his nails and was too restless to apply himself for any length of time to one subject. Although he thought of becoming a mechanic, he lacked initiative, industry, and self-control. He always seemed to want to attract attention to himself and he was inconsiderate of others. He "giggled" at anything and thought he was in school to entertain. "He could make anything funny and thought everything was funny." Thought to be insecure, he told tall tales that were obviously not true in an apparent effort to bolster his security. He got into no severe difficulty, although he was warned by the police because he had been shooting firearms illegally.

925. F:15:3   ACE IX, 50; XI, none   9'645-'2   2:4:8
     B:N:4   ENG IX, 44; XI, none
                  HSR DO 10th gr.
                  SVIB none

"Under proper supervision this girl might have had a fine personality." Taller than the average and very pretty, she carried herself in a regal manner. But there were few good things said about her. Her outlook on life seemed "completely warped." She could not take suggestions and would defiantly leave the classroom when she was displeased. She threatened one of her teachers in an anonymous note. During some trouble at the school both she and her mother "talked vulgarly to all of the school people and wrote obscene notes." The girl was "abjectly tied" to a young man whom she later married. The marriage was unstable and there was much quarreling. At the last time she was seen she looked "cowed, bruised, and battered." She had one child and was expecting another. Her problems had been recognized as early as age eleven, at which time a psychologist had suggested a possibly dangerous situation in the home. A majority of her ninth-grade teachers predicted future emotional maladjustment.

The mother was unstable. She felt persecuted and threatened many times to kill herself. She was exceedingly possessive of her children. She appeared bitter, cynical, and so forbidding that no one spoke to her. The father had died when the girl was about ten years old.

926. F:14:1   ACE IX, 99; XI, 93   '96<u>47</u>–5'1   2:1:17
    N:II:1   ENG IX, 98; XI, 97   '<u>43</u> 8<u>6</u>–'<u>520</u>   2:2:22
                   HSR 100
                   SVIB none

This girl's achievement in classes was good enough to make her the top student, but she so much antagonized others that she got little recognition for this achievement. She was "a talker who could not keep her mouth shut." "Adolescent in her reactions," she could show a nasty temper and would rarely stop to think, although she did well when she did stop. She liked to do as she pleased and did not like to have people get in her way. "Finally insulted, she clammed up and did not participate at all in her senior year." Apparently she was somewhat successful with her own group because she was president of a high school sorority. After graduation she went to college.

The father was a neurotic person who pushed his children. He had a permanent disability which may have been the reason for his defensiveness and cynicism. His attitudes were the same in his work as they were with his family. The girl did not get along well with him. The mother was a buffer between the father and the children. She much influenced the girl. Despite an incurable disease the mother seemed very stable and had many fine traits.

927. M:14:3   ACE IX, 89; XI, 88   9'65–2'1   2:6:5
    N:V:2   ENG IX, none; XI, 73   9'56<u>2784</u>–   2:9:6
                   HSR 85
                   SVIB 4'–9

This student was a leader and popular with his classmates and teachers. He was conscientious and competent, and he participated in numerous activities. His main interests were in radio and electronics. His teachers described him as conceited and "a go-getter." There were a few minor difficulties in school; he was somewhat of a nonconformist. After graduation he registered in a pre-engineering course in college but quit to go into the armed services, expecting to return for further education.

The father was a competent person without much push. The mother was friendly but not one who sought out others. The family was loving and close; most of its social life centered around church affairs.

928. F:16:1   ACE IX, 16; XI, 17   9'65<u>8314</u>–'7   4:9:8
    B:III:1   ENG IX, 37; XI, 14   986'14<u>37</u>–   4:13:17
                   HSR 27
                   SVIB none

Good looking and physically mature, this girl always had a lot of dates with older boys. She had a great deal of social grace but was not too intelligent. She was a member of one of the more snobbish groups in the school. She had good manners and a sparkling personality, and was kind, thoughtful, and sensitive. Although it was considered that she worked up to her ability, there was apparently some feeling of insecurity that contributed to difficulty she had in her schoolwork. She seemed rather unhappy during her final year of high school. With other boys and girls, she was involved in vandalism of public property. Someone said that she "would probably marry and lead a fine life as a wife and mother." One ninth-grade teacher thought of her as likely to get into legal difficulties. After graduation she went to a junior college. She became engaged to a boy who was from a good family but whose reputation was a little questionable.

The father and mother separated when the girl was in the eighth grade. The girl lived with her father but remained close to her mother.

929.	M:15:1	ACE IX, 91; XI, 91	9'6748–1'3	2:10:9
	N:VI:2	ENG IX, none; XI, 77		
		HSR 33		
		SVIB none		

Before his senior year this boy was considered a worthwhile student. His conduct then became so unbearable that he was expelled. He was lazy and hated to work; he was antagonistic and rebellious. Rules and regulations were challenges to him, and he could be mean and malicious in his attempts to break them. He went out for sports but could not stick with them, and he was dropped for lack of effort. There were repeated difficulties with the law: he was charged with shoplifting, illegal discharge of firearms, and other relatively less serious infractions. After school expulsion he joined the Marines, where he was reported to be adjusting well to military life.

The father, a not very intelligent or ambitious man, had a "weak personality." He tended to resent the teachers when his boy got into trouble in his senior year. The mother had to handle the discipline of the children, but she was not much more firm than was the father.

930.	M:15:1	ACE IX, 52; XI, 30	'9680–'43	2:5:7
	N:VI:2	ENG IX, none; XI, 62	'9–5'7 23	2:9:7
		HSR 76		
		SVIB 4'2–		

This was a pleasant, uncomplicated, and plain-spoken boy. At times he was a little gruff and crude, speaking his mind quite bluntly, but generally he was well adjusted, cooperative, and industrious, a quiet and serious "solid citizen." He was well liked and a good athlete. He had a part-time job outside of school and bought his own motorcycle, but he "was not a nuisance with it." Upon graduation he enlisted in the armed services.

931. F:15:6   ACE IX, none; XI, none   '97–23'6   2:2:19
     N:VII:3   ENG IX, none; XI, none
                     HSR DO 10th gr.
                     SVIB none

Shortly after she finished the ninth grade this girl dropped out of school in order to get married. Very little was reported about her except that she was irresponsible, both in and out of school. When she tired of a job she quit it without notifying anyone.

The father, an alcoholic, was very abusive when drunk. He beat his wife and was repeatedly brought into court because of his behavior. The mother, a practical nurse, was a good worker and a sympathetic person. However, she was guilty of promiscuity and she had a police record. One of the younger children was also frequently in trouble with the law. The family, of American Indian background, was generally unstable and lacked companionability.

932. M:15:3   ACE IX, 28; XI, 46   9'7–56324'1   1:10:11
     N:IVA:3   ENG IX, 49; XI, 34   '9–5'18 36   8:3:15
                     HSR 48
                     SVIB 4'–5

"A typical D student who rarely recited and cooperated only when it was convenient" was a description of this boy. Although he was not very interested in school, he did have a great deal of interest in farming. He was extremely quiet and somewhat of a "lone wolf," but he was fairly well liked and accepted by others. His parents gave him a great deal of freedom and he justified their confidence in him by not abusing this privilege.

The parents were industrious, religious, and ambitious. They were well respected and a strong influence in the community. They did everything they could to help their son get a start in farming.

933. M:15:0   ACE IX, 24; XI, 40   9'72–'560   3:5:13
     B:III:1   ENG IX, 15; XI, 15
                     HSR 14
                     SVIB 89'–2

This student liked sports and was fairly successful in them. He could be pleasant, but more often he had a bitter, hostile attitude. He talked excessively in class and had difficulty with some subjects. He worked almost full time outside of school and went with a very capable girl, who probably put him under pressure to be successful. She may have increased his uncertainty about himself. He was several times in trouble for traffic offenses. Both delinquency and emotional adjustment problems were anticipated for him by his ninth-grade teachers.

934. M:14:6   IQ (centile) 67   '9734865–'2   3:3:16
     N:IVB:3   HSR 32   '47 3596–   3:5:16
                        SVIB none

Unable to accept criticism, this boy if frustrated in class became angry, stubborn, and even "wild." Cross and mad, he would leave the classroom but return without holding a grudge. His school attendance was irregular and he was excluded from one of the athletic teams because he was caught smoking. Toward women teachers he seemed particularly disrespectful. His friends were said to be not of good character. He was guilty of repeated traffic violations, as well as of several disorderly conduct offenses. In spite of all these negative items, one person said of him: "He can be a gentleman." The juvenile judge characterized him as an obstreperous boy who always "carried a chip on his shoulder." During high school he was a "lone wolf" and for a period lived away from home.

935. M:15:3   ACE IX, 21; XI, 15   97'4823–   8:5:14
     N:IVB:4   ENG IX, none; XI, 11   '9–7'1   6:9:10
                       HSR 62
                       SVIB 4'8–0

An average student with an average number of friends, this was a quiet boy who did not cause any difficulty in school. He did not take any leadership role and was in few activities. During his senior year he was married, but he remained in school.

936. F:14:0   ACE IX, 65; XI, 58   9'7485–'216   4:9:16
     B:III:1   ENG IX, none; XI, 51   '39–'25   3:3:15
                       HSR 32
                       SVIB none

This girl's real mother died and the father remarried. The girl was nice looking, always neat and well dressed. She had a nice personality and was liked by teachers and fellow students. In school she was responsible, willing, and helpful. She was not a good student except for a couple of courses in which she was very good. She liked science, which was her worst subject, and seemed to work hard in spite of her poor achievement. She liked children and baby sat after school hours. In the ninth grade two teachers thought she might later develop some maladjustment. After graduation she began teachers' training and was reported to be making an average grade of C. She went steady with a boy who got into some trouble with the law; she remained loyal to him throughout this trouble.

937. M:16:3   ACE IX, 33; XI, none   9"7'4862–'3   1:10:10
     N:V:1   ENG IX, none; XI, none
                       HSR DO 11th gr.
                       SVIB none

A "hood type" boy, who was always playing practical jokes on people, this youth lacked the ability to make friends or mix with other students in an acceptable manner. He didn't like school and was ultimately suspended for excessive tardiness. Later, he dropped out completely. He was guilty of smoking in school and of other minor infractions of rules. He was an "individualist and apt to be disobedient." When he quit school he joined the Air Force.

938. F:15:1	ACE IX, 89; XI, 76	9′7<u>56</u>–0′23	4:3:15
N:I:1	ENG IX, 88; XI, 96	— —	— —
	HSR 94	′9<u>36</u>–02′5	6:0:21
	SVIB none		

Emotionally steady to the point of seeming somewhat insensitive, this girl was reliable and reasonably well accepted by the other students. Strongly motivated to get good grades, she seemed more worried about them than about acquiring knowledge. She was talkative and aggressive in a diplomatic and unobtrusive way. At times she was stubborn. She had little interest in the activities of the school, seeming to want to "get on top of the heap" and not caring how she achieved this. After graduation she went to a university.

939. M:15:2	ACE IX, 99; XI, 96	9′7<u>64</u> <u>8205</u>–	2:3:15
B:VI:2	ENG IX, 95; XI, 85	9′<u>42</u>–′0<u>16</u>	4:2:15
	HSR 59		
	SVIB ′4–0		

This boy was considered the most valuable football player on the team. A sociable, popular leader who was frequently elected to high student offices, he had a pleasant personality. He was called a "bright, even brilliant underachiever." Between the ages of eleven and thirteen he was in repeated trouble because of sexual offenses with younger girls. He made no attempt to excuse himself for this immoral conduct. According to a psychiatric evaluation made at that time, the behavior seemed unrelated to any other undesirable traits. There were no subsequent reported difficulties except for a peccadillo, nonsexual in nature, at the age of fifteen. After completing high school he continued his education at a small college.

The parents had both been previously married. The father, an irresponsible alcoholic, was occasionally in trouble with the law. He showed no interest in his family and eventually deserted them. The mother worked hard to support the family. She was concerned over its welfare, and she was very defensive about her son's problem.

940. F:14:6	ACE IX, 30; XI, 67	9′78–1′3	4:3:13
N:V:1	ENG IX, 75; XI, none	3′6478–5′	4:3:19
	HSR 16		
	SVIB none		

A girl with average intelligence who "succeeded on her personality," this student was probably the most popular person in her class. Very pretty and nicely clothed, she was friendly and boisterous, knew everyone, and seemed intensely interested in others. Appearing older than her actual age, she tended to date older boys. In her senior year she went into bars and was once recognized as a minor. In spite of her adult associations she was described as immature in some ways. She sometimes "giggled a lot" and her moods swung from happiness to depression, although she was usually happy and lighthearted. One person described her as "the perpetual queen candidate." Although her high school record was poor, she continued on to a junior college. She also continued going with the boy she had dated in her senior year.

The girl was said to be "the bright star" in the family. The father had been alcoholic but had straightened out. He remained a domineering person, stubborn and violent of temper. Some saw him as big-hearted, friendly, and "a dumbbell who talked too much." The mother was active and interested in school and community affairs. Several of the older children had been in trouble with the law.

941. M:15:1	ACE IX, 45; XI, 61	9'784–5'20	5:1:18
N:V:1	ENG IX, none; XI, 36	4"718'20639–	7:3:19
	HSR 42	784'20913–'5	6:5:15
	SVIB none		

This boy was average in his behavior and acceptance by others. He was well behaved and didn't get into any real trouble, but he was rather indifferent and not strongly motivated. More a follower than a leader, he was popular enough but never really active in school affairs. He had two very close friends who followed the same pattern. In general he was happy, cheerful, and well adjusted, but under some conditions he had a quick temper. His interests were mainly in outdoor activities. Of his school subjects he preferred mathematics. Outside of school he was "cooperative when convenient, easily depressed or elated, and a member of a marginal group of boys." After graduation he began college. During his first year he got into some behavior trouble. Apparently he was not very much to blame and the affair was dismissed as "adolescent carelessness."

The parents were much upset over the incident at the college and immediately made reparation for some damage that was caused. The family was a good one and well accepted in the community. Both parents worked outside the home, the mother's object being to make the family eligible for a higher social group.

942. F:14:2	ACE IX, 98; XI, 97	'9706–351'24	1:1:14
N:III:1	ENG IX, none; XI, 99	'078–45'23	3:0:14
	HSR 97	'06–35'2	1:11:15
	SVIB none		

Teachers could hardly say enough good things about this girl, who was "more like a college student than a high school pupil." Pleasant and happy, she had many friends among fellow pupils and teachers. Responsible and dependable, she was a leader and top student. She took part in many activities both in the school and outside. After graduation she went on to a university where she expected to take professional training.

943. M:15:0	ACE IX, none; XI, 28	98′1604–′5	6:16:10X
N:VII:3	ENG IX, none; XI, 10	′089–1′36	4:6:11
	HSR 07		
	SVIB ′4–		

This tall, gawky boy, immature in appearance, seemed to choose small boys for his friends. He was distinguished by always arriving at school before anyone else even though he lived some distance away. As the other students came, he would roam up and down the halls talking with them. He did a great deal of talking in class, but he was not a good student. He shunned girls and did not take part in any school activities. He was rather quarrelsome and quick to start a fight. When he finished his own schoolwork, "such that it was," he then wanted to help others with their work. Two of his ninth-grade teachers predicted emotional problems for him.

944. M:14:1	ACE IX, none; XI, 73	′98256–′34	4:5:8
N:II:3	ENG IX, none; XI, 65	78″9′36245–0′	1:4:15
	HSR 39		
	SVIB ′9–		

A handsome boy with curly hair and blue eyes, this youth had a sullen, petulant expression and gave the impression of having a chip on his shoulder. His actions were described as unfriendly and babyish. He was easily led by undesirable associates. He was popular among the younger boys because he had a good deal of spending money and a car. In school he did not accept responsibility and failed to work up to his capacity. One of the teachers felt that he was at cross purposes with himself — that he would have liked to be friendly but felt he shouldn't. He was competent in art and in music, and after graduation he continued his studies along these lines.

Both parents were witty and talented. The father was a small businessman, known and well liked by everyone. He was very fond of his children and tried to do everything possible for them. The mother liked reading but hated housework and cooking. She was a member of a fundamentalist religious group. It was a great blow to her when her daughter became pregnant and had to be married.

945. F:15:3	ACE IX, 95; XI, 98	9′834162–′5	2:5:20
N:III:1	ENG IX, 97; XI, 98	′8931 27–5′0	1:4:20
	HSR 95		
	SVIB none		

This was a nice, well-liked girl who was "a pleasure to have in class and always did what she was told to do without argument." She was an A student — "good college material." Particularly interested in music, she sought extra tasks and did them well. One teacher stated: "She is the kind that will probably never marry — just not that type of personality, very mature for her age." After graduation she took an office job.

946. F:14:0   ACE IX, 70; XI, 58   '984–1'20   1:4:9
     B:IVA:3   ENG IX, 95; XI, 98   '9348–'25   3:2:13
                      HSR 77
                      SVIB WR'

This was a mature and poised girl who was considered to be an overachiever. She took pride in her work and was well liked, pleasant, and cooperative. In some contrast to these qualities, she was colorless and without spark — a person who never seemed to have much motivation. She did not take part in school activities, although she took an average interest in the 4-H Club. After graduation she worked in a shop for a while but was soon married.

The mother had been divorced when the girl was a baby. She remarried, and this man was "a very good farmer." The home situation was described as good.

947. M:14:2   ACE IX, 63; XI, 58   9'84–1'63   1:3:10
     N:III:1   ENG IX, none; XI, 28   9'4–'0265   2:2:14
                      HSR 33
                      SVIB none

Most persons who came in contact with this boy described him as cooperative, well adjusted, friendly, and happy. Others readily felt in rapport with him, and he was very responsive when he felt trusted and understood. He could show a desirable amount of independence, and he was moderately ambitious. He was an "all-around boy with some athletic ability." There were a few who saw a different person, one with a high-pitched voice, who liked to tell dirty stories. He was also seen as lazy and a "fringe" character. In one episode he engaged in some minor vandalism and, in general, he was described by the police as overprivileged and an unstable "scatterbrain." He was one of the drivers in a serious accident in which some persons were killed. It was not certain that he was at fault in the accident.

948. M:15:1   ACE IX, 96; XI, 95   9'84375–'0   3:2:17
     N:II:1   ENG IX, none; XI, 89   '95–2'0   2:0:17
                      HSR 87   9'34–2'67   2:2:13
                      SVIB none

This was a "real fine boy" and a good student. He was conscientious, serious, exceptionally more "mature than usual, and a leader sought by others." With adults he was somewhat shy but polite and cooperative. He was active in youth programs in his church. Although it was said that he did not mix with girls, it was also said that he had regular dates with "better type girls." After graduation he began engineering training at a university.

The mother was quiet, intelligent, and deeply interested in her children. She wrote notes of thanks and appreciation to school people who had been able to help her children.

949. F:15:1	ACE IX, 97; XI, 91	9'84<u>56</u>–2'01	2:4:15
N:III:3	ENG IX, 91; XI, 89	'948<u>670</u>–'23	3:4:17
	HSR 71	'59<u>846</u>–'213	2:2:20
	SVIB none		

This was a good, "average" girl. She was fairly cooperative and a moderately good student with a nice personality. Interested in music and speech, she expected to continue her studies in college. She was particularly noted as having high ideals of conduct and she "always kept the best of company."

950. F:14:6	ACE IX, none; XI, 43	9'84<u>57</u>6–2'3	1:7:14
N:VI:1	ENG IX, none; XI, 51	5'9–<u>16</u>'327	4:6:12
	HSR 43		
	SVIB WR'		

This girl was flighty and flippant; she did not take things seriously. Her teachers considered her an underachiever who could not be trusted with responsibilities.

951. M:14:2	ACE IX, 50; XI, 61	9'846–'25	2:5:17
N:IVB:2	ENG IX, none; XI, 50	'98<u>43</u>–2'6	0:4:16
	HSR 41		
	SVIB 4'–		

This husky boy was "a solid farm kid, responsible and cooperative." He was sociable although rather reserved, and he was popular without seeming to put himself out to achieve this popularity. In his schoolwork he was dependable and trustworthy, but "a plodder with only moderate ambition." He was even tempered, never raising his voice or arguing. He played baseball, and in activities he was a strong leader who gravitated to leadership positions without effort. When a leader, he carried his duties through conscientiously. After graduation he went into the Navy and it was said that he would probably eventually return to farming.

The father was pleasant, kindly, and steady. He was not a leader in the community but provided an excellent example in conduct. The mother was quiet and sensible. There was no conflict in the family. Both parents were interested in the children and the home was well above average.

952. M:14:4   ACE IX, none; XI, 36   9'8462–'5   8:10:16
      N:II:3   ENG IX, none; XI, 20
                    HSR 48
                    SVIB none

Apparently neither bad nor malicious, this boy was usually pleasant and fun loving. Nevertheless, he got in considerable trouble because of his arrogance and "cockiness." He refused to study, and he became surly if pushed or if he felt not accepted. A great deal of the trouble seemed to stem from revolt against the father, who tried to control him. The boy's friends were "hot-rodders" and he was constantly in difficulties because of traffic offenses. At one time he left home but later returned of his own accord. His brothers were much brighter than he, but his teachers did not believe that this troubled him. As he grew older he appeared to mature.

The father was rarely at home and the family situation was poor. Not only this boy but his brothers were involved in various difficulties. The parents disagreed and quarreled over the discipline and the affections of the children.

953. M:15:2   ACE IX, 17; XI, 11   '98467–5'23   2:12:14
      N:IVC:3   ENG IX, 04; XI, 11   78'04–3'126   3:8:12
                    HSR 08
                    SVIB '9–5

This was "a big, hulking brute" who needed constant prodding. All his interests were in athletic activities outside the school. Because he was out so much at night, he was tired in the classroom. His schoolwork was poor; he had very little interest in it and merely filled a seat. Occasionally he became mischievous in class and had to be reprimanded. He barely got by and was easily led.

The family, although accepted by the community, was inconspicuous, and the parents were indifferent to education. They felt the boy was "picked on."

954. M:15:1   ACE IX, 86; XI, 58   '9847–'23   2:7:16
      N:III:1   ENG IX, none; XI, 63   '4730–   1:4:19
                    HSR 36
                    SVIB none

This boy was popular with many boys and some girls. He was nice looking, had a fine car, and wore good clothes. One teacher described him as "a smooth operator," and when he was reprimanded, the girls in the class always took his side. He was a "ladies' man." Restless and highly nervous, he never achieved well in class and did just enough to get by. He could not be trusted and on several occasions he forged excuses for absences. He excelled in athletics, and as he continued in school, this activity seemed to help him improve in his behavior. He was considered "hard to figure out," and he seemed noncommittal and bland, although it was thought that he did have strong feelings underneath this unemotional appearance. His behavior outside of school was not acceptable. His parents were often away and the home was frequently the scene of teen-age parties with drinking and promiscuous behavior. After police investigation of one of these parties, the boy tried to break away from the gang by putting more time into school athletics. Following graduation he went into pre-business training in college and apparently did well.

955. F:14:0	ACE IX, 02; XI, none	98'475–'2	1:5:16
N:V:1	ENG IX, 12; XI, none	'948–6'231	1:2:16
	HSR DO 12th gr.		
	SVIB none		

Many undesirable things were said about this girl when she was in the ninth grade. She was a big girl, sloppy in dress and "haughty and sexy" in manner. She wrote smutty notes which she left in her pocket for her mother to find, and she left other notes in fellow students' lockers with the intent of provoking them. Nothing seemed to bother her; she had few friends and did not seem to suffer from this lack. She had unrealistic goals, wanting professional training and seeming not well aware of her limitations. Much of her difficulty seemed to relate to the fact that she "hated her mother." She seemed to do things motivated by defiance of her mother. Police reports indicated that she was "chasing around and on the borderline of trouble, often openly defiant of authority and her parents." In spite of all these difficulties, she seemed to have improved by the time she was a senior. She quit school, however, and took a job. This job gave her some independence and she became better adjusted socially and a little more mature. A number of her teachers predicted that she would develop emotional maladjustment and possibly get into legal trouble.

The mother was very religious and dominated her whole family. She had "old school" ways of thinking and was completely unable to control the girl, although she even tried to get the police to help her.

956. F:14:2	ACE IX, 25; XI, 43	9'847 56–'120	1:5:12
N:II:1	ENG IX, none; XI, 76	9'–'1243	1:2:7
	HSR 57		
	SVIB none		

More concerned with boys than with grades, this girl was "cute and boy crazy." Always out for a good time, she was not, however, a discipline problem. She was chosen as a school homecoming queen. In her schoolwork she was barely average. After graduation she went on to a small college where she was reported to be much concerned about her grades because of the danger of being dropped at the end of her first quarter.

The parents seemed to be excellent people. There was an older sister who had had a great many troubles and had finally been institutionalized.

957. M:14:1   ACE IX, none; XI, 46   9'85–31'26   2:3:9
      N:IVB:2   ENG IX, none; XI, 50
                      HSR 69
                      SVIB '48–

This fine boy was cooperative and conscientious, a serious and hard worker. He stuttered, but he did not seem to be bothered by this speech problem. His chief interest was music. Vocationally he hoped to become a dentist.

958. M:14:6   ACE IX, 91; XI, 91   9'8'57–2'13   1:2:15
      N:IVA:3   ENG IX, 55; XI, 69   '596–2'40   3:2:14
                      HSR 72
                      SVIB '–

This was a farm boy who didn't like the farm and did everything he could to get away from it. He was generally well adjusted and well behaved. Tall and neat in appearance, he was well liked and friendly, although he was very quiet. It was said that he had been babied when he was small. He purposely did little things to "get the teacher's goat." He had particular difficulty with one teacher. He seemed to be good at planning things and expected to continue on to college.

The mother was an active churchgoer, but the father seemed "soured on church." He was called "peculiar." He was very strict and was not liked by his children, who were in continual conflict with him. The mother, who was pleasant and nice to work with, was an able and friendly person.

959. F:14:13   ACE IX, none; XI, 25   9'8570–1'23   2:10:5
      B:VII:3   ENG IX, none; XI, 89   '95807–1'236   1:5:6
                      HSR 54
                      SVIB WR'

This girl was not physically very appealing. Her face had blemishes that made her very self-conscious. She also had a slight speech defect. She did not like school and wanted her diploma merely to use it as a lever for a good job. She was quiet and not very dependable, and her behavior outside of school was considered to be questionable. She was frequently seen on the main streets in the evenings. It was a large family and she was often kept out of school to help at home. After graduation she went to another city, where she got a job that she lost after a few months. She then returned to live with her mother.

The father had died when the girl was about ten years old. The mother, an emotional woman and considerably overweight, had to have public assistance for her family. A number of the siblings got into various kinds of trouble.

960. M:15:1	ACE IX, 32; XI, 81	'986–2'3 75	4:5:13
N:II:1	ENG IX, 60; XI, 67	— —	— —
	HSR 47	'23–'406	3:2:17
	SVIB '4–		

This boy was conscientious, quiet, pleasant, and mature. Other students set him up as a leader both in class and in athletics. "He earned respect without actively seeking it." He had good speaking ability and took difficult courses in mathematics and science. He went to a university after graduation. His mother died before he entered college and his father became seriously ill shortly thereafter.

961. F:14:2	ACE IX, 89; XI, none	9'864–2'05	2:7:13
B:I:1	ENG IX, none; XI, none		
	HSR DO 11th gr.		
	SVIB none		

This girl's schoolwork and general behavior were very satisfactory. Her teachers considered her to be a very nice girl, well adjusted, poised, and pretty. Altogether she was quite mature and a "teacher's pride." She was a good worker in school and outside and had expected to become a secretary after graduation. In the eleventh grade she dropped out of school because of an illegitimate pregnancy. After the child's birth, she married a boy — not the father of the child — and was reported to be reasonably happy.

The father had died when the girl was a child. The mother, who was not a very adequate person, tried to carry on with the help of public funds. When a social worker wanted the mother to work for some money to help support her family, she refused, saying that her church and her daughters needed her. The mother apparently, however, did not supervise her daughters very closely and the daughters were known to have taken boys into their bedrooms.

962. F:15:1	ACE IX, 98; XI, 97	9''864'7132–'50	5:10:13
N:III:1	ENG IX, 94; XI, 85	'36–02'	7:1:20
	HSR 72		
	SVIB none		

This girl "had the appearance of being flighty but was a very efficient worker." She was pleasant and nice to work with. Very dependable, she was almost overly serious. She was socially accepted in the "right crowd" and was a leader, although not an outstanding one. Her interests were in dramatics and she wanted to become an air hostess.

963. F:15:6	ACE IX, 40; XI, 41	98'6475–	5:11:10
N:III:1	ENG IX, none; XI, 33	84'''975''62 31'0–	6:27:16X
	HSR 28		
	SVIB none		

This girl "thought she was cute." She was actually attractive in a "different sort of way" — she was a "pixie." Her ninth-grade adjustment was rather poor. She was defiant and highly active, having a poor attitude and seeming to need friends. She thought she was picked on and was at times depressed. She enjoyed the company of assorted boys and was considered "fickle." Occasionally truant in school, she was somewhat of a nonconformist and needed reprimanding to keep her quiet. A number of ninth-grade teachers expected that she would develop emotional maladjustment. She took a full-time clerical job after graduation.

One of the other children in the family was disabled and the parents gave much of their attention to this youngster at the expense of the others, who were "left on the outside."

964. M:15:0	ACE IX, 96; XI, 84	9″8′67–123′5	1:12:6
B:VII:2	ENG IX, 96; XI, 81	′6319748–2′	0:4:10
	HSR 78		
	SVIB 2′14–5		

This was a "nice average boy when in the tenth grade." Very close to his mother, he was quiet, shy, and without many friends. He complained of rheumatic pain. As he continued in school, he became a "black-leather-jacket type with a fancy haircut." He bought himself a "souped-up car," and he liked to show off in the town. He knew a great deal about automobiles. He became exceedingly demanding of his mother, expecting her to do everything for him. Ultimately he was caught in a theft, and was warned and released. After graduation he went to a junior college and helped support himself by an outside job.

The father was dead. The marriage had never been very good because the parents quarreled and the father drank heavily. The mother was a pleasant and respected woman who worked to support her son. She "doted on her son, spoiling him and waiting on him hand and foot."

965. M:16:1	ACE IX, 11; XI, 05	9′867–′53	4:11:17
N:VI:5	ENG IX, 10; XI, 17	′9–465′31	4:9:11
	HSR 41		
	SVIB 4′8–		

Neat and clean, a little gauche, slow in movement, this youth was not a very active mixer in social affairs. He was, however, a mature, hard-working boy, always willing to help out and generally at ease in situations that did not require an active, social manner. He was never a problem in or out of school, and as one got to know him, he seemed confident and self-controlled. He was also described as ambitious. He owned a car and took exceptional care of it. In his senior year he had a "very prim, sedate romance" with a girl. He was on the football team. After graduation he took a job as a semiskilled workman.

The father was a part-time farmer who did not have a strong personality and who was hard to talk to. The mother did not get along well with the father, and as a reaction to their quarrels, she developed skin disorders. A brother was frail and "a bit spoiled by the mother."

966. F:14:5	ACE IX, 90; XI, 94	9'8674–2'	3:5:7
N:IVA:4	ENG IX, 96; XI, 94	'6–2'7	0:5:11
	HSR 97	'809–'27	1:7:11
	SVIB none		

This girl was pleasant, responsible, very thorough, and mature. She had a good deal of initiative and took part in many extracurricular activities. She worked hard both at home and at school. After graduation she went to college where she majored in education.

967. M:15:6	ACE IX, 75; XI, 65	986'70–12'53	0:13:4
N:V:3	ENG IX, 47; XI, 50	'9–0'28	8:1:17
	HSR 63		
	SVIB 58'4–		

This boy was handsome and likable, but in the early high school years he was shy, backward, and an underachiever. He was self-conscious, bending over backwards to get attention. As he continued through school, he became more mature, and by his senior year he was active in student affairs and became "almost a leader." Although he was serious-minded, he owned a "hot-rod" and had a police record for speeding. After graduation he began training to be a minister. The boy's pastor, however, stated that he doubted the boy would complete this training because he really did not know what he wanted to do.

The father was a sociable person but not a leader. He was pleasant, acceptable, and active in church affairs. The mother, similarly, was outgoing and easy in manner. The children were well behaved but seemed to have an "inferiority complex" so that they tried too hard. Their behavior, consequently, was sometimes curiously inappropriate. The girls in the family were all said to be insolent.

968. M:16:4	ACE IX, none; XI, 12	'9860 457–	0:11:10
N:VI:3	ENG IX, none; XI, 10	'07–'9	3:3:13
	HSR 54		
	SVIB 4'–9		

When this boy first entered high school he was poorly dressed and shy about associating with others, particularly with girls. By his senior year he had gained poise and was acceptably social. He was cooperative and he tried hard in his schoolwork, but he had great difficulty keeping up with his class.

The home was a comfortable one. The parents were hard-working, good people who stayed close to home and had little social life.

969. F:15:6   ACE IX, 18; XI, 47   98'6075342–   8:12:12
     N:IVB:4   ENG IX, 04; XI, 03
                     HSR 02
                     SVIB none

This girl was neat, courteous, dependable, and poised. She was a hard worker at home and at school. In spite of her hard work her grades were poor and her progress through high school was "pretty much a matter of social promotions." The teachers did not expect her to finish school because of her poor ability and achievement. Her shorthand grades were an exception, and it was suggested that she would be a good stenographer. She was described as "deserving of admiration."

970. F:14:4   ACE IX, 72; XI, 90   '987–1'362   3:8:14
     N:V:4   ENG IX, 71; XI, 74   '967–1'32   1:3:9
                     HSR 40
                     SVIB WR'

This girl was mature and realistic. "A rascal but always lovable," and generally a "darling person," she was gay outside of class, and she seemed to like school and people liked her. She would talk to anyone who would listen and was a good and loyal friend. She had a tendency to be flighty and giggly, and at least one person said that she took responsibility poorly. Another mentioned "doubtful sincerity." It was felt that she did not work up to her capacity, but there was some improvement as she approached graduation. After graduation she went on to attend a small college, and although she had a boy friend, she appeared to put her college work first.

The father was described as opinionated, aggressive, and crude. He was tolerated but was thought of as taking the position of "a big shot." The mother was more quiet, pleasant, and probably dominated by the father. She was a willing and good leader in a community organization. The reputation of the siblings in the family was not very good.

971. M:15:0   ACE IX, 88; XI, 92   9'87–25'43   0:7:14
     N:V:1   ENG IX, none; XI, 95   '94–275'13   3:3:11
                     HSR 62   –45261'37   8:2:14
                     SVIB none

The band instructor saw this boy as "a fine, excellent person who was quiet, shy, well mannered, and cheerful." He was sensible, and his main interests were intellectual. He did not engage in extracurricular activities except for being on the second football team. Although he attended school dances, he "probably did not have his own date." He had many friends, however. He was seldom a leader and he did not show evidence of individuality. After graduation he went to a university to major in engineering.

The parents were fine people who were very much interested in the boy. They were active in school functions, and they opened their home to the boy's friends.

972. M:14:2	ACE IX, none; XI, 04	98'7260–'1	2:7:10
N:III:1	ENG IX, none; XI, 07	8'''9''7'61423–	2:16:10X
	HSR 04		
	SVIB '–		

This boy was "an average kid with a nice personality." He caused a few little disturbances and was at times indifferent, exhibiting careless work habits. His ability was considered to be low, and one teacher expected that he might become emotionally maladjusted.

973. M:14:0	ACE IX, 07; XI, 22	'9873–5'	0:8:8
N:V:5	ENG IX, 28; XI, 27	'3984–56'72	2:10:9
	HSR 22		
	SVIB '4–		

The description of this boy emphasized that he was a likable youth with a good personality. Although he was not malicious, he was energetic, had a lot of bounce, and caused trouble as long as he could get away with it. He would push the teachers as far as he could and he was "full of tease." He was a good athlete but was not a very strong leader in spite of being well liked. He was always neat and well dressed. After graduation he worked for his father, and was a dependable worker.

The father was a tense and excitable person who did quite a bit of drinking. The mother was also considered tense and likely to work herself into a "nervous state." She was an attractive woman and a good mother, active in church affairs. Although the parents were often at odds, the family had a good reputation in the community.

974. F:14:0	ACE IX, 18; XI, 30	9'873–'5	2:3:12
N:III:2	ENG IX, 51; XI, 34	'6–1'58	2:3:13
	HSR 33		
	SVIB 'WR		

This girl was attractive, sophisticated, and distinctive in her appearance. She was always well dressed and seemed to have good taste in clothes. An extrovert socially, she was well liked by everyone. She was trustworthy and self-confident. "An only child, she was not spoiled." She had the use of the family car whenever she wanted it. She was not very interested in boys. She worked hard in school, particularly in commercial subjects, and she "had to know the why of everything." After graduation she went to a junior college, but her adjustment there was not so satisfactory. She seemed to develop temperamental traits and refused to return for a second year because of some minor disagreement with an instructor.

The father was a skilled workman; the mother worked in the home and also took odd jobs outside. There was a very close mother-daughter relationship.

975. M:15:11	ACE IX, 05; XI, 09	9'8742–	2:10:11
N:IVC:3	ENG IX, 06; XI, 20	9''7486–'215	3:5:16
	HSR 07		
	SVIB none		

This boy was described as a "Horatio Alger type." He was always cleanly dressed and usually in good spirits. He was well accepted by others, reliable, and cooperative. Very religious in his thinking, he adopted austere ways of living. In his schoolwork he was well motivated; he tried hard but seemed to lack ability. With others he was quiet and self-effacing. In summary, he was "the kind of boy that people liked to work with and to help."

The family lived in a little shack in the country and were unable to pay their bills. The father was disabled. They seemed to be responsible people and to suffer more misfortune than most people. The father and mother were fanatically religious and held meetings in the home.

976. F:15:1	ACE IX, 70; XI, 71	9''87465–02'	1:5:20
N:III:2	ENG IX, 99; XI, 98	6'74895–0'2	1:3:16
	HSR 81		
	SVIB 'WR		

In grade school this girl was a tomboy who did everything the boys did. Other statements about her personality tended to be contradictory. In high school she still had "tomboyish qualities." By some she was was described as popular, well liked, well adjusted, a good student, but "a lone wolf." They further described her as cooperative, dependable, and possessing a good sense of humor. In contrast, she was said to be untrustworthy and "a very slippery little girl." She forged excuses for school absence and was "an operator." She had always wanted to be a boy but was very dependent upon her mother. She was guilty of several driving offenses and at one time was caught at a party where liquor was being consumed. After graduation she started college but shortly thereafter was forced to marry. She had gone with the boy for several years; he was from a good family.

The father was a successful businessman and a good provider. The mother was very extroverted, active in church and other club affairs. She was "almost too polite and friendly" and she dressed in "frilly clothes." "She shed many tears over her children."

977. F:14:2	ACE IX, none; XI, 34	9'8754–'12	6:3:8
N:IVA:3	ENG IX, none; XI, 39	'4983675–'20	3:3:10
	HSR 50		
	SVIB none		

This girl seemed to realize that she lacked imagination and had certain limitations; she had a very balanced view of herself. For example, she wanted to attend college but felt that she was not capable enough. She had many friends and was a nice person — "a contributor" to the school society.

978. F:15:5	ACE IX, 95; XI, 99	'98764–'1	2:3:17
N:III:1	ENG IX, 98; XI, 88	9'43–5'712	2:2:13
	HSR 74	'4–1'53	1:4:12
	SVIB none		

This pleasant and cooperative girl was dependable and a good student. In many activities she was a "semi-leader"; she was the type who could not delegate responsibility and had to do things herself. This meant that she was often slow to finish assignments and somewhat behind in her work. She was very popular with other students and was considered "boy crazy." In her schoolwork she often needed to be pushed, although she had the ability to be a top student. One report said of her, "I don't really care for her somehow; she had a slightly superior attitude." After graduation she enrolled in a university.

979. M:14:4	ACE IX, 24; XI, 47	9'80564–2'3	5:9:5
B:N:5	ENG IX, 65; XI, 70	'9–'836	2:4:11
	HSR 24		
	SVIB 4'–9		

A sullen boy who had a "don't get in my way" attitude, this youth was crude, uncooperative, and unwilling to accept criticism. His friends were always getting into trouble. He seemed to have no respect for authority and got away with anything he could. He was unpredictable, untrustworthy, and a "loner." He did nothing he did not have to do. He was dropped from an athletic team because he could not get along with the coach. Although he was described as reckless behind the car wheel, he was not known to have had any severe trouble with the authorities.

The father had died several years before the boy entered the ninth grade. The mother was high-strung and tense, and she talked so much it was hard to break off the conversation. She kept a close watch on her children but felt that she could not control them. The home environment was described as not good; the house was dirty inside and out.

980. F:13:8	ACE IX, 36; XI, 64	'90–'563	3:6:10
N:IVB:3	ENG IX, 34; XI, 31	'945–'631	2:2:13
	HSR 33		
	SVIB WR'		

This girl had a nice personality; she was extremely reliable and helpful. Serious and quiet, she made a fine adjustment in school. She was well liked by the students.

The father, a good farmer, was very strict and domineering in the home. He was well respected and active in community affairs. All the children were considered rather "quiet."

981. M:15:5   ACE IX, 50; XI, none   9′027–53′1   5:6:11
    B:IVC:2   ENG IX, 29; XI, none
                 HSR DO 10th gr.
                 SVIB none

Physically small and short, this boy did not like school. He was a poor student and took no part in school activities. There was a record of traffic violations for which his license was suspended.

The father died while the boy was still in grade school, but before his death he had deserted the boy's mother. The mother had lived with another man. She did not discipline the children and seemed indifferent toward them. The home was run-down and poorly kept.

982. M:14:1   ACE IX, 81; XI, 56   9′04278–′1653   0:8:3
    N:VI:2   ENG IX, 54; XI, 45   ′70985–′3   2:11:6
                 HSR 17
                 SVIB ′4–

Having an "I don't care" attitude, this boy was overbearing and rude. He was a constant discipline problem and others felt that he might become dangerous. Repeatedly truant and tardy, he had absolutely no interest in school. Most of his resistance was expressed in passive ways. He had no close friends nor did he engage in extracurricular activities. He suffered from dermatitis and asthmatic attacks. Before the ninth grade he had been caught stealing and he got into further trouble of this sort, as well as being a nuisance along with some other boys. After graduation he took a regular job.

The father was a meek, bashful, soft-spoken working man. The family was in average circumstances and was considered conservative, quiet, and respectable.

983. M:15:10   ACE IX, 50; XI, none   9′0452768–   1:7:9
    N:V:1   ENG IX, none; XI, none
                 HSR trans. 10th gr.
                 SVIB none

This boy was small and he had a congenital malformation. He was poorly dressed, uncombed, and not very clean. Quiet, mousy, and withdrawn, he was not well accepted by other students. Several teachers expected that he would develop emotional maladjustment.

He came from a "very bad family" where there were many nonconformists and odd members.

984. F:14:4   ACE IX, 32; XI, 24   9′0567–′13   6:6:7
    N:IVC:2   ENG IX, 40; XI, 60
                 HSR 26
                 SVIB none

Her bleached hair seemed out of character for this somewhat quiet and shy girl. Boys liked her but she did not seem to be interested in them. Usually happy, she was never moody or sullen and she was considered honest and wholesome. She was sensitive about being called a "farmer's daughter." One of the teachers listed her as likely to have emotional maladjustment.

985. M:15:2   N:VI:1
IQ (centile) 14
HSR none
SVIB none

9′064–′<u>57</u>   7:7:12

Careless, listless, and uninterested, this boy was always a minor discipline problem in school. He was a quitter, never finishing his assigned projects. He had a record of minor traffic offenses.

986. F:15:3   N:VI:3
ACE IX, none; XI, 83
ENG IX, none; XI, 74
HSR 90
SVIB none

′90<u>68</u>–132′   1:1:8

This girl was often absent from school without excuse and she got in minor difficulty because of an unauthorized slumber party that she gave. She was neat in appearance and rather unobtrusive in manner. Her teachers felt that she wanted to be better accepted by boys. In school activities she was likely to be late for minor appointments, but in important things she managed to be on time. Contrary to her desires, she was more a follower than a leader. She was usually cooperative but sometimes it took extra convincing for her to conform.

987. M:14:3   N:VI:2
ACE IX, 74; XI, 74
ENG IX, 79; XI, 66
HSR 48
SVIB 4′–90

′908–′<u>67</u>   9:5:14
4′<u>23 18 67</u>–′0   9:6:24

Though not a brilliant boy, this youth compensated for what he lacked in ability by determination and tenacity. He was well liked by faculty and students although he was reticent and shy. He was physically slight and frail. He had a steady job outside of school and when his mother died shortly after he graduated, he showed good emotional stability. In school he took an active part in classwork.

988. F:14:1   N:V:1
ACE IX, 58; XI, 88
ENG IX, none; XI, 86
HSR 47
SVIB none

9′08<u>24</u>–′1   6:2:12
′9–17′836   4:2:8

Attractive, dependable, and courteous, this girl was always well mannered, socially poised, and nicely dressed. She was described as "a realistic, down-to-earth type of person," a solid school citizen. She worked hard at tasks both in the school and at her job outside of school. She was well liked by girls and did not appear to be "boy crazy." Her grades tended to get worse during her school years. She married shortly after graduation. The mother had been hospitalized twice for alcoholism and the father was also a heavy drinker. Apparently the home was not a very bad situation in spite of these problems.

989. F:14:1	ACE IX, 36; XI, 43	'90<u>87</u>–6'2	6:4:12
N:III:2	ENG IX, none; XI, 43	'56<u>34</u>–'19	5:1:15
	HSR 81		
	SVIB WR'		

A "cute little minx," this student was a leader in her group, pleasant, well liked, cooperative, and reliable. She was vivacious, had numerous dates, and was a homecoming queen candidate. Her attitude was positive toward school and others. After graduation she began teachers' training but dropped out in mid-term.

The family seemed to be cohesive and acceptable. The father was popular and likable. The mother, somewhat high-strung and tense, did most of the disciplining of the children. She was described as efficient and a hard driver who made sure the children presented a good appearance.

990. F:15:2	ACE IX, 67; XI, 82	'0–<u>196</u> 84'7	6:1:8
B:VI:2	ENG IX, 88; XI, 93	'0–9'<u>8461</u>	7:2:14
	HSR 81		
	SVIB WR'		

This attractive, although somewhat overweight, girl was described as quiet and retiring, but responsible, cooperative, and reliable. There seemed to be no personality problem connected with her being overweight or with any other factor. She was well thought of by her classmates. After high school she went on to a vocational course of training, in which she did well.

The family seemed to offer a moderately good environment. The father died during this girl's childhood and the mother was forced to work after his death. A younger boy in the family was considered "not very bright."

991. F:15:5	ACE IX, 48; XI, 71	'0–3<u>16</u>'479	2:5:7
N:III:3	ENG IX, 42; XI, 43	'0–1<u>3</u>'6289	2:6:8
	HSR 70		
	SVIB WR'		

This was an exceptionally reliable girl, but one who lacked leadership ability. Her teachers noted that she had good judgment and stable emotional reactions. She was cooperative and friendly.

The home seemed very satisfactory and stable.

992. F:15:2　　　　　ACE IX, 70; XI, 84　　　　'0–3<u>19</u>'6　　3:1:13
　　N:IVB:2　　　　　ENG IX, none; XI, 93　　　'0–15'4<u>37</u>　　1:2:6
　　　　　　　　　　　HSR 96
　　　　　　　　　　　SVIB WR'

Shy and a little withdrawn, very quiet and hard working, this girl did not mix with the other students and had few friends. She was pale and slight in appearance. She seemed to enjoy school and studying, and she was considered an overachiever. Although cooperative, she did not show any evidence of leadership ability and seemed "lackadaisical."

　　The father and mother were described as superior persons who were respected in their neighborhood. Although their farm was rented, it was kept neat and in good shape.

993. M:15:5　　　　　ACE IX, 04; XI, 46　　　　'0–'<u>51</u>39　　7:3:12
　　N:IVC:3　　　　　ENG IX, 15; XI, 15　　　–91'86 <u>45</u>　　8:1:12
　　　　　　　　　　　HSR 36
　　　　　　　　　　　SVIB 4'–

One of twins, the other a girl, this boy was accepted by fellow students although he was very quiet and was in no activities at all. [The twin's MMPI codes were, ninth grade, '078–2'<u>63</u> <u>15</u> 0:3:12, and, twelfth grade, '<u>75</u>–4' 1:4:11.] Sometimes unreliable, he was, in general, fairly cooperative and did his required assignments. One person said that he was "a very fine kind of kid, hard working, who has risen above his environment." He hoped to go to a college or trade school.

　　The father and mother were hard-working people who did their best for the children. Both parents were older than most parents with children in this age group. They went into debt getting help for one child who was mentally retarded and handicapped. The father was an immigrant farmer. The family lived primitively in an old log house that was isolated in the woods.

994. M:14:1　　　　　ACE IX, 74; XI, 78　　　　'0–53'<u>846</u>　　3:1:8
　　N:V:2　　　　　　ENG IX, 59; XI, 62　　　'072–3'<u>46</u>　　3:4:11
　　　　　　　　　　　HSR 41
　　　　　　　　　　　SVIB 8'4–

This boy was quiet, plodding, industrious, and "sober-sided." Of good character, he was honest, reliable, and cooperative. He was a follower who did not contribute much to his class. While going to school, he had an outside job working with his father but was not particularly happy with this work. After graduation he continued on to college, planning for a business career.

　　The family was well thought of in the community and had an above average income. The father was a "fine mechanic." The mother worked outside the home. They were "a churchgoing family."

995. M:14:10   ACE IX, none; XI, 64   0'–5'78 2639   4:5:10
     N:IVA:3   ENG IX, none; XI, 22
                    HSR 49
                    SVIB none

Active in athletics, this boy never, however, excelled in sports or in anything else. He was uncooperative and negative in school, where he characteristically made a nuisance of himself by "much pointless questioning." He was critical of others and defensive toward himself. The other students did not like him very well.

The father, a "hard driver in everything," was considered mean and impossible to work with.

996. M:15:3   ACE IX, 59; XI, none   '0–61'873542   8:6:11
     N:IVC:3   ENG IX, 32; XI, none
                    HSR DO 10th gr.
                    SVIB none

This boy was described as "very quiet with a dead personality." He had no friends and was merely tolerated by others; he lacked initiative and gave nothing of himself. He was uninterested in school, "never said a word," and engaged in no activities. These same characteristics applied to his church affiliations. He soon dropped out of school, presumably because he was needed at home to help with work on the family's farm.

The parents "had low standards." The house was untidy and the parents associated with a "low crowd." In general the family had a poor reputation as "drifters and shiftless people."

997. M:14:6   ACE IX, 38; XI, 43   '0–635'142   3:7:9
     N:III:2   ENG IX, none; XI, 12   '07 89–'265   0:8:10
                    HSR 49
                    SVIB '8–

Although he was generally considered neat and well dressed, this boy was also described as "a little dirty." He was called quiet and cooperative, and yet was also regarded as an indifferent student who obtained below average marks. He was not a good mixer and did not go around with girls. He liked hunting and got into some trouble because of hunting in a prohibited area. Some minor stealing caused his exclusion from one of his classes.

The family lived in a fine house. The father, a small businessman, took his boy hunting and was described as having a lot of energy and enthusiasm. The father gave the children much freedom and would only occasionally "lay down the law."

998. F:14:5	ACE IX, none; XI, 21	'0–64'318	4:2:9
N:VII:3	ENG IX, none; XI, 28	'97–'518	5:3:13
	HSR 07		
	SVIB '–		

This girl was described as colorless and relatively unattractive. Overweight, she was very self-conscious about her appearance, yet she dressed unattractively. She was not popular with other students. She was not a troublemaker; her teachers said they felt sorry for her. Her school achievement was poor. After graduation she began doing housework.

All six children in the family had a wholesome attitude and were easy to get along with. The mother, also overweight, was considered to be a "nice person" who tried to do her best for her children. In general, the family relationship appeared to be satisfactory.

999. F:15:2	ACE IX, 82; XI, 62	'0–71'953	5:5:10
N:III:2	ENG IX, none; XI, 84	'70 289–'5	3:0:13
	HSR 99		
	SVIB WR'		

Many laudatory phrases appeared in descriptions of this girl: "mature," "efficient," "immaculate in appearance," "a good morale builder," "perhaps not strong in personality but able to fill responsible positions and an excellent citizen in every respect." Quiet and not too self-assertive, she loved to read. She was considered an overachiever in school; she took pride in her work and graduated with a very high class standing. After high school she went on to a small college, taking a professional course.

The father and mother were also described favorably. They were considered to be rather strict but affectionate with their children, and their method of control was to use persuasion rather than threats of physical punishment. The mother had a very close relationship with her daughter.

1000. F:14:3	ACE IX, 88; XI, 84	0'–941'358	2:4:11
N:III:4	ENG IX, 97; XI, 82	'89–2'41	2:2:17
	HSR 68		
	SVIB '–		

The descriptions of this girl varied among the informants. Some said she "dared to be herself and was well-liked." Others called her active and outgoing, said she did good work and seemed to enjoy life. In contrast, however, according to one informant, "even close friends were critical of her." She was considered by some "an enigma" who was alternately pleasant and outgoing, then quiet and reserved. She seemed to prefer reading to facing the reality of living. After graduation she went into nurses' training. She had a boy friend, but decided to wait for marriage.

The father, although easygoing and likable, never produced very well. He was discharged from his job because he seemed unable to follow directions. He was "slovenly and had no ambition." The mother, before her marriage, had been "accustomed to gracious living." She accepted the problems of the family "bravely and without complaining." She was capable and friendly.

1001. M:14:5	ACE IX, none; XI, 46	'01–2'39	6:4:16
N:IVA:4	ENG IX, none; XI, 53	'5934–	2:2:19
	HSR 60		
	SVIB none		

This boy, who felt he was a grown man and wanted the privileges of an adult, asked nothing of anyone. Outside of school he was a very hard worker and earned all of his spending money. In school he was lazy and made no apparent effort, although he was not a conduct problem; he saw no value in high school and could not be challenged. He was described as "headstrong."

1002. M:15:1	ACE IX, 14; XI, 19	'01–95'24	8:5:14
N:IVC:2	ENG IX, 37; XI, 06		
	HSR 13		
	SVIB none		

Although one person described this boy as likable, the general description was less favorable. His manner was characterized as loud and boisterous. He "thought he knew everything," and was "lazy and did not try." In the ninth grade, apparently to attract attention, he irritated teachers and classmates by interrupting and talking out of turn. He seemed to improve somewhat in later school years when he realized that his behavior was making him unacceptable except to his own small group.

The father was described as "easygoing and too tolerant." The mother did the subject's homework for him.

1003. F:15:4	ACE IX, none; XI, 19	'01362–'9	6:5:17
N:VI:1	ENG IX, none; XI, 12		
	HSR 12		
	SVIB none		

This girl had a record of truancy, and at the age of sixteen she was brought to juvenile court on a charge of drinking and sexual involvement with an older man at a party. She was placed on probation for a year. During her senior year she was much better behaved. At that time she was quiet and mature.

The probation officer felt that the home supervision was lax.

1004. F:15:5   ACE IX, 91; XI, 92   '0158–93'4   5:7:11
     N:III:2   ENG IX, 96; XI, 98   '09–'647   5:3:9
                    HSR 70
                    SVIB 'WR

Quiet, timid, and modest, this girl seemed "frustrated" in her senior year and her teachers felt that something was bothering her. However, if she was troubled, she managed to cover the cause and never admitted that anything was wrong. She was extremely reliable and cooperative in school. Because of a heart murmur, she was excused from physical education and was supposed to avoid overexertion. She became engaged just before the end of her senior year to a man who was said to be inferior to her in education, and she married him shortly after graduation. Following her marriage, she was less careful of her appearance than she had been previously. She was the youngest of six children, the next being seventeen years older.

The father was a retired skilled worker. The mother had had numerous jobs, but was also old and partially an invalid. Although the economic conditions of the home were poor, it appeared to be well kept up.

1005. F:14:4   ACE IX, none; XI, 19   '017823–9'   5:3:14
     B:V:3   ENG IX, none; XI, 45
                    HSR 04
                    SVIB none

Described as a "big, blowy blonde with a rather hard appearance," this girl was also unreliable. She was expelled from school for truancy but later she completed high school in a neighboring town. Her teachers described her as dreamy and unstable. She later married a classmate.

The father died when the girl was quite young and the mother took a job as a waitress even though it was not necessary for her to work. The school authorities blamed the mother for the children's problems because she left them to shift for themselves. The mother was amiable and readily agreeable to what was expected of her, but she did not follow through in action. All the children caused trouble in school, particularly by truancy.

1006. F:14:3   ACE IX, none; XI, 93   '018742–'96   4:2:16
     N:V:3   ENG IX, none; XI, 86
                    HSR 86
                    SVIB none

A fear of failure seemed to be the dominant characteristic of this "neurotic" girl. She was described as "lashed to fury by ambition." Studying was very important to her, and her father had to turn out the light at night so that she would not study too much. She appeared thin and worried, and was flighty and easily flustered.

The father was described as somewhat like his daughter, with worries over his business affairs. The family moved shortly after the ninth-grade testing and no follow-up information was available.

1007. F:15:3	ACE IX, none; XI, 01	'0<u>19846</u>5–	7:10:15
N:IVB:6	ENG IX, none; XI, 04	3'1<u>68</u> 45 <u>27</u>–	12:9:25X
	HSR 04		
	SVIB none		

Emotional maladjustment was predicted for this girl by her teachers, who observed her to be too easily depressed. Usually willing to follow the suggestions of others, she was never a leader herself. At the end of the ninth grade she transferred to another school. This school reported that she took no part in its extracurricular activities.

1008. F:14:4	ACE IX, 63; XI, none	'02–<u>45</u>'139	5:5:12
N:IVC:4	ENG IX, 90; XI, none		
	HSR DO 10th gr.		
	SVIB none		

The school record of this girl was satisfactory in spite of several interruptions. In the ninth grade she was described as "interested in people — mostly boys." After transferring to another school she became illegitimately pregnant. The pregnancy caused her to be very depressed and she attempted suicide. After the birth of the child she placed it for adoption and returned to school, where her teachers then described her as a "nice, pleasant girl." She later married.

Both the father and the mother were easygoing and without much ambition. The father's drinking was considered to be a factor in his lack of control over his children. An older sister also had an illegitimate child and lived a very irregular life. The mother felt that the older sister unfavorably influenced the behavior of the younger children, who were all arrogant, undependable, and undisciplined; the mother herself seemed to prefer dances and parties to staying home with her family.

1009. M:16:3	ACE IX, 09; XI, 29	'02–<u>61</u>'4	3:3:6
N:VI:2	ENG IX, 16; XI, 40		
	HSR 39		
	SVIB 4'1–0		

This boy missed a year of school because of chronic illness. Slow in speech and action, he seemed to take things easy. This manner was possibly caused by his physical condition. He made no trouble in school, but he did not exert himself. His work was never in on time and he offered no excuses for this tardiness. After graduation he took a job in the community.

The father was a good provider and the mother was a hard-working home-maker. The parents took no part in community affairs but were apparently accept-able enough as residents of the community.

1010. M:14:3	ACE IX, none; XI, 98	'02–81'<u>973</u>	6:5:6
N:III:2	ENG IX, none; XI, 93	'<u>26</u>–'8<u>15</u>	3:5:12
	HSR 98	'604–'<u>75</u>	3:2:17
	SVIB none		

Although he was immature, this boy was a good and very active student. He was conscientious and sincere, and he had a good disposition. He was an accomplished musician. After graduation he began technical training at a university.

1011. F:14:3	ACE IX, 02; XI, 04	0'21<u>837</u>–9'	6:10:9
N:IVB:4	ENG IX, 13; XI, 01	'<u>09</u>–'<u>41</u>	7:1:8
	HSR 14		
	SVIB '–		

Reports about this girl were somewhat conflicting. It was agreed that she was quiet, unassertive, and hard to know. She was also described as thorough, methodical, and likable, although she took no part in school activities. In contrast, however, she was said to have been caught cheating several times, and it was claimed that she frequently lied to a teacher. She was very fearful of not doing the right thing. Above all, she was inarticulate. She had many illnesses and was out of school nearly as many days as she was present. She would spend a few days in bed and then return to school, only to become ill again. There was no clear pattern in her illnesses and the school record did not list a particular diagnosis. Apparently her main complaints were weakness and headaches, and she always appeared listless. After graduation she continued to live at home, and her main interest was in finding a husband.

This family was described as "typical," although the mother was considered flighty and high-strung. The entire family was "health conscious" and their con-versation emphasized medicine and health in general. The three other children appeared to be lacking in initiative and had to be pushed to express themselves at all.

1012. M:14:5	ACE IX, 92; XI, 90	0'2<u>48</u>–1'<u>639</u>	0:5:7
N:VII:4	ENG IX, 88; XI, 95	0"48 27'5<u>69</u>–'1	0:9:8
	HSR 81		
	SVIB none		

Thin and undernourished looking, this boy had few friends and took part in few activities, with the exception of basketball. Although he was not considered a conduct problem, he was shy and very quiet in school. He had to work outside of school in order to earn money for his expenses. In his junior year he was involved in some vandalism directed against school buildings. The juvenile court ordered him to make restitution for the damage. Later he was found with beer in his possession and was rather severely treated because he was still on probation from the earlier offense.

The home situation was described as "lax." The father, a laborer, was a "hard drinker."

1013. M:15:1	ACE IX, 48; XI, 29	'025–'7349	4:6:12
N:IVB:2	ENG IX, 34; XI, 22		
	HSR 33		
	SVIB none		

Very little information was available about this boy. He was a hard worker, dependable, and liked by his teachers, but the other students merely tolerated him. His English usage was very poor, but he seemed eager to improve. He was described as "stolid and a plodder."

1014. M:14:7	ACE IX, 57; XI, 34	'027–138'496	4:3:6
N:V:2	ENG IX, none; XI, 14		
	HSR 06		
	SVIB '480–		

A well-built and nice-appearing boy, this youth caused no trouble, was quiet, and tended to stay by himself. Apparently he was self-conscious and a little lazy, although he was described as working hard. He was not in many activities. After graduation he continued to work on a job which he had held part time while he was in school. There was an episode in his freshman year when he was lectured and released because of vandalism.

1015. F:14:2	ACE IX, 50; XI, 37	'02784–'36 19	5:6:16
N:III:3	ENG IX, 59; XI, 56	'07268–3'14	3:7:13
	HSR 54		
	SVIB WR'		

This girl was described as shy, retiring, and withdrawn, although she had a ready smile and was fairly successful in her own circle of friends. She tended to concentrate on her schoolwork and to keep to herself rather than to engage in activities. In some respects she was considered immature and childish. She liked music and spoke with a soft, high voice. After graduation she began working in her father's office.

The family had a good reputation, although the father, who dominated the family, was considered stubborn and unreasonable in some of his contacts. The mother, a soft-spoken and relatively articulate woman, went through a period of nervousness and depression, and at that time she made things difficult for the family.

1016. M:14:2	ACE IX, 30; XI, none	02'8–951'346	3:6:10
N:IVB:5	ENG IX, 55; XI, 34		
	HSR 55		
	SVIB none		

This was a "nice-appearing, clean-cut" boy. He made friends with other farm boys, but was quiet and did not mix very well with the larger school group. The only additional item available about him was that he "worked to his capacity."

1017. F:14:2	ACE IX, none; XI, 61	'0284–'913	5:5:13
N:V:2	ENG IX, none; XI, 77		
	HSR 66		
	SVIB none		

This extremely reliable girl was considered "the soul of faithfulness." Friendly but not effusive, she was active in her church, where she was well accepted and respected as a member of the group. Less active in school, she was a moderately good student. She was large and not pretty, although there were no obvious defects in her appearance. In her senior year she became interested in a career as a medical technician or a nurse.

1018. F:14:2	ACE IX, 84; XI, 87	0'28764–'93	2:6:8
N:II:1	ENG IX, 91; XI, 84	— —	— —
	HSR 94	0'87263–'1	3:8:15
	SVIB none		

This "very quiet," nice-looking, pleasant girl was a good student, but she was so unassuming that her classmates considered her just average. She had friends and was described as "the type of girl that gets married within a year after high school graduation." Following graduation she continued her education at a university.

1019. F:14:9   ACE IX, none; XI, 91   '03–'26   4:3:13
      N:VI:1   ENG IX, none; XI, 87
                      HSR 69
                      SVIB none

Quiet, introverted, but friendly, this girl participated in class discussions and caused her teachers no difficulty, although she was an underachiever in her early high school years. She had been in a bad automobile accident in which a friend was killed and she may have suffered emotional aftereffects from this. She had to work in order to stay in school. Anxious to succeed, she hoped to go to college. By graduation she had improved her school standing by hard work.

1020. F:14:3   IQ (centile) 81   0'3174–9'5   6:3:13
      N:VI:3   HSR 75   0'746283–'59   3:5:12
                      SVIB none

This unobtrusive, easygoing girl rarely displayed emotion. Although she had high ability, she contributed nothing to classes and to other activities, with the possible exception of music, in which she had a considerable interest.

1021. F:17:7   ACE IX, 08; XI, none   '032–8'9467   5:4:7
      N:VII:4   ENG IX, 33; XI, none
                      HSR DO 9th gr.
                      SVIB none

Because this girl was not strong in her schoolwork, she had been held back one year and, when tested, was in the same grade as her younger sister. [The sister's MMPI codes were, ninth grade, –24'359 4:5:18, and, twelfth grade, '67–5'24 6:2:18.] Competition with this sister made her unhappy although apparently not resentful. The girl was said to be more sociable than her sister and to have a better sense of humor. Her health was not good and she had particular difficulty with her teeth. Shortly after the ninth-grade testing she left school to be married. The marriage seemed to be stable, and she had one child.

   This girl's father did odd jobs, and the home was not a very healthy environment, although it was said that the parents "meant well."

1022. F:16:0   ACE IX, none; XI, 77   '0361–'57   5:7:12
      N:IVA:3   ENG IX, none; XI, none   '4638 9517–   10:1:26X
                      HSR 64
                      SVIB '–

This mature and apparently well-adjusted girl was not a conduct problem in school. She had a select group of friends but did not engage in any school activities. She was described as "sickly."

1023. M:16:4   ACE IX, none; XI, 34   '04–'56   1:3:15
      N:V:1   ENG IX, none; XI, 22
                HSR DO 12th gr.
                SVIB none

Almost all that is known about this boy is that he was rather quiet and a "very poor achiever." He participated in no school activities and dropped out of school during his senior year. He did this, it was said, in order to go to work so that he could support his girl friend, "whom he was probably compelled to marry."

1024. M:15:3   ACE IX, 30; XI, 22   '04–5'63 79   5:7:14
      N:III:2   ENG IX, none; XI, 01   '08–'2375   2:4:16
                HSR 05
                SVIB '4–5

Although neat and well dressed, this boy was indifferent, uninterested, and negative in school. He occasionally created disturbances in class and took no part in class activities. His teachers regarded him as an underachiever because it was suspected that his intelligence was higher than tests indicated. In temperament he was quiet and withdrawn, and always seemed to be on the defensive. He was definitely a follower and when with poor associates he did very badly. After some of these friends had dropped out of school, his own work improved and he was more dependable; however, he still lacked initiative. Near the time of high school graduation he was arrested for illegal possession of liquor and for drunkenness.

The parents were said to have encouraged the boy to do better in school. Neither the mother nor the father, who was a skilled workman, had gone beyond the eighth grade in their education.

1025. F:15:3   ACE IX, 98; XI, 100   '04–9'135   4:3:15
      N:V:1   ENG IX, none; XI, 100   '34–'5718   5:0:13
                HSR 100
                SVIB none

This girl seemed to be outstanding in every way. Her high abilities were demonstrated in high achievements. Her moral and ethical standards were particularly good, and she was described as dependable, reliable, competent, and mature in accepting responsibility. She was active in many extracurricular activities and was a member of the student council. In some contrast, at least one teacher considered her to be "slightly introverted and not aggressive." She worked after school and took a considerable amount of responsibility in her family. She had a boy friend who was believed to be beneath her intellectually, but there was no mention of anything undesirable about him. She went to college after graduating from high school.

Her family background was good. The parents were active in school functions and interested in intellectual pursuits. They "maintained a strict home."

1026. M:15:12   ACE IX, 28; XI, 32   '0425–   5:10:5
      N:VII:5   ENG IX, 23; XI, 23   '042–   3:2:14
                       HSR 25
                       SVIB 4'–0

This boy was described as the only member of his family "mentally able to attend school." Although weak in his academic work, he made up for this limitation by his many virtues. He was a tireless worker, courteous, reliable, and dependable. He was in the band, played some football, and worked very hard to earn money for his support. He was well liked, even admired, by the other students for his efforts. Described as a "gentleman," he felt a strong loyalty to his family. After graduation he went to work at a service station.

The home, though run-down, was tidy and neat. The father was considered a "total loss." He was a laborer who, when he lost his job, appeared to have little incentive to get another one. He was retiring and did not want to talk to people. The mother was the strong force in the home and an influence for the better. In contrast to her husband, she was outgoing, friendly, and articulate. She worked outside the home as a domestic and was extremely capable, honest, and efficient. In summary, she was called "a good parent with a good type of control." With the passage of time she became unable to work because of a progressive illness.

1027. M:14:7   ACE IX, none; XI, 13   '042758–'96   7:4:19
      N:VI:3   ENG IX, none; XI, 38   20'87643–   6:3:18
                      HSR 28
                      SVIB '4–

"A little old man," this boy was small in stature, never laughed, and came and went alone. The teachers were somewhat puzzled by him, considering him odd and possibly shy, but they rated him an average student, and one said that he was "slow to learn but he never forgot what he learned." He took part in no activities and showed no particular interest in anything. After graduation he went to work in the community.

He came from a large family that lived in an isolated section of a suburb and kept to themselves, not socializing with the neighbors. The family was poor but they never asked for help, although they did receive some voluntary assistance. All the children attended school and all had a difficult time with their schoolwork.

1028. F:15:8   ACE IX, 38; XI, 36   '0428–'59   4:2:13
      N:IVC:2   ENG IX, none; XI, 51   '5–9'8   2:5:11
                      HSR 78
                      SVIB WR'

Repeatedly described as shy, this girl was very conscientious and dependable. She had a "quiet sort of confidence" and she could "say no when occasion demanded." She had made "a fine adjustment" and was described as having "high moral standards." She read a good deal and "worked up to her capacity." After graduation she took a clerical job.

The father, a farmer, was hard working but unprogressive. He was not at all forceful and was satisfied with the ordinary things of life. He was a person with a very even temper. The mother was a good housekeeper and a "good motherly type." The family was "cooperative and fine."

1029. F:14:4	ACE IX, 70; XI, 84	04'2867–5'1	4:13:8
N:III:1	ENG IX, none; XI, 85	4''''7''86'092–'5	1:10:13
	HSR 64	4''''78''29063–	1:14:17
	SVIB none		

The several descriptions of this girl were somewhat at odds, possibly because her behavior changed considerably as she continued through high school. The positive comments about her emphasized her good personality. She was generally well liked by both boys and girls and was generous and thoughtful in her social contacts. She "reflected a good home and appeared well brought up." She cheerfully accepted extra assignments. Contrastingly, one teacher thought she had little drive and initiative and that she did not appear as mature as other girls. She was also said to be dominating and frequently impolite. Described as "boy crazy," she had many dates, especially with older boys who did not attend the high school. She seemed to like to have a crowd about her: she was described as "a girl who would give a party in her home for members of a visiting band." A counselor spoke of her as a society girl. In the tenth grade there was a rumor that she had been intoxicated. She continued on to attend a university, and while there, she announced her engagement to be married.

The family was a happy one and the parents were interested in the welfare of the children. Both parents had some college education. The mother was reported to be very worried about this girl, but seemed unable to cope with her and gave in to her. One of the older sisters was considered to be the same type as the subject.

1030. F:14:4	ACE IX, 44; XI, 72	'043712–'9	14:4:18X
N:IVC:5	ENG IX, 43; XI, 48	'426 3871–'9	10:4:19X
	HSR 56		
	SVIB none		

This girl's vision was very poor and this handicap seemed to affect her schoolwork. She was shy and uncertain about being accepted by her classmates. She was neat and very conscientious but had poor coordination. Her manner was "a little silly and giggly and she was socially backward." She was "pathetic but unconscious of it." She worked very hard on her school assignments and was a plodder, always anxious to do anything to help the teachers. She was a friendly, "sweet girl" who would attach herself to a person.

Her father was "not active in anything." He was quiet and neat but did not have too strong a personality. The mother was more talkative but also mild mannered. She kept a close eye on her children and saw that they got all the necessary attention.

1031. F:15:0	ACE IX, 84; XI, 92	'0476–1'2<u>35</u>	3:1:6
N:IVC:3	ENG IX, 76; XI, 88	'43<u>758</u>–'<u>02</u>	2:1:22
	HSR 89		
	SVIB WR'		

Although pleasant and alert, this girl was shy and retiring in both social situations and school. She was conscientious, reliable, and hard working, but she was never a leader in social gatherings. After graduation she began to work in a clerical capacity.

She was an only child. The home situation seemed to be a very stable one, although the parents were not well known to the community and remained somewhat isolated on their farm.

1032. F:14:3	ACE IX, 52; XI, 64	'048<u>276</u>–<u>59</u>'	4:1:16
N:IVA:5	ENG IX, 69; XI, 67	'087–5'3	5:4:12
	HSR 69		
	SVIB 'WR		

While this girl was liked by many and was considered well adjusted, she was also described as relatively reserved and quiet, "not really fun and doing nothing well." Some persons viewed her as charming and poised; always well dressed, she made an attractive appearance. In her later high school years she became a friend of a girl who had a bad influence on her. This friendship was cited as the reason she lost many of her other friends. After graduation she continued in a relatively low type of semiprofessional training.

Both parents were very active in community affairs and were considered to be wholesome and attractive. The social status and reputation of the family were good, and the parents, who appeared compatible, were interested in their children. There were two male siblings who had speech defects.

1033. F:14:2	ACE IX, none; XI, 84	0'487–'95	4:8:11
N:II:2	ENG IX, none; XI, 95	'<u>70</u>–1'<u>89</u>	1:2:11
	HSR 84	'<u>53</u>–9'1	2:0:16
	SVIB none		

A teacher described this girl as "a parasite who depended upon everyone else for her work." She was poorly motivated and was considered an underachiever. Attractive in appearance, she worked part time as a fashion model. She had a restricted group of friends. After graduation, she went on to take university work. Two teachers expected her to develop emotional maladjustment.

1034. F:14:1	ACE IX, 96; XI, 92	'04987–'53	1:4:12
N:IVB:4	ENG IX, 99; XI, 88		
	HSR 91		
	SVIB 'WR		

"Probably tops in the senior class," this girl was described as having a good personality. She was well liked and appeared to have a good time in social situations, although she was never exuberant. She was not easy to know. In a quiet way she had a considerable drive to achieve and her teachers felt that she might come to show more leadership. After finishing high school she took further training and became a secretary.

The family had a good reputation. The father was a farmer and, although he was not outstanding in any particular way, he was fairly well accepted in the community. The mother, who was described as "substantial and wholesome," appeared to be compensating for a feeling of inferiority. The subject had one older sister. In general, the home situation was good. The parents were proud of their daughters and seemed to have done their best for them.

1035. M:14:7	ACE IX, 11; XI, 62	'05–'1239	3:5:14
N:IVB:2	ENG IX, none; XI, 33		
	HSR 72		
	SVIB none		

This boy was interested in farming and his friends were other farm boys. He was not a conduct problem in school, and he was pleasant and cooperative. Although he was considered a good student, one teacher did characterize him as "lazy, talkative, and not too eager."

1036. M:15:1	ACE IX, 72; XI, 88	'052–1'3	5:5:9
N:III:2	ENG IX, none; XI, 77		
	HSR 64		
	SVIB none		

Although not popular, this boy was called "likable." He was not aggressive and had an average number of friends. He took part in few school activities and appeared indifferent in school, although he said he liked it and he had a good attitude. He was not a conduct problem. He was anxious to finish school and go to work.

1037. F:14:3   ACE IX, 50; XI, 40   '052–'41   5:3:11
      B:V:3   ENG IX, 43; XI, 65   '435–   6:2:24
                      HSR 61
                      SVIB WR'

This "sweet little girl" who was "always a lady" had a nice personality and "was careful of her company." Shy, quiet, and lacking in initiative, she was considered stable and responsible. Although she did not give the impression of being very capable, she did what she was told and was an accurate and willing worker. These positive qualities seemed surprising to observers in view of her home background. She was going with a boy whose family did not have a good reputation, and the boy himself was "an unsavory character." In appearance she was a "pale-looking" girl. She did above average in her schoolwork although her teachers said she did not have much mental ability. She became a stenographic clerk after graduation.

Her father had left home and died before the girl entered the ninth grade. The mother, even before her husband had left her, was a drinker and promiscuous. Although the mother was locally notorious, she was said to be pleasant and outgoing; she tried to be a good mother and she kept her children "under control."

1038. M:14:3   ACE IX, none; XI, 33   '05278–1'9   3:6:7
      N:IVB:7   ENG IX, none; XI, 16   '508–6'21   1:6:6
                     HSR 01
                     SVIB none

Short, stocky, and strong, this boy tended to have friends who were younger than he was, partly because he was so short. He "chased" younger girls, sought publicity, and liked attention. His classmates tended to reject him. He was a nuisance in school and was considered unreliable. He was often late for classes and tried to get out of doing anything.

1039. F:15:5   ACE IX, 30; XI, 58   '054–'3   4:5:11
      N:VII:1   ENG IX, none; XI, 21
                     HSR DO 11th gr.
                     SVIB none

An unattractive girl, this youngster was described as having a "flat, broad face." Reports indicated a change in her behavior as she continued in school. In the ninth grade she was below average in scholarship but satisfactory in her general behavior. She worked outside of school, was active in the choir, and was, in general, a satisfactory student. In the tenth grade she began to change and became a problem in class. She talked out of turn, bothered others, refused to accept correction from the teacher, and was resentful and stubborn. When sent to the principal for reprimand, she was rigid with defiance, "almost as if in a fit of epilepsy." After a brief suspension from school she was somewhat better in her behavior. She had no close friends in school and her general character was withdrawn and reserved when she was not bothering others. Teachers felt that her father had been too strict with her. In her junior year she quit school, and shortly after this she married.

The home, although small and not very substantial, was well kept. There seemed to be a strong bond between the parents and their children. The neighbors considered the parents good people. The family income was irregular; the father, a day laborer, occasionally was out of work and the family had to apply for financial aid during these periods.

1040. F:14:2	ACE IX, 20; XI, 21	0'542–'196	4:6:13
N:III:1	ENG IX, 34; XI, 31	'7283 45169–	4:4:16
	HSR 08		
	SVIB none		

Apparently the school authorities did not expect much from this girl, and they received no more than was expected. Her only school activity was athletics in the twelfth year. No descriptive adjectives were available about her personality and it appears reasonable to conclude that she was working up to her capacity. After graduation she began working in a clerical position.

1041. M:14:1	ACE IX, 79; XI, none	'0568–'1	8:4:15
B:IVB:4	ENG IX, 57; XI, none		
	HSR DO 11th gr.		
	SVIB none		

This boy was considered too old and mature in his thinking for his age; it was felt that he was carrying too much responsibility. He "enjoyed school as much as the school enjoyed him" and would have liked to continue although he was forced to leave after his father died. He was pleasant and friendly with everyone, and after leaving school he married "a very fine girl."

Owing to irregularities in the behavior of the father and mother, the two boys of this family had been made wards of the state when they were younger. The father was unstable and alcoholic, and contributed little to the family. The mother was hard working and, as the years went by, established an excellent relationship with her two sons. Apparently, however, the mother had not been as reliable in earlier years and the boys lived with a paternal aunt.

1042. F:14:3	ACE IX, 17; XI, none	'0568–'193	4:5:17
N:VI:1	ENG IX, none; XI, none	–'9	6:3:14
	HSR trans. 11th gr.		
	SVIB none		

This was a quiet and inconspicuous girl who "just comes and goes"; she was little known to any faculty member, but she was considered happy because she had a ready smile. "Very dainty and nicely dressed," she was frail in appearance. She was handicapped by the fact that the family moved often, and they again moved at the end of her eleventh school year.

Both the father and the mother worked and the home appeared to be a good one, typical of modest-income families.

1043. F:13:6	ACE IX, none; XI, 62	'05<u>78</u>–'3<u>146</u>	5:7:8
B:IVB:5	ENG IX, none; XI, none	'54<u>76</u>–9'	4:4:17
	HSR 43		
	SVIB none		

This girl, a poor student, "to some extent put on airs and had haughty tendencies." She was not a conduct problem. She had a good circle of friends and was thought of as somewhat "extroverted." Her status after graduation was unknown.

1044. F:14:5	ACE IX, 07; XI, 22	'0<u>5847</u>–'2	3:7:12
N:VI:2	ENG IX, none; XI, 32	0'27 <u>4859</u>–	2:9:7
	HSR 11		
	SVIB '–		

This girl, who was nervous, unhappy, and withdrawn, seemed to suffer from inferiority feelings. In appearance she was overweight and unhealthy looking. She used physical illness to avoid school obligations such as recitations and special assignments. Her health problems, which often required visits to a physician, centered on allergic reactions. She was very quick to develop a rash when she felt any stress. Although she was not particularly disliked, she was psychologically inaccessible. She was particularly fond of jazz music of the most modern type. Around the time of the ninth-grade testing she was spending time with a group of teen-agers who were buying and drinking beer. Had her parents permitted, she would have quit school. But she did continue, although her achievement was poor. During her senior year she was known to the police as often being out late and going with a group of girls who on one occasion were found drunk and disorderly.

Like his daughter, the father was described by some people as seeming to feel that others were against him. He was, however, a steady worker and not known to be an obviously poor manager or a bad father. The mother was described as a "poor housekeeper" and irresponsible. The family was said to be without discipline. Both parents occasionally drank too much and the home was described as a "paper shack."

1045. F:14:4 ACE IX, 26; XI, 13 0'5867–1'3 3:11:4
      N:IVB:4 ENG IX, 38; XI, 32 '045–1'638 5:5:9
               HSR 40
               SVIB WR'

"Fat, dull, highly sensitive," and unaware of her own limitations, this girl was well enough liked by a small group. She was "chatty and vivacious," a good and hard worker both at school and outside. Teachers feared that she would some day be hurt as she came to realize her own limitations. Many persons rejected her, and yet she needed acceptance badly. She lacked initiative and was so untidy that she could not even keep a job doing housework. She was, however, willing to try everything: sewing, cooking, or any other household tasks. She was very religious and "very loyal." After high school she became a practical nurse. Two teachers thought she would have future emotional problems.

The father was a farmer and a poor one. A stern disciplinarian, he worked his children hard and dominated the family. The mother, who was treated badly by her husband, was quiet and unassuming. She seemed brighter than her husband. The parents had a good reputation, but they seemed insensitive to the needs of the children.

1046. M:13:7 ACE IX, 84; XI, 76 '05986–'42 0:6:8
      B:III:2 ENG IX, none; XI, 87 7'16350– 1:5:11
               HSR 83
               SVIB 4'1–90

Numerous complimentary adjectives, such as modest, cooperative, reliable, alert, mature, and conscientious, were used in the description of this boy. Although he did not usually take a leading position or push himself forward, he was liked by both teachers and students. He did not initiate conversations but could talk easily when they were under way. Apparently striving for perfection, he did his share of work and worked hard. He engaged in a few extracurricular activities and was considered an excellent school citizen. After graduation he went on to a professional college.

The father died when the boy was five and the mother remarried shortly thereafter. There were five children from the second marriage.

1047. M:14:1 ACE IX, 16; XI, 13 '06–91'58 3:7:9
      B:N:5 ENG IX, 18; XI, 09 '467–5'90 5:1:18
               HSR 02
               SVIB 4'–

A very thin, physically immature boy with a high-pitched voice, this youth was self-conscious because of his physical frailties. He also seemed immature psychologically, being described as "silly and giggly." In behavior he was considered lazy and a "fringe case on the edge of trouble." He was always in minor mischief and was considered a follower. The boys with whom he associated were rough and often got into trouble, but he was never with them at those times. When he was in the eighth grade he stole a gun and was apprehended for shooting it carelessly.

The father was away from home most of the time. He was a hard-working man with a good reputation. He was affectionate with the children. The mother often compared the boy unfavorably with his older sister, who was considered much superior. The mother seemed not to know how to control the boy.

1048. F:15:4	ACE IX, 63; XI, 61	'06287–9'5	3:3:16
N:V:2	ENG IX, 84; XI, 79		
	HSR 81		
	SVIB WR'		

Although not extremely attractive, this girl had many good qualities and was well liked. She was dependable, responsible, a strong leader, and emotionally stable. Considered a leader, she was also able to follow and be part of a group. It was mentioned that she had a fine sense of humor.

1049. F:14:4	ACE IX, 23; XI, 53	06'483712–'5	4:9:9
B:V:2	ENG IX, none; XI, 72	6024'738–5'9	3:4:10
	HSR 69		
	SVIB none		

Shortly before the ninth-grade testing this girl's mother had been killed in an accident, and following this loss the girl felt that there was no one with whom she could discuss her problems. This and the fact that the family frequently moved were said to have given the girl a sense of failure and insecurity. At the end of the ninth grade she transferred to another school. Although high school rank and psychometric information were obtained on her, information on her behavior subsequent to the ninth grade was not available. She was interested in entering some sort of professional training after high school.

The family was for many reasons unstable. The income was low and the father, who had a number of severe illnesses, was, at best, not a strong person. He had been hospitalized for both physical and mental illnesses. There had been constant strife between the parents; the father had blamed his wife for all his problems. He was described as a "habitual liar from youth." The home was poorly kept up and the furniture was "junky." As a result of the low moral standards, drinking, and infidelity on the part of both parents, the family was poorly thought of by the neighbors. The other children were considered thoroughly maladjusted.

1050. M:14:5   IQ (centile) 78   0′65–′13   2:6:10
      N:VI:2   HSR DO 11th gr.
                  SVIB none

Lacking in ambition and motivation, this boy gave the impression of being in school for a good time. Although vivacious and outgoing, he was also antagonistic and had a "pugnacious attitude." He was frequently truant and finally failed so badly that he dropped out of school.

1051. F:14:2   ACE IX, 42; XI, 71   ′06742–′935   5:7:12
      N:III:3   ENG IX, 54; XI, 58   ′5–′09   8:4:21
                  HSR 77
                  SVIB ′–

This shy, very conscientious, and quiet girl was well liked and pleasant. She was not a leader but was cooperative and reliable. She was "grade conscious," so that she achieved very well in school and was planning to go on to college. She was active in youth groups, both in and out of church.

   Her father, who was deaf, was a skilled craftsman who operated his own business. He was older than is usual among fathers of ninth-grade children. The mother was active in women's group work. There was one brother who found considerable mutual interest with the father. In all, the family was closely knit and there was no tension.

1052. M:15:3   ACE IX, none; XI, 02   ′068–51′23   3:4:11
      N:V:3   ENG IX, none; XI, 20   ′678549–   4:2:19
                  HSR 33
                  SVIB 4′8–90

A poor student, this boy was best described as immature and lazy but likable. He showed no interest in attending school or in engaging in school activities. He had athletic ability but lacked the "push" to excel. Unusually good looking, he had large, expressive eyes and curly hair. When a junior, he was tagged for reckless driving. After graduation he went to work at a local mill.

   The parents "lived for their children." The father, a semiskilled laborer, was a thoughtful person who went out of his way to help others. The mother, "a shy housewife," spent all her time at home or at church. All the children in the family were attractive, shy, and poor students.

1053. M:14:4   ACE IX, none; XI, 76   ′068–9′32   1:6:11
      N:III:1   ENG IX, none; XI, 35
                  HSR 36
                  SVIB none

The main thing emphasized about this boy was that he was uncertain, indecisive, not sure where he was going or what he wanted to do. His attitude toward school

'068213–

was "a little sour," and he did poor work. "A little on the quiet side," he was no particular conduct problem. There were several times in his senior year when he was tardy for school.

1054. M:15:3	IQ (centile) 35	'068213– 6:8:16
N:VII:1	HSR DO 12th gr.	
	SVIB none	

This boy appeared very unkempt and dirty, and wore his hair long with sideburns. His interest in autos led to several traffic offenses and his license was finally suspended. His school record revealed a long history of disturbances in this setting. He was truant and could get along with neither teachers nor classmates. He was described as moody, sullen, and withdrawn. He had several girl friends and may have been responsible for the illegitimate pregnancy of one of these. It was believed that he quit school at the beginning of the twelfth year in order to join the Army.

1055. F:14:3	ACE IX, 67; XI, 68	0'687–15'29 4:4:11
N:III:3	ENG IX, 85; XI, 85	
	HSR 80	
	SVIB none	

Attractive, well liked, and pleasant, this girl was vivacious and social. She was considered to be personally well adjusted. She transferred to another school during her sophomore or junior year.

The family was described as fine, solid, and well respected, and the children were given an opportunity to do things.

1056. F:14:1	ACE IX, 24; XI, 17	'069847–1'3 1:8:7
N:V:4	ENG IX, 48; XI, 45	06'28 79–5' 6:6:5
	HSR 56	
	SVIB WR'	

Reports about this girl were, in some ways, contradictory. She was described as pleasant, smiling, and well accepted by all. Consistent with these reports, she was active in music, declamation, cheerleading, plays, and the like. She was able to take teasing and criticism. In some contrast, she was also described as quiet and retiring. It was said that it was almost painful for her to speak. There was an interesting contrast between her final class rank and the evidence available relative to her intelligence. Possibly she was overachieving, although it seemed a little more likely that the test score was spuriously low. After graduation she took some additional vocational training and was placed in a very fine position.

The family situation was good, with a fine reputation and noted for participation in church and civic affairs. The father was a small businessman and, although considered uncultured, he was very good company and a "fine, down-to-earth person." The mother was quiet, reserved, and attractive.

1057. F:14:1	ACE IX, 85; XI, 78	'07–3<u>91</u>'	2:3:12
	N:IVA:4	ENG IX, 89; XI, 85	'0876<u>24</u>–1'5	3:6:10
	HSR 78		
	SVIB WR'		

At the time of testing, this girl was described as shy in reciting and reluctant to put herself forward in any way. She was also said to be charming and a pleasant person to have in class. During the following years of high school, her personality seemed to develop in a positive direction, and she became a good leader in church groups. After graduation she attended business college and subsequently became a secretary.

The father, a farmer, was described as quiet, inarticulate, and nervous. He had asthma. The mother was cheerful, pleasant, and a leader in the restricted community in which they lived. There was a younger brother described as quiet but with more "spark" than the girl. In all, it was an excellent family situation, closely knit and very respectable.

1058. M:14:4	ACE IX, none; XI, 44	0'7<u>25</u>–1'39	4:1:11
	N:V:1	ENG IX, none; XI, 43	0'529–13'	2:2:4
	HSR 73		
	SVIB none		

Overweight and physically lazy, this boy was withdrawn but rather good-natured. He "tended to his own business" and was slow to express himself. He seemed to work up to his ability or a little better. At times he was mischievous in class. He had been guilty of one minor traffic violation for which there was no punitive action. During his senior year, he supplemented his schoolwork by a night course.

1059. F:14:7	ACE IX, 82; XI, 46	0'726–5'9	5:0:12
	N:VI:2	ENG IX, none; XI, 65	'207<u>64</u>–'9<u>51</u>	5:5:12
	HSR 94		
	SVIB WR'		

This "very nervous" girl had many worries and anxieties which were half suppressed. Although it was difficult to get her to talk about her problems, when she did talk, she "really unloaded." She was described as an overachiever and a perfectionist who studied until midnight every evening and who could not relax. Not caring to go out, she preferred to stay home and study. She had no friends. A physician who examined her told the school counselor that "she was suffering from a disease and would not live very long." Neither the family nor the girl was told of this finding. She had several "blackouts" during her high school years. Contrastingly, she was said to be friendly, pleasant, and well liked by persons for whom she did odd jobs. One report also called her cooperative, neat, and "working to capacity." She was said to be mature and sensible. She was very close to her mother, although antagonistic toward her father. She went into secretarial work after graduation.

Both the father and the mother were in ill health and were considered inadequate. The father, an alcoholic, was sometimes abusive and he "had a chronic aversion to work." He had at least one period of hospitalization for mental illness. The mother, who seemed "worn down by her burden of work," was sometimes very depressed. She was thought to be of better than average intelligence. She was protective toward her husband and children, all of whom were sickly. Frequently she visited teachers to express her worries over the daughter's studying too much. The home, a "jerry-built affair," was "littered and crowded" and in such poor condition that at times it was almost unlivable.

1060. M:14:2	ACE IX, none; XI, 59	0"7'26514–'9	3:6:4
N:VII:3	ENG IX, 75; XI, 54	70'5682 13–4'	2:4:7
	HSR 57		
	SVIB none		

This was a nice-appearing, conscientious boy who liked school and had many friends. He did what he was told to do but was a bit quiet and engaged in few activities. He was not a conduct problem. While in school he worked at an outside job.

1061. F:14:4	ACE IX, 10; XI, none	'07524–'36	6:1:13
N:IVA:4	ENG IX, 22; XI, none		
	HSR DO 10th gr.		
	SVIB none		

This girl had many friends and was well liked in school. She was attractive, reserved, and always pleasant. Regarded as her father's pet, she would do everything for him. She was given opportunities that her brothers were denied. Not a conduct problem in school, she was believed to be a nice girl, and she caused considerable surprise when she became illegitimately pregnant. She had been going with a boy for a year and she left school to marry him after the tenth grade when the pregnancy became known. After the marriage the couple went to live with the boy's parents and the situation was reported as being good.

Her parents were brokenhearted over the pregnancy, but they made the best of it. The father was described in various ways. He seemed to be a pleasant person to meet but was also described as hardheaded and stubborn. He often kept the children home from school to help with the work on the farm because money and material things were very important to him. The mother was inconspicuous and hard to know. Quiet and retiring, she was dominated by her husband. There were four brothers, one of whom was described as a shy and bashful person who ran away from school because of these traits. By contrast, at least one of the other boys was described as open and friendly.

1062. M:14:9	ACE IX, 69; XI, 74	0'75<u>49</u>–'6	1:4:10
N:IVC:4	ENG IX, none; XI, 87		
	HSR 95		
	SVIB '4–0		

Although this boy was described as "tremendously capable," he was also called an "overachiever." He was class salutatorian and an honor student, and was also president of his class. His teachers said of him that "he would have been outstanding if he could have overcome his slightly shy characteristics."

1063. F:14:3	ACE IX, 46; XI, 56	'07<u>62</u>–'9	1:3:15
N:IVB:4	ENG IX, 72; XI, 88	'<u>60</u>–9'<u>34</u>	4:1:14
	HSR 72		
	SVIB WR'		

The subject was described as a "good average girl," well groomed and cooperative. She was not an active participant in church or school activities, but she did not appear to be rebellious. She did seem self-conscious and blushed frequently. It was suggested that this self-consciousness might come from the fact that she was overweight. She belonged to the girls' athletic association and the future homemaker organization. Her schoolwork was possibly somewhat above the expected achievement.

The father was a poor manager but very outgoing and jovial. In some contrast, the mother was brusque and more dominant, although described as a kind and loyal mother. In all, the family situation was a stable one with a very desirable pattern of social activities.

1064. M:15:5	ACE IX, none; XI, 11	'07629–	1:4:9
N:VI:3	ENG IX, none; XI, 08	6'''8''5<u>907</u>–'<u>23</u>	3:17:11X
	HSR 06		
	SVIB none		

The sole interests of this boy were "hot rods and hunting." Emotionally immature and shy, he was "utterly lacking in social graces." He could not talk to teachers and, when embarrassed, would giggle to cover up this embarrassment. His academic record was poor, although he never misbehaved and he seemed to be conscientious. The police had received complaints about him, but there was no record of any very bad behavior.

1065. F:14:3   ACE IX, 18; XI, 18   07'6852 49–'13   2:7:8
      N:III:2   ENG IX, none; XI, 50   '067825–9'   1:5:7
                    HSR 43
                    SVIB WR'

This girl had absolutely nothing to say and would hardly respond even when spoken to. She was mousy, afraid, and active in nothing. Always clean and well dressed, she was a follower and "a nice student to have around." She was friendly enough with a small group of girls. While still in school she wanted to be a nurse or a librarian, but after graduation she began business school training.

The father was rather lazy, shiftless, and undependable, always putting things off indefinitely. He was a careful but slow workman. He intimidated his children with his sternness. There was some conflict in the home and little affection between the parents. The mother was a fairly adequate person, although she complained a great deal and seemed "bent and worn." The children confided in their mother and were closer to her.

1066. M:14:3   ACE IX, 54; XI, 65   '0768529–1'3   3:5:7
      N:IVB:7   ENG IX, 65; XI, 31
                   HSR 68
                   SVIB '48–

There were very few items reported about this boy. He was not a conduct problem and his teachers considered him well adjusted. He was very popular and an outstanding athlete in several sports.

1067. F:14:3   ACE IX, 79; XI, 65   078'19342–'5   2:5:13
      N:V:2   ENG IX, none; XI, 97
                   HSR 38 DO 12th gr.
                   SVIB WR'

This very much overweight girl was "just too quiet and withdrawn." She rarely talked and when she did, she was noncommittal, never giving expression to her own thought and feelings. Never mixing with her schoolmates, she had few friends and participated in none of the school activities. She was described as a person with "a great deal of insecurity" who appeared to be very unhappy and frequently depressed. She hated school; seemingly, "she was afraid of it." Despite good ability she accomplished very little academically and seemed to be totally devoid of any drive or motivation to achieve. She was almost "habitually" absent, excusing herself on the basis of physical aches and pains. The school, however, took little stock in these complaints and considered her absences to be truancies. She became very discouraged over her schoolwork and wanted to quit during her junior year. Her teachers dissuaded her at that time, but finally she dropped out a few months before graduation. During most of the time she attended high school she worked as a maid. Reportedly she enjoyed working with small children.

She came from a good middle-class home. The mother dressed well, and she was considered friendly and intelligent. Quiet and slow in conversation, she was, nevertheless, rather high-strung. She was anxious for her daughter to finish high school, but she overprotected her and never gave her any responsibility. An older sister of the girl completed high school without difficulty.

1068. M:14:2	ACE IX, none; XI, 69	'082–'53	5:2:12
N:VII:3	ENG IX, none; XI, 27	782'01369–'5	5:4:19
	HSR 11		
	SVIB '489–5		

"Thin, undernourished, and mousy-looking," this boy was not particularly likable. He never took part in school activities; he was not interested in school and was often absent. Even when he came to class, he appeared to be half-asleep. He was most likely to be found on the streets driving either an automobile or a motorcycle. He drove fast and recklessly, seeming to wish to attract attention. He had a police record for careless driving. His ambition was to become a mechanic, and after high school, he took a job in that field.

The father was "kindhearted" but was in a tavern most of the day and night. This was only partly because he had a job as a bartender. After the boy's freshman year his parents separated. The mother was described as "irresponsible and no good"; "she didn't want to be bothered with children." Neither parent cared whether or not the boy attended school.

1069. F:15:5	ACE IX, 05; XI, 08	08'2361745–	3:10:6
N:VI:2	ENG IX, none; XI, 08		
	HSR 18 DO 12th gr.		
	SVIB none		

This girl, who appeared neither clean nor well dressed, was a hard worker with good motivation. Quiet, cooperative, and pleasant, she worked to her full intellectual capacity. She took part in no school activities other than those that were required of her academically. She dropped out of school before graduation to work as a clerk. It was also established that she was pregnant and was forced to get married. The marriage was said to be an unhappy one and the husband was described as "slovenly, sloppy, and rather stupid."

Her parents' home was a very poor one with low economic and moral status. Apparently the father and mother were reasonably affectionate and close to their children. The father, who was easygoing, earned just enough for the family. The mother was a poor housekeeper but was pleasant and interested in her family. One of the other girls in the family became illegitimately pregnant at the same time as our subject but did not know the father of this child. Another of the sisters was described as "wild."

1070. M:14:5   ACE IX, none; XI, 29   '085497–'3   3:5:13
      N:VII:3   ENG IX, none; XI, 32
                  HSR 54
                  SVIB 4'2–9

Although he was liked by his fellow students, this boy was not a good school citizen and was a continual truant. He wanted to do as he pleased and was more interested in hunting than he was in school. He was sent to the principal's office on many occasions and was finally expelled from school just before his graduation. He had been arrested and fined for a traffic offense shortly before he was expelled. After leaving school he worked on a farm for a while, although he finally joined the armed services as an enlisted man.

There was little supervision of the children in this home; they did as they pleased. Neither the father nor the mother was dependable and they never got along together. The father was occasionally fired for drinking, and the mother was considered irresponsible. The parents, who felt that the children were not at fault in their truancy from school, considered their responsibility for their children to be adequately met if they provided material things until each reached the age of eighteen.

1071. F:15:3   ACE IX, 54; XI, 82   '0862 57–'139   4:10:11
      N:III:1   ENG IX, 62; XI, 62   '0627–1'43   4:5:9
                  HSR 39
                  SVIB none

There was general agreement in the description of this girl as an "introvert" who "never registered an expression nor said yes or no." She was further described as shy and afraid to talk in front of a class or strangers. From a somewhat different view, she was described as a "nebulous, passive type of person who never seemed to listen or be interested." In spite of the feeling of her teachers that she did not present much with which to work, she had a high vocational interest in becoming a secretary. It was not known what she did after graduation.

The family, which did not seem to be unusual, was of an average status. The father was ill and hospitalized during one year when the girl was in school. An older brother, who was passive in his manner, was said to be very similar to the girl.

1072. M:14:4   ACE IX, 26; XI, none   0'8672–5'19   4:4:15
      N:IVA:3   ENG IX, 27; XI, none
                  HSR DO 11th gr.
                  SVIB none

In the spring of his junior year this boy dropped out of school after having shown complete indifference to the school situation. His teachers, who could get nothing from him, claimed that he "just filled a seat" and was often absent. He was described as "hardheaded and stubborn." An example of his behavior was his practice of retiring to his room whenever the minister visited the family. His parents let him have a car and permitted him a great deal of freedom, which may have contributed to the fact that he got into trouble for careless driving shortly after quitting school. He joined the armed forces on the spur of the moment and was attached to a unit that traveled about. He frequently wrote to his parents expressing his liking for the service.

The father was described as strong-minded, like the son, as opinionated, and as having "old-fashioned ideas regarding religion." However, he was also described as a fine man, pleasant, friendly, and fair. The mother was considered "jolly" and more easygoing than the father. The family relationship seemed harmonious, and in general the reputation of the family within the community was good.

1073. F:14:8	ACE IX, 34; XI, 36	'0875–'93	4:5:8
N:IVC:5	ENG IX, 29; XI, 34	'954–'1683	3:4:8
	HSR 56		
	SVIB WR'		

Described as a "good girl," although "a little shy and quiet," this youngster worked very hard but was only an average student. She avoided boys and was ashamed of the behavior of some of her sisters. Consciousness of this misbehavior of the sisters may have caused her to be withdrawn.

1074. M:14:5	ACE IX, 98; XI, 97	0'876–24'3	1:5:9
N:IVB:3	ENG IX, 94; XI, 93	78"0'59426–	2:11:8
	HSR 92		
	SVIB '2–5		

This was a nice, steady, highly motivated boy who was well liked by both boys and girls. It was said that he could have been valedictorian of his class but that he had not wanted the attention that this honor would focus on him. In the tenth grade he was considered an underachiever. He was generally described as unusually retiring and reserved. In spite of this tendency to withdraw from public view, he was active in athletics. He apparently had some difficulty in verbal expression. He was a winner of several college scholarships. After high school graduation he went on to a university to major in engineering. It was reported that his achievement continued high.

The boy's father was also described as quiet and reserved. The mother, considered a stronger personality than the father, was active in local affairs. The five other children were all described as outstanding, and several of them were considered leaders. In general it was considered to be a fine family background.

1075. F:14:2   ACE IX, 88; XI, 88   08'762–   3:8:6
      N:V:2   ENG IX, none; XI, 93   0'84–'71   2:4:7
                  HSR 76
                  SVIB '–

This girl was bright, sensitive, and physically attractive, and yet her schoolwork was little better than average and she had few friends. Unhappy, sad, and apparently holding herself in low esteem, she was hard to know and she seemed to some persons almost "sour in disposition." Lacking in enthusiasm, initiative, and drive, she said little, rarely participated in activities with others, and never led. Her teachers believed her schoolwork suffered from poor concentration and poor study habits. She was not always neat or clean and she did not have nice clothes. Her poor grooming and her limited participation in school social activities were attributed at least in part to a lack of money. One person said that her personality development was "thwarted because of the poor economic status of her family; she was a good, honest, hard-working girl starved for affection and luxuries." Although she seldom dated and never got into trouble, she was reportedly "a heavy necker." Thought to be deeply troubled, she did not discuss her problems with anyone. She lost the first job she had after completing high school because of her personality and lack of skill in meeting and working with people. She then found and kept a low-level job.

The home was dirty, untidy, and disorderly. There was little warmth or affection in the family, and the parents were said to be generally lax in supervision of their children. Another report claimed, however, that the father was very watchful of the girl and gave her little freedom. The father had been away from home much of the time when the girl was younger. The mother was eager that her daughter get a job, but she was described as lazy, unambitious, and oblivious of her children's needs.

1076. F:14:3   ACE IX, 77; XI, 81   0'879–'351   2:6:11
      N:V:4   ENG IX, 78; XI, 81   0'829 734–   4:4:9
                  HSR 71
                  SVIB WR'

This girl had a beautiful complexion, but she was much overweight. In general, she was described as dependable and responsible. "A good speaker who could think on her feet," she was poised and self-confident but without any particular talents. More critical description of her said that she was gossipy, careless, and not working up to capacity. She was too eager to please and lacking in the kind of social consciousness that would make her really acceptable. She wanted to go on to college, but her teachers doubted that she would succeed because she would not make the effort.

The father did not earn enough to provide the necessities in the home. The mother worked steadily and was the dominant member of the family. In general, the family appeared to be uncultured, untrained, simple, and sincere people.

1077. M:14:7   ACE IX, 11; XI, 43   '0892–31'47   3:6:6
      N:IVB:3   ENG IX, none; XI, 27   89'26703–   3:15:9
                      HSR 25
                      SVIB none

This boy was cooperative, and he worked up to his capacity. Described as shy and quiet, he was not a leader and very slow to make friends.

1078. F:15:2   ACE IX, 45; XI, 30   '09–1'83267   3:2:10
      N:V:1   ENG IX, none; XI, 22   '5439–'18   5:4:10
                      HSR 36
                      SVIB none

A twin, this girl was shy, timid, and not a leader. [The twin's MMPI codes were, ninth grade, '54–'912 5:1:16, and, twelfth grade, '59–2'6170 3:1:16. See p. 145 in this volume.] She was a mediocre student and seemed to be intent upon finishing high school as soon as possible in order to be married. She "had an eye for the boys" and the social aspects of life meant much more to her than any other interest. She was friendly and well liked. In the end she was forced into marriage and reported to be a poor homemaker, irresponsible, and immature as a mother, and although marriage had seemed to be her goal, she was described as unhappy with the problem of being a housewife and a mother.

There was little information about the family. The twin sister was said to be like the subject although perhaps of somewhat higher ability. This twin sister was also married early.

1079. M:14:1   ACE IX, 72; XI, 53   '09–2'6517   2:4:8
      N:V:5   ENG IX, 75; XI, 85   9'43–'250   0:2:14
                      HSR 43
                      SVIB 4'–

Relatively mature and personable, "this boy was attractive and he knew it." He "thought he was a woman charmer and would show off to the female teachers." In general, he had many social graces and was well liked by other students. It was particularly mentioned that he was good in English. He liked sports, went hunting and fishing, and was interested in music. After graduation he entered the armed services.

The family reputation and home situation were fairly good, chiefly because of the qualities of the father, who was a skilled workman. The boy was very close to him; and, like his son, the father was a hunter and a fisherman. He was an active leader in the community and in church. He tried very hard to keep the children at home and well taken care of. The mother, who was never home, was said to prefer a career. Although admired for her competence, she was criticized for not being a good mother. A daughter, who was insecure and much in need of her mother, was rejected and sought to compensate by confiding in a school counselor.

1080. M:15:3   ACE IX, none; XI, 50   '09248–1'36   2:5:10
      N:V:1   ENG IX, none; XI, 35   '0497 28–'6   3:6:17
                      HSR 11
                      SVIB none

A boy with "a happy disposition," this youth was also quiet, a dreamer, and slow to perform. He was neither well dressed nor very mannerly. In class he put forth little or no effort except under pressure, and he was not a good student. Careless, restless, and lazy, he directed his energies toward looking for ways to get out of work. His teachers felt he could have done better work if he had tried. Despite this, he caused no trouble and was not a discipline problem in school. Outside of school he was "a motorcycle boy," wearing the traditional garb and associating with friends who were described as "a crumby bunch." Troubled by a chronic physical disorder since the age of twelve, he was nevertheless accepted for military service after completing high school.

1081. M:14:1   ACE IX, 95; XI, 84   '0956–1'   5:10:5
      N:III:2   ENG IX, none; XI, 74   '90 35–'6   6:4:12
                      HSR 89
                      SVIB 4'12–

This was a "good substantial boy," who made a fine adjustment and was well liked. He was neat, dependable, industrious, mature, cooperative, and trustworthy. In manner he was quiet, somewhat reserved, but not withdrawn. He had some leadership ability and held minor class offices. He was on the honor roll and took part in several extracurricular activities. After graduation he entered a teachers' college with the hope of eventually going into pharmacy.

The father, although pretty strict with his children, was close to them and trusted them. He had a strong personality; he was intelligent and a successful skilled workman. He was not very active in community affairs. No information was given about the mother. The family lived in a good home, relatively luxurious in furnishings.

1082. F:14:7   ACE IX, 08; XI, 20   '095742–1'6   2:5:12
      N:IVB:6   ENG IX, 27; XI, 24
                      HSR 30
                      SVIB none

Neat and well liked, this girl was very quiet, unassuming, and tended to mind her own business. Although she was "worth while," she was not outstanding in anything. It was said of her that "although she might get silly, she never overstepped." She was active in some musical areas and in a science club.

1083. F:15:4   ACE IX, 59; XI, 90   '0968–'531   4:6:12
      N:V:3   ENG IX, 57; XI, 61
                 HSR 74
                 SVIB WR'

A "shy, blushing blonde," this girl lacked confidence and was "easily confused." She was well accepted by students. She did well enough in her schoolwork, except that she seemed to be limited in her vocabulary development. She took an active part in 4-H projects.

1084. M:15:8   IQ (centile) 21   '0974–5'1   4:9:14
      N:VII:2   HSR DO 11th gr.
                 SVIB none

"A pleasant kid who enjoyed life," this boy was "forever truant." He was also said to have "a chip on his shoulder." Indifferent to school, he found excuses for everything, and he dropped out of school in his junior year. Two of his teachers expected that he would get into trouble with the law, and there were some minor delinquencies which were not specified.

1085. M:15:3   ACE IX, 17; XI, none   '09758–1'3   2:7:4
      N:VI:2   ENG IX, none; XI, none
                 HSR DO 11th gr.
                 SVIB none

Large for his age, this boy was sloppy in dress and was dirty looking. Although robust and healthy, he was absent from school nearly one day out of five and his mother always wrote his excuses. At the beginning of his junior year he dropped out of school and joined the armed forces. It was believed that he would have been a discipline problem if he had continued in school, and he would no doubt have had difficulty finishing with a satisfactory record. He daydreamed, puttered, and was indifferent, needing constant prodding to do the work that he finally turned in. Socially he did not mix well and he engaged in no activities. He spent a relatively short time in the armed forces and returned home, where he was reported to be idle.

In general, his home was not badly kept, although it was "a bit dirty." The father was "a big, pleasant fellow on the quiet side," who was steady, calm, and a good provider. The mother was nervous and high-strung and tended to defend the children when they got into any trouble. She was often ill and made much over her illnesses. A younger brother was described as rebellious and surly.

1086. F:14:1   ACE IX, none; XI, 73   0'978–31'52 1:3:7
   N:IVB:3   ENG IX, 63; XI, 74   07'82–431'5 4:5:12
           HSR 57
           SVIB none

This girl was unobtrusive and nonassertive. She "kept busy at activities." She had many friends, most of them from her church group. She liked school and her teachers. She seemed well adjusted and was not a conduct problem.

1087. M:15:4   ACE IX, 90; XI, 82   '09784– 2:10:14
   N:VI:3   ENG IX, 81; XI, 52
           HSR 09
           SVIB '90–

This boy, an underachiever in school, mostly liked outdoor activities. He often went hunting, fishing, and swimming, and liked to work in the fields. He had very little interest in schoolwork and needed to be prodded. He was a "mature boy."

1088. F:14:6   ACE IX, 02; XI, 26   '0986–1'25 3:9:5
   N:VI:2   ENG IX, none; XI, 09 '954–2'16 3:4:7
           HSR 25
           SVIB WR'

Considered well adjusted, well balanced, cooperative, friendly, and solid, this girl "never gave any trouble." She was exceedingly quiet and a little "hayseedish." Her scholastic achievement was reasonably good in the light of her abilities. She improved in scholastic and personality development as she progressed through school. After graduation she worked in a clerical capacity.

  The family lived on a very modest income in a small community. The parents had an elementary school education. The relationship between the mother and the girl was said to be especially close.

APPENDIX TABLES AND INDEXES

Appendix Tables

Appendix Table 1. General T-Score Norms for the Statewide Sample

| | Boys [a] | | | | | | Girls [b] | | | | | |
| | Valid | | High L | | High F | | Valid | | High L | | High F | |
Scale	Mean Score	S.D.	Mean Score	S.D.	Mean Score	S.D.	Mean Score	S.D.	Mean Score	S.D.	Mean Score	S.D.
L	4	2.2	11	0.1	4	2.3	4	2.1	11	0.1	3	2.1
F	6	4.7	5	3.3	18	1.7	5	3.3	5	3.5	18	1.6
K	14	5.0	20	4.3	11	4.5	14	4.6	20	4.7	9	4.2
1	50	9.2	57	10.3	60	13.6	48	8.6	53	8.6	54	9.4
2	52	10.7	60	9.4	63	13.6	49	8.8	53	8.3	56	9.9
3	52	8.4	59	8.6	57	10.5	52	8.5	56	8.3	55	10.1
4	59	10.3	62	9.9	68	11.6	59	9.3	60	10.1	70	12.9
5	50	9.3	50	7.7	54	9.4	53	9.8	56	8.7	58	10.5
6	55	9.7	54	9.1	72	10.5	56	9.7	54	8.6	73	12.2
7	58	10.0	57	8.0	73	11.3	57	8.3	54	6.7	67	9.0
8	61	11.8	61	9.8	88	12.6	59	9.8	58	8.0	80	11.8
9	59	11.5	55	8.8	71	10.8	57	11.7	53	9.4	70	11.6
0	54	8.9	53	7.4	61	7.3	55	9.3	53	8.4	61	9.0

[a] The mean valid profile for the boys had the code '84976-.
[b] The mean valid profile for the girls had the code '48 7960-.

Appendix Table 2. Code Stability for the Boys

| | Frequency as High Scale in 9th-Grade Profiles | | | Percentage of Boys with Highest 9th-Grade Scale in 1st or 2nd Place on Retest Code | | | Percentage of Boys with Highest 9th-Grade Scale among 1st Three Low Points on Retest Code | | |
Scale	T < 70	T ≥ 70	Total	T < 70	T ≥ 70	Total	T < 70	T ≥ 70	Total
1	0.9	0.9	1.8	8	22	15	0	7	3
2	2.1	2.0	4.1	16	39	27	14	6	10
3	2.5	0.2	2.7	37	44	38	2	0	2
4	10.5	7.7	18.2	51	75	60	0	0	0
5	3.3	1.3	4.6	44	73	52	8	0	6
6	3.2	2.6	5.8	26	16	22	5	1	3
7	3.7	4.0	7.7	24	38	31	4	1	3
8	5.9	12.7	18.6	31	39	37	6	3	4
9	9.6	11.4	21.0	41	59	50	3	4	4
0	6.2	1.3	7.5	31	55	34	10	0	9

375

Appendix Table 3. Code Stability for the Girls

Scale	Frequency as High Scale in 9th-Grade Profiles			Percentage of Girls with Highest 9th-Grade Scale in 1st or 2nd Place on Retest Code			Percentage of Girls with Highest 9th-Grade Scale among 1st Three Low Points on Retest Code		
	T < 70	T ≥ 70	Total	T < 70	T ≥ 70	Total	T < 70	T ≥ 70	Total
1	0.2	0.2	0.4	0	33	17	17	0	8
2	0.9	0.6	1.5	7	24	15	10	0	6
3	3.0	0.9	3.9	54	50	53	0	3	1
4	12.0	7.9	19.9	47	65	53	2	1	2
5	8.4	3.6	12.0	29	45	34	10	10	10
6	5.1	3.8	8.9	25	25	25	4	7	5
7	3.6	1.6	5.2	24	33	36	2	0	2
8	4.6	5.6	10.2	24	31	28	1	2	1
9	8.1	9.3	17.4	37	56	47	7	4	5
0	9.3	2.8	12.1	42	64	47	6	3	5

Appendix Table 4. Percentage of Valid and High L and F Profiles

Validity Scale	Boys	Girls	All
L			
Valid (L = 0–9).....................	97.4	97.7	97.6
High L (L ≥ 10)......................	2.6	2.3	2.4
F			
Valid (F = 0–15).....................	91.4	96.5	93.9
High F (F = 16–21).................	5.6	2.9	4.3
UHF (F ≥ 22).......................	3.0	0.6	1.8
Both L and F valid (L < 10; F < 16)........	88.8	94.2	91.5

Appendix Table 5. Rates per Thousand of the First Two High and Low Points in Profiles of the Boys and Frequency of Delinquency and Dropouts among Boys in Each Two-High-Point Code Class [a]

Code Class	Rates per 1000 [b]				Percentage of Delinquents among Boys in Each Code Class			Percentage of Dropouts among Boys in Each Code Class
	T < 70	T ≥ 70 [c]	Total High	Total Low	T < 70	T ≥ 70 [c]	Total	
Invalid Profiles								
L ≥ 10			26				23	20
F = 16–21			56				41	32
F ≥ 22			30				45	48
? ≥ 40			8				37	16
Valid Profiles								
Indet.[d]	55	8	63	37	30	41	34	10
No high point..	16	0	0	16	28	0	28	14
1–	0	0	0†	29	67	0	67†	33†
12	1	0	1†	12	43	33	40†	10†
13	2	1	4	33	30	69	44	11
14	1	2	3	4	36	41	39	21
15	0	0	0†	8	0	0	0†	0†
16	1	1	1†	4	0	33	20†	20†
17	1	1	2†	3	25	18	21†	5†
18	1	3	4	3	36	40	39	11
19	1	1	2†	3	10	60	27†	20†
10	1	1	2†	3	38	33	35†	29†
Total 1.......	9	9	18	103	32	42	37	16
2–	3	0	3	37	21	0	21	36
21	1	1	2†	20	20	33	25†	6†
23	1	1	2†	16	25	14	21†	16†
24	4	4	8	5	44	32	39	25
25	1	1	2	22	8	33	21	8
26	1	1	2†	7	36	20	31†	0†
27	2	3	5	5	40	33	35	18
28	1	4	5	1	47	15	25	14
29	2	1	3	4	37	0	23	7
20	4	4	9	19	29	18	24	24
Total 2.......	21	20	41	134	33	23	33	19
3–	3	0	3	25	40	0	40	13
31	2	1	3	20	30	33	31	4
32	2	0	2†	5	24	0	20†	10†
34	6	1	7	2	23	0	22	9
35	2	0	2†	6	33	0	33†	11†
36	3	0	3	3	23	100	26	4
37	2	1	3	1	13	33	17	0
38	2	0	2†	0	20	100	24†	10†
39	2	0	2	1	28	0	26	5
30	1	0	1†	1	25	0	25†	0†
Total 3.......	25	2	27	64	26	26	26	7

[a] An asterisk (*) indicates the two-point code is among the fifteen most common; italics set off the corresponding rates and percentages. A dagger (†) is used to indicate that there are fewer than eleven in the total two-point code class.

[b] Rates per thousand are used because of the small numbers that occur in many of the code classes. Since numbers are rounded off, the figure in the total column is not always the sum of the figures in the preceding columns.

[c] The height of the first point only in each code class was considered.

[d] Included in the "indeterminate" class are all codes with underscoring on the first three or more high points. If underscoring occurred on the first two high points only, one-half a tally was assigned to the first high point and one-half a tally to the second high point.

377

Code Class	Rates per 1000				Percentage of Delinquents among Boys in Each Code Class			Percentage of Dropouts among Boys in Each Code Class
	T < 70	T ≥ 70	Total High	Total Low	T < 70	T ≥ 70	Total	
4–	10	1	10	7	35	67	37	16
41	4	4	8	3	28	22	25	36
42	7	6	13	3	32	46	39	17
°43	*14*	6	*20*	3	*28*	*40*	*31*	*14*
45	6	3	9	1	46	52	48	11
°46	*10*	9	*19*	1	*43*	*60*	*51*	*20*
°47	*9*	*10*	*19*	1	*29*	*43*	*36*	*17*
°48	*15*	*22*	*37*	1	*43*	*55*	*50*	*21*
°49	*24*	*17*	*41*	2	*50*	*60*	*54*	*25*
40	6	1	7	0	52	14	44	17
Total 4.......	105	77	182	23	40	51	45	20
5–	4	0	4	72	10	0	10	10
51	0	0	0†	11	0	0	0†	0†
52	2	2	4	13	15	33	23	9
53	2	1	3	15	5	44	17	10
54	6	2	8	2	24	39	28	11
56	4	2	6	11	24	21	23	10
57	3	1	4	3	43	31	40	7
58	3	3	6	1	22	27	24	5
59	4	2	6	11	44	28	39	9
50	3	1	5	15	26	9	22	9
Total 5.......	33	13	47	154	24	28	26	9
6–	4	0	4	21	53	0	50	10
61	1	0	1†	5	0	0	0†	0†
62	1	0	2†	4	10	50	21†	14†
63	2	1	3	6	13	29	16	0
64	4	5	9	2	31	44	38	22
65	3	2	5	10	39	53	44	6
67	2	2	4	2	13	33	23	23
68	4	8	12	1	26	24	24	15
69	5	5	10	4	42	47	44	20
60	5	2	7	4	18	11	16	20
Total 6.......	32	26	58	59	29	34	31	16
7–	2	0	2†	2	20	0	20†	0†
71	1	0	1†	3	50	50	50†	20†
72	2	3	5	3	14	17	15	8
73	2	1	3	1	35	0	23	7
74	5	5	10	1	34	48	41	21
75	2	1	3	2	24	50	30	0
76	3	2	5	1	36	24	31	10
°78	8	*20*	28	1	*45*	*21*	28	*18*
79	5	4	9	1	22	31	26	13
70	7	4	11	2	26	33	29	10
Total 7.......	37	40	77	17	31	27	29	14
8–	2	0	2	1	8	0	8	17
81	2	5	8	3	42	52	49	19
82	1	6	7	0	58	29	34	34
83	3	1	4	0	23	50	31	14
°84	*10*	*20*	*30*	0	*33*	*38*	*36*	*26*
85	3	2	5	1	11	24	17	15
°86	*6*	*13*	*19*	1	*28*	*42*	*38*	*26*
°87	*11*	*43*	*54*	1	*35*	*34*	*35*	*19*
°89	*12*	*31*	*44*	1	*36*	*38*	*37*	*20*
80	8	5	13	0	18	30	23	20
Total 8.......	59	127	186	8	30	37	35	22

Code Class	Rates per 1000				Percentage of Delinquents among Boys in Each Code Class			Percentage of Dropouts among Boys in Each Code Class
	T < 70	T ≥ 70	Total High	Total Low	T < 70	T ≥ 70	Total	
*9–	*18*	*2*	*21*	44	*41*	*33*	*40*	*11*
91	2	1	3	4	33	22	30	9
92	2	1	3	2	46	11	36	15
93	6	2	8	2	33	44	35	7
*94	*21*	*30*	*51*	2	*41*	*48*	*45*	*17*
95	6	6	13	11	21	34	28	10
*96	*7*	*12*	*19*	5	*29*	*42*	*37*	*12*
*97	*7*	*10*	*18*	2	*27*	*35*	*32*	*8*
*98	*17*	*46*	*63*	2	*31*	*34*	*33*	*12*
90	9	3	12	3	22	44	28	18
Total 9.......	96	114	210	77	34	39	36	13
0–	11	1	12	42	33	33	33	18
01	1	0	1†	3	9	0	8†	8†
02	7	2	8	10	8	17	10	1
03	1	0	1†	1	16	0	15†	8†
04	5	1	6	0	22	50	25	12
05	6	1	7	11	12	0	11	5
06	6	1	7	2	20	55	26	14
07	8	4	12	2	25	30	27	13
08	9	3	12	0	22	18	21	13
09	8	1	8	5	17	25	18	13
Total 0.......	62	13	75	76	21	27	22	11
Total valid sample					31	38	34	15

Appendix Table 6. Rates per Thousand of the First Two High and Low Points in Profiles of the Girls and Frequency of Delinquency and Dropouts among Girls in Each Two-High-Point Code Class [a]

Code Class	Rates per 1000 [b]				Percentage of Delinquents among Girls in Each Code Class	Percentage of Dropouts among Girls in Each Code Class
	T < 70	T ≥ 70 [c]	Total High	Total Low		
		Invalid Profiles				
L ≥ 10			23		5	18
F = 16–21			29		28	32
F ≥ 22			6		21	29
? ≥ 40			5		13	13
		Valid Profiles				
Indet.[d]	62	8	70	46	8	13

[a] An asterisk (*) indicates the two-point code is among the fifteen most common; italics set off the corresponding rates and percentages. A dagger (†) is used to indicate that there are fewer than eleven in the total two-point code class.

[b] Rates per thousand are used because of the small numbers that occur in many of the code classes. Since numbers are rounded off, the figure in the total column is not always the sum of the figures in the preceding columns.

[c] The height of the first point only in each code class was considered.

[d] Included in the "indeterminate" class are all codes with underscoring on the first three or more high points. If underscoring occurred on the first two high points only, one-half a tally was assigned to the first high point and one-half a tally to the second high point.

Code Class	Rates per 1000				Percentage of Delinquents among Girls in Each Code Class	Percentage of Dropouts among Girls in Each Code Class
	T < 70	T ≧ 70	Total High	Total Low		
No high point......	16	0	0	16	2	7
1–	0	0	0†	41	0†	0†
12	0	0	1†	21	0†	50†
13	0	0	1†	38	9†	9†
14	0	0	1†	5	20†	20†
15	0	0	1†	13	25†	50†
16	0	0	0†	9	0†	0†
17	0	0	0†	3	0†	0†
18	0	0	1†	3	20†	30†
19	0	0	0†	7	0†	100†
10	0	0	0†	4	0†	0†
Total 1..........	2	2	4	144	12	26
2–	1	0	1†	48	0†	20†
21	0	0	0†	31	0†	0†
23	1	1	2†	18	0†	21†
24	1	1	2	4	0	12
25	0	0	0†	10	0†	33†
26	1	0	1†	9	0†	9†
27	1	1	2†	6	0†	8†
28	1	1	2†	0	11†	33†
29	0	0	0†	5	0†	25†
20	3	2	5	36	2	21
Total 2..........	9	6	15	166	2	19
3–	3	0	3	22	7	0
31	1	2	3	25	9	12
32	1	1	2	8	5	5
34	9	3	12	2	8	18
35	2	0	3	2	0	13
36	4	0	4	4	7	12
37	2	1	3	1	13	13
38	4	1	5	0	7	11
39	2	0	3	4	13	20
30	1	0	1†	0	0†	0†
Total 3..........	30	9	39	69	7	13
4–	9	0	9	3	7	9
41	2	1	2	3	25	33
42	4	2	7	3	7	17
°43	*14*	*8*	*22*	*2*	*10*	*15*
°45	*17*	*4*	*21*	*1*	*13*	*15*
°46	*14*	*15*	*28*	*1*	*22*	*26*
°47	*14*	*7*	*21*	*2*	*10*	*13*
°48	*17*	*17*	*34*	*0*	*17*	*21*
°49	*19*	*20*	*39*	*3*	*20*	*18*
40	10	4	14	0	14	19
Total 4..........	120	79	199	20	15	18
5–	17	4	21	70	9	9
51	1	0	1†	16	9†	0†
52	2	1	3	12	4	18
53	4	1	4	4	4	12
°54	*14*	*7*	*21*	*2*	*6*	*16*
56	5	4	9	3	9	13
57	5	1	6	1	4	11

| Code Class | Rates per 1000 | | | | Percentage of Delinquents among Girls in Each Code Class | Percentage of Dropouts among Girls in Each Code Class |
	T < 70	T ≥ 70	Total High	Total Low		
58	9	5	14	1	9	17
*59	13	9	22	12	9	11
50	15	5	20	10	9	11
Total 5	84	36	120	131	8	12
6–	5	0	5	8	4	4
61	0	0	0†	8	0†	0†
62	1	0	2†	8	5†	10†
63	4	1	5	5	2	12
64	9	10	18	1	11	17
65	4	1	5	2	4	19
67	6	5	11	2	11	6
68	6	12	18	1	10	17
69	7	5	12	5	5	10
60	9	4	13	2	5	5
Total 6	51	38	89	52	8	12
7–	3	0	3	3	13	13
71	0	0	1†	1	0†	0†
72	1	1	2	2	0	0
73	2	0	2	1	8	8
74	5	2	7	1	12	7
75	3	0	3	0	11	11
76	3	2	5	2	9	5
78	9	6	15	1	9	14
79	4	2	5	2	11	5
70	5	2	7	1	6	5
Total 7	36	16	52	12	9	9
8–	2	0	2	1	9	0
81	0	2	2†	1	25†	30†
82	1	1	2†	0	6†	17†
83	2	2	4	0	14	11
84	8	6	14	0	11	13
85	5	3	8	0	7	13
86	5	11	15	0	8	20
*87	10	13	23	0	12	14
89	7	13	20	1	10	25
80	6	5	11	0	6	19
Total 8	46	56	102	4	10	17
9–	8	1	9	48	6	10
91	0	1	1†	13	9†	9†
92	1	0	1†	6	8†	15†
93	3	2	5	6	2	4
*94	16	25	41	5	17	17
*95	15	12	27	12	13	16
*96	8	13	21	5	16	18
97	8	7	15	4	7	11
*98	14	30	44	3	12	15
90	7	3	10	5	6	17
Total 9	81	93	174	107	12	15
0–	13	1	14	27	3	5
01	1	0	1†	4	15†	15†
02	5	4	9	18	7	11
03	2	0	3	1	0	11

381

Code Class	Rates per 1000				Percentage of Delinquents among Girls in Each Code Class	Percentage of Dropouts among Girls in Each Code Class
	T < 70	T ≧ 70	Total High	Total Low		
04	9	4	13	0	5	10
°05	18	2	21	6	9	9
06	11	4	15	2	7	15
°07	15	6	21	1	7	6
08	11	6	17	0	4	11
09	6	1	7	3	4	43
Total 0	93	28	120	62	6	9
Total valid sample . .					10	14

Appendix Table 7. Adjective Ranks for Single High-Point Codes among the Boys

Adjective or Pair	Rank	Adjective or Pair	Rank
Scale 1		*Scale 4*	
Stubborn-hostile	2.5	Stubborn-hostile	2.5
Leader-very popular	2.5	Truant	3.5
Introvert-quiet	3	Follower-indifferent	4
Pleasing-well mannered	4	Leader-very popular	5.5
Cooperative-conscientious	5	Lazy-undependable	7.5
Erratic-unhappy	8	Mature	8.5
Mature	8.5	Unlikable	9
Unlikable	9	Erratic-unhappy	10
Lazy-undependable	10.5	Cooperative-conscientious	10
Truant	10.5	Introvert-quiet	12
Follower-indifferent	11	Pleasing-well mannered	12
Scale 2		*Scale 5*	
Pleasing-well mannered	5	Mature	1
Erratic-unhappy	5	Leader-very popular	2.5
Lazy-undependable	6	Unlikable	3.5
Cooperative-conscientious	6.5	Cooperative-conscientious	4
Introvert-quiet	6.5	Stubborn-hostile	6
Mature	7	Pleasing-well mannered	7
Truant	8	Truant	8
Stubborn-hostile	8	Follower-indifferent	8.5
Follower-indifferent	8.5	Introvert-quiet	8.5
Leader-very popular	9.5	Erratic-unhappy	11
Unlikable	11	Lazy-undependable	12
Scale 3		*Scale 6*	
Cooperative-conscientious	1	Leader-very popular	1
Introvert-quiet	2	Lazy-undependable	4
Pleasing-well mannered	2	Mature	4.5
Leader-very popular	4	Pleasing-well mannered	6
Mature	4.5	Follower-indifferent	6.5
Erratic-unhappy	5	Truant	8
Truant	6	Introvert-quiet	8.5
Unlikable	6.5	Cooperative-conscientious	9
Lazy-undependable	7.5	Erratic-unhappy	9
Stubborn-hostile	10.5	Stubborn-hostile	9
Follower-indifferent	12	Unlikable	12

Adjective or Pair	Rank	Adjective or Pair	Rank
Scale 7		*Scale 0*	
Pleasing-well mannered...........	3	Introvert-quiet	1
Mature	4.5	Unlikable	2
Erratic-unhappy	5	Mature	2
Cooperative-conscientious	6.5	Cooperative-conscientious	3
Unlikable	6.5	Lazy-undependable	3
Introvert-quiet	6.5	Follower-indifferent	5
Follower-indifferent	6.5	Truant	5.5
Lazy-undependable	9	Leader-very popular.............	7.5
Leader-very popular	9.5	Stubborn-hostile	10.5
Truant	12	Pleasing-well mannered	11
Stubborn-hostile	12	Erratic-unhappy	12
Scale 8		*High L*	
Follower-indifferent	3	Erratic-unhappy	1
Unlikable	3.5	Pleasing-well mannered	1
Stubborn-hostile	5	Unlikable	1
Lazy-undependable	5	Lazy-undependable	2
Erratic-unhappy	7	Cooperative-conscientious	2
Cooperative-conscientious	8	Follower-indifferent	2
Pleasing-well mannered...........	10	Truant	2
Introvert-quiet	10	Mature	4.5
Truant	10.5	Introvert-quiet	4.5
Leader-very popular.............	11	Leader-very popular.............	5.5
Mature	12	Stubborn-hostile	7
Scale 9		*High F*	
Erratic-unhappy	2.5	Stubborn-hostile	1
Stubborn-hostile	4	Lazy-undependable	1
Introvert-quiet	4.5	Follower-indifferent	1
Truant	5	Truant	1
Unlikable	5	Erratic-unhappy	2.5
Leader-very popular	7.5	Pleasing-well mannered	8
Mature	8.5	Mature	8.5
Pleasing-well mannered...........	9	Unlikable	9
Follower-indifferent	10	Introvert-quiet	11
Lazy-undependable	10.5	Cooperative-conscientious	11.5
Cooperative-conscientious	11.5	Leader-very popular.............	12

Appendix Table 8. Adjective Ranks for Single High-Point
Codes among the Girls

Adjective or Pair	Rank	Adjective or Pair	Rank
Scale 2		*Scale 3*	
Cooperative-conscientious	2	Mature	2
Introvert-quiet	3	Pleasing-well mannered...........	2
Unlikable	5	Leader-very popular	3.5
Truant	7	Peppy-scatterbrained	4
Erratic-unhappy	7	Cooperative-conscientious	6
Peppy-scatterbrained	8	Follower-indifferent	8.5
Pleasing-well mannered...........	8	Erratic-unhappy	8.5
Lazy-undependable	9	Stubborn-hostile	9
Leader-very popular.............	9.5	Introvert-quiet	9
Follower-indifferent	10	Unlikable	9.5
Stubborn-hostile	11	Truant	10.5
Mature	11	Lazy-undependable	11

Adjective or Pair	Rank	Adjective or Pair	Rank
Scale 4		Introvert-quiet	4
Truant	1	Stubborn-hostile	4
Mature	2	Mature	6
Stubborn-hostile	2	Cooperative-conscientious	9.5
Lazy-undependable	3	Pleasing-well mannered	10
Leader-very popular	5	Leader-very popular	11
Peppy-scatterbrained	6		
Introvert-quiet	6	*Scale 9*	
Unlikable	8	Peppy-scatterbrained	1
Erratic-unhappy	8.5	Truant	2
Follower-indifferent	8.5	Stubborn-hostile	3
Pleasing-well mannered	9	Leader-very popular	3.5
Cooperative-conscientious	11	Pleasing-well mannered	3.5
		Mature	4
Scale 5		Lazy-undependable	4.5
Peppy-scatterbrained	2	Cooperative-conscientious	5
Leader-very popular	2	Erratic-unhappy	5.5
Follower-indifferent	3	Unlikable	7
Unlikable	4	Follower-indifferent	11
Pleasing-well mannered	5	Introvert-quiet	11
Introvert-quiet	5		
Erratic-unhappy	5.5	*Scale 0*	
Cooperative-conscientious	7.5	Introvert-quiet	2
Stubborn-hostile	8	Erratic-unhappy	4
Truant	8.5	Lazy-undependable	4.5
Lazy-undependable	9	Truant	5
Mature	10	Follower-indifferent	5
		Unlikable	6
Scale 6		Pleasing-well mannered	6
Cooperative-conscientious	3	Cooperative-conscientious	7.5
Pleasing-well mannered	3.5	Mature	8
Stubborn-hostile	5	Leader-very popular	9.5
Leader-very popular	6	Peppy-scatterbrained	10
Lazy-undependable	6.5	Stubborn-hostile	10
Follower-indifferent	7		
Mature	7	*High L*	
Introvert-quiet	8	Introvert-quiet	1
Truant	8.5	Pleasing-well mannered	1
Peppy-scatterbrained	9	Erratic-unhappy	2
Unlikable	9.5	Follower-indifferent	2
Erratic-unhappy	11	Unlikable	2.5
		Cooperative-conscientious	4
Scale 7		Mature	5
Cooperative-conscientious	1	Stubborn-hostile	6.5
Leader-very popular	1	Leader-very popular	7
Mature	2	Lazy-undependable	9
Follower-indifferent	6	Truant	10.5
Truant	6	Peppy-scatterbrained	11
Peppy-scatterbrained	6		
Lazy-undependable	6.5	*High F*	
Stubborn-hostile	6.5	Erratic-unhappy	1
Pleasing-well mannered	7	Stubborn-hostile	1
Erratic-unhappy	10	Lazy-undependable	1
Introvert-quiet	10	Unlikable	1
Unlikable	11	Follower-indifferent	1
		Truant	3.5
Scale 8		Peppy-scatterbrained	6
Lazy-undependable	2	Introvert-quiet	7
Unlikable	2.5	Leader-very popular	8
Erratic-unhappy	3	Mature	9
Peppy-scatterbrained	3	Cooperative-conscientious	9.5
Truant	3.5	Pleasing-well mannered	11
Follower-indifferent	4		

Appendix Table 9. Frequency of SVIB Primary, Secondary,
and Reject Codes [a]

Code Group	Primary	Secondary	Reject
Boys			
1	2%	10%	3%
2	3	7	7
4	35	27	0.3
5	2	4	22
8	8	25	0.3
9	5	13	8
0	2	6	15
Girls			
WR	53	18	0

[a] 5 per cent of the boys' profiles and 28 per cent of the girls' profiles were classified as '– codes.

High Point Index

OF TWELFTH-GRADE AND COLLEGE CODES

All twelfth-grade and college codes are listed in one numerical order in this index, with the college testings differentiated by a dagger after the code. On the indented line below each entry is the subject's ninth-grade code, under which in the numerical sequence followed in the body of this volume the summary for the case is to be found. Permutations of twelfth-grade or college codes having the first two or more digits underscored are *not* listed. The reader should keep in mind that there is frequent underscoring among these codes — mainly because MMPI profiles from more average persons such as these juveniles show little dispersion of score values over scales. Thus the index should be consulted for all points of a reference code when it shows several underscored or relatively equal high points.

-21'75† F
  '4572038-'91
-'2178 M
  -4'
-2178'063 M
  '56439-1'20
-24'671 F
  '7-21'60
-45261'37† M
  9'87-25'43
-45'62† F
  '6-5'231
-4'58 F
  '954-631'2
-'460† F
  -1'385
-7'928 M
  6'458-1'73
-'9 F
  '0568-'193
-91'86 45 M
  '0-'5139
-9'4650 F
  -1'385
-9'781 F
  '130724-95'
-05'6 M
  '4-819'73
'1-9'75† M
  '26-'5
'12348-'596 F
  31'74 28960-'5

12'80374-'59 M
  '1056-
1203'78465-9' F
  123"7860'45-9'
'13248-'5 M
  9'4827130-5'6
'132748-9'5 M
  '26-'5
134'"287"65- M
  84'0-
1"3487'26905- M
  18'03 27645-
'135-'09 M
  1'637502-
'130-98'56 M
  '89-5'1
'1439-'076 M
  '387954-'02
'149- M
  2'904-'1
'17 3420-6'9 M
  '8310694-
'19342-5'6 M
  94'87 263
19'874-'05† F
  9'458-'2
'10 236478- F
  '4835-'0
2'"1'07'38-'96 M
  1'037825-
'23-'406† M
  '986-2'3 75

'231 78495-0'† M
  '819375-0'
'238-'4† M
  '5-
'2387- F
  '5678-'24
'24-'5 M
  '4062378-'9
'2453-'6 M
  '5-
2"48'67013-5' M
  2'"84"731'06-'9
2'4017 89- M
  2'807194-'6
2'59-7'41680† M
  9'-231'50
'26-'815 M
  '02-81'973
'26-'930 M
  4"26'5791 830-
'2678540-'9 M
  2'75683-9'
'27163458-'0 M
  '143589-'0
'274 603-5'1 F
  20'67458-9'
'27084-'3 M
  '4-5'36
'283465- F
  '52-'379
'20 4678-5'9 F
  278"031'469-5'

'206 47-95' F
  -3'9461
'20764-'951 F
  0'726-5'9
20'785- M
  '401-'8
20'87643- M
  '042758-'96
'3-1'045† M
  '3-9'24 580
'3-'20 F
  '5-'39
'3-4'871 F
  '9-'0
'3-'529 F
  '9480-'23
'3-'56 M
  '4-9'
'3-9'45 F
  '46-'29
'3-98'7526† M
  '89-5'1
'3-0'2 F
  '38974-'20
'3-'025 F
  '49-'32
'3-'0496 M
  '20738-'9
'31-'29 M
  '834-'509
'31-0'92 M
  '56-'09

3'162-9'5 F
5'361-97'428

3'168 45 27-X F
'0198465-

'317-'5 M
41'93 86-

'319-2'50 M
8179'4063-5'2

3"21'0784-5'9 F
32'40 817-'5

'325178-9'46 M
'54-9'6

'34-'297 F
734062-'5

'34-2'09 F
'93-'2410

'34-5'718 F
'04-9'135

'34-'05 M
3'74189-'06

'34-'079 M
'381-0'2

'3416-'09 F
4'6798-5'2

'3416 57- M
341'8672-'09

341'782 506- F
'32719-'6

'34 518-'90† F
31'74 28960-'5

3'452-9' F
'5318-'0

'346-2'9 M
'436817-'0

'34618-'0 F
'34256-'09

3'4672180-'95 F
6"3240'718-'5

'346897-0'† M
'20738-'9

'3469-02'† F
'395687-20'

'348-'5 F
94'8765-21'0

3'481679-'05 M
'32416-'09

34'851 9672-'0 M
84"61'7932 50-X

'34857 16- F
'648-9'2

'34 89 67-5'2 F
-21'509

'349-'26 F
9'4851-

'3495-0' M
'2-7'9016

'349 56-20'7† M
'4580-1'793

'35-'69 F
'758-'1

'35467- M
'256378 40-'9

'354 69-'270 M
'5-12'43 90

'35678-'9† F
7120 5843-'9

'3579- F
'5478-

'36-'25 F
'89347-'205

'36-'207 M
'63-2'094

'36-9' M
'3-5'6

'36-02' F
9"864'7132-'50

'36-'0529 F
'634-5'1

'364-0'95† M
2'5376-'90

3'6478-5' F
9'78-1'3

'365-'09† M
'63-2'094

'367-5'40 F
'6-5'231

3'6785291- M
6'5789 21304-

'368-2'50X F
'347-'2

'374-'65 F
'4320-

'374812-5' F
'39-'5

'37485-'9 F
4"321 789-'65

'374 96 81-'50 F
'7965-'2

3784'261-'5 F
4'8967-'10

'3791 45-'0 M
'927-'1

'3790-'5 F
'32670-5'4

'38-'6 M
'4378152-

'38-'05 F
'3489-'0X

'3856742- M
'16390-2'75

'3861-25'0† F
'4876-'5

'389-'056 M
'9-'6

'39-'25 F
9'7485-'216

'39-5'20 F
9"163847-

'39-0'857† M
'734258-'96

3"918'647-'0 F
'37-'052

39'6874-5'0 F
8'7906-

'398-'2 F
68'9027-

'3984-56'72 M
'9873-5'

'304725-'9 M
2'746318-'5

'4-X F
'65-'91

'4-1'53† F
'98764-'1

'4-17 80'5† F
'4-'1

'4-'290† F
'3-'798

'4-5'81 37 M
87'90-1'32

'413786-'05† M
7'43218-

4"163978- M
'6134-

4'17832-'9 F
'476-'902

'42- M
4'87123-'0

'42-1'3 M
68'4713952-

'423-9'6 M
'49813-5'02

4'23 18 67-'0 M
'908-'67

'426 3871-'9X F
'043712-'9X

4'270816-'9 F
7'068 34-9'

'42807-'53 M
4'67-'95

'420 587- M
8'972450-'6

'43-'6 M
'4-6'8

'43-'05† M
'13-'5

'4317982-'05 M
'42693-'0X

43'19782-5' F
3'17954-'0

'43258-'0 F
5'2347-'9

'435- F
'052-'41

'435-'02 M
6"489'27-'15

4'3578- F
'4-'963

4'36-'5029 F
'4-'15

'436-'05918 M
'24-5'9

'4365-2' M
'4580-1'793

4'367819-5'0† F
3'4678-5'0

'436789-5'0 F
'74-'9

'4368-2' M
6'47835-'9

'4368751-0'9† M
'53-9'

'43687 915-'0† M
'89436-'02

'4369-0'527† F
9'63-2'

'437185-'9 M
'52-4'3781

'4372-'60 M
'3-'926

'43758-'02 F
'0476-1'235

'437896-0'5 F
'437-0'2

'4370- F
5'402-

'438-X F
'3856-'20

'438-'659 M
80'74926-'51

'438-0' F
'4-2'507

4'38567 29-0' M
4'61378 59-

4'3859 167-'0† F
'56-'90

'43 86-'520 F
'9647-5'1

4'3862715- M
78"9'6423-

'438 75-† F
94'8765-21'0

'4391 78- F
4'076-

'43 9578-'02 F
'6-'24 18359

'439 587-0' M
4'867935-'02

43'96187-5'0 F
'41-'50

'4398-2'506 M
8'945673-2'0

43'98167- F
7'98456-

4"39'85612- F
'379 2468-

'43986-0'† F
'20678-9'

'43906- M
'49728-'3

4'536-2'0 M
14'86357-'90

'4568 2790- M
4'072658 31-'9

'45689-2'0 F
'5-'87

'45 73 869- F
'495-'21

'4579-'6 M
'45167-'2

'459 63-0' M
4'81357-'60

459'73-'0 M
'65-31'2

'46-1'59 F
6'9078-2'13

'46-'7 M
-1'3429
462'79830-5' F
8'6179402-
4'63-'5170† F
4'9678-'1
46'317289- F
'587-
4'637-'05 F
'80475-9'1
'46372- F
'75-'2
'4638 9517-X F
'0361-'57
'4653- F
6'7894-
'467-5'90 M
'06-91'58
'46 7893-'2 F
9'458-'2
'46813-'0 M
'784-23'65
'46837-0'29 F
-62'7
'468 79- M
'6498-'3
'46953- F
4'806793-'2
'469823-0'† M
4'32165-'09
'47136-'5 M
1'768093-'4
4"718'20639- M
9'784-5'20
'47 3596- M
'9734865-'2
'473861-'0 M
84'76 391-
'473915- M
86'"2"413'79-X
47'39802- M
73'501 846-
'4730- M
'9847-'23
'4753- M
'24089-5'6
'476-1'5 F
'485693-'1
4'768103-'2 F
8'749 361-'5
47'68239- F
'72098-'531
47'68'092- F
8'"5"764'9120-X
4""'78"29063-† F
04'2867-5'1
4'7839-5'2 M
9'480-'63
4'7856-'92 F
5'6-'237
4'786 913-'20 M
'46381-'5
4'78609- F
5'807-

4""'7"86'092-'5 F
04'2867-5'1
'479 683-'50 F
3'4678-5'0
'4798-'65 F
'287406-
'47983562- F
5'437986-
47 06'235891- F
8'"49"67301'25-
'48-5'209 M
'1348-5'920
'48-50'29† F
'4-'15
'481736-'9† F
'476-'902
'482 37-5'60 M
4'819-5'0
48 31'27 695-0' M
'819375-0'
'483 17-'90X M
'7-0'26
486'312 075- M
'6094 825-
48"6'7923-'5 M
2'897406-
'4860-'25X F
'5-'6793
'487-'59† F
'648-9'2
48'725 30-'9 M
'204-6'9
48'720-'6 M
8"72'356094-
'4876- F
'7416 0358-'9
4'87936-'50 F
'468-2'0
4'87963-'0 M
4'7189 63-
'489-'02 M
68'9740-'1
4'8956- M
8"64709'25-'3
'489573-0'† M
'8634715-'0
489'63-0' M
'489713-
4'897- F
'594-21'37
'49-12'5 F
'72834-'9
4'9-'2 M
9'4781-'2
'49-21'38 570 M
'946-2'13
'49-2'05 F
'7905-'1
'49-5'23 M
94'873-2'0
'491658-2' M
'948-2'73
'4935-21'867 F
'59-1'206

4'9385- F
'954-'6
495'372861-† M
29"7438'61-'0
'49538-0'2† M
4'867935-'02
4'9568 73-'20† M
'79680-13'4
49"5876-'1 M
49'8523-'1
'496-750'812 M
4'6398-'0
4"9'67-52'01 F
'4-'1
4"9'67832-5'0 F
4'9678-'1
4'"968753-'0 M
'459-6'20
4'"972'186305- M
'724-5'0
'49730- F
8'40567 31-
4"981'6372-'0 M
9'4173-5'62
'49 83-'0† F
'37-'25
'498367-'2 F
-'96
'4983675-'20 F
9'8754-'12
4'9875-'0 F
'4978-'0
'406879- F
4"02'678-'15
'5-1'280 M
'734258-'96
'5-1486'3 M
'7-'216
'5-2'† F
'4-1'79
'5-'20 F
'654-
'5-'4918 M
'53-9'
'5-'72809† M
'386-'0X
'5-781'† M
'3-'679
'5-9'8 F
'0428-'59
'5-'09 F
'06742-'935
5'2-'84 913 M
'507-'463
'523 49-6'† M
'5-'9
'524-'9 M
'649-'7520
'53-2'768 F
'386-'7
'53-'429 F
'7120 5843-'9
'53-'9 M
'5-'9

'53-9'1† F
0'487-'95
'532-'90 F
4'2583 0617-'9
'534-2'† F
'6-'24 18359
'534-'029 F
'4235-'6
'538-'92 M
'5806-1'423
'54-'26 M
5'38-4'6
'54-'61780 M
'3-'679
'54-0'2 F
'487-
'543-2'6 F
'7-9'
'543269-0' M
4'32165-'09
'5439-'18 F
'09-1'83267
'546893-20' M
9'42-'0
'5476-9' F
'0578-'3146
5'483 67-'92 F
5'487 31-'20
'548397-'21 F
8'695312-
5'634-'19 F
'9087-6'2
'564-'219 M
'63-'1
'564-0'2 F
'35-2'017
'5649- M
5'0684 972-1'3
'5670-31'49 F
9'5483-'012
'56974-'23 M
'5467-2'9
5'608947-'3 F
8'"7'601 593-X
'57-1'32 F
'5-24'13768
'57 2390-'6 M
7'2840136-9'5
'578-'6 F
'23517-
'58234 71-'9† M
'52-4'3781
58"3'74961- M
8'94673-'0
'584-2'10† M
'83165-0'9
'584-2'09 F
'5194-'0
'58 41 37-'0 M
84'723-
'58436-02' M
'59-'72 06
'5896-0' M
9'573-2'4

5'9–16'327 F
9'84576–2'3
'59–2'6170 F
'54–'912
'5934– M
'01–2'39
'59 36–0' M
'95–270'6
5'94–'02† M
49'8523–'1
'59 478–'0 F
'76820–'5
'596–2'40 M
9''8'57–2'13
'59 687– F
6'0985–1'34
5'978–0'2 M
'7891–5'6
'59 78–0'2 F
84'796–31'25
59'8–'1 F
5''–2'37 19
'59846–'213† F
9'8456–2'01
'598463–20' M
254'731–
5''9'873–'42 M
5''489'3671–'2
59'874–'1† M
5''489'3671–'2
'50–'129 M
'506–'41279
'50–41'98 M
'7094–6'
'50–91'687 F
2'483506–'9
'5046–'91 F
'8507–'92
'5046 27–† M
5''2'46173–9'
5''07'62–9' M
'751082 34–9'
'508–6'21 M
'05278–1'9
'5089–'31 F
2'408135697–
'6–1'58 F
9'873–'5
'6–2'7 F
9'8674–2'
'6–4'7125 F
9'63–2'
'6–5'† F
'364–29'5
'6–'529† F
'7685 42–
'6–5'7 M
46'183725–X
'6–81'79 M
–3'29
'6–85'94 F
'673948–5'
'6–'9 F
'3–'798

'6–'9 F
'498–'5
'6–'9210 F
'457–'2
'6–0'71† M
9'–7'0
'62 58–'0 M
9'10–2'
'6319748–2' M
9''8'67–123'5
'634–5'0 M
'4–'59
'6349–0'5 F
'946378–0'521
'635–'780X M
'8361457–
6'378–2'5 F
'59–'6
'639148–0' M
'3146–
'64–15'2 90 F
'8–'4659
'64–5' F
'36417280–9'5
'64–51'2 F
–9'713
6'''4'28'39705–X M
47'98625–
'6435–'92 M
'3–'9
'64379–'20 F
9'548–21'3
'648–'3 M
8''7'490513–
'648–90'7 F
423'167805–X
'6483 701–'5X F
7'08641259–
'648710–9' M
78'45 13 96–
'6498–'0 M
'496–2'15
'640–9' F
'80476–'2
'65–9' M
'60–'91384
'654–'0 M
5''2'46173–9'
'67–5'24 F
–24'359
'672 84 31– M
6'782341–X
67'4502831–'9 M
'675834–'1
6'74895–0'2 F
9''87465–02'
'678–'09 M
4'5867931–'2X
'678549– M
'068–51'23
6'78043952– F
'7045–9'
'679–20'18 F
9'64–21'803

6'794–1'5 F
5'908–3'12
'68–1'0 F
'4785–'01
'6837–'40† F
8''749 361–'5
68''473'902–'5 F
49'6378–'5
68''''4'''9''7'05 231–X F
8'''64''937'0521–X
6'''8''5907–'23X M
'07629–
6'''8''72'49103–X M
897'062–
6'87 4105–'9† M
2''75683–9'
'6890–'2 M
1'387249–'5
'69–0'8 M
'9–'7015
'6937–45' F
'731468–5'
'6954–173' M
'4068–'31
'697–15' F
6'57–'13
'60–9'34 F
'0762–'9
'602–94'15 F
'7685 42–
6024'738–5'9 F
06'483712–'5
6'0283714–'5 F
'86749–
'603–'9 F
6'4789–1'
'604–'75† M
'02–81'973
'7–'13 F
'8095–36'4
'7–'2 F
'3–'871 69
'7–'319 F
'76048–3'1
'7–'413 F
'950–321'
71'48935–† M
8'734–'50
7'16350– M
'05986–'42
7''21'43805– F
3'178–'20
'72403–'5 F
'802731–'59
'726–5'4 F
7'896 42–5'
'7283 45169– F
0'542–'196
7'29408– M
8'497 2365–
72'01385–'9 M
'314207–'5
7'2068 43–'59 F
'407–39'81

'731564–'0 M
8'9670–'4
'736 2458–'0† M
'256378 40–'9
'738–'659 F
'938–2'05
'7384–5'02† M
8'9670–'4
'74213–'6 M
1''7'435280–
74''236'581– M
6'5780 1249–
743'281690– F
9'4783 162–
7'4823 69– F
8'947 60–'1
74''8'2963–'1 M
'42783–5'9
7'48321–'5 F
'6–'19
7'4806239– M
8''17'234069–
74'80965– M
6'087 94–'31
758'024639– M
7'2854–'9
'7684310–5' F
'637–5'129
76'8902543– F
6''2'809 74–
'76034– M
2''178'0634–'5
'78–'1 F
'7–1'4932
78129'453–'6 M
8'7209–'346
78'13 42659– M
'78246–9'
7'8290–'6† F
3'178–'20
782'01369–'5 M
'082–'53
7''''820''64'9– M
89''76'3–'1
'78421–'6 M
'8634715–'0
784'20913–'5† M
9'784–5'20
78'459 36– M
'53–6'1
'786–'120 M
'7680–'59
'7862–'59 F
7'6948–5'
78'623904–5'1 F
8''0247'631–'9X
'78 6032–'9 F
3'718654–
'789–25'143 M
9'6–'413
78''9'36245–0' M
'98256–'34
'78964230–1' F
2430'86719–5'

'943–20'6 M
'59738–6'4

9'43–5'712 F
'98764–'1

'9436–205' M
'346719–0'

'9436–20'7 M
'6947–5'2

'9438–0'25 M
'3–'20

'94 30–2'1 F
'94538–2'1

9'45–'13† M
9'458–'2

9'45–1'326 F
9"5'487–23'10

'945–1'6 F
9'546807–312'

'945–'631 F
'90–'563

9'453–2'01 F
9'47–'01

9'45 68–20' F
94'68–21'3

9'457–'026† M
'65–31'2

9'4586–0'12 M
'79680–13'4

9'46–'712 F
'948–'105

'946–0'52† M
9'3468–'7

9'463–02'5 M
'4680–2'135

'94638–0'5 M
–1'3689

9'465–2'0 F
'57943–

'94685–20'1 F
'58–'20

9'4687–30'2† F
'496–1'53

'947–5'6 F
'78023–'95

94"7328 51'6– M
29"7438'61–'0

9'4768–1' F
'496–1'53

'9478–'5126 F
'8657–1'2

'948–52'6 M
'243–'50 67

'948–6'231 F
98'475–'2

94'8327– M
4"98172635–

'9485–0'21 M
'34517–'9

9"'486'73–† F
8""96"'743'15–X

'948670–'23 F
9'8456–2'01

9'487–'13† M
8'96704–

9'487–5'2 10 F
'8–1'20 35

'94 873–'52 M
'9134–

9'4873–'65 F
9'58467–2'01

94'87635–'1 M
8'609 75–'2

'95–'17 F
'49087–

'95–2'0 M
9'84375–'0

'95–4'62 F
'3–'925

9'54–127' F
5'49–2'60

'954–'1683 F
'0875–'93

'954–2'16 F
'0986–1'25

9'54–21'0 F
'49860–1'27

9'54–06'271 F
59'84–0'21

'956–'238 M
'35–8'1

9"561–'20 F
'5948–0'2

9'562784– M
9'65–2'1

'9563–8'7† M
5'64239–

'95 78–0'6 F
'589–0'

'958–02' M
'596–2'170

'958 24–1'3 M
9'458–'2

'95807–1'236 F
9'8570–1'23

9'638–02'† M
'927–'1

'964–'15 M
9'4683 75–2'

'964–'372 M
'8–'75

9'6438–127'0 M
'894–'725

96'48 57–'21 F
8"4639'7120–X

'965–2' M
'2649–'51

9'65–2'10 M
'6724 59–'01

'967–1'32 F
'987–1'362

'9678–14'325† M
8"6'10937–'45

9'68 7452–'3 F
'68245 79–'1

96'8047–51'23 F
'60–85'1973

'97–'518 F
'0–64'318

'97–6'523 M
8'9067–2'31

9'734–20' M
'53–6'7

9"7486–'215 M
9'8742–

9'76–'132† M
'7–69'385

9'76384–† M
'7398–2'

97'68–'312 M
'789–2'354

9784–2'53 M
'9–832'165

9'786– M
'8473–

'9786 042–'135 F
87'603492–5'

'98–'12 M
'9134–52'06

'983–2'0 F
'89–'241

9'834–'27 M
9'3814–'06

'983416–0' M
9'587–312'6

'984–'61 M
87'61304 25–

'9843–2'6 M
9'846–'25

'9843–2'05† F
'78023–'95

'984371–'20 65 M
'89436–'02

9'8453–'0 M
8"4'9605173–

9'846–5' M
69'4782–

9'847–20'1 F
6""84"'7"239'01–X

9"8476'5–'2 M
'8970–'6135

9'8513– M
'938–'65

'98 53–0' M
4'53167289–0'

986'1437– F
9'658314–'7

'9864–'2 M
9'–7'0

9'864–2'51 M
8"9'6714–'5

9'864370–'5 F
8""96"'743'15–X

9'867–2'0† M
'6537890–'1

986'7204–31' M
8"7'0942163–X

9"874–6'20 F
5'–273 10'468

9876'2 3405– F
'70342–

'90 35–'6 M
'0956–1'

'90 38674– F
'5048–'123

9"08367–24' F
'5–246'1

'0–13'6289 F
'0–316'479

'0–15'437 F
'0–319'6

'0–21'34569 F
'84–'92

'0–3615'2 M
7'0846–'235

'0–5'913 68 M
8"7'246153–

'0–9'2 F
'406–'5

'0–9'8461 F
'0–196 84'7

'02–5'13 M
4"9'67283–'15

0'27 4859– F
'05847–'2

'03–9'451 F
'506–'213

'036745–'9 F
'6–14'59827

'042– M
'0425–

'0438–'9 F
'51–'47

'045–1'638 F
0'5867–1'3

0"48 27'569–'1 M
0'248–1'639

'0497 28–'6 M
'09248–1'36

0'529–1'3' M
0'725–1'39

'053–9'2 M
52'0876–

0'54–61'3 289 F
5'0–31'4

'0546–'2719 F
'605–1'2379

0'56–913' M
'48602–

'057–4'21 F
56'9748–'2

'06–35'2† F
'9706–351'24

'062–5'1 F
'67042–'95

'0627–1'43 F
'0862 57–'139

06'28 79–5' F
'069847–1'3

'0678–1'3 F
8'9760–21'45

'067825–9' F
07'6852 49–'13

0'687239–'4 M
'369718–

'07–'9 F
6'409873–'52

'07–'9 M
  '9860 457–
'072–3'46 M
  '0–53'846
'07268–3'14 F
  '02784–'36 19
0'74 286– F
  6'02874–'9
0'746283–'59 F
  0'3174–9'5
'07468–'9† M
  '401–'8
'078–'139 M
  '6085–1'39
'078–45'23 F
  '9706–351'24

07'82–431'5 F
  0'978–31'52
'07 89–'265 M
  '0–635'142
'08–'2375 M
  '04–5'63 79
'08–259'14 F
  –51'429
'08257–6' F
  5'098–4'2
0'829 734– F
  0'879–'351
0'84–'71 F
  08'762–
0'84216–5'3X M
  6'8490–'53X

'085–'49 M
  '6075–'19
'087–5'3 F
  '048276–59'
0'87263–'1† F
  0'28764–'93
'087624–1'5 F
  '07–391'
'089–1'2463 F
  '57–
'089–1'36 M
  98'1604–'5X
'08 97–5' M
  86''''7''19'32405–X

'09–'41 F
  0'21837–9'
'09–4'213 M
  68'0794–'5
'09–'647 F
  '0158–93'4
'0962–'14 F
  '8240–
0'97285–1'3 F
  8'065 972–'1
'0978– F
  –2'65
'09873–'12 M
  '1–5'9

Low-Point Index

OF NINTH-GRADE, TWELFTH-GRADE, AND COLLEGE CODES

The codes in this index are inverted to place the low-point scales first. A period divides the low and high points of each code. If a code is from the twelfth-grade or college testing, there is an indented entry on the line immediately below which gives, in normal order, the ninth-grade code under which the case summary is to be found.

'1. 2'79– M
'1. 2'904– M
'1. '35– F
'1. '3587– F
'1. '4– F
'1. '43– M
'1. 46'8702– F
'1. 46'89057– F
'1. '485693– F
'1. 4'89076– M
'1. 49"5876– M
   49'8523–'1
'1. 4'9678– F
'1. 4"'96'8 270– M
'1. 49'8523– M
'1. 56'9708– M
'1. 58'6427– M
'1. 59'8– F
   5"–2'37 19
'1. 59'874– M
   5"489'3671–'2
'1. '63– M
1'. 6'4789– F
1'. '6490– M
'1. '6537890– M
'1. '67– F
'1. 675834– M
'1. '68245 79– F
'1. '68740– F
'1. 68'9740– M
'1. 74"8'2963– M
   '42783–5'9
'1. '758– F
1'. '7658– M
'1. '78– F
   '7–1'4932

'1. 7'8459 62– M
1'. '78964230– F
   2430'86719–5'
'1. '78052– M
'1. '7905– F
'1. 82'07935– M
'1. 8"46'0279– F
'1. 8"570 296– M
   8"'6794'13502–X
'1. 8"709'465–X M
   8062'7549–
'1. 8'947 60– F
'1. 89"76'3– M
'1. 8'065 972– F
1'. '9– F
1'. '92– F
'1. '927– M
1'. 9'4768– F
   '496–1'53
'1. 94'87635– M
   8'609 75–'2
'1. 98'7260– M
'1. '98764– F
'1. 9'0824– F
'1. 0"48 27'569– M
   0'248–1'639
'1. '0568– M
'1. 0'87263– F
   0'28764–'93
1'. '0956– M
1'2. '8657– F
1'2. '9354– F
   '2–1'3
'12. '98– M
   '9134–52'06
'12. 9'8754– F

'12. '09873– M
   '1–5'9
'123. '5048– F
1'23. 8"469'075– F
   4"896'703–
'123. 9'5– M
1'23. 9'8570– F
'12 35. 9'478– M
123'5. 9"8'67– M
1'235. '0476– F
1'236. '95807– F
   9'8570–1'23
1'2379. '605– F
'1239. '05– M
'1243. 9'– F
   9'847 56–'120
12'43 90. '5– M
1'2463. '089– F
   '57–
12'5. '49– F
   '72834–'9
1'25. '0986– F
12'53. 986'70– M
125'06. '8– M
1'26. '79– M
1'27. '49860– F
127'. 9'54– F
   5'49–2'60
127'0. 9'6438– M
   '894–'725
1'280. '5– M
   '734258–'96
'129. '50– M
   '506–'41279
1'20. '56439– M
'120. '756– F

'120. '786– M
   '7680–'59
1'20. '984– F
'120. 9'847 56– F
1'20 35. '8– F
1'206. '59– F
12'086357. 9'– F
13'. NHP. F
1'3. '2– F
'13. '2650– F
1'3. '29486 75– M
1'3. '42– M
   68'4713952–
1'3. 5'0684 972– M
'13. 6'57– F
'13. '7– F
   '8095–36'4
1'3. '7980– F
   '94–'167
'13. '7089– M
'13. '8– M
'13. 9'45– M
   9'458–'2
'13. 9'487– M
   8'96704–
'13. 9'54087– F
1'3. '958 24– M
   9'458–'2
1'3. 9'6748– M
1'3. 9'78– F
1'3. 9'0567– F
1'3. '052– M
13'. 0'529– M
   0'725–1'39
1'3. 0'5867– F
'13. 0'65– M

LOW-POINT INDEX

9'5. 0'31<u>74</u>– F
'95. 0'487– F
9'5. '06<u>287</u>– F
'951. '<u>20</u>7<u>64</u>– F
0'726–5'9
951'<u>346</u>. 02'8– M
95'24. '01– M
95'81. '30– F
95'02. '463–X F
'96. NHP. F
'96. 2'''1'07'<u>38</u>– M
1'037825–
9'6. '4– M
9'6. '423– M
'498<u>13</u>–5'02
9'6. '54– M
'96. '7342<u>58</u>– M
'96. '018<u>742</u>– F
'96. '042758– M
'963. '4– F
'965. '87<u>431</u>– M
'8–5<u>62</u>'3
'97. 5'348– F
'971. '2– M
9'7<u>13</u>. NHP. F
97'<u>428</u>. 5'3<u>61</u>– F
9'7<u>5</u>. '1– M
'26–'5
9'781. NHP. F
'130<u>724</u>–95'
9'8. '5– F
'04<u>28</u>–'59
9'<u>8461</u>. '0– F
'0–1<u>96</u> <u>84</u>'7
98'<u>56</u>. '130– M
'89–5'1
98'7<u>526</u>. '3– M
'89–5'1
'90. 14'86<u>357</u>– M
'90. 2'5<u>376</u>– M
'<u>90</u>. '32– F
'90. '<u>34</u> 5<u>18</u>– F
31<u>74</u> <u>28</u>960–'5
'90. '4<u>83</u> <u>17</u>–X M
'7–0<u>26</u>
'90. '53– F
'90. '532– F
4'2<u>583</u> <u>0617</u>–'9
'<u>90</u>. '56– F
'<u>90</u>. 5'7– F
'902. '476– F
'902. 6'3 M
'905. '34– F
90'7. '648– F
423'1<u>67</u>805–X
'0. '14<u>3589</u>– M
0'. '<u>231</u> 78495– M
'81<u>9</u>375–0'
'0. '271<u>63458</u>– M
'14<u>3589</u>–'0
'0. 29''7<u>438</u>'61– M
'0. 3''1'<u>478</u> <u>962</u>– F
'0. 3'1<u>7954</u>– F

'0. '34<u>618</u>– F
'34<u>256</u>–'<u>09</u>
0'. '34<u>6719</u>– M
0'. '34<u>6897</u>– M
'20<u>738</u>–'9
'0. 34'8<u>51</u> <u>9672</u>– M
84''61'7<u>932</u> <u>50</u>–X
'0. '3489–X F
0'. '3495– M
'2–7'9<u>016</u>
'0. 3''7<u>841</u>'26– M
'0. '<u>3791</u> <u>45</u>– M
'927–'1
'0. '386–X M
0'. 3''9<u>18</u>'647– F
'37–'0<u>52</u>
'0. 39'7<u>48261</u>– F
'0. 4'1<u>28</u>376– M
'0. '41<u>35</u>– F
0'. '4136957– F
'0. 4'<u>23</u> <u>18</u> <u>67</u>– M
'908–'<u>67</u>
'0. '4<u>2693</u>–X M
'0. '43<u>258</u>– F
5'2347–'9
'0. '43<u>6817</u>– M
'0. '43<u>687</u> <u>915</u>– M
'89<u>436</u>–'02
0'. '438– F
'4–2'<u>507</u>
0'. 4'3<u>8567</u> <u>29</u>– M
4'6<u>1378</u> <u>59</u>–
'0. 4'<u>3859</u> <u>167</u>– F
'56–'<u>90</u>
0'. '4<u>39</u> <u>587</u>– M
4'867<u>935</u>–'02
0'. '43<u>986</u>– F
'20<u>678</u>–9'
0'. 4'5<u>3167289</u>– M
0'. '4<u>59</u> <u>63</u>– M
4'81<u>357</u>–'<u>60</u>
'0. 459'<u>73</u>– M
'65–31'2
'0. 4'6<u>398</u>– M
'0. '46813– M
'784–23'<u>65</u>
0'. '46<u>8375</u>– F
0'. '46<u>9823</u>– M
4'32<u>165</u>–'09
'0. '473861– M
84'<u>76</u> <u>391</u>–
0'. 48 31'27 <u>695</u>– M
'81<u>9</u>375–0'
'0. '48<u>35</u>– F
'0. 4'87<u>123</u>– M
'0. 487'<u>93</u> <u>15</u>– M
'0. 4'87<u>963</u>– M
4'71<u>89</u> <u>63</u>–
0'. '48<u>9573</u>– M
'86<u>34</u>715–'0
0'. 4<u>89</u>'63– M
'48<u>9713</u>–
'0. 4'89<u>763</u>– M

'0. 4'''9<u>68</u>753– M
'459–6'20
'0. '49<u>78</u>– F
'0. 4'''9<u>81</u>'6372– M
9'41<u>73</u>–5'62
0'. '<u>49</u> <u>83</u>– F
'37–'<u>25</u>
'0. 4'9875– F
'49<u>78</u>–'0
'0. '5194– F
'0. '53<u>18</u>– F
0'. '543<u>269</u>– M
4'32<u>165</u>–'09
'0. '<u>58</u> <u>41</u> <u>37</u>– M
84'723–
0'. '589– F
0'. '5<u>896</u>– M
9'5<u>73</u>–2'4
0'. '<u>59</u> <u>36</u>– M
'95–2<u>70</u>'6
'0. '<u>59</u> <u>478</u>– F
'76<u>820</u>–'5
'0. '<u>62</u> <u>58</u>– M
9'10–2'
0'. '6<u>39</u>1<u>48</u>– M
'31<u>46</u>–
'0. '6<u>498</u>– M
'496–2'15
'0. '6<u>54</u>– M
5''2'46<u>173</u>–9'
'0. '73– M
'0. '7<u>31564</u>– M
8'9<u>670</u>–'4
'0. '7<u>36</u> <u>2458</u>– M
'25<u>6378</u> <u>40</u>–'9
0'. <u>78</u>''9'3<u>6245</u>– M
'98<u>256</u>–'<u>34</u>
0'. '81<u>9</u>375– M
'0. 8<u>19</u>'432– M
'85<u>349</u>–
0'. '<u>836</u>– F
'85<u>94</u>–'2
'0. '84<u>796</u> <u>53</u>– M
'6984–2<u>5</u>'3
'0. 854'<u>3679</u>– M
24'70–9'
'0. '86<u>34</u>715– M
0'. '8<u>79</u> <u>23</u>– M
6'7<u>0</u>854–
'0. 8'94<u>673</u>– M
'0. '9– F
0'. 9'<u>34</u> 7<u>5826</u>– M
'895–6'2
'0. 9'42– M
'0. 94''8'<u>3765</u>– F
0'. '98<u>3416</u>– M
9'587–<u>312</u>'6
'0. 9'84<u>375</u>– M
'0. 9'8<u>453</u>– M
8''4'96<u>05173</u>–
0'. '98 <u>53</u>– M
4'53<u>167289</u>–0'
'<u>01</u>. '4785– F

'01. '67<u>24</u> <u>59</u>– M
'01. '9– F
'<u>01</u>. 9'47– F
'01. 9''4'7685– M
0'<u>12</u>. 9'4<u>586</u>– M
'79<u>680</u>–1<u>3</u>'4
'<u>012</u>. 9'5483– F
'01<u>578</u>. '6– M
'0<u>16</u>. 9'<u>42</u>– M
9'7<u>64</u> <u>8205</u>–
0'2. '3– F
'38<u>974</u>–'20
<u>02</u>'. '<u>3469</u>– F
'39<u>5687</u>–20'
02'. '36– F
9''8<u>64</u>'7<u>132</u>–'50
0'2. '381– M
'<u>02</u>. '387<u>954</u>– M
0'2. '39<u>76458</u>– M
'<u>02</u>. '41<u>389</u>– F
'02. '435– M
6''489'27–'15
0'2. '437– F
'<u>02</u>. '43<u>758</u>– F
'0476–1'2<u>35</u>
'02. '<u>43</u> <u>9578</u>– F
'6–'<u>24</u> <u>18359</u>
'02. 4'867<u>935</u>– M
'<u>02</u>. '489– M
68'9740–'1
0'2. 4''89<u>56</u> <u>17</u>– M
0'2. '<u>49538</u>– M
4'867<u>935</u>–'02
02'. 4'9<u>638</u>– M
0'2. '54– F
'487–
0'2. '<u>564</u>– F
'35–2'0<u>17</u>
<u>02</u>'. '58<u>436</u>– M
'59–'<u>72</u> <u>06</u>
'02. 5'94– M
49'8523–'1
0'2. '59<u>48</u>– F
0'2. '<u>59</u> <u>78</u>– F
84'7<u>96</u>–3<u>1</u>'25
0'2. 5'978– M
'78<u>91</u>–5'6
'<u>02</u>. '63<u>478</u>– F
0'2. 6'74<u>895</u>– F
9''87<u>465</u>–02'
'02. 84''7<u>53</u> <u>69</u>– M
4'9<u>785</u> <u>63</u>–'20
'<u>02</u>. '869– M
'8–1<u>25</u>'06
'02. '89<u>436</u>– M
0'2. '<u>8946</u>– F
'34<u>256</u>–'09
<u>02</u>'. 9'– F
'58–'<u>20</u>
02'. '9– F
'487–
'<u>02</u>. '9<u>35</u> <u>48</u>– F
9'4<u>687</u>–1'<u>35</u>

400

Index of Invalid Profiles

The codes for testings on which deviant L or F scores were obtained are listed numerically in this index. Following each main entry are the L, F, and K scores, in that order. If a code is from the twelfth-grade or college testing, there is an indented entry on the line immediately below which gives the ninth-grade code under which the case summary is to be found.

INVALID L

3'168 45 27–   12:9:25   F
  '0198465–
'3489–'0   13:1:25   F
'368–2'50   11:2:24   F
  '347–'2
'386–'0   13:2:22   M
'4–   10:1:20   F
  '65–'91
423'167805–   13:10:24   F
'426 3871–'9   10:4:19   F
  '043712–'9X
'42693–'0   10:2:18   M
'438–   11:4:23   F
  '3856–'20
4'5867931–'2   11:6:21   M
'4638 9517–   10:1:26   F
  '0361–'57
'483 17–'90   10:1:25   M
  '7–0'26
'4860–'25   10:2:20   F
  '5–'6793
'493–05'   11:4:21   M
'5867–   11:4:21   F
'635–'780   11:5:15   M
  '8361457–
'6483 701–'5   10:3:24   F
  7'08641259–
8'421 397–'6   10:4:24   M
  84'7105–
'843127–'9   11:5:24   M
  '5–'6
'9–'467   10:2:15   F
  '92–1'

'943–'20   10:3:21   M
'043712–'9   14:4:18   F
0'84216–5'3   10:3:20   M
  6'8490–'53X

INVALID F

42"879'6351–   6:18:10   M
46'183725–   8:18:15   M
462'79830–5'   6:16:8   F
  8'6179402–
'463–95'02   1:21:3   F
4"'98"6'507231–   3:26:8   F
50'6489–31'2   0:20:7   F
6"'4"28'39705–   6:22:9   M
  47'98625–
'65–2'3   2:16:8   M
6""84'"7"239'01–   2:21:7   F
68""4'"9"7'05 231–   0:23:7   F
  8"'64"937'0521–X
6'8490–'53   7:16:8   M
6"'8"5907–'23   3:17:11   M
  '07629–
6""8"72'49103–   3:16:11   M
  897'062–
68'94753–   7:16:11   F
8"'124 709–'5   3:23:16   M
8"'1"6729'350–   6:30:13   M
8"'2175'49360–   5:16:20   M
8"'46'13725–'9   7:16:20   F
84"61'7932 50–   6:22:16   M
8"4639'7120–   2:16:15   F
84"72'36510–   3:16:12   M
  61'4837–

84"9'620–'53   5:17:11   M
84"'975"62 31'0–   6:27:16   F
  98'6475–
8"'5"764'9120–   5:18:19   F
86"'2"413'79–   6:19:20   M
86"'42'731 90–   8:23:12   M
86"'47"93'205–   3:28:9   F
8"'64"937'0521–   7:28:7   F
8""'6"5274'1093–   1:37:6   M
86""'7"19'32405–   5:27:14   M
8""'6"'74"20195–   1:25:11   M
8"'6794'13502–   6:20:16   M
8"'69'"74'2105–   6:24:20   F
8""'71"'32'6459–   6:25:14   M
8""'72"'51'96430–   7:22:18   M
8"'"7"69'250413–   1:21:9   M
  8'679'130 254–
8"'7'601 593–   7:18:12   F
8"'792'4650–   3:16:11   M
  '807459–'3
8"'7'0942163–   2:21:9   M
8"'709'465–'1   2:16:6   M
  8062'7549–
8"'9"467'5013–   1:22:7   M
89"'64'13 07–   2:24:4   F
8""'96"'743'15–   2:22:8   F
8"'9"7'61423–   2:16:10   M
  98'7260–'1
8"'0247'631–'9   3:17:10   F
94'56087–'3   5:16:4   F
9'54738021–   4:20:10   F
98'1604–'5   6:16:10   M